The Churches in England
from Elizabeth I to Elizabeth II

Kenneth Hylson-Smith

The Churches
in England
from Elizabeth I
to Elizabeth II

Volume I: 1558–1688

SCM PRESS LTD

(cased) 0 334 02645 8

(limp) 0 334 02638 5

First published in Britain 1996
by SCM Press Ltd
9–17 St Albans Place, London N1 0NX

Typeset by Regent Typesetting, London
and printed in Great Britain by
Mackays of Chatham PLC, Chatham, Kent

Contents

Acknowledgments

Any writer attempting to provide an overview of the churches in England during such an action-packed, complicated, and exceptionally important period as that from 1558 to 1688, is soon made aware of almost total dependence on the work of others. It is to the many scholars who have laboured long and hard describing and analysing the religious history of those years, and who have striven to address some of the countless questions such a fraught yet formative time poses, that the first and most heartfelt acknowledgment is made. The extensive references throughout the text will amply testify to my reliance on the excellent work of a host of historians. And working in Oxford has been so beneficial. Where else in the world is there such ready access to this material than in Oxford, where much of it has originated, and all of it is held? Therefore, my second debt is to the most courteous and helpful assistants in the many libraries of Oxford, and more particularly to those in the Bodleian Library, and the libraries of the theology and history faculties.

Other historians are far more able and better equipped to do what is attempted in this work, but it is put forth with but one justification: no such book at present exists, and a gap needs to be filled.[1]

The actual writing of a book like this is a collaborative venture. In addition to the scholastic work of others, there has especially been the immensely gratifying support and encouragement of the Revd Dr John Bowden, the Managing Director of SCM Press, and the unfailing friendliness and help of Margaret Lydamore and other members of his staff. Valuable advice has been received from Dr Tony Hobbs and Dr Peter Thompson; and I have greatly benefitted from the reassuring comments of the fifty and more historians who kindly responded to my enquiry about the need for a trilogy of books covering the period from 1558 to the present day. Then, finally, there is the immeasurably precious companionship of my wife, Gillian, to whom this work is dedicated.

Introduction

Until about the 1970s it was customary for church historians to regard the English Reformation as fundamentally a product of the reigns of Henry VIII and Edward VI. Books on the English Reformation almost invariably concluded at or before 1558, when Elizabeth ascended the throne.[1] Twentieth-century historians have, until quite recently, neglected the period 1558 to 1688. But in the last few decades the whole character, content, timing and pace of change of the English Reformation and the post Reformation period have been subjected to intensive and extensive scrutiny, and there have been vigorous debates on a wide range of topics covering the religious history of England from the 1520s to 1688. There has been a massive and impressive outpouring of works covering that period, mainly in the form of unpublished theses, articles and monographs. This is perhaps an opportune time to attempt to produce a synthesis, and also to bridge the divide between the Tudors and the Stuarts which has so far to quite a noticeable extent determined the chronological limits of monographs and general histories.[2] The purpose of the present book is therefore simple and possibly naive. It is to provide a comprehensive, clear, analytical account of the churches in England in the period 1558 to 1688 which recognizes recent research and different historical perspectives and views, and which is attractive and useful to students of history and theology, clergy and ministers, interested laymen and, hopefully, a wide range of the general public. There is value in such works which give an overview of the history of the churches during a given period, which try to discern the most important elements and trends in that history, which give a framework for more particular and specialist studies, and which make the relevant findings of scholars known to a wider audience than would otherwise be the case. Also, by the judicious use of references, footnotes and a full bibliography the main body of the text can be liberated from some of the more detailed data and discussional topics appropriate to the specialist historian, and this allows for a flow of narrative which might be helpful to the non-specialist.

Historiography

A brief indication of some of the topics of recent debate among historians, all of which will be explored in depth at the appropriate points as our story unfolds, will give some idea of the complexity of the historiographical scene.

There is first of all the varied picture which is painted of the pre-Reformation English church. The 'Whig' interpretation of the English Reformation, which held the field until it started to be seriously contested in the 1970s, has a distinguished pedigree which ran from John Bale, *The Image of Both Churches* (1545) and John Foxe, *Acts and Monuments* (1563, 1570), via John Strype, *Ecclesiastical Memorials* (1720) and the works of many other outstanding historians, before it received its most sophisticated modern exposition in A. G. Dickens, *The English Reformation* (1964). Foxe was a protagonist for a newly emergent Protestantism, and others in this Whig tradition were markedly and explicitly partisan in their writings, whereas Dickens writes with sensitivity as a highly professional historian who only produced his magnum opus after thirty years of careful research. Nonetheless, all of those in this historical tradition, including Dickens, contrasted the superstition, corruption and tyranny of the mediaeval, pre-Reformation Catholic Church with the piety of the discontented proto-Protestants. As will be seen in chapter 1, the 'revisionists' take a contrary view. They emphasize the rarity of negligence and immorality among the pre-Reformation clergy, the value of monasteries in offering charity, education, employment, and prayers for departed souls, the small amount of anticlericalism, the high level of benefaction and good-will towards the church, the persistent popularity of images and prayers for the dead, and, in general, the way the pre-Reformation church was an accepted, lively and relevant institution in the society of its day. Such a portrayal has itself been challenged, and in the meantime valuable local studies continue to illuminate the period and provide data for further debate.[3]

Then we move on to the Reformation itself. The Whig interpretation stresses the rapid and radical changes resulting from the Henrician Protestant Reformation, and the triumphant progress of Protestantism as it increased in power and swiftly commanded the allegiance of people in all ranks of society. The revisionists emphasize the deep-rootedness and persistence of the 'old faith'. They depict the legislation of Henry VIII and Edward VI as mere precedents, the first for royal supremacy and the second for a Protestant establishment, both of which would have been abortive but for the long reign of Elizabeth. It was only during the Elizabethan era that England was truly converted to Protestantism, and even then the transformation was far from complete: before 1558 there was little support for the Reformation, and after 1558 there was a continuation of the popularity and prestige of the Catholic Church to an extent which has hitherto generally been underestimated. The whole process of protestantization was largely from above and slow, and it was not a result of any speedy and spontaneous popular movement. But again, the revisionists have themselves been challenged. Their critics applaud their valuable exploration of neglected evidence and their meticulous regional studies, but qualitative considerations are postulated as of overriding importance rather than quantitative assessments. Thus, for example, it is acknowledged by the critics of revisionism that hostility to the traditional church and positive enthusiasm for Protestant ideas were confined to a small minority of the population before 1558, but it is pointed out that the small minority was vociferous and highly committed and was able to emerge victorious against a lukewarm, unorganized and largely leaderless majority. And this applied throughout the remainder of the sixteenth century and, indeed, well into the following century. All these topics will be studied in detail in the first and second chapters of the present work.

Within this overall re-evaluation there has been a considerable re-appraisal of the internal dynamics and varying fortunes of Catholicism during the sixteenth century and beyond, and various, often conflicting descriptions and analyses have been offered. These will be examined fully in chapters 4, 9 and 10, and elsewhere.

The whole phenomenon of 'Puritanism' has also evoked a lively and extended interchange of views among historians, as they have discussed the features which distinguished the Puritans from others within the established church, the relationship between Puritanism and Calvinism and, indeed, the justification for even attributing a separate identity to such Christian believers. The animated cut and thrust on these issues has been enlivened by a particularly protracted and searching exchange of views about 'the rise of Arminianism'. This in its turn has contributed to the wider historiographic consideration of 'the causes of the Civil War'. These matters will be addressed in detail in chapters 3, 5, 6 and 7 in particular.

Other specific issues in the period which have come under the microscopes of historians of religion include the economic and structural aspects of church life; the Marxist explanation of church life and development; the nature and content of the Elizabethan Settlement, which will be encountered in chapter 2; the analysis of the Hampton Court Conference and the differing views on the religious attitude and policy of James I, both of which topics will be examined in chapter 5; the religious beliefs and policy of Charles I, which will be considered in chapter 7, and of William Laud, which will command attention in chapters 6 and 7; the religious ideals and policy of Oliver Cromwell, which will be explored in chapter 8, where the recent historiography of the Interregnum sects will be considered; and the varied interpretations of the Restoration settlements, which will be addressed in chapter 10.

In the present study I will carefully draw upon the work of Whig historians, revisionists and post-revisionists. I will place the events described in an historiographical context, and will, in most cases, suggest how the data and theories should be viewed. I will attempt to cast light upon the period by giving a narrative account of the salient events and by appropriate analysis which takes account of the painstaking work of historians of different schools. Perhaps the prime requirement in undertaking any historical work is humility. 'It cannot be emphasized too many times that there are few "correct" interpretations in the study of history. In reaching conclusions about the past historians rely on primary sources for evidence. One of the first things that students of history ought to learn is that there are many questions to which historical evidence simply does not provide clear cut answers. Many historians may use the same primary sources but reach different conclusions about the past.'[4]

Amid such a welter of historiography, and the profusion of theses, articles, monographs and books, it is obviously desirable to undertake our task of synthesis with explicit guidelines: a clear structure and a few identifiable themes will help us to avoid being overwhelmed by an ocean of new information and so many cross currents of conflicting theories.

Themes

There are four particular threads which will run through the present analytical narrative.

First, in the endeavour to take account of recent historiography and local studies I will not remain neutral and uncommitted. I will attempt to integrate the complicated array of 'facts', and the competing historical interpretations into a coherent picture of how the churches in

England changed from the early sixteenth century to the late seventeenth century. Broadly speaking I will portray a transformation from a country which was dominated by traditional Catholicism with all its interlocking structural, behavioural, liturgical, theological and social aspects, described briefly in chapter 1, via the 'protestantization' of the next one hundred and eighty years or so, both 'from above' and 'from below', the varying nature and pace of which will be considered as we progress through the period, to the predominantly Protestant country which welcomed William and Mary. We will see how Catholicism was marginalized, but how it retained its distinctive place in the life of the nation, and at times surfaced with real or illusory hopes of regaining something of its past, perhaps imagined, glory. I will trace how those who were impatient with the speed and thoroughness of the protestantization process asserted themselves, but were in their turn opposed. And we will see how, throughout, the Church of England assumed its distinctive form, and Dissent/Nonconformity was born.

In considering the establishment of the Church of England, I will suggest that the reign of Elizabeth 'was not conspicuously a post-Reformation age, as some Anglican interpretations of history would have us believe, but the age of the English Reformation *par excellence*, when Protestantism was for the first time taking a strong hold on families of the country gentry and on the urban middle classes'.[5] It was 'only in the half-century after 1559, even somewhat later in some regions of northern England, that the real shape of the established church became clear'.[6] Indeed, I believe that no 'future history of the English Reformation will end in 1559. Elizabeth's reign is now seen to be of crucial importance because it saw the completion of the Protestantization of the English people and witnessed the creation of a uniquely English style of Protestant church which was later to be labelled Anglicanism'.[7] This process of consolidation and the achievement of identity went on through much violent change of fortune until, by 1688, the Church of England was a far more comprehensive, cohesive and recognizable entity than it had been in 1558; through the trials and testings of a century and a half it had come of age. 'Its boundaries and fundamental characteristics had been established, its continued existence was assured, and it was ready to embark on a career which would eventually see it emerge as a leading Christian denomination with an influence extending throughout the modern world.'[8]

Alongside this, and as a second thread or theme to be explored, there was the emergence and early formative years of the English

Presbyterians, Congregationalists, Baptists and Quakers, as well as the temporary but interesting spectacle of the radical sects of the Inter-regnum period. In 1558 there was no sign of any such Dissent, and yet by 1688 it was thriving, with the four main Dissenting bodies dis-tinguished by their particular beliefs and practices, and worshipping in their own meeting places.

In following the variable fortunes of Dissenting bodies I will bring to my aid helpful sociological work on 'church, denomination and sect'. Perhaps no other period in the history of the churches in England is better able to test the validity of the sociological distinction between these three categories of collective religious belief and behaviour. But in order to appreciate this theme in the present study, it is necessary to summarize how the sociological typology of 'church', 'denomination' and 'sect' was suggested, developed and refined by Max Weber, Ernst Troeltsch, Richard Niebuhr, and such recent sociologists as Howard Becker, Bryan Wilson and David Martin.

It was Weber who first focussed the attention of sociologists on the distinction between church and sect,[9] a distinction which he attempted to formalize. He suggested that a church is characterized by the existence of a professional priesthood removed from the 'world', with salaries, promotions, professional duties and a distinctive way of life; and by its claim to universal domination which transcends familial, tribal, and ultimately national, boundaries. Members are born into the church rather than having to join it. Its dogma and rites which must have been recorded in the holy scriptures, have become part of a systematic education. A church is also characterized by the fact that all these features occur in some kind of compulsory organization, as charisma is separated from the person and attached to the institution and to the office.

Because of its claim to be the custodian of all things sacred the church is able to make demands on political power. In fact its jurisdiction extends in principle to all areas of conduct, and no area is seen to be outside the limits of its authority. Weber maintained that the church was therefore able to deploy sanctions in the furtherance of its monopoly. Because of its claims to charisma of office the church is irrevocably opposed to all forms of personal charisma, that is, to any individual claim to prophetic or other illuminatory powers.

The sect, by contrast, opposes charisma of office. Within the sect the individual can partake of the sacred only by virtue of his own personal charisma, namely, by experiencing the sacred directly. Thus he can only become a member as a result of publicly established qualification, for example by rebaptism as a qualified adult. Because the emphasis is on personal charisma as opposed to charisma of office there is no separate stratum of specialists whose task it is to mediate the sacred to the rank and file. In its purist form the sect would therefore insist upon democratic administration under which clerical officials, in so far as they existed, would be treated as servants of the congregation.

Weber's pupil Ernst Troeltsch elaborated on the basic conceptual framework of his mentor. He tried to show that the tensions between radical and conservative elements in Christianity manifest themselves in different forms of organization.[10] The church accommodated itself to the prevailing social and political life, but the the anarchic communism inherent within the gospel lived on in various forms although tightly controlled, for instance in the lip service paid by the church to the ideal of brotherly love. The radical element in Christianity is either contained by the church, realized temporarily but then ultimately contained, or re-vitalized in the sect.

H. Richard Niebuhr's main interest was in denominationalism.[11] He claimed that in Protestant history the sect has always been the child of an outcast minority, taking its rise in the religious revolts of the poor, of those who were without effective representation in church and state. The sociological character of sectarianism is such that it is always modified in the course of time by the natural processes of birth and death. By its very nature the sectarian type of organization is valid only for one generation. The sects of the poor all become middle class sooner or later, and then they loose much of the enthusiasm which grew out of their necessities.

Howard Becker built on the ideas of Weber and Troeltsch and, for example, refined the sociological concept of denomination by proposing that it was in essence simply a sect in an advanced stage of development and adjustment to other religious collectivities and to the secular world.[12] The early fervour of the self-conscious sect has generally disappeared by the second or third generation and the problem of training the children of believers almost invariably causes some compromise to be made in the rigid requirements for membership which were characteristic of earlier phases.

Other sociologists, such as Liston Pope, J.M.Yinger, J. Wach and David Martin have, in a variety of ways, questioned or modified the concepts of Weber, Troeltsch, Niebuhr and Becker, but there has remained the core of characteristics distinguishing the three categories, which we have briefly outlined, which most sociologists tend to recognize, and which are useful in our present analysis.[13] However, before we conclude this review of pertinent sociological interpretations it will be helpful to summarize the characteristics of sects and denominations offered by Bryan Wilson.[14]

For him, a sect is a voluntary association. Membership is by proof to the sect authorities of some claim to personal merit, such as knowledge of doctrine, affirmation of conversion experience or recommendation by members of good standing. Exclusiveness is emphasized, and expulsion exercised against those who contravene doctrinal, moral or organizational precepts. A sect's self-conception is of an elect; a group of individuals possessing special enlightenment. Personal perfection is the expected standard of aspiration, and the sect is indifferent to or hostile to the secular society and the state. Sects differ among themselves in terms of internal characteristics, but the commitment of the sectarian is always more total and more defined than that of the member of other religious organizations. The ideology of the sect is much more clearly crystallized than that of the denomination or church, and the sectarian is much more distinctly characterized than is the member of one of the other types of religious organization. The behavioural correlates of his ideological commitment set him apart from the world. Sects have a totalitarian rather than a segmental hold over their members, in that they tend to regulate the totality of their lives. Ideological conformity may be achieved by compulsory participation but the method of control varies from sect to sect.

A denomination is recognizably different. It is formally a voluntary association, but it accepts adherents without the imposition of prerequisites of entry and employs purely formalized procedures of admission. It emphasizes breadth of belief and practice, and tolerance. Since membership is not tightly controlled, expulsion is not a common device for dealing with the apathetic or wayward. A denomination's self-conception is unclear and its doctrinal position is unstressed. It is content to be one movement among others, all of which are thought to be acceptable in the sight of God. The sociological idea of the denomination is that of HM loyal opposition, of disagreement within consensus. The denomination accepts the standards and values of the prevailing culture and of conventional morality. There is a trained professional ministry. Lay participation occurs but is typically restricted to particular aspects of the divine economy and to particular areas of activity. Services are formalized and spontaneity is largely absent.

Education of the young is of greater concern than evangelism of the outsider. Additional activities are largely non-religious in character. Members are drawn from any section of the community but within one church or one region membership will tend to limit itself to those who are socially compatible.

To whatever extent the sociological appraisals I have outlined are accepted as valid, and they may be questioned in certain details, they have an obvious relevance to the church life of England in the period 1558 to 1688, and this does not need to be greatly elaborated. Increasingly, the Church of England found itself set amidst a proliferation of sects and denominations, and, without the aid of latter-day sociological conceptions to help them, its members were confused and anxious about what was happening. It more and more found itself in an anomalous position as the established, national, church in an increasingly pluralist society. Indeed, immediately after the end of the period covered by this book an act of Parliament gave substance to what had been happening gradually throughout the preceding one hundred and fifty years. 'The Toleration Act of 1689 marked the end of the Church of England's claim to be the national church, the single all-inclusive church of the English people.'[15] Clearly there were countless men and women, and indeed the majority of churchmen, who believed, like William Sancroft, that the Church of England was 'a lily among thorns', and 'the purest certainly upon earth',[16] but they were now faced with the need to justify the role of the church in a much changed situation.

Thirdly, I will attempt to place the church, in its widest connotation, embracing the Church of England, the various forms of Dissent and Catholicism, within the total matrix of society. With the dramatic, eventful reigns of Elizabeth, James I and Charles I, the national trauma of the Civil War and the Interregnum, the impact of the Restoration and the reigns of Charles II and James II, and finally the epoch-making Revolution of 1688/89, there were political, constitutional, social and economic transformations which altered for ever the relationship of the church to the state, and transmuted the status and role of the church and the place of Christianity within the nation. I will try to discern what the faith meant to ordinary men and women at all levels of society. Clearly such an ambition is constantly thwarted by lack of evidence, by variations as between the regions, by the sheer complexity of an ever-changing population, and by the impossibility of entering into the inner life of any one person, let alone the population of a country over such a span of time. But due consideration should be given to what local studies reveal, and what can be learnt of the inner dynamics of the various Christian traditions which will be encountered.

Fourthly, these momentous years gave birth to the first modern manifestations of atheism, agnosticism and freethinking. 'Christianity remained far and away the most potent intellectual influence on Tudor Englishmen; and all allowance made for religious minorities and for magical and non-Christian beliefs, the Church remained central to the lives of the great majority.'[17] But this situation changed in the course of the seventeenth century. The probings of philosophers which gathered momentum around the mid-seventeenth century could not help but breed a certain scepticism and, in the hands of Thomas Hobbes, 'materialist scepticism about the grounds of knowledge could prove devastating to claims to religious certainty'.[18] The seventeenth century also witnessed the early growth of modern science and, albeit in a very restricted and undramatic way, the emergence of a 'scientific attitude', which, while not being inherently anti-religious, raised questions which before had largely lain dormant.

I

Prelude

Never, since the fifth, sixth and seventh centuries, and the era of St Patrick, St Columba, the Iona community, the coming of St Augustine and the subsequent spread of Christianity in the south, St Aidan, St Cuthbert, the Lindisfarne settlement, and the conversion of great tracks of the north, did England experience such concentrated, dramatic and important changes in her religious life as in the period from 1530 to 1689. In the early sixteenth century she was more or less secure in the Catholic fold, despite many stirrings of discontent, and church and state could reasonably be regarded as aspects of one entity. By the end of the seventeenth century she was well and truly a Protestant country: there was an independent national church with its clear identity, and well-defined and recognized body of belief and practice, but still somewhat uncertain about its relationship with the state; there were strong, well-established nonconformist bodies to some extent protected by law; and there was dawning the Age of Reason and the Enlightenment during which the very fundamentals of Christian belief were to be questioned more and more explicitly and passionately.

The pre-Reformation church

There is much disagreement over the degree of health enjoyed by the late mediaeval English church, but most historians would probably acknowledge that it was 'a collection of practices, habits and attitudes rather than an intellectually coherent body of doctrine'.[1] Whatever the extent of imperfection, and indeed corruption, that tarnished the late mediaeval church in England, and the church of the early sixteenth century, it appeared to contemporaries to be impregnable. It faced no formidable challenges, either from below, in the form of an attack upon its shortcomings, let alone upon the whole basis of its existence, or from above, in the form of an assault by the monarch or the central government to usurp its jurisdiction, redefine its theology or seize its property and lands. There was no widespread campaign for the non-payment of church tithes, or any other form of agitation to undermine the national, diocesan and parochial work of the church. There were a few heretics around, but this had been so for a century and more, and there was no reason to think that they would cause much trouble. The church had many and obvious failings, and it had its critics, but this had been so throughout most, if not all, of its history. 'And whatever the difficulties the church faced, little and usually local, it was secure, for it offered the sinners of England security in this world and eternal bliss in the next.' There were 'no Reformations on any visible horizon'.[2]

The church was an integral part of society, and for most of the population as they went about their daily tasks it was accepted as the only expression of the Christian faith known to them. It had no serious rival in its claim to be the spiritual home of all people. It exercised a great, diverse and vigorous hold over the imagination and the loyalty of the vase majority of citizens from the most humble to those of high rank. By providing opportunity for worship, by its cult of saints, by the visible expression of saintliness in images, by its claims to invoke the aid of the supernatural to help ordinary people to cope with the spiritual and physical hazards of everyday life, by its festivals, processions and special services which were so much part of the routine of life, and above all by the mystery of the mass, and the comforting rites of confession and absolution, the church was omnipresent and powerful in its sway over the population as a whole. The liturgy conducted within its walls was at the core of its life and that of the community which the local church served, 'for within that great seasonal cycle of fast and festival, of ritual observance and symbolic gesture, lay Christians found the paradigms and the stories which shaped their perception of the world and their place in it'.[3] The church, both in villages and urban areas, was the most usual gathering-place for the community, so that its liturgical life was enlarged and reinforced by other wide-ranging functions.

The liturgy lay at the heart of mediaeval religion, and the Mass lay at the heart of the liturgy. In the Mass the redemption of the world, wrought on Good Friday once for all, was renewed and made fruitful for all who believed. Christ himself, immolated on the altar of the cross, became present on the altar of the parish church, body, soul, and divinity, and his blood flowed once again, to nourish and renew Church and world. As kneeling congregations raised their eyes to see the Host held high above the priest's head at the sacring, they were transported to Calvary itself, and gathered not only into the passion and resurrection of Christ, but into the full sweep of salvation history as a whole.[4]

There is evidence that parish churches on the eve of the Reformation were in many respects flourishing, still regarded with awe as the places above all where lay Christians could encounter God, and that it was common for the local communities to take great pride in them. Although there were great variations from place to place, there was an overall huge demand for masses, and therefore for the priests to say them. And the mass was not just the supreme occasion when the individual believer offered devotion, and found a means of forgiveness and sanctification; it was a source of human community.

This sense of community went beyond the living to the dead, in the form of devotion to the saints. Such devotion was imposed by the church, with over fifty days of the year apart from Sundays being *festa ferianda*, days solemnly dedicated to the saints on which all except the most essential agricultural work was forbidden. And the pressure from above was met by a widespread enthusiasm from below. Candles lit before images of saints in churches and pilgrimages to the shrines of saints were common features of English church life. The saints were seen as being totally dependent on Christ but able in a special way to mediate the benefits of Christ's passion. They were regarded as intercessors for those who came to them seeking such aid, not only in the present but also at the last day. They were perceived as friends and helpers.

By the beginning of the sixteenth century the heyday of the great national shrine at Canterbury was over, but regional and local shrines, as well as the well established pilgrimages to Rome, Jerusalem and Compostella, remained the focus of much devotion until the very moment when they were outlawed. Likewise, devotions to Mary proliferated in late mediaeval and early sixteenth-century England, and her cult towered above that of all other saints.

As well as great value being placed upon the power of saints, and especially Mary, to intercede with God on behalf of sinners, there was almost universal belief in the efficacy of indulgences to shorten the torments of souls in purgatory. Despite the theological objections implicit in the notion of indulgences, they were eagerly sought by every class in English society in the later Middle Ages. The concept of purgatory itself loomed large in lay awareness, and provided the rationale not only for indulgences, but also for the immense elaboration of the late mediaeval cult of intercession for the dead. 'The whole structure of mortuary provision of Masses, alms, pilgrimage, and the adornment of churches and images, which to a greater or lesser degree characterized almost all the wills of fifteenth- and early sixteenth-century English men and women, was raised on the belief that such largesse would hasten the soul's passage through the pains of Purgatory.'⁵ The miseries and pains of purgatory offered powerful inducements to present right living, and full provision for the after life, and they were evoked by preachers consistently and persistently.

In the context of the small communities in which people spent their lives, the church, which was often the only substantial building for miles around, was a symbol of God's presence and the proud centre of local corporate life. Late mediaeval society was still 'implicitly Christian, even if there were conflicts between the ideal and the reality. Equally, the mediaeval church and its religion were explicitly social, catholicity defining its membership rather than its beliefs'.⁶

The late mediaeval church has been accused of blatant superstition. In response the revisionists claim that in the late fourteenth and early fifteenth centuries the kind of religious beliefs and practices to which I have alluded, which formed the conventional religion of the day, provided what in daily life were regarded as supernatural protection against the hazards of rural life, mechanisms of social conciliation and pathways to eternal life, but in such a way that the modern mind regards them as far-fetched superstition. At the popular level the sacraments and other ecclesiastical rituals, prayers and devotional practices 'were credited with an inexorable and compelling power'.⁷ Whether there was rampant superstition is to the revisionists largely a matter of definition. 'One man's superstition is another's spirituality: what mattered was that the simple rituals of village religion were functional – they apparently worked!'⁸ The vast majority of the English people were, on this understanding of the situation, at least passively satisfied with the manner in which the church undertook its religious and its social role. The church had many failings, but it was neither moribund nor oppressive, and ecclesiastical institutions were not for the most part corrupt or anachronistic.⁹

So the debate continues. It must be acknowledged that there is no easy answer. 'Investigating how far the people of late mediaeval England believed in and acted on the demands of Christianity encounters major obstacles. Contradictions and contrasts abound, now stressing belief in the church and in its creeds, and manifesting orthodox piety; now suggesting ignorance, anticlericalism and impiety.'[10] Any simple conclusion would be facile. The local studies[11] and new historiography of recent decades has shed much light, but it has also tended to increase the complexity of interpretation, and made it harder to reach a right judgment on the various issues involved. Nonetheless, on the basis of the evidence so far the pre-Reformation church in England does not seem to have been particularly degenerate. It was, for example, probably more open to legitimate criticism at the end of the fourteenth century than at the beginning of the sixteenth century. In the pre-Reformation era the church in England enjoyed the security of its long history, its integration into the whole life of the nation at all levels, and its subjection to Rome in matters of faith. In the church life of the country, and especially in 'popular religion', there were semi-pagan survivals, sub-Christian folk-lore and magic, and pre-Reformation Catholicism was vulnerable to the kind of attacks it was to receive from the Reformers, but it commanded the allegiance of most of the people, and in the early sixteenth century most observers would have considered it established and safe in its existing form for the foreseeable future. From the perspective of the distinctive Protestant emphasis upon personal faith, the vernacular Bible, the reform of the liturgy and the rejection of transubstantiation and the Catholic mass, the whole system appeared to be riddled with superstition and corruption. But, at the same time, the beliefs, and more especially the practices, of Catholicism were so well entrenched that it would not readily and quickly be displaced. The spread of Protestantism was therefore due, on the whole, to be slow, piecemeal and painful, with many setbacks.

The extent of negligence and corruption among the pre-Reformation bishops and clergy is also an unresolved issue. By the early sixteenth century the bishops had assumed a role in the life of the nation which demanded that they participate in both national and local political life and play their part as members of the landholding ruling elite. Many of the higher clergy were civil servants who had been rewarded with ecclesiastical promotions for the service they had rendered to the crown. Many church dignitaries grew immensely rich from ecclesiastical preferments. They were largely immersed in secular affairs, and they quite commonly left their religious duties to be performed vicariously, or not at all. It was a state of affairs which had developed over many centuries, but to its Protestant critics it was an open scandal. Although inherent in the accepted conduct of church and state affairs, it attracted criticism from those who considered that the wealth of the church was its spiritual bane, and that the secular ambitions and entanglements of its bishops were a hindrance to its spiritual well-being. There is little to indicate widespread episcopal profligacy or irresponsibility; it was more that the system militated against the exercise by its chief pastors of those functions which were essential for a spiritually healthy church.[12] And, despite the impediments, there were bishops who fulfilled their diocesan tasks in a way which even the severest critic would applaud. For example, in her study of John Langland, the bishop of the massive diocese of Lincoln from 1521 to 1547, Margaret Bowker describes a man who worked conscientiously to serve the clergy and people under his charge, and to uphold the Catholicism to which he was so devoted; and when he died it seems reasonably certain that 'he left a diocese with priests and laity as conservative as he was'.[13] Other examples could be presented of scrupulous episcopal conduct.[14] Nonetheless, as with the whole state of Catholicism previously mentioned, the work of bishops in general fell far short of the Protestant ideal, and they were therefore also wide open to the onslaught which was about to come.

Although the ignorance, negligence, indiscipline and avarice of the pre-Reformation clergy may have been unjustifiably magnified by commentators, they, like the higher clergy but for different reasons, were a ready target for criticism.[15] Absenteeism was certainly common, but probably less than has often been assumed. The clergy on the whole were neither illiterate nor incompetent, although preaching seems to have been poor. In such matters it is difficult to generalize, but it does appear that the sermons of the day were mostly stereotyped, and followed conventional and somewhat wooden forms, with a lack of personal inspiration and liveliness. They were efficient, for instance in conveying a Catholic understanding of the meaning of Easter, but they tended to follow a rather stylized and crudely materialistic view of the host, and it may be that the average sermons 'with their violent fantasies and pagan narratives, insensitively marshalled to support Christian doctrine, and not always even that, in fact smothered Christian truths in the minds of artless congregations'.[16] With their evident shortcomings, and as the frontline guardians of the ecclesiastical and religious system which was anathema to Protestants, they were very public and obvious targets for Protestant attacks.

The extent of pre-Reformation criticism levelled at the church in general and the priesthood in particular is difficult to gauge. The revisionists declare that anticlericalism was not widespread or pronounced. J.J. Scarisbrick claims that there was a partnership, or sym-

biosis, between laymen and cleric. There was a measure of anticlericalism, as there will presumably be in even healthy Christian societies.
There were rubs and rows as, for instance, over the ever contentious
issue of tithes; there were unpopular clergy who were criticized, but
these were attacks upon individuals rather than upon the office they
held; and there were areas of the country and remote regions which had
scarcely been Christianized at all, and where the people had little
time for Catholic clergy or the Catholic Church. But overall the level of
anticlericalism was not high, and it certainly did not match the bitter
and violent anticlericalism that was to be found on the continent.[17]
Christopher Haigh also considers that anticlericalism was not acute.
There were parishes where there was friction between priest and people,
but there was not a general clash between laity and clergy, and anticlericalism was not a cause of the Reformation. 'Anticlericalism', he
declares, is a 'convenient fiction', based on 'an embarrassingly narrow
range of examples'.[18] And these are typical remarks of those who project
an essentially harmonious relationship between the late mediaeval
priests and the lay people.[19] In contrast, others from A. G. Dickens
onwards have unearthed ubiquitous discontent with clergy. To cite
but two examples. J. F. Davis has drawn attention to the heresy trials
of 1511, and asserted that one of their features was rampant anticlericalism,[20] and W. J. Sheils maintains that contemporary evidence
reveals widespread dissatisfaction with the church in the early sixteenth
century among all sectors of society.[21]

There was clearly scope for the development of anticlericalism. There
is ample evidence of individual hostility and violence against clerics,
presentments at visitation, resentment at tithe and other payments,
murmurings when absenteeism deprived the community of pastoral
oversight and church services, and complaints in some of the reformist
literature, but there seems to be remarkably little evidence of serious
and extensive anticlericalism.[22] For a good proportion of the parishes of
the land the parishioners displayed a quiet, unostentatious devotion to
the faith of their fathers, with the parish church as the focal point not
only for their religious life, but also for their social and administrative
affairs.[23] This is not to say that there was not much against which the
reformers could justifiably rail. Indeed, the whole Catholic system was
shot through with features which were abhorrent to the proto-
Protestants and Protestants. Nevertheless, at the local level the church
was continuing in its way of life, its practices, and in its role as regula-
tor of the moral behaviour of the English laity, much as it had done for

centuries before the Reformation. Of course there was great diversity
and variation in the type and quality of parish ministry from one region
to another, and between different parishes,[24] but I am concerned with
an overall assessment.

John Colet, the Dean of St Paul's, in an influential sermon in 1511,
pinpointed four fundamental evils which beset the clergy: ambition,
which resulted in a scramble for office, and pluralism; carnal and moral
laxity; covetousness, which resulted in the clergy being over zealous in
exacting dues from the laity; and, perhaps most importantly, too great
a concern for the affairs of the secular world.[25] Recent studies have cast
doubt upon the validity of Colet's criticisms as applied to the generality
of the English clergy, and have shown that any generalizations are
dangerous. Much of the parochial ministry was conscientiously undertaken within the accepted Catholic norms of the day.[26] And it needs to
be borne in mind that there were undoubtedly serious economic
problems facing the average parish and parish clergyman in the early
sixteenth century which had unfortunate repercussions: pluralism
and seeking after all possible tithes and dues often appeared to be
undesirable but necessary. The clergy were often local men, perhaps
mostly conscientious, but certainly, in the majority of cases, poorly-
paid.[27]

In the immediate pre-Reformation years the church was exercising its
social influence chiefly through the sermons and homilies delivered by
the clergy, and by means of the sacrament of confession and penance,
but it was also doing so through the ecclesiastical courts. There were
notorious cases of gross injustice perpetrated by the pre-Reformation
church courts, of which the most infamous was that of Richard Hunne
in 1514, but in general they offered a local and relatively cheap way of
settling disputes in a wide range of matters concerned with moral and
property law.[28] It has been the conclusion of all historians who have
recently examined the records of individual courts that there was
remarkably little hostility to the jurisdiction of the courts in matters
of religious belief and practice, and of morality. Indeed, those who
have studied specific categories of business have admired the conscientious discharge of their duties by all the court personnel, especially the
judges.

Although the pre-Reformation church and its associated institutions
was not particularly degenerate or ineffectual, it represented a form of
Christianity which was regarded by proto-reformists and Protestant
reformers as having seriously drifted from the biblical norm; and it was

therefore fundamentally flawed. It needed to be radically reformed, or replaced. It needed a Reformation. And this brings us to the Lollards; for they, perhaps more than any other pre-Reformation group in England, called for a reformation and renewal of the church.

During much of the fifteenth century the Lollards were a diffuse and unfocussed popular movement. There were Lollard groups, or cells, which persisted for more than a century, but they had no church of their own, no organization, and no creed or clearly formulated body of doctrine which made them distinctive and around which they could rally.[29] They variously attacked papal authority, transubstantiation, the veneration of images, clerical endowments, purgatory, indulgences, pilgrimages and the use of music during the liturgy; they championed the provision and use of the scriptures in the vernacular, and gave priority to the role of the godly prince. They proclaimed the scriptures as the sole authority for belief and practice, preached, and circulated Bible translations and religious tracts. Divergent strands appeared within Lollardy, but that it survived and 'contributed in some significant degree toward the Protestant Reformation is a fact based upon incontrovertible evidence'.[30]

After the initial impulse which the founder, John Wyclif, gave to the movement, Lollardy had been driven underground by the repressive measures of Henry IV and his successor. But during the late 1480s it revived and, in the absence of any vigorous attempts to subvert it, began to flourish. By the end of the first decade of the sixteenth century it had developed into a serious menace to the church, and, if the number of cases coming before the courts is taken as a true indicator, this surge continued until the 1530s.[31] 'There was no straightforward move from pre-Reformation dissent into the post-Reformation Church, but the specific beliefs of the Lollard tradition were to play their part in shaping that Church's religion.'[32]

The ground had also been prepared for the reception of Lutheran doctrines by subtle theological, philosophical and ideological trends. There was the *devotio moderna*, the deepening of the spiritual life in the later Middle Ages. Throughout Europe it tended to assume the form of a quiet pietism among both lay people and secular clergy. It was an example of taking piety into the market place, and it existed alongside the more demanding, austere and elevated mysticism which was prevalent within a small elite of the monastic orders. It inclined to deflect interest from the ecclesiastical institutions to an interior and personal religion.

Such a re-focussing of spiritual life was reinforced by the decline of scholasticism. After a protracted period in which it had, to quite a large extent, been discredited, Luther opposed the whole scholastic theological system with his biblical theology. But even before his onslaught Erasmus and Colet were applying the New Learning to the study of the scriptures. The shift of standpoint and method in English theological life showed itself clearly in 1496–7 when Colet returned from Italy and delivered his momentous Oxford lectures on Paul's Epistle to the Romans. His commentary was not to be compared in its radical deductions with that of Luther, but it nevertheless had a remarkable freshness, appeal to common sense, breadth of outlook and vigour when compared with its mediaeval predecessors. He took a new look at the book and applied the humanist critique to the text. He was fascinated by the life and thought of Paul, and he treated him as a real man in a real historical setting. He was influenced by mediaeval methods of exegesis, but the novelty was the way in which he departed from the established methods of exposition. In a similar way Erasmus made his contribution to a change in the intellectual and religious climate in England by his humanism, and his demands for a scriptural Christianity and vernacular Bibles for the people. Tyndale and others responded by attempting to meet such demands.

William Tyndale (*c*.1495–1536) was the greatest of the Bible translators. Born in an area of Gloucestershire where the Lollards had once been strong, at a young age he made it the single dominant object of his life to produce a worthy and scholarly English version of the Bible in language which was readable by the boy who followed the plough. Despite being a Latin and Greek scholar of considerable erudition, he had no private means and was not able to gain preferment in England. He was eventually financed by sympathetic members of the Merchant Adventurers Company, whom he met in London. This enabled him to emigrate to Germany, live there while he undertook his translation work, print his translation on German presses and clandestinely import and distribute it in England. His translation of the New Testament, with some renderings which excited the wrath of some conservative churchmen, arrived in England in 1526. It was the work of a genius, and was substantially preserved in the Authorized Version of 1611. The authorities disapproved. The church burnt it, and would gladly have assigned the translator to the flames as well. By 1530 Tyndale had also translated and printed the Pentateuch and the Book of Jonah. His self-appointed task was, however, abruptly terminated in 1535 when he was betrayed by a fellow Englishman and, after eighteen months in prison, strangled and burnt in October 1536 under the heresy laws of the Netherlands.

The ex-friar Miles Coverdale (1488–1568), an associate of Tyndale's later years, turned to Protestant Switzerland for protection and there completed the translation of the whole Bible. He made full use of Tyndale's work, and a literal translation from the Hebrew into Latin by the Italian Dominican Santes Pagninus. He was not a Hebrew scholar, but, with his complete command of German, he was able to take advantage of two German translations, one of which was by Luther. And he made his own distinctive contribution, for he had a remarkable ear 'for the well-turned phrase and for the ring of a sentence'.[33] This talent was well displayed in his version of the psalms which was incorporated into the Anglican Prayer Book. He was also a far more amenable collaborator with the government than Tyndale, and did not offend Catholic susceptibilities in the same way as Tyndale, with abusive marginal comments. His Bible was approved by Thomas Cromwell, and via Cromwell by Henry VIII. The enterprising printer James Nicholson was permitted to print it, and such was its success that in 1537 he issued two revised editions.

At the same time a translation came from the pen of John Rogers, chaplain to the house of English merchants at Antwerp, who adopted the pseudonym Thomas Matthew. This so-called 'Matthew Bible' attracted the attention of Thomas Cranmer, who brought it to the notice of Thomas Cromwell in August 1537; and Cromwell prevailed upon the King to allow its sale throughout the country. Rogers later won distinction as protomartyr of the Marian persecution, when he was burnt at Smithfield in February 1555 in the presence of his Flemish wife, her infant baby, and their ten other children.

Over a number of years Cromwell planned a new and authoritative English Bible. He entrusted the revision to Coverdale. The work, which came to be called the Great Bible, duly appeared in July 1539. By the end of 1541 it had run through seven editions.

Even during the short span of years which is the subject of this book, the vernacular English Bible was the bedrock for the development of Anglicanism and Dissent; it was the means whereby multitudes came to a living and vital faith; it gave inspiration to George Herbert, John Milton, John Bunyan and a host of other major or lesser poets and writers; it fortified the spirit of the Pilgrim Fathers and the pioneers in the New World; it gave courage and inspiration to Oliver Cromwell;

and it helped to mould a nation during a time when it was forging its own identity.

Despite all these influences, it appears that at any one time during the first seventy years of the sixteenth century the number of enthusiastic, fully convinced and committed Protestants, whether they be Lollards, Lutherans or English reformers, was small in total and minuscule as a proportion of the entire population. But their energy and determination made them effective. They had a message which was in many respects antipathetic to the prevailing beliefs and practices of official Catholicism and the accepted norms of the population as a whole. As we have seen, in the popular and conventional religion of early sixteenth-century Englishmen salvation was sought through devout observances, and there was a great emphasis on saints, relics and pilgrimages. A powerful preaching of justification by faith was bound to play havoc with the cults of such popular religion. 'It struck at the foundations of saint-worship, pilgrimages, formal penances, pardons, indulgences, intercessory masses, chantries and a host of other institutions, since not merely the abuses and superstitions associated with them, but even the beliefs underlying them became suspect; they seemed to be futile attempts to build up human "merit" and distractions from the creation of the new relationship between God and man.'[34]

The Henrician Reformation

In the second quarter of the sixteenth century Protestantism was promoted by a stalwart band of resolute men. Robert Barnes and Thomas Garret were selling Tyndale's New Testament wherever they could elude the vigilance of the bishops. John Frith helped Tyndale and then published a number of provocative tracts. He finally perished at the stake in 1533. The heresy of Thomas Bilney consisted of little more than a repudiation of the practice of intercession to saints and a denial of the contemporary purgatorial doctrines, yet he suffered martyrdom at the stake in 1531. Bilney had been one of a group of students who discussed Lutheran writings and Erasmus' Greek Testament at a meeting-place in Cambridge known as Little Germany. Others in the group included Thomas Cranmer, William Tyndale, George Joye, William Roy, Robert Barnes, John Frith, Nicholas Ridley, Rowland Taylor, Thomas Arthur, Matthew Parker and Hugh Latimer. They were all feeling their way. Although they avoided making spectacular pronouncements and shunned controversial criticism, a body of opinion was beginning to grow which was neither traditional nor Lutheran.

Then, in the midst of all this largely uncoordinated, and often somewhat covert, activity came the very coordinated, extremely public, staccato-like Acts of State of the 1530s and the dissolution of the monasteries. In quick succession a number of Acts transformed the official national religious scene. In a few years the King and his chief minister, Cromwell, 'consummated a dual revolution, severing the English Church from the Papacy and subjugating it to the control of the Crown in Parliament'.[35] The Acts were not introduced because of a tide of public opinion pressing for change, but because of the personal circumstances of the King who was assisted in his policy by the determined and purposeful Cromwell. They were made possible because the church had a weak hold upon political opinion. Without them the spread of English Protestantism would have been retarded.

The series of enactments and actions I am about to review were triggered by Henry's tortuous manoeuverings in order to effect an annulment of his marriage with Catherine of Aragon. But the 'great matter' must not be seen either as the mere 'occasion' or as the sole cause of the English Reformation. It was neither. Without it the schism with Rome would not have been consummated by 1533–4, and who can say how much longer England would then have remained within the Roman fold? On the other hand it was not the chief cause of the cataclysm, without which England would have remained Catholic, for there were forces at work in society by that time, as we have noted, which made a reformation likely at any time, or over a period of time, given the right circumstances.

Under Henry and Cromwell something like a planned revolution was enacted between 1532 and 1540. First came the acceptance by the Commons of the King's demands as expressed in a document known as 'the Submission of the Clergy', whereby they acknowledged Henry in place of the Pope as their supreme legislator. 'From that point the English Church ceased to be a potential obstacle in the progress of the breach with Rome.'[36]

Next came the bill for the abolition of annates, the payments made by the bishops to the Pope on accession to their sees, rated at one-third of a year's income, and a long-standing grievance in the whole Western church. The bill also provided for the independent English consecration of bishops-elect if the Pope retaliated by refusing bulls of consecration. As the time for such extreme measures had not yet come, Henry hesitated to sanction the bill, and Cromwell inserted a clause which held it up until the King should confirm it by letters patent. The act thus became a means whereby Henry could demonstrate his restraint on parliament. It was a useful diplomatic weapon in his armoury.

The 1533 Act in Restraint of Appeals was Cromwell's masterpiece in statute-making and a crucial piece of legislation. It extended the provisions of Richard II's statute of praemunire to appeals lodged at Rome. In its preamble England was called an Empire and her sovereign was said to owe submission to no other human ruler.

After the divorce issue had been settled, Cromwell expeditiously produced a succession of statutes designed to elaborate a new legal relationship between church and state, and passed them through Parliament during the two crowded sessions of 1534. A further Act in Restraint of Annates confirmed the prohibition of payments to Rome and laid down the procedure for the election of bishops and abbots. Election henceforth became purely formal, for the chapters and monasteries were bound to elect those nominated in the royal licence. The Dispensations Act finally stopped all payments to Rome and then stipulated that dispensations, which meant licences to allow departures from the canon law, should be issued by the Archbishop of Canterbury. The Act of Submission of the Clergy gave statutory form to the existing submission and forbade Convocation to legislate except by the licence of the Crown. A yet further statute ordered the payment of first fruits (one year's income for the new incumbent of any benefice) and tenths (an annual levy of one tenth of the annual value of every benefice) to the Crown. Lastly, the Treason Act in the second of these two historic sessions made the calling of the King or Queen a heretic or schismatic a treasonable offence. In total, these acts completed the work of establishing the royal supremacy in the church and of destroying the power of the Pope in England.

Cromwell was the driving force behind all this legislative activity, as he was in the ensuing dissolution of the monasteries. In 1535 he was appointed vicar-general, and in that capacity undertook a thorough investigation and reconstitution of the church, over the heads of the bishops, and this included a visitation of the religious houses. All the smaller of these institutions with an income of less than £200 a year, except for any the King identified as fit to be an exception, were first of all targeted, and then the greater monasteries. The property was assigned to the Crown, the heads of the houses given a pension and the monks given the option of being transferred to the greater houses or of seeking employment as secular clergy. The work was largely accomplished between 1536 and 1540. In terms of its social effects it was the most far reaching enactment of the government in those revolutionary years.

'Historians of widely different religious persuasions are today remarkably agreed that the monasteries of early Tudor England were no longer playing an indispensable role in the spiritual life of the country, certainly not one to justify their continued employment of so large a part of the landed wealth of the kingdom.'[37] The monasteries still had their defenders, and some of the risings in the North were animated in part by a rallying call to defend them against their detractors.[38] But, for the most part, they had ceased to be communities dedicated to holy living, which set an example to laymen and their secular brethren. Monasteries were owners of great tracts of land, and they had mostly come to play a part in the more mundane aspects of contemporary town and country public life which was more or less commensurate with their status as landowners. Nonetheless, there is little known about contemporary views on these long-established institutions. The evidence from official pronouncements concerning moral shortcomings among monks and nuns can be largely discounted, as it was gathered with a particular end policy in mind, and the pronouncements of bishops and other 'visitors' also needs to be viewed in its true perspective. 'But the attitude of ordinary early Tudor laymen, and the extent to which they regarded the monasteries as a necessary part of their present and future life, still largely eludes the historian.'[39]

The dissolution of the monasteries created a massive change in landownership, which was second only to that which followed the Norman Conquest, but it was far less revolutionary than it might have been. The purchasers of the land seem mostly to have been the former lessees or local landowners, often of gentry status, who wished to consolidate their estates. There were very few new men or outsiders who exploited the market, so that the general pattern of landownership among the laity was not too radically disturbed. As a consequence, the poor, and the customary tenants, did not usually lose their traditional rights, and they were not normally exploited by their new landlords.

Many of the monasteries' critics were adamant that their very considerable wealth could be used more positively for the common good, and in particular for the social and religious, but more especially educational, betterment of the people. This expectation was frustrated, for Henry VIII failed to make such a transfer of resources. Although some monastic property was used to establish new bishoprics out of large dioceses, as with the creation of Peterborough and Oxford out of the former diocese of Lincoln, and Chester from parts of York and Lichfield, their endowment was inadequate and resulted in administrative difficulties.[40] The sum total of educational endowment was the founding of Trinity College, Cambridge and Wolsey's college at Oxford, later to be renamed Christ Church. Although the Chantries Act of 1547 was more significant as a gesture of reform than as an act of plunder, it did result in the refounding of their schools, and the placing of these schools on a more secure base. But even this planned redistribution of wealth, albeit quite sizeable, was piecemeal and haphazard. It was not the sort of programme envisaged by the humanist reformers of the 1530s, and the growth in educational provision in Tudor England was mainly the result of private benefactions rather than of Crown policy.

Nevertheless, it was perhaps the dissolution of the chantries that had a more devastating local effect than the abolition of monasteries. There were probably over four thousand of them or similar institutions in pre-Reformation England, each capable of supporting at least one priest.[41] There were regional variations, with a great concentration in London, largely because of its wealth. There were more in the North than in the South-East or Midlands, with one in two churches housing a chantry of some sorts in the former and about one in five in the latter two regions. The chantries, and what they undertook, appear to have had quite widespread support, and it seems that the enthusiasm for chantry foundations was a national phenomenon which persisted into the sixteenth century.

The abundance of chantries is but part of the evidence of a desperate desire for intercessory masses, which they were able to gratify for people of substance. For an infinitely larger number of people this yearning was satisfied by membership of confraternities or religious gilds. Such voluntary associations proliferated in England in the late fourteenth and fifteenth centuries. Most were local and based in the parish. Their popularity is accounted for by both the widespread fear of sudden death, especially in the wake of the Black Death, a deep lay devotion, and a craving for mutual aid in the search for salvation.[42]

To accompany all these radical actions, there was some attempt to achieve a measure of doctrinal definition. This took the form of the Ten Articles of 1536 which, after the failure of the bishops to produce an agreed statement, was largely dictated by the King himself. In defining the faith of the newly constituted church, the Articles showed a compromise between the old and the new, but retained a very clear Catholic element. They were orthodox on the sacraments of the altar, penance and baptism, and on the place of good works in the total economy of God; but they deemed no other sacraments necessary, and they cautiously advanced towards the Lutheran view on the vexed problems of prayers to saints and prayers for the dead. Cromwell followed the Ten Articles with Injunctions which made the Articles binding on the clergy; ordered a Bible in English to be placed in every parish church; and instructed the clergy to preach against the usurped power of the Bishop of Rome, to discourage veneration of images and relics and the making of pilgrimages, and to teach children the Lord's Prayer, Creed and Commandments in English.

It is questionable how far these enactments were effective in practice. To take but one example, there is strong evidence to show that in the 1530s, on the eve of a wave of iconoclasm, icons were of considerable importance to the average man and woman. And this cleaving to traditional values and practices extended to other well-established acts of devotion. 'Time, energy and expenditure were still faithfully bestowed upon the maintenance of traditional figures, the erection of new additions, the provision of clothes, ornaments and lofts, and the offering of lights, of gifts and pilgrimage.'[43]

Nonetheless, for whatever combination of reasons, the revolution which was effected in the 1530s only met limited and disjointed opposition. Amid the ruling classes there was no split along doctrinal lines. The Duke of Norfolk and the Earl of Shrewsbury were the leading magnates who strove to preserve Henry's throne when sedition and rebellion appeared, and yet they held Catholic beliefs, and detested Cromwell and his reforming outlook. The higher clergy were compliant. Only John Fisher, Bishop of Rochester, accepted martyrdom over the question of the Supremacy, and only one, Reginald Pole, chose exile on account of his beliefs, although many of the bishops, headed by Stephen Gardiner and Cuthbert Tunstall, were opposed to Cromwell and Cranmer. Those heads of monasteries accused of treason and complicity in rebellion, with a few exceptions such as Abbot Cooke of Reading, seem to have been unfortunate victims rather than deliberate martyrs. And, in general, the parish clergy appear to have accepted the decisions of authority with little demur. The most notable champion of the old order was Thomas More, 'the most distinguished but most controversial adversary of the English Reformation'.[44] More was resolutely orthodox and explicitly advocated the burning of heretics, but such was the weight of learning and the sanctity of character with which he upheld his orthodoxy that he commanded the respect and even the awe of many of those who strongly repudiated his views.

The most forthright and public demonstration against the new measures was the northern rising known as the Pilgrimage of Grace, which convulsed Lincolnshire, Yorkshire, and finally all the North at the end of 1536. For a time it appeared to threaten not only Cromwell's programme of reformation but even Henry's throne. The causes were complex. Basically the North was more feudal and conservative than most areas of the country, and the interference of central government in its affairs, which had markedly increased under Cromwell, was resented. The nobility and gentry objected to the invasion of their rights, and the agricultural fraternity cried out against enclosures and raised rents. Roman Catholicism was especially entrenched, and the reforms, although barely begun, were seen by many as heretical. Monastic institutions abounded in Lincolnshire and Yorkshire. They were seemingly valued as part of the rich northern religious tradition and way of life, and there was widespread indignation at the policy of dissolution.

In Yorkshire, Robert Aske, a country gentleman and lawyer, assumed the leadership of what was to him essentially a Christian cause – he popularized the banner which displayed the five wounds of Christ and used the terminology of a pilgrimage. His followers took York, where he set up in state, issued ordinances for the government of the north, received the adherence of such dignitaries as Edward Lee, the Archbishop of York and Lord Darcy, and amassed a band of 30,000 armed men. But the uprising came to nothing, for after some negotiations between the Duke of Norfolk, representing the King, and the rebels, and vague promises which were not fulfilled, the pilgrimage was ended and, with an additional excuse provided by a further, untimely disturbance, Norfolk preceded to execute men all over the North, including Aske and Lord Darcy. Henry would not tolerate opposition.

It appears that the King had never been an enthusiastic religious reformer, and he had retained much of his ingrained Catholicism. When a Catholic reaction to the reformation process became evident in the late 1530s he therefore introduced the Act of the Six Articles of 1539 which attempted a definition of the Christian faith with a view to 'abolishing diversity of opinions'. The articles consisted of an assertion of the doctrine of transubstantiation; and declarations that communion should be administered to laymen in one kind only, that the marriage of priests was forbidden, that private masses should continue, that vows of charity must be perpetually observed, and that auricular confession should persist. Such requirements demonstrate that the Henrician Reformation was not a capitulation to Protestantism, and Protestants denounced the Act as a whip with six strings. Indeed, at the end of his reign, in 1546, the Catholic party remained energetic in the Privy Council, still with high hopes of stamping out what it regarded as heresy.

The Edwardian Reformation

However, with the death of Henry VIII and the coming of Edward VI, with a Protectorate under the Duke of Somerset and then the leadership of the Duke of Northumberland, the pendulum started to swing more markedly in a Protestant direction. Somerset sanctioned the publication of books by reformers, such as Luther, Tyndale, Wyclif, Barnes, Bullinger and Frith. Persecution under the Six Articles ceased; popular preachers denounced images, and in various places Protestants smashed them and interrupted traditional ceremonies; a campaign was launched both by the bishops and the Council with equal zeal, for the removal of all stone altars and for their replacement with wooden communion tables; an Act of Parliament censured anyone reviling the mass, but approved communion in both kinds; legislation dissolving the chantries was approved; clergy were required to recite homilies from the pulpit which attacked the doctrines of purgatory and salvation by good works, and proclaimed salvation by faith alone; and the Council authorized Cranmer and the divines to draft 'one convenient and meet order, rite, and fashion of Common Prayer' for use in England, Wales and Calais.

The first Prayer Book was issued in 1549, and enforced by the first Edwardian Act of Uniformity. The book was a compromise between Catholicism and Protestantism, with concessions to Catholicism, especially regarding ceremonies, which greatly disappointed Protestants. In fact Stephen Gardiner was able to give it an orthodox Catholic reading: and that convinced the reformers that it was unacceptable. It was basically a translation of the Sarum Use, and it was more a liturgical work than a formulary of religious doctrine. Its main theological significance lay in its treatment of the eucharist. And in this there is evident a mixture of the old and the new. Thus, the Prayer Book gave the eucharist the title – 'The Supper of the Lord and the Holy Communion Commonly Called the Mass'. Thomas Cranmer was in the midst of a personal re-appraisal of his own eucharistic thought. In the late 1530s the archbishop had seriously begun to question the Catholic doctrine of transubstantiation, and in 1546 he started to waver on the doctrine of the real presence. During the debate over the new Prayer Book he was initially influenced by John à Lasco, and spoke of the bread and wine as merely 'figurative' elements, reflecting the teaching of Zwingli, but by the end of the debate he echoed the opinions of Bishop Ridley. This doctrinal shift is to be seen in the words of consecration in the new Prayer Book, which state that the body and blood of Christ 'may be unto us'; a departure from the words 'may be made unto us' in the old Use of Sarum. The wording permitted the denial of transubstantiation but was compatible with either a real presence or a true presence. It was also important from the point of view of the protestantization process that there were a few significant liturgical changes, such as the omission of the elevation of the host. But the most significant short and long-term novelty lay in the language used. Here was an authorized manual of worship in English, which drew heavily upon the Great Bible of Tyndale and Coverdale and the Lutheran Church Orders as well as the Catholic rite according to the Use of Sarum. Together with the Second Prayer Book (1552) and the Forty-Two Articles (1553), the foundations were being truly laid for the impending Elizabethan Settlement.[45]

The Act of Uniformity which enforced the Prayer Book provided graduated penalties. For refusal to use the new Prayer Book, for using other forms of worship or for 'depraving' it, the offending cleric rendered himself liable to loss of the profit from one of his benefices for a year and to suffer imprisonment for six months. A second offence would result in the permanent loss of all benefices and one year's imprisonment. Life imprisonment was the penalty for a third offence. No penalty was specified for laymen absenting themselves from church, but any person attacking the Prayer Book or procuring a cleric to use other forms of service would incur a fine of £10 for the first offence, £20 for the second and loss of all goods for the third.

By 1549 England had been greatly influenced by continental Protestant theologians who came and settled in the country, significantly from Strasbourg, Zurich and Geneva rather than from Wittenberg. Of particular note were Peter Martyr, Bernardino Ochino and, most outstandingly, Martin Bucer. He was the leader of the Strasbourg churches and a close friend of John Calvin. He combined tolerance with a strong commitment to the Swiss reformation, and he shared with Cranmer an interest in and talent for liturgical revision.

From 1549, when he was appointed Regius Professor of Divinity at Cambridge, he advised on the compilation of *The Ordinal* of 1550, the service for the ordination of priests, in which the traditional rite was followed quite closely, but a pronounced and unequivocal Protestant strain was introduce with the stress placed on the function of the clergy. Previously the newly ordained priest was assured that he was to 'Receive authority to offer sacrifice and celebrate Mass both for the living and the dead', whereas the new instructions were 'Take thou authority to preach the word of God and to minister the holy sacraments in the congregation.' The new emphasis on preaching was symbolically expressed by the presentation to the ordinands of a Bible in addition to the traditional chalice and paten.

The Protestant cause was considerably furthered by the Second Prayer Book of 1552, the second Act of Uniformity of the same year, the reform of the common law and the codification of the beliefs of the church in the form of the Forty-Two Articles.

The second Prayer Book acknowledged many of the Protestant objections raised to the first Prayer Book, including about two-thirds of those expressed by Bucer. It made some deliberate breaks with the past, especially in its form of communion service. It was based on the premise that 'everything without scriptural warrant should be omitted and a form of worship evolved which the Apostles themselves could have sanctioned'.[46] What were attacked as the 'papal' remnants in doctrine, gestures and vestments in the 1549 communion service were dropped, so that even the most vehement critics, like John Hooper, could be satisfied that the mass had been abolished in England. The so-called Black Rubric also made it clear that kneeling at the communion denoted only respect for and not adoration of the sacrament, and this helped to placate the more extreme reformers. The congregations up and down the country would have been most aware of the replacement of the altar by the communion table in a different and more accessible position, and the substitution of the traditional vestments by a plain surplice. Those who were more learned or zealous would have observed that the structure of the communion service had been radically changed and that the canon had been redesigned to give emphasis to the congregational or communal features of the service.

The most important doctrinal change in the new Prayer Book was the use in the administration of the sacrament of the words 'Take and eat this, in remembrance that Christ died for thee, and feed on him in thy heart by faith with thanksgiving', instead of the former words 'The

Body of Our Lord Jesus Christ which was given for thee, preserve thy body and soul unto everlasting life.' This new form did not deny belief in a real presence in accord with what Ridley had set out in 1549, but it was open to an interpretation which was acceptable to the most radical of the Swiss 'memorialist' reformers. In this and other respects the new Prayer Book allowed for differences of view on the eucharist, but within the ranks of the Protestants rather than between Protestant and Catholic.[47]

The second Act of Uniformity was passed in 1552 to enforce conformity to the new Prayer Book. It reasserted the authority of the former Act of Uniformity and imposed penalties on those who attended any other form of worship. It met with little overt protest or signs of disapproval, for the parish clergy who were ill at ease about the new liturgy were not organized to resist, and no one gave them the lead to do so.

Cranmer also applied himself to the arduous, but much needed, task of reforming the law administered in the church courts. His *Reformatio Legum Ecclesiasticarum* made a major contribution to the process, although it remained unpublished until 1571.

In June 1553 the Forty-Two Articles, which Cranmer had compiled after consultation with the bishops, received the royal assent. They were issued largely in response to the pressure, especially since 1549, for a doctrinal declaration. They represented a decisively Protestant interpretation of the faith, with attacks upon such traditional Catholic views as transubstantiation, the sacrificial mass, purgatory, clerical celibacy and papal supremacy. But they also expressed strong opposition to the continental Anabaptists: to the denial of original sin, the dispensing with moral law, to lay preaching, communal property, forswearing of oaths, millenarianism and the belief in universal salvation. They sought to encompass Lutheran, Calvinist and Zwinglian creeds without accommodating the Catholic faith, except where it did not, in any case, differ from the main Protestant interpretations. The articles also reinforced the status and standing of the King in relation to the established church, declaring him to be 'Supreme head on earth, next under Christ, of the Church of England'. The articles were sanctioned by Convocation without debate, and Northumberland and the Council promulgated them. But it was too late for them to have much impact at the time, for within a few months the young King was dead, and his successor, Mary, immediately abandoned her brother's religious policies.

England's Reformation was not speedy, and it took time for the ideas to penetrate the country. It was largely led from above, at national and local levels, by monarchs and Parliament and by clergy and local leaders. There was a gradual educational process, which was aided by the growth of the printed word and means for its dissemination, so that each new generation was more fully educated in a Protestant direction than their elders, and familiar with no other order. 'The concurrent generational and familial dislocations which affected many adolescents meant that, by Mary's accession in 1553, a whole generation had been brought up in many places on the reformed doctrines, or had discovered them for themselves. In such cases a process of veritable reconversion would be needed to re-establish Catholic truth among them.'[48]

The Marian Reformation

The reign of Mary lasted only five years, yet it had an enduring effect and left an indelible impression; but in a way, and in a form which was the very opposite of what the sovereign intended. She attempted to restore the realm to its former papal obedience, and, as she saw it, to save the country from mortal sin. She may have succeeded but for the shortness of her reign and a series of actions which militated against her one set purpose. Prominent among these was her marriage to Philip of Spain, the son and heir of Charles V, after resolute resistance to all attempts to persuade her not to do so, and the consequent widespread alarm which the marriage caused, with the spectre raised among Protestants of restored Roman Catholicism and possible incorporation within the Habsburg dominions. She compounded this particular mis-understanding of her subjects' prejudices by also delighting openly in her Spanish blood. She showed no sympathy for the financial concerns of those influential subjects who were anxious about surrendering the monastic property which they had so recently acquired. She embarked upon a persecution which aroused widespread distaste even in an age accustomed to suffering and brutal punishment. She undertook an unpopular war and lost Calais disastrously. She employed the services of Reginald Pole, the papal legate, and thus reposed her greatest trust in a man who almost totally miscalculated the mood of the nation.

The first Marian Parliament, called in September 1553, showed that while its collective view was decidedly not Protestant, it was also not papalist. It broadly represented the religious position as it had been in the final years of Henry VIII. It was undoubtedly a distinctive departure from the Edwardian Parliaments. In these early days of the new monarch there were indications of the general willingness of the nation 'to take its religious colour from the Crown, which had not as yet shown its full papal intentions'.[49] But it was not long before such intentions became clear. When, with Philip at her side, she summoned her third Parliament in the autumn of 1554, her main purpose was to obtain the necessary approval for the national submission to Rome. At the time of this parliamentary session Cardinal Pole arrived as the papal legate and the chosen instrument of the reconciliation. The Queen received him joyfully, and a week later the two Houses almost unanimously petitioned that the realm should be readmitted to the Roman communion. The ceremony of absolution and reconciliation was duly performed by the Cardinal. After some debate appropriate legislation was agreed by Parliament. Philip was included with the Queen within the scope of the treason law, and it was made a treasonable offence to pray for the Queen's death or assert that her title to the throne was defective. The church was empowered to condemn heretics and the Crown to burn them. The legislation of Henry VIII against the powers of the clergy and the papal jurisdiction was repealed. But, perhaps as evidence that all this was not totally indicative of a genuine repentance, ex-church lands were declared to be, like all other land, within the protection of the common law and not subject to the decisions of any canonical court.

It was at this point that the burning of the Protestants began. The number of fully convinced and dedicated Protestants in the country at the time cannot be computed, but it was far in excess of the Lollards and the pioneers of the New Learning in Henry's middle years, and they were far more influential than their forebears. The Queen was determined to suppress them, and at whatever cost. In this resolve she was supported by Edmund Bonner, Bishop of London, and Stephen Gardiner, Bishop of Winchester, both of whom were ambitious to strike down the leading Protestants and, indeed, humbler folk who were found to be heretics. By the end of her reign many more of the bench of bishops shared this outlook. But the responsibility for what was done must rest upon the Queen and Cardinal Pole.

The most prominent victims were the first martyr, John Rogers, John Hooper, Bishop of Gloucester and one of the most extreme Protestants, Hugh Latimer, Bishop of Worcester, Nicholas Ridley, Bishop of London and, as a climax which shook the country, Thomas Cranmer, Archbishop of Canterbury. Cranmer's human weakness and final courage as he first of all recanted and then boldly repudiated his recantation, affirmed his Protestant beliefs, walked resolutely to the stake and calmly held to the hottest flame the hand that had signed away his truth, aroused deep emotions and won much sympathy and admiration. The burnings were mostly in the strongest area of Protestantism in and around London, in East Anglia and in the South-East. The numbers were not great compared with what happened in the Netherlands, but it was stupendous and traumatic for England, which had never seen anything approaching it before. As an attempt to destroy Protestantism it was an utter failure. It rather alienated the non-partisan majority and emboldened the Protestants who met in conventicles and preached openly. The gentry, other than churchmen, and the prosperous merchants, appear not to have furnished one martyr. Most of the victims were poor people, craftsmen, tradesmen and apprentices.

The burning of heretics was not novel. It happened before and after the reign of Mary, and most of those who were burned believed that heretics should suffer such a fate. Almost everyone in the country thought that there should be only one religion, and that there should be penalties to ensure this. Two things were unusual in the Marian persecutions. One was the numbers involved, with just under three hundred victims, which was greater than during any other reign, although this might be thought inevitable when the attempt was to extirpate the beliefs of the people who were a well-established minority who had governed England three years earlier. The other was that three years later the supreme power had passed to the friends and colleagues of the martyrs.

The martyrs died in defence of a distinctive theology. This was essentially Protestant and was in defiance of what were considered unacceptable and dangerous dogmas which had grown up in Catholicism. The beliefs held so fervently by the reformers were enshrined in the Second Prayer Book of 1552 and in the Forty-Two Articles, which we have considered. They also died in a conflict over authority. Cranmer, Ridley and Latimer died because they stood for a theology which was temporarily in eclipse.

Cranmer, Ridley, Latimer, and many others, died for a vision of the divine will in the world which was totally contradictory to the official theory . . . Partly through their own efforts, and partly through circumstances which played into their hands and the hands of their followers, their theology triumphed. It was less coherent than that which it replaced, but more dynamic; more spiritually satisfying, but less stable. Moreover it carried within it the seeds of a radicalism equally obnoxious to its opponents and its first protagonists.[50]

In the wake of persecution there was an outpouring of Protestant propaganda on an unprecedented scale. Between 1554 and 1558 the publications noticeably changed in tone and content, from devotional works to polemical and political treatises. The increasing Protestant confidence and radicalism is indicated in the culminating work, Christopher Goodman's *How Superior Powers Ought to be Obeyed* (1558), which stridently called for a godly revolution, and appealed for the overthrow of Athalia as an unnatural as well as an ungodly ruler. Such a shift was a far cry from the resignation of Hooper and Cranmer and presaged the emergence of Elizabethan Puritanism. It also raises the question whether the next generation of English reformers would have been revolutionaries in the mould of the French Huguenots had not Mary died in 1558 and Elizabeth come to the throne.[51] It was also during the reign of Mary, in 1554, that John Foxe first published his history of Christian persecutions. But this was done while he was an exile in Strasbourg, and it was issued in Latin. It was only when the work was published in an expanded English edition in 1563 as the *Acts and Monuments of matters happening in the Church*, commonly known as 'Foxe's Book of Martyrs', that it was to help so significantly in promoting the Protestant cause.

When Foxe wrote his martyrology he was sharing exile with some of the foremost Protestants of the day. Protestant historiography has portrayed the exodus as a near-miraculous deliverance from adversity, whereas modern historians have tended to see the migration as 'neither hasty, nor improvised, nor to any conspicuous extent a response to persecution'.[52] The Marian authorities may even have encouraged the emigration of these opponents of the Queen's religious policies. But, whatever the interpretation, their first hand encounter with the continental Reformed Church in its various forms was to prove of particular importance when the exiles returned to their native country. Many of them were to assume important roles in the Elizabethan church, and their period of exile made them even more determined than they might otherwise have been to steer the church in a distinctive Protestant direction. There were about eight hundred men, women and children who went into exile. Of the four hundred and twenty-seven who have been identified by name, one hundred and sixteen were gentry, including two who were to be Elizabethan Privy Councillors, Sir Francis

Knollys and Sir Francis Walsingham; sixty-seven were clergymen, including twelve who were destined to be Elizabethan bishops and three, Edmund Grindal, Edwin Sandys and Thomas Young, who were to be Elizabethan archbishops; one hundred and nineteen were theological students, including an Elizabethan Regius Professor of Divinity at Oxford, Laurence Humphrey; and forty were merchants, among whom was a future leader of the Elizabethan Puritan classical movement. Some went to Henry Bullinger's Zurich; some to John Calvin's Geneva; some to the Strasbourg of Peter Martyr; and some to Valerand Poullain's Frankfurt. All was not harmony and light. At Frankfurt there were differences of opinion on liturgical matters. On the one hand, there was William Whittingham and the minister, John Knox, who supported a hybrid order of church service which incorporated the substance of the Second Prayer Book, but minus the litany and surplice and certain other features, and the Genevan order, and in opposition to this there were John Jewel and Richard Cox in favour of including the litany. The Coxians managed to have Knox and his followers expelled, and they restored the Second Prayer Book with only minor changes. Within two years the Frankfurt church divided again over their attitude to a new reformed discipline.[53] But despite such unhappy events, the whole experience of the exiles helped to enthuse them with the distinctive ethos and teaching of the reformed faith, and to prepare them for their crucial part in the life of the church under Elizabeth.

The fleeing into exile of so many able men also helped to weaken the opposition in England to the Marian regime. In the House of Commons there was, perhaps, less resistance to formal proposals put forward by the government than has traditionally been supposed.[54] When there was such resistance it was not very successful. There were convinced Protestants such as Ralph Skinner sitting in Mary's Parliament, but those with strong feelings were not generally in a position to appear in Parliament, and those who cared most either went into exile or were martyred. Parliamentary members who opposed the Crown on religious grounds needed to find support from broader interests, and this was only accomplished in a very limited way by enlisting the aid of those who feared for the future of their former church lands; and even then such an alliance was only effective in the case of the defeat of the exiles bill, where concern for property operated.

What can be said of Mary's religious policy and achievements as a whole? Again we are faced with contradictory assessments. The general conclusion of most historians before the entry of revisionism was not favourable. She was portrayed as a sad and increasingly lonely person as she pursued what she perceived as her God-given mission. Although a kind women in personal relations and merciful to political offenders, she was ruthless and relentless in her religious crusade. Her health was bad; Philip left her for the continent and failed throughout 1556 to return; her fourth Parliament, which met in the autumn of 1555, disappointed her as it refused to approve Philip's coronation or the restitution of any church land; public criticism became louder and more offensively expressed; the burnings were increasingly resented, and caused many local commotions; Protestant manifestos were imported from exiles abroad and widely disseminated; plots instigated on the continent were discussed in England, and may have involved members of Parliament; little support was given to her in the wars with France; and Cardinal Pole became very sick, knowing, as his health deteriorated, that he was alienated from Pope Paul IV, out of favour with the Spanish and unpopular throughout England. Pole and his sovereign died on the same day, 17 November 1558; both of them aware at their end that the task they had set before themselves was not completed.

But an alternative view has been cogently argued. According to J. J. Scarisbrick, writing in 1984, one of 'the most notable things that has been happening to the study of Tudor history in recent years is the accumulation of evidence by people who have no ideological axe to grind that Mary Tudor's reign was not so unsuccessful after all'.[55] He acknowledges that there were disasters and failings, but asserts that in 1553 there was a real sense of a fresh beginning after years of confusion and upset; Mary's regime tried to be broad-based and to face up to some of the urgent tasks confronting it, and it produced much sensible housekeeping and reform. Reginald Pole was less anachronistic and clumsy than he is often depicted. The bench of bishops of which he was a member was able to stand comparison with any bench of bishops in the previous history of the *Ecclesia Anglicana*, or, perhaps many that followed. The old religion was tenacious and survived throughout much of the country, and it was reanimated by the policy of Mary, together with the ministry of her Catholic-minded bishops and clergy. This portrayal is elaborated by Christopher Haigh who maintains that there was, without doubt, a speedy return to Catholic worship in most places, without compulsion, and to the delight of large majorities.[56] It is an interpretation which is still further expounded and illustrated by Eamon Duffy, who points to evidence that the Marian church was widely accepted, and was establishing itself in the parishes. He regrets the burning of the Protestants, and reckons that the hounding down of so many religious deviants over so wide an area in so short a period of time was self-defeating. But he perceives a certain re-casting of Catholicism in the Marian era, in conformity to a European-wide redirection in the Counter-Reformation, whereby there was a more self-conscious emphasis on the cross and redemption. R.H. Pogson also concedes that there were shortcomings in the Marian regime, and that Mary and Pole may have made political errors and misjudged English opinion, but he attributes to them impressive preparations for Catholic reform, which were abortive mainly because the Queen and the papal legate faced colossal administrative problems of a complexity which would have baffled any politician, and which could not be surmounted in such a short reign.[57] David Loades also awards an accolade to Mary and Pole who, he says, managed to halt, and indeed to reverse, a process of inexorable decline that went back well before the Protestant reformation process began some twenty years before. But, he adds, 'it would have required not only more time, but also a more positive policy, to have achieved more'.[58]

It is too simplistic to portray the reign of Mary as a reaction that failed, and as a short interruption in the process of protestantization. In many respects that is true, but the reality is somewhat more complex. When she came to the throne the Roman Catholics were at a low ebb spiritually, and bereft of authority and leadership. She failed in her aim of full Roman Catholic restoration, with the elimination of rival creeds, but she left the Catholics more healthy than they had been at the time of her enthronement.[59] They were to a greater extent than in 1553 united in allegiance to the Pope and set to play a continuing part in the religious history of England.

The reformations I have so cursorily surveyed clearly affected the church's structure, and its role in society, but massive and dramatic though many of the changes were, the fundamental framework remained intact. Apart from the introduction of six new dioceses (one of which, Westminster, was suppressed in 1550), the geographical map changed little; except in some towns, the parochial landscape was scarcely altered; and bishops and chapters continued to hold sway. There had been a major diminution in the extent of the church's land-holding, but it remained a powerful possessor of land and property. Economically the church remained a force, with tithes and other fees a continuing bone of contention. Nonetheless, the Reformation had set in motion some basic changes. The breach with Rome was to result in the disappearance of the concept of the unitary church, and its replacement by denominational pluralism, and this, as I have previously stated, was to be effected within a few generations, and within the span of my present study. The other major change was to take much longer to surface. For it was perhaps not until the nineteenth century that the Church of England came to terms with the severance from the mediaeval relationship between church and society which was inherent in the Reformation, and introduced radical structural and administrative reforms.[60]

2

The Elizabethan Settlement

By the time Elizabeth ascended the throne in 1558 the contest between Catholicism and Protestantism to win the hearts of the people of England and to become the official faith of the nation was inconclusive. Despite the fact that the protestantization of the country had gone a long way by the beginning of Mary's reign, and was not significantly reversed by the time she died, the future religious allegiance of the nation was still in doubt in November 1558, and a multitude of people would have conformed to whichever of the two competing systems was triumphant. The theological positions had not yet been sharply and irrevocably defined; the disputants, in England at least, were neither integral Tridentines nor fully Protestant or Calvinist; they were indeed not wholly clear in their own minds where they stood, or whither the world was moving.[1]

Elizabeth's intentions concerning a religious settlement were as unclear to her contemporaries as they have subsequently been to historians.[2] One interpretation, and that the oldest, goes back to John Foxe, and claims that the Queen and her Protestant councillors had intended to introduce a settlement based on the 1552 Prayer Book, but were forced to make Catholic concessions because of the implacable opposition of both the bishops and some lay peers in the House of Lords. An alternative view, proclaimed by Sir John Neale in the 1950s, and received by historians generally for a generation as the accepted orthodoxy, dramatically altered this picture. It asserted that Elizabeth wished to do no more than reintroduce her father's national church, and the more conservative 1549 Prayer Book, but had to adopt a more radical programme under pressure from a group of determined Protestants in the House of Commons who insisted that the 1552 Prayer Book should be adopted.[3] The most recent and most generally accepted account claims that the 1559 religious settlement was a delicate operation to balance a variety of forces ranging from the conservatives to the returned Protestant exiles.

But even if this is so it is questionable if Elizabeth herself preferred the

1552 rather than the 1549 Prayer Book, and possible that she only accepted the former because of lack of support from her lay and clerical advisers at court for her preferred option. Perhaps she rightly decided that if she was to acquire the Royal Supremacy she would have to deal with the only important clerical group which was willing to accept it, the Edwardian Protestants. It is noticeable that the new Elizabethan council and administration was, for the first time, staffed wholly by laymen, and was positively Protestant. No fully committed Roman Catholics were included, and even 'trimmers' in religion who had been closely associated with Marian policies were excluded. But those from the other end of the theological spectrum, from what was called the Genevan camp, who were known to be extremists, were likewise not represented. The majority were men such as William Cecil, Nicholas Bacon, Walter Mildmay, Francis Knollys, William Parr, Francis Russell and James Haddon, who all exhibited a firm attachment to the moderate Protestantism associated with Thomas Cranmer, Martin Bucer and Peter Martyr. Almost all the members had been major post-holders under Edward, and a significant number had also served under Henry VIII. With such a membership, the government managed to secure the adoption of its programme for a religious settlement without great modification.[4] This does not mean an entirely Protestant settlement, because the Catholics were still a force to be reckoned with, especially in the Lords and in various areas of the country. It was a lopsided compromise, with a distinctly Protestant bias.

At the death of Mary England was technically Roman Catholic and reunited with Rome. Elizabeth was hostile to the Roman Catholic mass but favoured the pomp and splendour of the old religion; she liked candles, ornaments and vestments, and in another age might have liked images. But she appreciated the complexity of the situation and would not hazard the delicate balance necessary for a satisfactory settlement by attempting to impose her own predilections on the nation. She did not want to make windows in men's souls, but she did want to ensure as far as possible that whatever men believed they should obey her government. When she rode into London on 23 November 1558 amid the genuine plaudits of the people she was a mature, intelligent woman who had learned in twenty-five years of changing fortunes how 'to measure political forces and effects, to comprehend the emotions and desires of the people, and to assess the characters of the leading men through whom she would have to act'.[5] As a ruler she controlled policy more than any other Tudor, but she was politically astute in the course she took. 'She was talented, engaging, and hard-working, yet cautious, conservative, imperious, and petulant in the face of change.'[6] She dedicated all these talents to the service of the country as she conceived such service, and to achieving her aim of a strong and united nation, which demonstrated its unity by its conformity to the faith and practice of the one national church.

A powerful influence in these early years of the new reign was exercised by the so-called Marian exiles, whom we have already encountered. Under the Elizabethan regime they came into their own, and took up influential posts. Among them there were Dr Richard Cox, who had been Dean of Christ Church and Vice-Chancellor of the University of Oxford from 1547 to 1550, Laurence Humphrey, Thomas Bentham, William Cole, who had been Lady Margaret Professor at Oxford, Christopher Goodman, William Whittingham, Thomas Lever, Master of St John's College, Cambridge, James Pilkington, Perceval Wiburn, Edwin Sandys, who was Vice-Chancellor of Cambridge at Mary's accession, John Knox and John Jewel. They returned imbued with the spirit of the continental reformers among whom they had stayed. 'The spirit we have seen in the martyrs becomes even more explicit and conscious in the exiles; it is the spirit of the self-reliant oppositionist, the man with the hard core to his mind, the man with "civil courage", proof against even the claims of the Tudor dynasty.'[7] They were strong individuals, but they never became a single and united party; they were not a Calvinist faction. They had imbibed the Calvinist doctrines, but they shrank from the full rigours of Genevan church government and social organization. They accepted episcopacy and a considerable amount of state control. They honoured Cranmer and were content with the Protestantism of the 1552 Prayer Book.

From the beginning the Elizabethan government was intolerant in matters of religion. Its policy was constructed with the clear intention of making it possible for all people to attend the same churches. William Cecil, Elizabeth's chief minister, believed that 'the state could never be in safety, where there was toleration of two religions. For there is no enmity so great as that of religion, and they that differ in the service of God can never agree in the service of their country.'[8] The concern of Queen and government was not for full agreement but outward conformity. The aim was not unprincipled. It was a recognition that full agreement from the heart in matters of religion was hard to come by, if not impossible, and that outward conformity at least committed those concerned to the view that the settlement was merely erroneous, and not sinful, and therefore avoided the compulsion to rebel for the sake of religion and conscience. This of course embraced the Roman Catholics, who it was hoped would support the national church on the ground that they would probably be disloyal if they did not. Even if the Elizabethan religious settlement may, with much justification, be regarded as dictated by expediency rather than by religious principle, it was an attempt to establish a mid-Tudor coalition, 'to preserve the uneasy compromise which had enabled Cranmer and Gardiner to sit together on the bench of bishops'.[9] But such an ideal was difficult, and probably unobtainable, in practice, because of the way both sides had moved on from their former postures as a consequence of the reigns of Edward and Mary. So the Elizabethan settlement was rejected by Cuthbert Tunstall as too radical, and by Miles Coverdale as not radical enough. Even among laymen, the Earl of Shrewsbury on one side and the Earl of Bedford on the other had moved too far to be able to share common ground. In such a situation, where Elizabeth and her government could not satisfy the Protestants and the Catholics, they found it expedient and more congenial to err in a Protestant direction.

The Acts of Supremacy and Uniformity and the new Prayer Book

The religious and ecclesiastical system as settled by Elizabeth and maintained by James I was based upon the Acts of Supremacy and Uniformity. Setting aside the revolutionary epoch of the mid-seventeenth century, there was in fact no departure from the lines laid down by Elizabeth until they were modified by the 1689 Act of Toleration just after the end of the period covered by the present book.

The Act of Supremacy of 1559 was based on the assumption that the ecclesiastical changes effected by the statutes of 1529 to 1536 were a restoration rather than a revolution. By means of them the ancient jurisdictions which of right belonged to the Crown had been restored to it, and the nation was delivered from a usurped foreign authority. These recovered rights had been resigned by Mary. The Act of Supremacy therefore restored 'to the crown its twice-lost authority' and freed the nation 'a second time from the "bondage" into which it had fallen'.[10] It swept away all foreign authority, both spiritual and temporal, and vested in the Crown the supreme power over the national church, although it was careful to restrict such power and, for example, did not restore the title of 'supreme head'. Elizabeth herself declared that such supremacy did not involve the right to exercise strictly spiritual functions. The general right of Parliament to legislate for the church, subject to the royal assent, was no new issue, but in the matter of the definition of doctrine the act recognized a limitation, and expressly reserved the right of the clergy to assent.

In throwing off the yoke of Rome, Parliament had no intention, as I have previously mentioned, of introducing religious toleration, and the Act of Uniformity authorized a certain form of public worship which prohibited all others. It revived the use of the 1552 Prayer Book with certain modifications, and enjoined its use throughout the kingdom. Any minister who declined to use it in the form prescribed, or used any other form of worship, was to be severely punished, and for a third offence would suffer deprivation and imprisonment for life. Heavy penalties were also threatened against anyone 'depraving' the Book of Common Prayer or hindering its use, and a general conformity was enforced by the imposition of a fine on all who refused to go to church. The duty of executing the various provisions of the Act was particularly laid upon the bishops and the ecclesiastics, but it was also entrusted to the judges and other lay officials.

The Act of Supremacy was not a sweeping or tyrannical act either in the nature of its provisions or with regard to the number of people whom it directly affected. It was a reflection of the fact that, with foreign complications and domestic uncertainty, Elizabeth was obliged to proceed with care. Initially it pleased Protestants who welcomed the Prayer Book as substituting a purer form of worship for the breviary and the mass, and it was conservative enough not unduly to alarm either the Pope or the King of Spain.

The 1559 settlement 'implied, in substance if not in every detail, a return to the 'state of religion' which had prevailed at the time of Edward VI's death',[11] but it made three significant concessions to conservative opinion. First, the alteration of the Queen's title from Supreme Head of the Church to Supreme Governor was widely acclaimed as a move to avoid the headship of a woman over the church. Secondly, the royal Injunctions which expanded the detail of the settlement allowed 'the use of many of the old vestments in services and remained diplomatically silent about destroying other items of liturgical furniture'.[12] Thirdly, and perhaps most importantly, the 1552 communion service was modified to add the words of administration in the 1549 book to the words in the 1552 book. Thus, the communicant receiving the bread would hear the words, 'The body of our Lord Jesus Christ, which was given for thee, preserve thy body and soul unto everlasting life' (1549);

'take and eat this in remembrance that Christ died for thee, and feed on him in thy heart by faith with thanksgiving' (1552). The words at the administration of the wine had a similar combination of formulae, which suggested on the one hand a real presence, which was congenial to conservatives, and on the other hand the idea of communion as a memorial only, which was following the theology of Zurich. 'Placing this ambiguity at the moment when a communicant was likely to be most attentive to what was happening was a masterpiece of theological engineering.'[13]

Although the Elizabethan Prayer Book essentially revived the Second Edwardian Prayer Book, against the known wishes of the Convocation of the clergy and the Roman Catholic bishops in the House of Lords, and was part of the move towards greater protestantization, it made some concessions to those of a more conservative persuasion. Catholics would take comfort from an Ornaments Rubric which brought back the altar and the vestments of the First Prayer Book until such time as the Queen, upon the advice of her ecclesiastical commissioners, wished to make changes. The new Prayer Book also retained the word 'priest' and the specifically sanctioned priestly power of absolution. And Roman Catholics would have been pleased about the removal of the prayer to be delivered from 'the tyranny of the bishop of Rome, and all his detestable enormities'.[14] The Queen seems to have been chiefly concerned to preserve the external appearance of parish church services and life, and she insisted on the use of all the vestments which had been in use in the second year of Edward VI; but a further definition of doctrine along lines which were generally acceptable to Protestants was left until 1563, when Convocation agreed the Thirty-Nine Articles.

The Thirty-Nine articles, the Injunctions and the royal visitation

The Thirty-Nine Articles of Religion were based on the Forty-Two which had received the royal assent on 12 June 1553. 'In very large part they represent what was most sensible and maturely-considered in the Reforming thought of the mid-century.'[15] The Calvinist element is evident throughout the Articles, and more especially in some, such as xiii :

Works done before the grace of Christ and the inspiration of his Spirit, are not pleasant to God, forasmuch as they spring not of faith in Jesus Christ, neither do they make men meet to receive grace, or (as the School-authors say) deserve grace of congruity: yea rather, for that they are not done as God hath willed and commanded them to be done, we doubt not but they have the nature of sin.

And this Calvinistic influence is perhaps even more pronounced in Article xvii :

Predestination to life is the everlasting purpose of God, whereby (before the foundations of the world were laid) he hath constantly decreed by his counsel secret to us, to deliver from curse and damnation those whom he hath chosen in Christ out of mankind, and to bring them by Christ to everlasting salvation, as vessels made to honour.

This is not just the expression of a moderate Calvinistic or 'sublapsarian' theology, which would not have included the Fall in the predestined plan of God, and would have asserted that the election of the redeemed took place only thereafter. Taken as a whole they appear to represent a rigorous 'supralapsarian' position in which the salvation of some men, and, by implication, the damnation of others, was from the beginning built in to the very order of the universe. And yet the Articles affirmed that the free will of man is expected to cooperate with the grace of God rather than remaining inactive, by stating that good works, though ineffectual in putting away sins, are 'pleasing and acceptable to God'.

In various ways the Articles, like the earlier Elizabethan Prayer Book, were basically Protestant, but with some gestures in a conservative direction. They took a strong anti-Catholic position by adding communion in both kinds, by designating only baptism and the Lord's Supper as 'gospel' sacraments, and by declaring forthrightly that priests could lawfully marry. But, in their interpretation of the Lord's Supper, although Cranmer's view of a true or spiritual presence was upheld, by the declaration that the body of Christ is eaten by faith 'after a heavenly and spiritual manner only', the specific denial of the real presence was dropped. A totally new article, which reflected the Reformed view of the precisianists, or Puritans, asserted that the 'wicked' are not 'partakers of Christ', but this was dropped when the Queen gave her approval to the remaining thirty-eight articles, and was only introduced in 1571.

The other constituent of the settlement, the Queen's Injunctions of 1559, was a further mixture of the traditional and the new. They covered almost every aspect of church life. Preaching was controlled in that it was stipulated that only those licensed by the bishop might preach. Such licensed clergy were ordered to preach at least once every month and to devote at least four sermons a year to the Royal Supremacy. On the other Sundays they were required to read one of the official homilies which provided the sole diet for any congregations which did not have a licensed preacher. All churches were to hold an English Bible and an English version of the Paraphrases of Erasmus. Every minister was obliged to instruct the youth of the parish in the Ten Commandments, the Lord's Prayer and the Catechism. Shrines, images and any 'monuments of feigned miracles, pilgrimages, idolatry, and superstition' were to be removed. The communion table, though retained at the east end, was to be brought into the middle of the church at service time, which, in practice, because of the difficulty of moving heavy furniture about the church, tended to mean that each church kept the table in the place it preferred. But the Injunctions were not all Protestant biased. Some aimed at preventing any further move towards Protestantism. All books and pamphlets were to be licensed. The clergy were to wear 'such seemly habits, garments, and such square caps' as were used in Edward's reign. Bowing to the altar was prescribed, and the use of wafers in the communion was required - 'another calculated gesture towards simple catholics'.[16]

'The celebrated *via media* which characterized all these formularies was a note sounded by the Queen for pragmatic reasons but which, with the passage of time, would seem a faithful expression of reformed catholicity and of a characteristic Anglican centrality and moderation.'[17]

The terms of the settlement, as detailed in the acts and the Injunctions, were enforced by the royal visitation which was mounted in the summer of 1559. It was an early example of 'the extent to which the effective control of ecclesiastical policy lay with its agents'. Although our knowledge of the visitations is slight, 'events in London suggest that the zeal of the visitors exceeded the terms of the Injunctions, to the extent of effecting an almost irreversible alteration in the physical setting of Anglican devotions'.[18] In London there was such widespread and enthusiastic iconoclasm by late 1560 that a royal proclamation was issued which attempted to restrain the spoiling and breaking of tombs and other monuments. A permanent legacy of this whole operation was the Ecclesiastical Commission.

But there was another side to the picture as it emerged from the visitations. There were regional, and indeed parochial variations, and in some areas conservatism was very evident. The Archbishop's commissary, after the investigation of the diocese of Chichester, concluded pessimistically:

Except it be about Lewes and a little in Chichester, the whole diocese is very blind and superstitious for want of teaching . . .; even in the city of Chichester few of the aldermen are of good religion. They use in many places ringing between morning and the litany, and all the night following All Saints' day, as before in time of blind ignorance and superstition taught by the Pope's clergy. Many bring to church the old popish Latin primers, and use to pray upon them all the time when the lessons are being read. Some old folks and women used to have beads in the churches, but these I took away from them but they have some yet at home in their houses.

The explanation given by Bishops Barlow and Curteys for this failure of the Reformation to win popular support in Sussex in the 1560s accord with those expressed in the report of the visitation of 1569:

Many churches there have no sermons, not one in seven years, and some not one in twelve years, as the parishes have declared to the preachers that of late have come thither to preach. Few churches have their quarter sermons according to the Queen's Majesty's injunctions. In many places the people cannot yet say the commandments, and some not the articles of their belief, when they be examined before they come to communion, and yet they be of the age of forty or fifty years. The ministers there for the most part are very simple.[19]

The early years of the settlement

In the first five years of her reign the Queen carefully completed the foundations of the Elizabethan church, ably assisted by her chief minister William Cecil, and her first Primate Matthew Parker (1504–75). Parker was ideal for the task. He was a learned and modest man who was genuinely reluctant to assume responsibility as archbishop, but then conscientiously and judiciously undertook the onerous duties entailed. He was an historian and antiquarian; a non-exile who had avoided rigid continental allegiances and had not become embroiled in bitter doctrinal controversy, and yet he could appreciate and sympathize with Protestant aspirations. And he was fortunate in having as his main colleague the admirable and erudite Bishop of Salisbury, John Jewel, who provided a magnificent defence of the national church in his *Apologia Ecclesiae Anglicanae* (1562). This was followed a year later by John Foxe's *Acts and Monuments*.

John Jewel (1522–71) was greatly influenced by Peter Martyr, and while still a young man he held distinctly Protestant views.[20] During the Marian persecution he recanted in terror, and signed an anti-Protestant declaration. He subsequently fled abroad, to Frankfurt, in 1555 and confessed his fault before the congregation. While on the continent he came in close touch with some of the reformers, and he returned, greatly influenced by them, to participate in the Westminster disputation, and to assist in the drawing up of a Protestant confession of faith. Nonetheless, with his scholarship and wide knowledge of antiquity, and with a considerable awareness of, and respect for, more Catholic forms of theology and churchmanship, he maintained his independence of view and, for example, opposed John Knox and the advanced Calvinists. He was appointed to the bishopric of Salisbury in 1560, and was a strong supporter of the Anglican settlement. He remained hostile to Roman Catholicism, but although sympathetic to Geneva, he based his theology only on assertions which he thought could be justified by reference to the double standards of the scriptures and the doctrine of the primitive church, as these were expressed by the authoritative councils and the teaching of the Fathers of the first six centuries.

In his *Apologia Ecclesiae Anglicanae*, in a terse form and with powerful and convincing arguments, he endeavoured to prove that general reformation had been necessary for the English church. No charge of heresy could be proved against it, as it only made what were considered necessary changes within its competence, which were consistent with a Catholic position. The reformers had not laboured to create a new church but to reform the old. This was a theme which was echoed by Whitgift, who taught that the church was reformed and not transformed. Jewel emphasized that the reformers had departed from Rome because of its errors and its false doctrine, rather than because of the unholy lives of its leaders. The catholicity of the English church was secured by virtue of its retention of true Catholic doctrine. Jewel rebutted accusations of sectarianism and antinomianism, asserted that reform by such a body as the Council of Trent was impossible, and declared that local churches had the right to legislate through provincial synods. The book promptly established itself as the best defence of the Anglican claims which had yet been published.

Foxe's book in many respects represented a contrast to Jewel's measured arguments and restrained tone. It was a very extended pro-Protestant, anti-popery tract. It was a massive book which attempted to portray in vivid, not to say gruesome, language, the whole history of Christian martyrdom from the time of Christ to the Marian persecution.

One skilfully painted picture after another rehearsed the countless and fearsome sufferings of Christians throughout the ages, and the message which was constantly and persistently inserted in the text was the anti-Christian, persecuting, nature of popery. Foxe expatiated on the theme of the godly elect, the faithful witnesses throughout the ages, and the concept of an elect nation which was crystallized for him by the Marian persecution. By this means he was able to give his story a climacteric experience which heralded the advent of Elizabeth. Basing what he wrote on the Book of Revelation, he postulated four ages in the history of the church. The time in which he lived was the fourth age. Rome was the Antichrist, and the true servants of God, of whom Wyclif was the first in the new age, were raised up by God to testify against the anti-church. He believed firmly in the royal supremacy, and in Elizabeth as the specially ordained pinnacle and vindication of the Reformation. And this interpretation was promptly built into the national myth. *Acts and Monuments* rapidly became a companion volume to the Bible and the Prayer Book in countless homes, and for many generations it fuelled the enthusiasm and dedication of Protestants. Indeed, versions of it, abbreviations, or selected passages, have continued to be published right up to the present day.

An event of major importance in helping to establish the reformed English church in these early years of the new reign was Elizabeth's well-timed intervention in Scotland in 1560 whereby, through the Treaty of Edinburgh, French influence was largely removed and control was placed in the hands of the redoubtable John Knox, William Maitland of Lethington and the Protestant Lords of the Congregation. At a stroke there was initiated a steady convergence of the two countries, which Queen Mary Stuart could not prevent. And one consequence of this was the profound Protestant influence which the northern kingdom exercised for a long time over its southern neighbour.

But the whole process of protestantization in England was slow. Elizabeth and her government were cautious. They saw the dangers of moving too rapidly, as they beheld the somewhat radical removal of altars and rood-lofts, organs, vestments and chalices which continued throughout the 1560s. They saw how many Catholic and quasi-Catholic practices continued with a minimum of concealment. They saw how many Englishmen 'clung to their traditional ceremonies, to their processions and holy water, and above all to the mass, long after the legislation of Elizabeth's first Parliament had finally made such things illegal'.[21] Although the accession of Elizabeth and the 1559 Settlement, with all its political in-fighting, had resulted in Protestant leadership of the Church of England, it had not resulted in Protestant control of those parishes where Roman Catholic priests and traditionalist laity were in a large majority. There was a long struggle by bishops and officials of the Church of England to impose the Prayer Book and the Injunctions on the parishes. And seeing these things, the Queen and her advisers applied the brakes and proceeded gently with the enforcement of conformity.

Nonetheless, the process of protestantization had been set in motion, and it was only a matter of time before it percolated down and became the norm.

> For a while, it was possible to sustain an attenuated Catholicism within the parish framework, by counterfeiting the mass, teaching the seven sacraments, preserving images of saints, reciting the rosary, observing feasts, fasts, and customs: by what some historians have called 'survivalism'. But as times changed and generations passed, as memories faded and rosaries were lost, as new ministers cajoled and bishops imposed penances, survivalist Catholicism was diluted by conformity, until . . . after 1578, it disappeared completely.[22]

The religious and parochial life of the 'ordinary' churchman

The Church of England and Wales was governed by two archbishops and twenty-four diocesan bishops. Twenty-one of the dioceses were mediaeval and the others had been endowed by Henry VIII out of his spoils from the dissolution of the monasteries. There were about 9,400 parishes, served by a total of about 8,000 parish clergy.[23] Some livings were too poorly endowed to attract a minister or suffered because of insufficient recruits to the ministry. A statute of 1545 authorized amalgamations of parishes worth less than £6 a year, but this had little or no effect in changing a structure which was frozen in the geographical pattern of the thirteenth century. And after three hundred years it was beset with anomalies. In the lowland area of southern England it generally produced small, compact units, so that the well nigh thousand parish churches and parochial chapels of Norfolk came near to equalling the entire parochial provision for Scotland. On the whole lowland England fared best and offered the chance of thorough pastoral provision, whereas in the north some parishes consisted of large empty uplands. This disparity was ameliorated in the case of traditional religious patterns by the more pronounced continuance in the north of active monasteries, which helped to overcome the deficiencies in the parish system, or chantry chapels which could stand as independent units, rather than as subordinate structures, as was more commonly the case in the south. Shifts in population and the effects of the Reformation changes on the ministry also made the parochial structure in some major towns anachronistic, as a large number of parishes found themselves served by poorly-paid clergy. In such situations some local initiative, such as the raising of a voluntary levy in order to provide a decent salary for a minister, was necessary in order to secure a ministry of any description.[24]

Let us look more closely at the religious and parochial life of the people. And first at the clergy. The lowest group in the church were the unbeneficed curates. Evidence which has been culled from such dioceses as Lincoln and Coventry and Lichfield, and the counties of Kent and Lancashire indicates that they were poorly paid and insecure.[25] Although the beneficed clergy were more prosperous, they were very frequently in a parlous state, other than the minority who served in the more lucrative parishes. Although there is some evidence that there was economic improvement for at least some of the clergy in the course of the sixteenth century and on into the seventeenth century, especially among those rectors and vicars who farmed their own glebe or collected and sold their own tithe and who thereby benefited from price rises,[26] it is likely that until well into Elizabeth's reign, and indeed until after the bad harvest decade of the 1590s, the parochial clergy suffered from problems which must have made the improvement of their revenue very difficult.[27]

The Elizabethan church was, however, very successful in improving the knowledge and education of the clergy. In the middle of the century the evidence indicates widespread ignorance among the clergy. One of the most notorious illustrations of this was the 1551 visitation of his Gloucester diocese by Bishop Hooper, in which it was revealed that of the 311 clergy he examined, 168 could not repeat the Ten Commandments, 34 did not know the author of the Lord's Prayer and 10 could not repeat it. Peter Heath has questioned whether this survey can be taken entirely at face value, but he concedes that 'with so tenuous a grasp of the basic essentials of their faith' the clergy 'were patently ill equipped to cope with the increasingly curious layman'.[28]

One, albeit imperfect, measure of the Elizabethan success in trying to overcome this deficiency in the ministry is the increasing proportion of university graduates among the clergy. In the diocese of Canterbury this rose from about 18% in 1571 to 60% in 1603, in Worcester from 19% in 1560 to 52% in 1620, and in the poorer Lichfield diocese from 14 to 24% between 1584 and 1603.[29] From training the clerical elite only, the universities turned their attention to training almost the entire ministry of the Church of England. The founding of Emmanuel College, Cambridge, by the Puritan politician Sir Walter Mildmay, for the specific provision of clergy training, was but the most ambitious attempt in a campaign to achieve such an objective. And the improvement in clerical education was matched by the improved religious education of the laity.

It is exceptionally difficult to gauge the religious beliefs of lay people at the parish level four hundred years ago, and then to make any generalizations. This is especially so for a period in which Protestant ideas were supplanting traditional beliefs. There is difference of opinion among historians about the extent of the penetration of Protestant beliefs and practices at this time, and the pace at which the protestantization process progressed. In a splendid text, *The Stripping of the Altars*, Eamon Duffy asserts that the English people did not expect a Reformation, that most of them resented it when it came, and that it impoverished them spiritually, ritually and materially. Although there were of course those for whom the Protestant gospel was light and liberty, and although the impact of such believers was disproportionate to their absolute numbers, 'for most of the first Elizabethan adult generation, Reformation was a stripping away of familiar and beloved observances, the destruction of a vast and resonant world of symbols which, despite the denials of the proponents of the new Gospel, they both understood and controlled'. But even Duffy acknowledges that by the 1570s, after so much Protestant influence, 'whatever the instincts and nostalgia of their seniors, a generation was growing up which had known nothing else, which believed the Pope to be Antichrist, the Mass a mummery, which did not look back to the Catholic past as their own, but another country, another world.'[30]

Full scope was given to those who were conservative in belief, and wished to be conservative in practice, within the Church of England, when they lived in parishes served by Roman Catholic priests. But there were also conservative believers in parishes served by 'godly' preachers. Christopher Haigh gives the name 'parish Anglicans' to those conservatives who put stress on the Prayer Book and emphasis on the harmony and vitality of the village unit, at play and at worship. Their ideal minister was not the godly preacher, but 'the pastor who read services devoutly, reconciled quarrellers in his parish, and joined his people for "good Fellowship" on the ale bench'.[31] These were the lay people described by Judith Maltby as 'Prayer Book Protestants', who 'struggled to compel reluctant ministers to supply the restricted ceremonial and ritual prescribed in 1559, and whose initiatives for liturgical conformity represented an enthusiastic defence of the "imperfect" Established Church'.[32]

But it was the ideal of the reformers and a large proportion of their Elizabethan successors for every church in the land to have provision for a biblical sermon at all the major acts of worship which was winning the day. No longer was the prime duty of the clergy seen as the faithful performance of the mass and the traditional liturgical round. The new model entailed emphasis upon the communication of abstract ideas in a compelling form to the laity. This required skills and training which were in short supply, as well as theological motivation of an order which many did not posses. Mediaeval ministry had involved preaching, but it was accorded less prominence than the pastoral and liturgical roles of the priest, and there was an assumption that the graduate priests would occupy senior clerical posts rather than undertake the local, confined, responsibilities of parish ministry. At the Reformation the order of friars, with their dedication to preaching, had been swept away, thus casting more onus on the parish priests to preach effectively. With the Elizabethan improvement in the quality of education among parish clergy, and with this new focus for ministry, there is little doubt that many parishes experienced a quite radical change during the last three decades of the century. And this was enhanced by the 1575 requirement that prospective deacons must be at least 23 years of age and must have served a minimum of a year before proceeding to priest's orders.[33] Then, in addition to this planned move to improve the quality of the ministry of the established church, and to change its character, there was the supplementary, unplanned, but widespread, funding of new 'lecture-ships'. These were instigated largely in market towns, often in places where there were insufficient churches or where the churches were ill-endowed. They helped to contribute to the improvement of religious education among the laity, and they were an important feature in the Protestant campaign, but they were a cause of contention at national level, as we will see in the following chapter.

As far as the actual physical setting for worship is concerned, it is of note that the buildings changed very little, but the ornaments, furniture and fittings in them changed very much. 'Perhaps the most remarkable fact about Anglican Church architecture is not the Gothic revival which flourished in the nineteenth century, but the Gothic survival which continued from 1558 to 1662.'[34] In fact this survival lasted longer, and with less variation from mediaeval precedents, than was the case among the Lutherans of Germany and Sweden. It may have been yet one more, and in this matter a highly visible, way of expressing the continuity of the mediaeval with the reformed Church of England.

Unquestionably, there was a strong iconoclastic element in English Protestantism: and it was fought with vigour by the English Catholics of the time.[35] The result was the almost complete smashing of the figures on the roodscreens, and the discontinuance of the making of religious sculptures in wood. It also meant the almost total elimination of painting on walls or windows of churches. Some of the monastic churches were kept as parish churches, but most of the others must have suffered great despoiling, as they were deprived of their often ornate windows. Much of the mediaeval art was destroyed, and much of the former priestly paraphernalia was removed from the celebration of the liturgy. Low-backed straight pews or benches were arranged about the pulpit and reading desk. Representations of God and the saints were removed, and increasingly clear glass replaced coloured panes. Carved and painted figures of Christ, the virgin and the apostles, were pulled down, and the painting of the doom on the tympanum was washed over. Statues of saints were cast out. Painted wooden boards were introduced which bore the Royal Arms, the Lord's Prayer, the Creed, and the Tables of the Ten Commandments, and were affixed by royal commandment, and sculptured tombs were placed in the churches by prosperous families.

But, whereas Edwardian Anglicanism[36] had been highly functional, Elizabethan Anglicanism was less so. It combined the functional approach to the church as the house of prayer, and a place of preaching and teaching, with a concern for worship, and a recognition that church buildings, clergy dress and ceremonial symbolism were capable of contributing to a sense of holiness and of the numinous. In ceremonials and externals many of the Catholic features were retained. The 1559 Prayer Book contained an Ornaments Rubric which ordered the use of vestments and the alb and cope during the communion service; and the 1559 Injunction required the clergy to wear the surplice during services. The Black Rubric of 1552, which had declared that kneeling when receiving the communion did not in any way imply a real presence, was deleted from the 1559 Prayer Book. And such 'popish' remnants as the sign of the cross in baptism, the ring in marriage, crucifixes and candles were permitted.

The Elizabethan liturgical reforms also included a reinforcement and application of previously introduced innovations in church music. It was generally agreed by Catholics as well as Protestants of the sixteenth century that there was a great need for choral reform because of the chaos in musical practice. The need for church and domestic psalmody in metre was first met by Sternhold, probably in 1548, in a version which was completed by Hopkins. It was not an outstanding work, being rather awkward and obvious, but at times it was capable of a sustained dignity. The two composers of genius of the period, who provided church music, were Thomas Tallis (*c.*1505–1585) and William Byrd (1543–1623).

And where did the Queen stand amid all this change and activity? It is not easy to interpret her attitude and the nuances of her own personal religion, but her general policy seems somewhat clearer. Even if the settlement of 1559 did not exactly match her own personal preferences, she was determined that it should persist, and she resisted any change to it. The Church of England was neither created nor re-created by the Acts of Supremacy and Uniformity. Over the years of her reign it was gradually consolidated, but even at her death it had not achieved its full potential, or that poise between Protestant and Catholic ideals which Richard Hooker so fully and so well expounded in his *Laws of Ecclesiastical Polity*.[37] There were conflicts within the church itself which needed to be faced, between the 'establishment' and the Puritans, over the issues raised by the Presbyterians and the proto-Arminians; between the Church of England and the Separatists, and between the Church of England and the Roman Catholics; all of which will now be examined in some detail.

3

Elizabethan Puritanism and Separatism

Puritanism in profile

There has been much debate over many years about the definition and identification of Puritanism. Whig, Marxist, revisionist and post-revisionist historians have tried to determine the part it played in the religious and more general history of its day; and still there is not a consensus view. In its modern phase, the discussion places Puritanism in the context of the causes of the English Civil War. The traditional, pre-revisionist, political historians perceived the Civil War as the climax of mounting political tensions and crisis largely between Crown and opposition, an interpretation which could readily accommodate the traditional presentation of the polarity in the church between an established 'Anglicanism' and an oppositional Puritanism. This identified 'the rise of Puritanism' with the march towards the 'liberty and reformation in the Puritan revolution'.[1] Such a view, which was most cogently expressed by William Haller,[2] assumed a background provided by S.R. Gardiner.[3] Sir John Neale entered into this historiographical inheritance, and read back the interpretation into the reign of Elizabeth.[4] In turn Patrick Collinson followed Neale, and portrayed Elizabethan Puritanism as an ideology and a movement, with its potential revolutionary aspect focussed in the person of John Field: Elizabethan Puritanism 'was the precursor of that revolutionary Puritanism which helped both to cause and then to fuel the English civil war'.[5]

In parallel with this historiography, Christopher Hill was developing and applying the earlier insights of R.H. Tawney, and providing a Marxist interpretation of the sixteenth, and especially the seventeenth-century course of events. In essence he saw Puritanism as playing a crucial role in social and economic changes and class conflicts, which were central to the causes of the English revolution.[6] He gave particular attention to the influence of Puritanism on the emergent godly middling sort, who played an equivocal but vital part in the move towards revolution.

The pre-revisionist views I have so far outlined held the field until the early 1970s.[7] The notion of long-term social causes of the Civil War was sketchily and sceptically discussed by Conrad Russell in 1973.[8] Then the groundwork for a profound reassessment was laid by Patrick Collinson, who questioned the traditional concept of a coherent Anglican estab-lishment during Elizabeth's reign.[9] This was succeeded by Nicholas Tyacke's assertion of the prevalence of Calvinist predestinarianism amongst the theologically sophisticated in the reigns of Elizabeth and James. Such a picture of a predestinarian consensus raised questions about the validity of any separate existence for the Puritans at all. Perhaps it was relevant as a descriptive term for a particular style of individual or collective piety, but it was of no consequence when it came to political action and discourse.

The debate is far from over, for the revisionist wheel has turned full circle. Historians like Conrad Russell and John Morrill have returned to religion as the basic cause of the conflict which lead to the Civil War.[10] A number of historians have entered the lists.[11] There is also a recon-sideration of the internal dynamics of Puritanism: a re-examination of it phenomenologically in its own terms as an expression of deeply held religious convictions.[12] Puritanism is back at the centre of explanations.

So, with this somewhat complicated historiographical background, we will focus our attention upon the Elizabethan Puritans. Who were they, what did they believe, and what did they achieve?

On one thing all historians and commentators appear to be agreed. If the existence of Elizabethan Puritanism is conceded, then it was that movement 'which sought further reformation and renewal in the Church of England than the Elizabethan settlement allowed'.[13] It was the quest for 'the logical completion of the process of reconstituting the national Church, which in their view had been arrested halfway'.[14] 'Further reformation' had a double meaning, for on the one hand it implied the attempt to secure reform in the whole body of the church, and the intention of completing the English Reformation; and, on the other hand, it involved the fulfilling of a further reformation within the Puritan brotherhood, in those parishes, communities and households where Puritan influence was not resisted. In this respect there was a characteristic ambivalence in Elizabethan Puritanism. 'This paradoxical and somewhat untidy combination of what Ernst Troeltsch differen-tiated as the "church type" and the "sect type" of Christian societies was the hallmark of early Puritanism.'[15]

In the Elizabethan period, as indeed in the succeeding decades,

Puritan was an imprecise term, mostly used in contemptuous abuse, and applied to at least four overlapping groups.[16] There were the clergy who scrupled some Prayer Book ceremonies and phrasing; the advocates of Presbyterianism; clergy and laity who were rigid doctrinal Calvinists and who practised a serious Calvinistic piety; and certain of the gentry who showed a particular public concern for godliness, the laws of England and the rights of subjects. Perhaps one can identify features shared by all four groups: a cluster of convictions, which were biblicist and Calvinist in character, about Christian faith and practice and about the essential nature of congregational life and pastoral office; a sense of realizing the New Testament pattern of true and authentic church life by means of 'eliminating Popery from its worship, prelacy from its government and pagan irreligion from its membership';[17] and a common body of literature, catechetical, evangelistic and devotional, with a homiletical style and experiential emphasis that were all its own, among the authors of which William Perkins was the most formative and Richard Baxter the most distinguished.

Puritanism was a dynamic factor in the history of the churches in the reign of Elizabeth, which was 'as much or more an age of movement as of conservation'.[18] The Puritans, as a group of convinced and fervent Protestants, could be distinguished from the general mass of those who merely conformed to the established religion. The 'godly' for the most part attended their parish churches and mingled with the less godly. Yet they were united among themselves by a close bond. They were aware of their doctrinal unity, but in the last resort they

> were denoted and united less by theological dogma than by attitudes of mind and by a way of life. Like the Lollards and other sectarians who formed a part of their historical ancestry, they were characterized as much by domestic withdrawal as by doctrinal expansion. They met in private houses to study the Scriptures, walked around together singing psalms, made excursions to hear their favourite 'godly' preachers. So far as they bred fanatics, even these tended to be disciplined rather than demonstrative.[19]

Puritans gave great importance to preaching. 'They wanted more preaching, as much more as possible, so as to carry the Gospel into all corners of the land, even the darkest, and to raise the educational and disciplinary level of all members of all congregations. Since salvation came through the Word, it could not be preached too much.'[20] Indeed, salvation and sanctification were central preoccupations in the individual and communal life of Puritans. Puritanism was essentially a spiritual movement, passionately concerned with God and with godliness. It was 'a movement for church reform, pastoral renewal and evangelism, and spiritual revival; and in addition – indeed, as a direct expression of its zeal for God's honour – it was a world-view, a total Christian philosophy, in intellectual terms a protestantized and updated mediaevalism, and in terms of spirituality a reformed monasticism outside the cloister and away from monkish vows.'[21]

The Puritans had a dream of what they wanted the church and society as a whole to be. Their goal was to complete what the English Reformation had begun. They wanted to finish the reshaping of Anglican worship and to introduce effective discipline into Anglican parishes. They sought to establish righteousness in the political, social, economic and domestic spheres of national and local life, and to convert Englishmen to a vigorous evangelical faith. They yearned for England 'to become a land of saints, a model and paragon of corporate godliness, and as such a means of blessing to the world'.[22]

The years of uncertainty: 1558–1570

The Marian exiles who returned to England in the early years of Elizabeth's reign, and who had tasted of the wine of reformed church life on the continent, either in the form of the strong and potent doctrines and practices of Geneva, or the less heady teaching and life of Frankfurt or Zurich, returned with high expectations of what was possible for the Church in England. And many of them, together with like-minded supporters who had remained in the homeland, did not regard the 1559 Settlement as final. They had experienced on the continent what they regarded as a true reformation, and the 1559 Settlement fell far short of their model. They acknowledged that it was a beginning, and even a good beginning, but it was inadequate, and they looked forward with some measure of confidence to better days. After all the Queen had no obvious alternative but to offer some of them important posts in the church, and they were prepared to wait for the time when their godly princess would complete the reformation she had begun. But the Queen had no such intention. Her concern, as we have previously noted, was for conformity, at least in matters of worship and practice rather than details of belief, and the establishment of a comprehensive national church along the lines laid down in the 1559 Settlement. Far from identifying herself with the aspirations of the Puritans, she may have resented the concessions she had made to them in coming to that settlement. A clash of interest between her and her government and the more uncompromising Puritans was therefore almost inevitable.

Nevertheless, in the first decade or so of the reign there was little or nothing that could be called an organized Puritan movement. Powerful and determined individuals held strong Puritan views, but they were not coordinated in a united effort to achieve their desired ends. They did not form a party. They were small in number and were not agreed about what ought to be done. And their effectiveness as a pressure group was actually lessened by the fact that a number of them accepted high office in the church, and then somewhat modified their stance.

> Jewel as bishop of Salisbury, Sandys as bishop of Worcester, Grindal in London, Cox in Ely, Pilkington in Durham and Scory in Hereford proved less radical than they had been in exile. Inevitably, the responsibilities of office made them more conservative, limited their freedom of speech and action, and inclined them to the view that rather than desert their flocks and leave them a prey to Romish wolves, it was better to accept the considerable gains already made and not to risk everything by demanding what the Queen would certainly refuse to grant.[23]

There were also a number of returning lay *émigrés* in Elizabeth's first Parliament. Among these were Sir Anthony Cooke, the father-in-law to Sir William Cecil, Sir Nicholas Bacon, Sir Francis Knollys, the Queen's cousin and a member of the Privy Council, and Sir Edward Rogers, the Vice-Chamberlain. There was a vital core of a dozen or more such 'Puritans', and they were powerful and influential. Some of them were, like their clerical equivalents, hampered by the constraints of holding office, but they were supported by a large body of determined Protestants in the House. In addition, there were a number of gentlemen scattered throughout the country who sympathized with the views of their zealous Protestant representatives in Parliament. Finally, the universities, and especially the University of Cambridge, were a breeding ground for Puritanism.

With all these pockets of Puritanism in the country there was clearly much discontent with the national church, and at least a possible nucleus for a Puritan movement. Despite the fact that those who wanted change constituted less of a movement than a climate of opinion, from 'the earliest months of the reign there were signs of the beginning of future puritan associations, if not a coherent party'. This focussed particularly upon those 'repatriated exiles who, whether by choice, or of necessity, remained on the periphery, devoting themselves to the pursuit of an ideal which differed materially from the official policy of the Church'.[24]

The Queen and her government played their part in avoiding a confrontation with the Puritans. They concentrated on removing the more obvious and offensive manifestations of popery, and they also allowed Protestant deviationists a good deal of licence. There appears to have been a considerable amount of liturgical nonconformity in the 1560s, which entailed negligence or ignorance of what had been laid down by authority; and, at least in some cases, the use of particular liturgical practices was symbolic of theological views different from those officially prescribed. Services and prayers were said in the chancel, or sometimes in the body of the church or from the pulpit. Some of the clergy wore a surplice and cope, some a surplice only, and some wore neither. The communion was variously received, kneeling, sitting or standing. At baptism some ministers used a font, others an ordinary basin, and some omitted the sign of the cross when administering the sacrament.[25] Such disorder and lack of conformity if it persisted might have spread and encouraged even more pronounced defiance of authority.

Archbishop Parker attempted to meet the problem by sweet reasonableness. In 1564 he tried to persuade Thomas Sampson, Dean of Christ Church, Oxford, and Laurence Humphrey, President of Magdalen College, Oxford, to wear the surplice and to conform in other respects with the requirements of the church, and he also put pressure on others, including William Whittingham, Dean of Durham. This began what became known as the vestiarian controversy, since it was concerned with the question of vestments and clerical dress in general, as well as with other liturgical and ceremonial matters. Although it might appear a somewhat unfortunate issue for a confrontation between the Puritans and Parker, representing the established order, since it was not fundamentally to do with dogma, it was argued by Parker's opponents that clerical dress could not be regarded as a thing 'indifferent', for it was associated with the idolatrous worship of the Church of Rome. The Queen also saw it as important and had no sympathy with those who would not obey her laws. They were a threat to uniformity throughout the realm and, in a letter of 25 January 1565, she berated Parker and the bishops for slackness in not enforcing conformity.

Parker was not in a strong position. The Queen and the Privy Council avoided direct involvement, so there was no Injunction issued by the

Queen's authority under the Act of Supremacy. Parker was left to cope as best he could. In 1566 he circulated a general directive for the whole church, in a document which later became known as the *Advertisements*, which was published by his authority and that of a number of bishops and ecclesiastical commissioners. It declared that the Queen knew how necessary it was for the advancement of God's glory and the establishment of Christ's pure religion that all her subjects should be joined 'in one perfect unity of doctrine . . . and one uniformity of rite and manners'. She had consequently instructed the archbishops and bishops to take action 'whereby all diversities and varieties among them of the clergy and people . . . might be reformed and repressed, and brought to one manner of uniformity throughout the whole realm'.[26] The *Advertisements* stipulated that communion was to be received kneeling and not sitting or standing, and fonts were to be used in baptisms. Unlicensed preaching was forbidden, and existing licences for preachers were to be cancelled and replaced by new ones. The new code discarded the unrealistic requirement of the eucharistic vestments, except for the cope and that only in cathedral and collegiate churches, but it was most explicit in its insistence on the surplice and every detail of outdoor dress. All these requirements were not new. The novelty lay in the fact that the ecclesiastical authorities were going to make an effort to enforce them and put an end to the toleration which nonconforming clergy had hitherto enjoyed. For minds disposed to compromise all this might have been acceptable, and could have been seen as not an unreasonable standard for the sake of uniformity. But the 'precisians' were not in such a mood.

The Queen's letter to Parker and the *Advertisements* revived the conflict between those who held that 'in the Lord's action nothing ought to be used that the Lord Jesus hath not sanctioned neither by precept nor practice', and those who claimed even Calvin on their side in the view that 'certain things though not positively approved must be tolerated'.[27] The active opponents of the *Advertisements* were few in number, but they were determined and resourceful. They used the press to produce a tract, edited by Robert Crowley, and entitled *A Briefe Discourse against the Outwarde Apparell and Ministering Garmentes of the Popishe Church*, which attacked the established church. But Henry Bullinger wrote to Laurence Humphrey and Thomas Sampson in effect advising them to conform. He urged every one of the nonconformists to consider 'whether he will not more edify the church of Christ by regarding the use of habits for the sake of order and decency, as a matter of indifference . . . than by leaving the church . . . to be occupied hereafter if not by evident wolves, at least by ill-qualified and evil ministers'.[28]

English Puritanism was also influenced by the foreign reformed communities in London. They were fascinating to English Puritans, as they were organized Calvinist churches which enjoyed a high degree of self-government, and they were free to elect their own officers and to exercise reformed, congregational discipline. Within about ten years of Elizabeth's accession, a small group of English Puritans were copying these congregations. Secretly 'and in defiance of the law, they were using among themselves orders of reformed worship and discipline akin to those used publicly and with permission by the stranger churches'.[29]

The contribution of the foreign congregations to the developing Puritan movement was particularly important because of the special significance of the London Puritans within the total national scene. And this was most notably so in the period 1566 to 1572. 'In these six years, the Puritan protest grew from a relatively trivial objection to vestments and certain ceremonies retained in Anglican worship to a more fundamental rejection of the Prayer Book in toto – a protest against the whole ethos of Prayer Book worship – and of the unreformed, episcopal government of the Church.'[30] And in this development the Puritan group in London played a crucial role.

Elizabethan Puritanism, although often described in terms of a movement, owed much to what was going on spontaneously at the local level, not only in London but in various communities throughout the land. Indeed, these local agitations for the reform of the ministry, for the freeing of the church from all traces of Popery and, more generally and fundamentally, with the reform of a society corrupted by sin, often 'had little to do with the grand national puritan campaign'. And, further, they had frequently 'come into being many years before and embraced people who would not normally be regarded as puritans'.[31]

An example of such local Puritanism was to be found in Cranbrook in Kent. Richard Fletcher was the minister of this Wealden township from early in the reign of Elizabeth until his death in 1586. He was no Puritan, and 'the whole town did not reverberate with psalm-singing and godliness', but between 1575 and 1585 he employed, in succession, three curate-preachers who were Puritans, and under his ministry there was an active Puritan minority in the town. There were various clashes with church authorities. There were also visiting preachers who helped to maintain a high profile for Puritanism in the town and to arouse the opposition of traditionalists. 'Puritan Cranbrook' acts as a sort of microcosm to particularize two large issues, and to throw some light on them. The first of these is 'the nature of the interface between the officially inspired Reformation of the national church and what might be called the local and unofficial Reformation, with its ancient Lollard roots'. The second is that process of 'the bifurcation of English Protestantism towards, on the one hand, those conservative religious sentiments which approximate to our understanding of Anglicanism, and on the other through a transitional Puritanism to the Dissent of the later seventeenth century'.[32]

The beginning of English Presbyterianism

The most radical expression of English Puritanism in the first half of Elizabeth's reign was the Presbyterianism which emerged in the 1570s; and yet its cardinal doctrines – a parity of pastors and churches, the congregational eldership and regional synods – had been seen in action in London well before 1570, in both the refugee churches and in some native English Puritan congregations. London Puritans had paved the way for the message of Thomas Cartwright.

During the spring of 1570 Thomas Cartwright, the Lady Margaret Professor of Divinity at Cambridge, lectured on the first two chapters of the Acts of the Apostles, and thereby caused a storm which spread throughout the country. Using as a standard his interpretation of the system of ecclesiastical organization which he believed was described in the Book of Acts, he severely criticized the state of the Church of England. In unambiguous language he forthrightly declared that the name and office of archbishop should be abolished. In place of the existing prelates there should be bishops with purely spiritual functions. The deacons should care for the poor. The government of the church should not be in the hands of chancellors and archdeacons, but entrusted to local ministers and a local presbytery. Each parish should choose its own minister, and no one should seek the office, nor receive it at the hands of a bishop. Cartwright had not yet worked out the implications of what he was advocating, neither had he developed a full-blooded Presbyterian system. He had no personal experience of continental Calvinistic churches, and he was not as yet directly influenced by them. But what he proposed was radical enough and would have revolutionized the Church of England. The model he recommended differed profoundly from what had been established by law. It was a very explicit challenge to the established church and to the doctrine of royal supremacy. It was strong meat indeed.

In Cambridge the most determined and energetic opponent of Cartwright was the doughty John Whitgift. Whitgift (1530–1604) had been born into a Yorkshire gentry family. He took his Cambridge MA in 1557. Like Matthew Parker, he stayed in England during the reign of Mary and had not experienced the full impact of continental Protestantism. In 1570 he became Vice-Chancellor of Cambridge University, just in time to ensure that Cartwright was deprived of his professorship. Cartwright left Cambridge, possibly accompanied by another future Presbyterian leader, his friend Walter Travers, and went to his spiritual home, Geneva.

There was nothing new in the teaching about synodical organization as expounded in England in the early 1570s, or in its practice. But it was novel to claim that the particular form of church order and discipline which was found in the Calvinist churches was alone apostolic and was necessary for all times and in all places. Presbyterianism also represented a development and deepening of the already evident split between 'the internal spiritual dynamic of edification and growth of godly consciousness on the one hand and the demands of external order and formal obedience to the prince on the other'.[33] It in effect shifted the Christian prince from the centre to the periphery of Protestant concern. The conformists believed that in any reformation of the church the prince's will was limited by scripture and the need to conform with the will of God. In practice Presbyterian teaching left no place for the prince in the ordinary, daily government of the church. It was handed over, lock, stock and barrel, to the godly.

There was a widespread urge at that time among those who held Presbyterian views to draw together in classes and synodical assemblies, and through these to strive for uniformity of faith, worship and order. But the numbers of those involved was not great. Presbyterians were a sub-set of Puritanism, and only a few Puritans were Presbyterians. Presbyterian Puritans wanted many of the reforms demanded by other Puritans; they were not obsessed by matters of church government and church discipline. Also, the Presbyterian leaders differed considerably among themselves about what they wanted as a replacement for the existing system of church government. For all these reasons there could be no sudden and universal change. Presbyterianism evolved.

It was at this point, in the early 1570s, as Puritanism was becoming more militant and Presbyterianism more prominent, that John Field came into the picture. For some time he had been schooling himself in preparation for his role as 'the organizing secretary of Elizabethan presbyterianism'.[34] Field (1545–88) was born and bred in London and supported at Oxford by the Clothworkers' Company. It was his ministry in London, and especially at Holy Trinity, Minories, where an extreme form of Puritanism had taken root, that nourished and strengthened his natural pugnacity, and turned him into 'a dedicated revolutionary, a militant Calvinist whose capacity for leadership was acknowledged internationally as well as within English puritan circles'.[35] He rapidly became, and for some time remained, the principal character in the dramatic early years of English Presbyterianism.

He first achieved national fame for his part in the writing and dissemination of the brilliant manifesto, *The Admonition to Parliament* (1572). It was a public polemic in the guise of an address to Parliament. It consisted of two parts. The first, which was the Admonition proper, specifically advocated the Presbyterian system of church government:

> . . . as the names of archbishops, archdeacons, lord bishops, chancellors, etc, are drawn out of the Pope's shop together with their offices, so the government which they use . . . is antichristian and devilish, and contrary to the scriptures. And as safely may we, by the warrant of God's word, subscribe to allow the dominion of the Pope universally to rule over the word of God, as of an archbishop over a whole province, or a lord bishop over a diocese which containeth many shires and parishes. For the dominion that they exercise . . . is unlawful and expressly forbidden by the word of God . . . And as for the apparel, though we have been long borne in hand, and yet are, that it is for order and decency commanded, yet we know and have proved that there is neither order nor comeliness nor obedience in using it . . . Neither is the controversy betwixt them and us . . . for a cap, a tippet or a surplice, but for great matters concerning a true ministry and regiment of the church according to the word . . .[36]

In order to make the kind of radical reforms advocated by Field and his friends successful, there would have to have been far-reaching changes in the structure of politics and society which neither the Queen nor her subjects wanted. It would have been one of the most dramatic revolutions in English history. And, ominously, the authors also said that if their petition did not find favour with the Queen, they would, by God's grace, address themselves to defend his truth by suffering, and willingly by submitting their heads to the block.

The Admonition had an immediate and startling effect, made more telling by its vigorous and lively style. John Field and his colleague Thomas Wilcox were tracked down as its anonymous authors and sentenced to a year's imprisonment for offending against the Act of Uniformity. But a *Second Admonition* soon appeared, followed by Whitgift's *Answer to the Admonition*, Cartwright's *Reply*, Whitgift's *Defence*, Cartwright's *Second Reply* and a version of Walter Travers' *Full and Plain Declaration of Ecclesiastical Discipline*. The lengthy controversy was not pleasant. Both sides were completely unyielding in their opinions and showed little if any understanding or appreciation of their opponents views. Cartwright in particular wrote 'with a bitterness that justifies Hooker's rebuke that three words uttered with charity and meekness may be more blessed than three thousand volumes written with disdainful sharpness of wit'.[37]

It was also at that time that there appeared an English version of *De disciplina ecclesiastica* (1574) by Walter Travers, which was probably the most systematic exposition of Presbyterian churchmanship during that period.

John Field continued to exercise an effective Presbyterian leadership. It was no doubt largely due to his efforts and those of his immediate friends and fellow-believers that during the 1570s the Presbyterians became much more organized. And one very important aspect of this was what became known as 'the classical movement'. It seems that spontaneously there came into existence a number of conferences and assemblies, perhaps mostly, and in many cases exclusively, for ministers, which became known as classes. Attempts were made to weld these into some kind of unity and to spread the movement by establishing more gatherings of this type. John Field was secretary of the London group and both he and his group played a leading role in trying to achieve these objectives by means of a number of provincial and national synods. A loose federation emerged rather than a centrally directed and united organization. It appears that lay 'elders' did not participate in classes or synods, although there were a number of parishes which endeavoured to associate 'elders' with the ministers in various unofficial 'presbyteries'. By 1582 these classes had become so well established that at least one, at Dedham in Essex, kept a regular minute-book. Two national synods, and possibly more, were held – in London in 1586 and Cambridge in 1587. The Puritan clergy attending them deliberated in such a way that they 'showed that they regarded themselves as the General Assembly of an English Presbyterian Church'.[38]

It was in the context of such a development that John Field and his friends were able to organize what has been described as 'the first really effective pressure group in parliamentary history'.[39] In addition to petitions from different areas of the country, surveys of clergy were organized in a number of dioceses to provide statistical and other evidence to support their criticisms. They were remarkable documents, giving lists of ignorant and unpreaching ministers, of those who were non-resident or pluralists, and of those who led scandalous lives. For instance, the list for Essex contained entries like the following:

Mr Bulie, parson of Borlie, a man of scandalous life, a drunkard
Mr Hall of West Ham, a drunkard
Mr Warriner, of West Mersey, an adulterer.[40]

The 1586/87 Parliament included a band of members resolved to promote an out-and-out Presbyterian reformation: Peter Wentworth, Sir Anthony Cope, Job Throckmorton, Robert Bainbridge, Edward Lewkenor, and Ranulf Hurleston.[41] On 27 February 1587 Cope set before the House of Commons a most immoderate and ridiculous bill which proposed two measures to remedy the parlous condition of the Church of England. The first was that an annexed book, which was a revised Genevan Prayer Book incorporating a scheme of Presbyterian church government, should be 'authorized, put in use and practised'; and the second was to make utterly void and of none effect all such existing laws, customs, statutes, ordinances and constitutions which defined the worship, ceremonies and government of the church. Thus, at a stroke, it was recommended to the House that the entire fabric of Tudor ecclesiastical legislation, including the Prayer Book, together with all the surviving pre-Reformation canon law, ecclesiastical institutions, offices and foundations, should be obliterated. Not surprisingly the bill was opposed even by such a convinced Puritan as Sir Walter Mildmay, and it led to the imprisonment of Cope, Wentworth and three others. There was little support for so radical a proposal: many members of Parliament were Puritan in their sympathies, but few were Presbyterian.

Around 1586/87 the Presbyterian movement was at its strongest; during the next six years it rapidly declined and became almost extinct. There were several reasons for this striking change. First, the death of John Field in 1588 removed the key inspirational and organizational figure, and there was no one to replace him. He had been the lynch-pin of the movement for a long time, and Walter Travers who succeeded him as coordinator did not have Field's genius for organization. Other lesser, but important, leaders and friends of the movement also died at this time: notably the Earl of Leicester in 1588, Sir Francis Walsingham and Sir Walter Mildmay shortly afterwards. With such losses the Presbyterian influence in the Privy Council and in central government generally was severely weakened.

Then there were the Martin Marprelate tracts in 1588–9. These were a series of clever, witty and sarcastic attacks upon the church and its leaders. But they were somewhat excessive in their gibes against individual bishops, and especially against Whitgift, and they provoked Whitgift, with the support of the Queen, into taking counter-measures. The joint campaign of Whitgift and his able fellow-worker Richard Bancroft resulted in the general suppression for the time being of Puritanism as a whole. We will return to these matters more fully in a moment, when we consider the final years of Elizabeth's reign, but after we have given some attention to those Puritans who were so exasperated with the established church that they decided they could not 'tarry for the magistrate'.

Separatism

It was perhaps inevitable that sooner or later some of the more extreme and determined Puritans would not be content just to make their protests about the established church, and propound their views of what 'further reforms' were necessary, but would, through impatience, frustration or uneasy conscience, break away and form Separatist congregations. In a somewhat confused account, but one which is valuable to historians, John Stowe recorded that in about 1567 there appeared in London congregations of 'anabaptists' who 'called themselves puritans'.[42] It has been accepted quite widely that the word Puritan first came into use in connection with these groups. It was in the mid-1560s that there originated that tension between nonconformity and conformity, Puritanism and anti-Puritanism and, eventually, the schism between the Church of England and Dissent which was to become so central in the future history of the churches in England.

It was on 19 June 1567 that the sheriff's officers in London discovered a meeting at Plumbers' Hall of about one hundred people, gathered ostensibly for a wedding but in fact to hear sermons and to celebrate the Lord's Supper. Seventeen or eighteen of them were arrested, but treated with kindness. They were questioned by the Lord Mayor and by Bishop

Grindal. 'The replies of the prisoners to Grindal's questions show that while their intentions were Puritan their actions were Separatist, that they stood at the parting of the Puritan and Separatist ways.'[43] But, if the Plumbers' Hall group was a mixture of Puritan and Separatist elements, there soon emerged outspoken Separatist congregations, so that even the strongly Protestant Grindal grew impatient. The most notable of these was led by Richard Fitz. The members of his congregation had 'set their hands and hearts, to the pure unmingled and sincere worshipping of God'. They shared with the conforming Puritans the belief that in order to be a true Christian community they should strive to have first and foremost, 'the glorious word and evangel preached, not in bondage and subjection, but freely, and purely. Secondly, to have the sacraments ministered purely, only and all together according to the institution and good word of the Lord Jesus, without any tradition or invention of man, and all together agreeable to the same heavenly and almighty word of our good Lord Jesus Christ.'[44] They also shared a belief in the need for effective church discipline, in order that godliness and true worship might prevail in the fellowship of God's people. Where they differed from the conforming Puritans was in their belief that such further reform could not be accomplished within the established church. They believed that they must separate from the Church of England in order to erect a rightly constituted church structure. 'With such protests and such assertions as these the wheel had now turned full circle, and the principles and practices forged in the furnace of the Marian persecution for use against the Church of Rome were now turned directly against the inadequately reformed Church of England.'[45]

It is difficult, with the amount of evidence at present available, to know to what extent the Fitz congregation was indicative of a nascent separatist tradition, but it seems that there was such a tradition, at least in London, before Robert Browne appeared on the scene. Among these early Separatists there were the first stirrings of the theology of the gathered church which was to become such a potent force in the following century. Although Grindal made well-intentioned efforts to contain the conventiclers within the established church, he failed, and his failure, together with the subsequent intensification of persecution, only helped to reinforce the resolve of the Separatists, and to distinguish them from the conforming Puritans. Such a process of increasing group consciousness was further promoted by martyrdoms, as first Richard Fitz was imprisoned and died in prison, and then other pioneers suffered for their beliefs.

At this stage we encounter the growing popularity of meetings known as 'prophesyings', or latterly simply as 'exercises'. They were 'periodic gatherings in market towns of the clergy of the surrounding countryside for the study and exposition of the Scriptures'.[46] Such assemblies were open to the public and this proved a useful and fruitful means of providing fellowship and education for clergy as well as stimulating instruction and theological debate among the laity. The meetings consisted of sermons preached on a selected text by three or four of the company under the presidency of a moderator: this was done before the other members present and, in most cases, before a lay audience. The public preaching was followed by private 'censure' and conference among the ministers alone, and there was finally a dinner where there might be some discussion of matters of common interest. Few of these associations were Presbyterian. Indeed, the system was sanctioned by the bishops, and the bishops in a few diocese required all the clergy to attend the gatherings and gave permanent moderators powers of discipline. Bishop Curteys, who was appointed to the see of Chichester in 1570, introduced the clerical exercises into his diocese at the beginning of his episcopate. There was an exercise conference in all of his eight rural deaneries and each met six times a year. Either the bishop himself or his chancellor acted as moderator at the exercises in the western deaneries, and his commissary at Lewes fulfilled the same role in the eastern part of the diocese. And the bishop found them to be of great value:

> The Profitablenesse of the said Exercise is thys. That whereas before the Exercise began, There was not in the whole Diocese three that were able to preach to any ordinary Audience, & the rest of the Ministers generally knew not the Principles of Religion. God be thanked now, viz. within the space of six years ther[e] be upon thirty well able to preach at Pawle's crosse, with great commenda[ti]on; & upon forty or fifty more that make good & godly exhortations to the common people with gret edifying in their own parishes.[47]

Nevertheless, despite such endorsements, the prophesyings were far removed from Elizabeth's conception of the functions of a national church: she believed that free expression among the clergy and open theological debate among the laity would lead to sedition. She therefore ordered Grindal to suppress the prophesyings and reduce the number of licensed preachers to three or four for each county. The archbishop, with his strong Protestant sympathies, refused to comply and boldly questioned the Queen's command. In a measured but defiant statement he wrote to the Queen:

> And for my own part, because I am very well assured, both by reasons and arguments taken out of the holy Scriptures and by experience (the most certain seal of sure knowledge) that the said exercises for the interpretation and exposition of the Scriptures and for exhortation and comfort drawn out of the same are both profitable to increase knowledge among the ministers and tendeth to the edifying of the hearers: I am forced, with all humility, and yet plainly, to profess that I cannot with safe conscience and without the offence of the majesty of God give my assent to the suppressing of the said exercises; much less can I send out any injunction for the utter and universal subversion of the same. I say with St Paul, 'I have no power to destroy, but only to edify'; and with the same apostle, 'I can do nothing against the truth, but for the truth'. If it be your Majesty's pleasure, for this or any other cause, to remove me out of this place, I will with all humility yield thereunto and render again to your Majesty that I received of the same . . . Bear with me, I beseech you, Madam, if I choose rather to offend your earthly Majesty than to offend the heavenly Majesty of God.[48]

Grindal was promptly suspended from office and confined to his palace. It was a further indication that the kind of reforms sought by the more persistent and determined Puritans would not come from above, that is from the Queen and her bishops. The scene was set for the activities of a few dominant Separatists who were to lay the foundations for the long-term development of English Dissent and Nonconformity.

The first two of note were amongst the most important: Robert Browne (1550–1633) and Robert Harrison. They were both undergraduates at Cambridge in 1570 when Cartwright was electrifying the university with his lectures on the Acts of the Apostles. Browne adopted Puritan views, and was dismissed from his first post as a school teacher because of his outspokenness about the 'woeful and lamentable state of the church'. He started to make it plain that he rejected the idea of a national church. Against such a mixed church, containing those who were not really Christians because of the compulsion upon all to join, Browne and his fellow Separatists set up the model of independent 'gathered' congregations whose members would be bound together by a covenant. The congregation of each church would choose its own pastor and elders. Although different congregations might consult each other, there was no need to do so and there were to be no bishops or national synod to supervise them.

Browne's career from the time of his dismissal from his first post to his death was full of action and drama. In 1579 he attached himself to the household of the minister of Dry Drayton, Richard Greenham, and, although he had no licence to preach, he began preaching in a most provocative way in Cambridge, challenging the authority of the bishops, and denouncing them as 'ravenous and wicked persons' who sought rather 'their own advantage, or glory, or mischievous purpose, than the welfare and benefit of the church'.[49] Browne declared bishops to be Antichrists. They had no right to licence preachers, he maintained, and when his brother obtained two preaching licences for him he lost one and burned the other. By 1581 he had advanced beyond the point of rejecting episcopal authority and was repudiating the established church itself. He decided to set in train his own reformation.

He joined forces with Robert Harrison, who he mistakenly thought shared his extreme views, and, in 1581, formed with him a Separatist church in Norwich with its own liturgy. The members of the congregation covenanted with each other to choose their own minister, and entered into an agreement 'for cleaving to the Lord in greater obedience'.[50] It was a tough city in which to undertake such a venture, as the bishop, Edmund Freke, was anxious to show his conformity to the royal will and he conducted a systematic silencing of Puritan preachers. Undaunted, Browne preached openly, not only in Norwich but widely in Norfolk. It was not long before he and others were sent to prison. Such was the difficulty of worshipping as they wished that Browne and Harrison decided to leave England and to breath the freer air of the Netherlands.

Their new home, however, did not prove to be the expected promised land. They and their followers settled in Middelburg in Zeeland, but 'the strains of exile acted on their sensitive and scrupulous spirits to produce what was to be the common experience of English exiles in the Netherlands: dissension, divisions, and sometimes disillusionment'.[51] Browne and Harrison quarrelled over such matters as whether children of believing parents should or should not be regarded as members of the church, and what attitude to take towards those who conformed to the Church of England. The quarrelling reached a climax in 1583 when Browne was expelled from his own church. He went to Scotland where his views met with little sympathy and where he was imprisoned for a while. In 1584 he returned to England where, much to the chagrin of his fellow Separatists, he submitted to Whitgift. In 1591 he was ordained and presented to the living of Thorpe-cum-Achurch in Northamptonshire. But his adventurous and changeful life still had remaining quirks, and at his death in 1633 he was once more a Dissenter, and once more in gaol, this time in Northampton for striking a village constable. He was no doubt an awkward and cantankerous man, but he had courage and vision and can be considered as one of the true progenitors of modern Dissent.

When Browne wavered in his commitment to Separatism others appeared to take his place, and most notably John Greenwood (d.1593), who followed Wright as chaplain to Lord Rich of Rochford, and Henry Barrow (1550–93), a gentleman of independent means. Greenwood moved to London when the unauthorized services he was conducting in Lord Rich's house were suppressed, and there he either found or created the 'Ancient Church' in a house in St Paul's churchyard. For this he was cast into prison in 1586. A month later Barrow was also arrested when he went into the Clink to visit Greenwood and other imprisoned Separatists.

The importance of Greenwood and Barrow lies largely in their teaching and in their deaths, rather than in their actions during their lives. They made it plain that they left the Church of England because, for four reasons, they regarded it as in a state of total apostasy. First, the members of the parish congregations were not usually people converted by the preaching of the gospel who 'were able to make a personal confession of faith, and who were committed to a life of obedience to God'. Rather, they were a mixed multitude, some of whom were converted and committed, but the majority of whom were not. Secondly, the parochial ministry was not patterned on the apostolic ministry of presbyters and deacons appointed by the congregation to preach the word and administer the sacraments, sustained by the free gifts of the people whom they served. Rather, the Church of England ministry had many and varied functions and offices, with the ministers appointed and ordained by bishops and others, and paid from rents, fees, tithes and stipends. Thirdly, parish worship was directed by a book whose instructions derived not from scripture but from Rome, not from God but from the inventions of men. And, fourthly, the government of the parish churches was not shared by the total congregation seeking the will of God, but was rather composed of an unholy mingling of the rights of the parish priest, the diocesan bishop with his courts, and the secular power of the state.[52]

The persistent and strong attack upon the Church of England by Greenwood, Barrow and others, and their emphasis upon the ideals of a separated, godly congregation of converted people dedicated to the will of God, did not indicate a marked breach between the conforming Puritans and the Separatists. The 'close alliance, in thought if not in deed, between the left-wing Puritans within the church and the Separatists outside it affords important evidence of the close theological ties between the two. For many it was but a short step from impatient Puritanism within the established church to convinced separatism outside it. So close in many ways were the ideals of the two groups that for many the step from Puritanism into separatism was often but the step between yearning and fulfilment.'[53]

The Separatists continued to meet despite being deprived of their leaders. The informer Gamble revealed that in the summer they gathered 'in the fields a mile or so about London' where 'they sit down upon a bank and divers of them expound out of the Bible'. In the winter 'they assemble themselves by five of the clock in the morning to that house where they make their conventicle for that Sabbath day . . . they continue in their kind of prayer and exposition of Scripture all that day'. They did not use the Lord's Prayer or any form of set prayer as they repudiated 'all stinted prayers and read service' as 'babbling in the Lord's sight'. They permitted laymen to speak in their meetings, since 'every man in his own calling was to preach the gospel'. And they excommunicated offenders. After their religious exercises they shared a meal together. They then had a collection to cover the cost of the meal, taking any surplus to the prisons where any of their fellowship was committed. And the number of such incarcerated brethren increased, so that, by March 1593, a Separatist petition complained that there were some 'threescore and twelve persons, men and women, young and old, lying in cold, hunger, dungeons, and irons', seventeen or eighteen of whom had died 'in some noisome goals within these six years'.[54]

Greenwood and Barrow remained imprisoned for seven years. Both of them, but especially Barrow, continued to produce a formidable flow of propaganda. By March 1593 the authorities tired of this. They were convicted of devising 'seditious books', and on 6 April they were hanged at Tyburn. A few weeks later John Penry, who had played an important part in the printing of the Marprelate tracts, suffered the same fate. 'Imprisonment, judgment, yea death itself,' he had declared to his accusers, 'are not meet weapons to convince men's consciences, grounded on the word of God.'[55]

The Act passed in April 1593 for Retaining the Queen's Subjects in their due Obedience, which imposed imprisonment and then the alternative of exile or death for refusal to attend church, resulted in an exodus of Separatists abroad. Francis Johnson, a former Fellow of Christ's College, Cambridge, had stepped into the breach at the imprisonment of Barrow, Greenwood and Penry, and had become the pastor of Greenwood's church in London. In response to the 1593 Act this congregation decided to emigrate, and most of the prisoners were released to join them in Amsterdam. In 1597 the government released Johnson after five years in prison, and he and his brother George joined the bulk of the London flock. Francis became the pastor of a church which by the end of the century had almost three hundred members. But the history of the reunited church was far from happy. The 'separatist curse of contentiousness soon settled on them'. George Johnson accused his brother of appropriating too much authority to himself. And then there was further trouble over the dress of the women. While in prison Francis had married a wealthy widow. At the time her fashionable clothing had shocked the little band of shipwrights, joiners and shoemakers.

> Now the clothes controversy burst out anew. Stays became literally great bones of contention. Breastpieces were discussed in bated breath, while the husband solemnly offered to produce the offending gown for inspection at a formal meeting of the congregational officers. Eventually the pastor excommunicated his brother and also his father, who had come across the channel in a vain effort to settle the controversy. Such were the sad extremes to which the separatist principles carried their followers.[56]

John Whitgift and the decline of Puritanism

The decline of Puritanism as a force acting within the Church of England for 'further reformation' can be attributed to a number of factors and circumstances, but one in particular can be dated very precisely. On 23 August 1583, the disciplinarian, anti-Puritan John Whitgift was elected Archbishop of Canterbury. Less than two months after his appointment, and even before he was enthroned, he issued a set of articles which caused alarm among the Puritans. To some extent they were non-controversial, for they were in part concerned with wide-reaching reform and with discipline, but the focus of Puritan attention was almost exclusively on the requirement they contained for clerical subscription to three articles as the condition for exercising any ecclesiastical function:

> 1. That her Majesty, under God, hath, and ought to have, the sovereignty and rule over all manner of persons born within her realms and dominions and countries, of what estate ecclesiastical or temporal soever they be. And that none other foreign power, prelate, state or potentate hath, or ought to have, any jurisdiction, power, superiority, pre-eminence or authority, ecclesiastical or temporal, within her Majesty's said realms, dominions and countries. 2. That the Book of Common Prayer and of ordering bishops, priests and deacons containeth nothing in it contrary to the word of God. And that the same may be lawfully used, and that he himself will use the form of the said book prescribed in public prayer and administration of the sacraments and none other. 3. That he alloweth the book of Articles of Religion agreed upon by the archbishops and bishops in both provinces, and the whole clergy in the Convocation holden in London. And that he believeth all the articles therein contained to be agreeable to the word of God.[57]

The first article was unexceptional to Puritans, as was the third if, as decreed by the statute of 1571, subscription was confined to the more strictly doctrinal of the Thirty-Nine Articles. But it was the second of Whitgift's articles which caused most problems, and, indeed, problems for perhaps the majority of the clergy, and certainly for Puritans defined in the broadest sense. At first almost four hundred clergy refused to subscribe, and a series of petitions were sent to bishops and the Council by clergy and country gentlemen. They were sympathetically received, and Whitgift found himself opposed by men like Walsingham, Knollys and Leicester, together with the clerk of the Council. He bowed to the opposition and compromised. He allowed a more limited form of subscription, with modification to the article about the Prayer Book. Eventually only a handful of clergy were deprived.

Whitgift had made a tactical error in his first set of articles as he had united the moderate as well as the radical Puritans against him. The following year he was more tactful when he issued a set of twenty-four questions which were to be enforced by the newly strengthened Court of High Commission by means of the *ex officio* oath. This time the interrogation was limited to the leaders, and the moderate Puritan clergy were exempt. The questions were also designed to elicit what those concerned had done rather than what they believed. Nonetheless, Whitgift's policy of trying to achieve an unattainable degree of uniformity made it more difficult than it might otherwise have been to deal effectively with the hard core of extremists, and it also placed his own episcopal order in grave danger. 'In the long run, the Whitgiftian policy, continued in their generations by Bancroft and the Laudians, was as much responsible as any puritan excess for destroying the comprehensiveness of the Church of England and its fully national character.'[58]

The work of Richard Hooker

Richard Hooker (1554–1600) published his magisterial book, *Of the Laws of Ecclesiastical Polity* in 1594 and 1597 as an extended answer to the Puritan case against the Church of England.[59] It was of major importance as an *apologia* for the Anglican Church in its infancy, and it was effective in what it sought to do. But its importance goes far beyond the circumstances which gave birth to it, and the age in which it appeared. It is the 'most creative contribution to the literature of Anglicanism'. It is 'a manifesto to which the Church returns at every crisis to seek justification and vindication'.[60] No brief summary can convey the richness, variety and scope of this monumental work, but a bald outline will at least serve to indicate the range of what Hooker undertook and the main lines of his argument.[61]

Hooker's genius was immediately shown in the way he widened the previously rather narrow and sterile debate. In the first Book he examined the different kinds of laws which operate in the world, which all come from God, the one law-giver, and which affect every aspect of the world and man's part in it. He tried to establish that there was not just one set of laws by which man should be governed: life was far more complex than was suggested by the Puritans. In this he differed radically from the central Protestant position as elaborated by Calvin, which portrayed man as totally corrupted and therefore not able to comprehend God's law, except in as far as God chooses to reveal himself. For Hooker some laws are known from God's revelation, but some can be known by reason. Thus, as a logical continuation of this theme, in the second Book he considered the arguments of those who urged reformation of the Church of England on the ground that 'scripture is the only rule of all things which may be done by men'. If there are laws to be followed other than the revelation of God in scripture, then, in things indifferent, such as ceremonies, the church is free to adopt music, set prayers, the sign of the cross and other such practices which were anathema to Puritans. In the third Book he attacked the assertion that 'in scripture there must of necessity be contained a form of church polity, the laws whereof may in nowise be altered'. The fourth dealt with the Puritan contention that the Church of England was corrupted with popish orders, rites and ceremonies and that it ought to follow the example of the reformed churches in removing such corruptions. The fifth Book, which was published after the first four in 1597, went into great detail in an extended examination of the charge that the Church of England retained such corruptions in its Prayer Book, in its ceremonies and its methods of government.

Hooker's great work played its part in the decline of Puritanism because it was 'the most effective and authoritative defence of the established church against its Puritan critics that had so far been produced'; although it should not be given too much contemporary significance in this respect as it may well not have been accepted as authoritative in the years immediately after its publication, or indeed have been very widely read. Hooker recognized the existence of different national churches and different schemes of church organization, but he did not admit the possibility of different churches within any one state. ' He opposed what he regarded as one of the perversions of truth perpetrated by the Puritans', who 'separated State and Church as two corporations independent of each other'.[62] Hooker did not recognize the right of Separatists or Roman Catholics to dissociate themselves from the national church.

Despite the overall decline of Puritanism in the last decade or so of the sixteenth century there was a flowering of Puritan writings and a steady spreading of Puritan ideals in the parishes. William Perkins was a pioneer, and in 1589 started a series of popular books which were written in sermon style to promote Puritan piety. Richard Rogers followed where Perkins led, and Nicholas Bound made a contribution. They helped to establish what was to become an outstanding corpus of distinctive devotional works, the influence of which was to extend into the centuries ahead.

Religion and the people

It is well to recall that the issues of Puritanism and Separatism which we have been considering, and which aroused such passion and, in some cases, extremes of statement and action, only involved a small proportion of the population. 'The complete triumph of Puritanism would have submerged other religious values developing within Anglicanism. It would also have imposed an undue strain upon that large proportion of the English people who were willing to worship in church but not to embrace so intense and so disciplined a religious life. A national church cannot become a club for religious athletes.'[63]

For many people Christian belief and practice was an integral part of the 'daily round and common task' in one of the countless hamlets, villages or small towns which provided the setting for their lives. England was a largely rural country, with but a few scattered urban areas. For various, not easily identifiable, reasons, the fourteenth and fifteenth centuries witnessed a massive reduction in the total population, so that, by 1500, it hardly topped two million, which was scarcely higher than just after the Norman Conquest. By the end of the century it had risen to over four million, with a very uneven distribution throughout the land, but even at that level the majority of the population lived in widely dispersed small communities. The only great town was London, with a population of about 60,000 at the beginning of the sixteenth century and 215,000 by the early years of the seventeenth century. When Henry VIII ascended the throne in 1509, the largest other towns were Norwich (12,000), Bristol (10,000), Exeter, York and Salisbury (8,000 each), Coventry (7,500) and Kings Lynn (4,500); and probably none of these exceeded 20,000 a hundred years later. Approximately 10% of the Tudor population lived in towns, about half of whom resided in London. The size of the average settlement was small, probably not more than two to three hundred, and the vast majority of the population made their living by agriculture, or in agriculturally related occupations.

Within this society, and more particularly within these unnumbered small communities, the church occupied a central place and fulfilled a crucial role. The local church was typically accepted as an essential part of the matrix of society, and its teaching was accepted by most people as axiomatic. Most Tudor Englishmen and women were probably far less interested in theology than many books suggest, but belief in God was universal. Although a few men like Marlowe and Raleigh were reputed to be atheists they were scandalous oddities. Atheism and agnosticism scarcely existed, and almost no one dared openly to deny the existence of God.

At least on paper, the religious needs of the population were well catered for. There were approximately 9,400 parishes, and there were ample priests to serve them. In addition there were large numbers of men in minor orders who ranked legally as clergy but filled posts such as tutors or secretaries. The influence of ecclesiastics permeated the whole of society. Ecclesiastical authorities, and after 1559 the state, expected everyone to attend church. Whether they were pious, committed Christians or not, prayers, homilies and biblical passages must have become deeply imprinted on the minds of congregations.

Such religious socialization does not imply universal piety and commitment. For most people the Christian faith was the accepted norm and the primary determinant of their world view, but this was not invariably the case. At first glance it appears that the official religion of the Elizabethan era must have embraced the great majority of the people, and that it must have held an almost impregnable position in the life of the nation and its inhabitants. After all, in theory at least, the Anglican Church was nothing less than society itself in one of its most important manifestations. It was the nation at prayer. 'Every child was deemed to be born into it. He was expected to be baptized by the local clergyman and sent by his parents or employer to be catechized in the rudiments of the faith. It was a criminal offence for a man to stay away from church on Sundays, and the very mode of worship there symbolized the society in which he lived.'[64] A second glance, however, reveals that there were varieties of belief, and even non-belief, which were expressed in a multitude of ways. Not only were there a range of Puritan and Separatist views, but there was the beginning of a distinctive anti-Calvinist trend, albeit at this stage a small minority movement; there were the Catholics; and there was an ill-defined 'folk' religion which probably permeated society to a greater extent than has generally been appreciated, which was a mixture of religion and magic. And, of course, much of the religious belief, even when it was deep-rooted, genuine and central to the life of the individuals concerned, may not have been very dogmatically sophisticated. For many, and especially for those in the artisan and middle-order socio-economic groupings of the population, to whom the Protestant faith was sincerely held and yet not particularly well articulated, Foxe's *Book of Martyrs* was a prime source of inspiration and instruction, with its simple, highly-emotionally charged Protestantism and strong anti-Roman Catholicism.

More people than has hitherto generally been acknowledged either did not attend any place of worship at all, or, if they did, put in a reluctant appearance at the parish church, and so behaved that the services were, as far as they were concerned, a travesty of what was intended. 'Presentments made before the ecclesiastical courts show that virtually every kind of irreverent (and irrelevant) activity took place during worship. Members of the congregation jostled for pews, nudged their neighbours, hawked and spat, knitted, made coarse remarks, told jokes, fell asleep, and even let off guns.'[65] There was plenty of scope for religious heterodoxy, and even some self-conscious rejection of religious dogma. There was quite widespread ignorance of the most elementary doctrines of the Christian faith. One historian has described the Elizabethan period as 'the age of greatest religious indifference before the twentieth century',[66] and 'although this may seem an exaggeration it is certain that a substantial proportion of the population regarded organized religion with an attitude which varied from cold indifference to frank hostility'.[67] Although there was little openly expressed atheism, an historian of the period has declared that 'of tavern unbelief there was a great deal'; and he concludes that despite the enforced church attendance, it is doubtful whether more than a quarter of the population 'can be said to have had any religion at all'.[68]

It appears that a disproportionately large number of the 'godly' were literate, and of the multitude who were less religiously committed a considerable proportion were illiterate.[69] Protestantism was a religion of the word – the scriptures, books and sermons – and it more readily reached, and was embraced by merchants, tradesmen and artisans in towns, than by country folk.[70] Illiteracy was widespread, and particularly prevalent in the countryside; and there was a huge variation in the educational level and intellectual sensibility within Elizabethan society, with grammar schools and the two universities providing education for many among the social elite in contrast to the lack of any such provision among the mass of the uneducated.[71]

But this broad divide must not be over-emphasized. Many of the illiterate in country areas as well as towns were numbered among the 'godly', and there were many of the more literate who were indifferent to religion, and certainly not ardent Protestants. Margaret Spufford and Patrick Collinson among a number of historians have questioned any very close link between religious, and more especially Protestant, commitment and educational levels or class situations.[72] Spufford concludes that the 'close study of the wills of orthodox villagers bears out the general impression . . . of a society in which even the humblest members, the very poor, and the women, and those living in physical isolation, thought deeply on religious matters and were often profoundly influenced by them'.[73] This may be somewhat of an overstatement in view of the evidence she adduces, but it does draw attention to 'a broad spectrum of unspectacular orthodoxy'; and it and other studies justify the conclusion that it would be mistaken 'to over-emphasize either the presence of "godly" groups or the existence of people largely indifferent to religion'. It is reasonable to reckon that most 'people were located somewhere between these poles'.[74] As Collinson states it: 'The multitude doubtless conformed in great numbers to the prayer-book religion of the parish church, which became part of the fabric of their lives.'[75]

Beyond the bounds of the parish, it is of note that church courts continued to play an important part in the life of the nation, and in the promotion of discipline and conformity within the established church. They exercised an omnipresent influence, not only by their jurisdiction in matters of a purely ecclesiastical nature at the levels of province, diocese and archdeaconry, but by the way their powers and activities 'extended to some of the most intimate aspects of the personal life of the population as a whole'.[76] Law and legal institutions were of immense importance in the society of Elizabethan and early Stuart England. Government, whether it was national or local, political or ecclesiastical, was largely channelled through legal forms, and there was a less clear boundary between judicial and administrative action than there is today. There was a considerable expansion of legal activity throughout the reigns of Elizabeth and James i, in which the church courts were key elements.

But were they effective in the values they purveyed? Martin Ingram, who made a thorough study of them, believes that they were. He argues that they did not promulgate outmoded or unwanted values. He asserts that 'many of the courts' activities were either in line with the existing attitudes and expectations of honest householders in the parishes (as in the pursuit of notorious sexual offenders), or represented a realistic attempt, normally supported by at least a section of local opinion, to nudge the mass of the people towards improved standards of morality and religious observance'.[77] He also portrays them as effective in what they did. They were not vitiated by lack of teeth. They had a socially relevant task to perform, and they did it remarkably well.

A postscript like this, with its reminder of the 'religion' of the mass of the people in the latter half of the sixteenth century, is a necessary counterbalance to a chapter on Elizabethan Puritanism and before we consider Elizabethan Catholicism, lest, despite the importance of both of these belief systems, we forget that life was less religiously intense and hazardous for the bulk of the people who were content to live in a more humdrum conformist way, than for the highly committed believers who mainly tend to attract the attention of historians.

4

Elizabethan Roman Catholicism

Historiography

Elizabethan Roman Catholicism has been the subject of much historical debate during recent decades. Like so many facets of the church history we are reviewing, various, and often contradictory, interpretations cause complications. Simple, unqualified, conclusions are unwarranted. There is first of all the disagreement over the degree of continuity or discontinuity between pre- and post-Reformation Roman Catholicism. A. G. Dickens and J. Bossy are the leading proponents of fundamental discontinuity.[1] Dickens was very influential in postulating a distinction between 'survivalism' and 'seminarism': there was, he asserted, a quite rapid decline in the conservative attachment to old traditions, and after some time there arrived a new, dynamic, imported brand of post-Reformation Catholicism, brought by missionary priests. Bossy reinforced this view, and suggested that the post-Reformation community was created by the seminary priests and Jesuits after 1570. It owed nothing to what had gone before.

The revisionists proceeded to challenge the prevailing interpretations of an heroic post-Reformation Catholicism in the characteristically decisive and vigorous style with which we are by now familiar.[2] As we have already seen, they claim that there was little demand for change from below and Catholicism continued to grip the hearts of a large portion of the population. They suggest that there was much more continuity between 'mediaeval Catholicism' and 'Counter-Reformation Catholicism' than has often been allowed, and the emerging recusancy owed much to what had preceded it. They argue that recusancy was well-established before 'survivalism' disappeared. There was a certain amount of Catholic withdrawal from the parish church to the gentry household, but 'the separation of Catholics from the worshipping community was a very slow process, which began early with non-communicating, took the next step in refusal to attend regular services, but achieved severance in baptism, marriage and burial much later'.[3] By the time the seminary mission and then the Jesuits undertook their work there already existed the essential concept of a separated Catholic church. There was possibly no dramatic growth in recusancy at any time, but a fairly steady transition from the one state of affairs to the other.

J.C.H. Aveling and P. McGrath detect some continuity between pre- and post-Reformation Catholicism, and see in the Elizabethan period the reconstruction of English Catholicism.[4] McGrath accepts that it was highly unlikely that there was a distinctive break between the 'old' Catholicism of the pre-1530s and the 'new' Catholicism of the 1570s. 'There was a different attitude towards certain practices like fasting, frequent confession and communion, and so on, and the influence of the Counter-Reformation in England became more marked, but not-withstanding all this, the seminary priests had more in common with the Catholicism of the earlier period than they had differences.'[5] But he differs from Christopher Haigh in some of the secondary themes elaborated by Haigh. Thus, he questions Haigh's assertion that those clergy who conformed, but who nevertheless sought to maintain some remnants of Catholic belief and practice within the established church, and those laity who became church papists, were contributing to the possible restoration of Catholicism. On the contrary, McGrath considers that such a fifth-column might well have made the Church of England more acceptable to Catholics than if it had been more distinctly Protestant, and it also weakened Catholicism by blurring the differences between the old and the new traditions. McGrath also expresses regret at the fierce criticism levelled by Haigh at the work of the seminary priests. He acknowledges shortcomings but defends them against Haigh's accusations, that they were guilty of major errors of strategy and tactics, that they were seeking an easy life as domestic chaplains, that they concentrated over-much on the care of Catholics and did not give enough attention to the conversion of heretics, and that, as a general conclusion, their mission was a failure. McGrath also denies the suggestion that numbers of the priests had a death-wish or a martyr-wish. He appreciates the value of Haigh's work, and its stimulus to the study of Elizabethan Catholicism, but he regrets what he considers to be Haigh's partisanship in his assessment of the work and achievements of the seminary priests and the Jesuits.[6]

This chapter will elaborate on the view of Catholicism which was briefly adumbrated in the Introduction. It will be suggested that Catholicism did not disappear with the slow protestantization process;

it was gradually replaced – more speedily at some times, and in some areas, than at others, and occasionally with some measure of recovery, but inexorably overall – and in its place there emerged various forms of Protestantism. This process was continuous; but the 'old' was not sunk without trace, to be replaced by the 'new'. Rather, the 'old' continued, albeit in a modified form, and the 'new' reinforced some features of the 'old', discarded others, and introduced new elements.

It is well to recall that Elizabeth came to the throne a mere twenty-five or thirty years after the Henrician reforms had been inaugurated, and that those years had included massive swings from Catholicism to Protestantism and back again to Catholicism, before the 1559 Settlement restored Protestantism to favour once more. In retrospect we can see that 1558 was the beginning of a period of protestantization which was to continue until the present day, but this was not evident to those living at the time, and was especially not part of the perception of the 'average Englishman' who was the inheritor of centuries of Catholicism. The real impact of government ecclesiastical legislation, certainly in the areas of the country away from London, the cathedral cities and the main towns, was slight. The pattern of church life and the religious beliefs and life-styles of ordinary people were dictated to a great extent by custom, and it took a considerable time for changes to be integrated into the corporate life of the small rural communities which were the setting for the life of most Englishmen, and for the individuals composing those communities to adopt any fundamental alteration in their beliefs and practices. Thus, despite the legislation of the 1559 Settlement, and the efforts made to implement it, there was a transition period in the 1560s at least when there were survivals from the former Catholicism, and a continuance of former Catholic dogmas and modes of behaviour.[7] Indeed, as indicated in the previous chapter, there was also a persistence throughout those years, as throughout the whole sixteenth century and into the seventeenth century, of scepticism and the tacit or explicit rejection of both Roman Catholicism and Protestantism. The 'hold of organized religion upon the people was never so complete as to leave no room for rival systems of belief'.[8]

At the parochial level English Roman Catholicism during the 1560s and into the 1570s was not marked by a strong body of opinion which stressed union with Rome and conscious rejection of a heretical Church of England.[9] The issues were blurred, and for the peasantry at least the old religion entailed a complex of religious practices, many of which remained available. 'The altars, images, holy water, rosary-beads and signs of the cross, which visitations from many parts of the country show remained prominent in the churches, kept aspects of Catholic worship in the public arena, and many clergy made the Prayer Book services as much like masses as circumspection allowed.'[10] Some ostensibly 'conforming' clerics provided services as officially required in their churches and Catholic ones in secret. By such behaviour throughout the country these clergy arguably did as much towards the survival of Catholicism in England as did the determined recusant priests or the brave seminary missionaries whom we will soon encounter. Such conservative parish priests 'held the loyalty of their flocks to as much of the old faith as circumstances permitted, until official pressure, personal frustration and a clarification of issues made more laymen willing to move into recusancy'. They 'thus fulfilled an essential bridging role between the Marian Church and separated Elizabethan Catholicism'.[11]

But this continuance of Catholic belief and practice noticeably declined at parochial level as the reign advanced. For example, at the beginning of the reign, although Roman Catholicism ceased to be the established religion of England, in Northumberland, it continued, though illegal, to be the religion of the majority for a time.[12] But with the defeat of the rising of 1569 it seems to have almost totally disappeared, only to re-emerge under the influence of some seminary priests and Jesuits as the religion of a minority led by a few recusant gentry. The recusants included some yeomen and poor people, but they were a small group, largely confined to the Tyne valley and the edge of the Western Highlands. This social pattern helps to give credence to the theory that between the accession of Elizabeth and the Restoration English Catholicism was essentially a seigneurial religion, with its survival dependent on 'the unity and independence, the traditions of hospitality and the social dominance of a neighbourhood of numerous gentry households which were geographically scattered but linked by bonds of kinship and spiritual affinity'.[13]

The Elizabethan Settlement was not totally repugnant to Catholics. The laity were more concerned with ceremonial than with doctrine, and in the early years of the reign, if not for a longer period, the ceremonial emphasis of the services was left largely as a matter of local option. The major problem for Catholics was the insistence of the authorities on the acceptance of the royal supremacy, but in the 1560s most of the Romanists made some show of conformity to avoid trouble. It was the previous Marian bishops who were most unwilling to conform, and all of them, with the exception of Kitchin of Llandaff, remained loyal to

Rome and were deprived. The parish clergy as a whole were not as uncompromising. Of the total of about 8,000 of them, only between 200 and 1,000 suffered deprivation.

'Church papists' were quite widely distributed in the Church of England congregations. It is evident in a publication in 1582 that they were publicly recognized. In an acrimonious exchange between two interlocutors 'Professor of the Gospel' expresses his obvious detestation for the churchmanship of his fellow debater:

> Pa[pist]: Wherefore shoulde yee call me Papist, I am obedient to the lawes, and do not refuse to go to the Churche.
> Pro[fessor of the Gospel]: Then it seemeth you are a Church Papist?
> Pa[pist]: A Church Papist, what meane ye by that?
> Pro[fessor of the Gospel]: Doe not you knowe? I will tell ye, there are Papists which will not come at the Churche: and there are Papists which can keep their conscience to themselves, and yet goe to Church: of this latter sorte it seemeth you are: because yee goe to the Churche.[14]

We will see how, in an era of disorder and dislocation, it is excessively difficult to erect clear boundaries between conforming Catholics, and those ingenuous, and often inconspicuous 'parish Anglicans' and 'Prayer Book Protestants' whom we have already encountered. Church papists may provide one answer to the decline in numbers and zeal of English Catholics. Catholics and potential Catholics may have found a spiritual home in a church which still retained Catholic elements. Certainly, as we will see, the Catholics were increasingly discouraged to conform to the Roman Church, which was generally a despised religious community, with countless negative historical and political associations and connotations. The missionary movement may have failed to have any significant effect upon the beliefs and practices of ordinary people; and yet there was also ever present and at hand a church which was comprehensive enough to accommodate the crypto-Catholics with conciliatory opinions.

A period of Roman Catholic activism

By the late 1560s and early 1570s it was clear that Protestantism was becoming well entrenched, and the overall Roman Catholic passivity was replaced by a more aggressive stance. Certain positive steps were taken in an attempt to re-assert the claims of Roman Catholicism.

The first of a series of crucial events was the Northern Rising of 1569.[15] In the north of England, for a variety of reasons, adherence to the 1559 Settlement, and even perhaps to the regime, was more qualified than in most other areas of the country. Mary, Queen of Scots, exercised a powerful influence. The dioceses of Carlisle, Durham and York were particularly hostile to Elizabeth, and in Cumberland and Westmorland the Catholic mass was openly retained. Aware of actual or potential opposition, Elizabeth and Cecil completed Henry VIII's policy of displacing the Percies, Nevilles and Dacres from offices of military and political importance in the far north. The various deprivations and replacements destabilized the area. By 1569, the Earls of Northumberland and Westmorland had reached a position where they put their hope in a *putsch* linked to the succession of the Queen of Scots.

The Northern Rising was the immediate consequence of somewhat convoluted political manoeverings, the object of which was a proposal to marry Mary, Queen of Scots, to the Duke of Norfolk, England's premier peer, who would then use his influence to settle the succession to the throne, and would promote Catholic interests, by replacing Cecil as chief minister. The campaign collapsed when Elizabeth discovered what was being plotted, and the Earls of Northumberland and Westmorland, who had been implicated, were abandoned by their southern allies and left to fend for themselves. There was an uprising, but the revolt was quelled, and Elizabeth and Cecil seized their opportunity to subdue the north and enforce compliance. A number of the leaders were hung and Cecil planned a comprehensive redistribution of northern patronage. The Council of the North was reconstituted in 1572 under the presidency of the Puritan Earl of Huntingdon, the Queen's cousin; and he used his powerful position to attack Catholic recusancy and to foster Protestantism by appointing sound Protestants as preachers in the market towns of the region.

The second development of significance in these pivotal few years surrounded the activities of William Allen (1532–94) who made a greater contribution to preserving Roman Catholicism in England than any other individual.[16] He came from a gentry family and appeared set for a distinguished career in Oxford, where he was appointed principal of St Mary's Hall in 1556. But he resigned a few years later and eventually joined the Roman Catholic exiles in Louvain. For a while he returned to England where he was among a small number who actively tried to persuade English Catholics that they should not in good conscience attend the services of the established church. This uncompromising stance put him in danger from the authorities, and in 1565 he once again went into exile. After studying theology at Louvain he was ordained priest. In 1568 he established a college in Douai which was intended as a centre for English Catholic scholars abroad, a training place for priests who would restore the Catholic religion in England when the time was ripe, and an educational establishment for English youths. In the ensuing years he gathered a remarkably able group of men about him. The first ordinations were in 1573, and the first Douai priests went to England the following year. The college struggled against shortage of funds and considerable opposition and criticism from both Catholics and non-Catholics. The missionary priests travelled in disguise, visited Catholic families and 'worked with success to check the easy-going conformity that was changing nominal Catholics into effective Anglicans'.[17] They declared conformity unacceptable; conform to Catholicism or be cut off from the church was the simple option offered. And, confronted with such a stark alternative, some became Protestants while others became active Catholics who before had been inactive or lukewarm. The Crown and its officers regarded this missionary, or seminary, movement as an insidious and dangerous attack, made more so by the papal bull of 1570 which we will consider in a moment.

William Allen remained an exile and died a cardinal at Rome. He had set a pattern which was followed in 1579 with the foundation of another English college in Rome under Jesuit direction. The flow of Jesuit missionaries began in 1580. They were to be even more active and successful than the earlier seminarists.

The third important event at this time was the bull *Regnans in Excelsis*, issued by Pius V on 25 February 1570, which pronounced the Queen excommunicated and deposed. It was a stark, uncompromising document which unmistakably declared what powers were possessed by the Pope and what were the consequences of the use of those powers. There was no salvation outside the one Holy Catholic and Apostolic Church. God had committed that Church to Peter, and to his successor the Pope of Rome, whom 'alone He has made ruler over all peoples and Kingdoms, to pull up, destroy, scatter, disperse, plant and build, so that he may preserve His faithful people . . . in the unity of the Spirit and present them safe and spotless to their Saviour'. Despite all the efforts of the Pope to maintain the unity and the Catholicity of the Church, the bull complained that the number of the ungodly in England had grown, and Elizabeth merely promoted corruption. She was 'the pretended

Queen of England and the servant of crime'. She had 'seized the crown and monstrously usurped the place of supreme head of the Church of England', and she had reduced the kingdom to a miserable ruin. She had embraced the errors of heretics, oppressed the followers of the Catholic faith, instituted false preachers, abolished the mass, celibacy and Catholic ceremonies, and in these and other ways had put herself beyond the pale of the Church. 'Therefore', the bull continued, 'we do out of the fullness of our apostolic power declare the foresaid Elizabeth to be a heretic and favourer of heretics, and her adherents in the matters aforesaid to have incurred the sentence of excommunication . . . And moreover [we declare] her to be deprived of her pretended title to the aforesaid crown and all lordship, dignity and privilege whatsoever.' The bull then went on to pronounce the nobles, subjects, and people of the said realm, and all others who had in any way sworn oaths to her, to be forever absolved from such an oath . . . We charge and command all and singular the nobles, subjects, people and others aforesaid that they do not dare obey her orders, mandates and laws. 'Those who shall act to the contrary we include in the like sentence of excommunication.'[18]

The bull was most unfortunate and unwise. The condemnation of the Queen was belated and there was no provision for enforcement by Catholic princes. It seems that it was not meant as a general invitation to Catholic rulers to take action against Elizabeth, but was intended to reassure the consciences of Englishmen, who, it appears, the Pope perceived as eager to rise in rebellion. But, if this was so, it came too late to encourage and support those participating in the Northern Uprising, which had already ended in disaster. It immeasurably heightened the bad consciences of Catholics, and increased the tension for them, by facing them with the agonizing alternative of being loyal, obedient Catholics, and traitors as well, or loyal citizens who had to disobey the Pope. In the event most English Catholics ignored it. The vast majority could, with all honesty, say that they had not seen it and it had not been officially communicated to them. They continued loyal to the Queen, but the government could, and did, use the bull to great effect to argue that Papists were henceforth bound to be traitors. And such an accusation was apparently endorsed by the bull not being withdrawn, and by the way the papacy strove to overthrow the Queen.

The next in the quick succession of events which were at the same time both productive of intensified anti-Catholic feeling and an encouragement to further Catholic militancy and intransigence was the Ridolfi plot.[19] Roberto Ridolfi was a Florentine banker who had been settled in London for many years. He had been arrested in 1569 on suspicion of providing money for the northern rebels, but had been released. He continued to reside in London, where he was ostensibly engaged in commercial business but actually an agent of the Pope, charged with the task of organizing all the actual or potential enemies of Elizabeth and Cecil into one great act of defiance. After conferring with Guerau de Spes, the Spanish ambassador who conceived it his duty to stir up treasonable discontent in order to bring the country back to the Roman fold, it was agreed that the Duke of Alva should land a force in East Anglia while Philip of Spain should send another force from Spain to the West Country. With his usual admixture of optimism and fantasy, Ridolfi unrealistically expected that at the appearance of these two forces the English Catholics would rise up in great numbers and with unbounded enthusiasm, liberate Mary Stuart, and join with the invaders in ousting Elizabeth. He then obtained the reluctant concurrence in the plot of the Duke of Norfolk. Philip was quite sanguine, and there was even mention in Spanish court circles of rounding off a revolution with the assassination of Elizabeth. Alva was less compliant, perhaps because he sensed the shallowness of Ridolfi's thinking and the high risk that the whole scheme would end in ruin and probably the death of Mary Stuart. He agreed to send troops only in support of an actual serious and effective English Catholic rising led by the Duke of Norfolk. Largely as a consequence of carelessness by Ridolfi, the plot was discovered, and the Duke of Norfolk was sent to the Tower. This was the immediate signal to Philip and Alva to drop the invasion plan. Elizabeth's retribution was mild. She remained satisfied with foiling her enemies. She took no steps against Mary other than a tightening of surveillance. Angry Protestants bayed for the blood of Mary, but Elizabeth satisfied them with the execution of Norfolk.

Within two months of the death of the Duke of Norfolk another event, this time abroad, helped to yet further fuel anti-Catholic emotions. After her unsuccessful attempt to assassinate Admiral Colingny, Catherine de Medici plotted with Henry of Guise the massacre of the Huguenots in Paris, having won the support of Charles IX by a tale of a Huguenot plot against Catholics. The massacre began in August 1572 and soon spread throughout France. Colingny was killed, together with thousands of Huguenots, and the survivors took up arms in the fourth civil war. The horror with which the news of the massacre was received in the English court and more widely in the country at large was heightened by the accompanying revelation of the Spanish satisfaction at the event and the rapture at Rome.

'The ten years which separated the papal bull of excommunication of 1570 from the arrival of the Jesuits in 1580 saw the turn of the tide in the ebbing fortunes of the Papists in England.'[20] This is true from two points of view. On the one hand the various events, activities and developments I have briefly reviewed reanimated a somewhat lethargic and moribund English Catholicism. There was a distinct danger in the 1560s that, despite the activities of various priests and a limited number of laymen who strove to keep the Catholic flame alight, Catholicism would quietly perish as the older generation died, especially because a lack of priests made it more difficult for Catholics to practice their faith. The priests who helped in the survival of Catholicism in the 1560s assisted in providing a bridge between the halcyon days of Mary and the new Catholic surge in the 1570s, but it was a bridge of finite length, for they were only helping to hold the situation. A new dynamic was needed to ensure the long-term continuation of English Catholicism, and the work of the Douai missionaries helped, in quite a small but significant way, to provide such an impetus.

But, on the other hand, there was a growth in anti-Catholicism as the threat of a revived, often aggressive, Catholicism became increasingly apparent. The government thought that the papal challenge called for more drastic legislation than had formerly been considered necessary. Thus, the Treason Act of 1571 made it high treason to signify in any way that Elizabeth was not the lawful Queen, or to suggest that she was a heretic, schismatic, tyrant, infidel or usurper. A further act in the same year prohibited the bringing in and execution of any bulls or other instruments from the see of Rome. A third enacted that anyone who had gone or who should go overseas without licence and who did not return within six months would forfeit the profit of his lands and all his goods and chattels. And the government clamped down on the new Catholic missionaries. In 1577 Cuthbert Mayne became the first seminary priest to suffer under the more severe government policy, when he was hung, drawn and quartered. This was followed in 1578 by the execution of a second Douai priest, John Nelson, and a layman, Thomas Sherwood. By 1580 the stakes for being a Catholic had been raised, and English Catholicism had assumed a higher and more pronounced profile than it had enjoyed for a generation.

By then Catholics had organized themselves as a distinct church which was outside the framework of the Church of England. 'They were conscious members of a Roman Catholic Church, with local congregations worshipping secretly together. They had their own priests and their own sacraments, and their exiles provided encouraging propaganda and works of piety. But this underground church had three potentially fatal weaknesses: it suffered from leakage as some church papists drifted away into full conformity; there were too few priests to sustain loyalties and provide the sacraments for those who wished them; and the supply of priests was contracting rapidly as the older generation died.'[21] An energetic attempt was about to be made by the Roman Catholic Church to meet these problems.

The 1580s

In the 1580s there was a pronounced papist challenge from within and without the realm. During that decade the regime was under its greatest threat from papists. In particular, there was the energetic activity of the Jesuits, the growth in the number of Papists, and the growing danger of foreign invasion, which culminated in 1588 with the Spanish effort to overthrow the Queen and restore once more the Catholic religion.

With the landing in England of two Jesuit priests and a lay brother in the summer of 1580 the Catholic attempt to win England back to Catholicism entered a new phase. The Society of Jesus had not responded immediately and enthusiastically when Cardinal William Allen had urged that Jesuits should join the Douai priests in a concerted effort to convert the country. They first of all wanted and obtained papal clarification of the 1570 bull. They were reassured when the Pope informed them that the bull applied to heretics and not Catholics, and that English Catholics were under no obligation to take any action in the present situation. The Jesuits were told that they should not involve themselves in affairs of state; they were on a spiritual and not a political mission. One of that small band of first missionaries, the Jesuit martyr-priest Edmund Campion, later expressed this well: 'My charge is, of free cost, to preach the gospel, to minister the sacraments, to instruct the simple, to reform sinners, to confute errors, and, in brief, to cry alarm spiritual against foul vice and proud ignorance wherewith my dear countrymen are abused. I never had mind, and am strictly forbidden by our fathers that sent me, to deal in any respect with matters of state or policy of the realm, as those things which appertain not to my vocation.'[22]

The arrival of the first Jesuit priests was tremendously important, largely because the first two, Robert Parsons and Edmund Campion, were in their different ways men of quite exceptional ability who were to make a remarkable impact. Parsons was a Fellow of Balliol and making a successful career in Oxford when, as a result of a college dispute, he resigned his Fellowship and left under a cloud. He was probably a Catholic at heart but not deeply committed. He subsequently went to the continent, and his experiences, especially at Louvain, where he undertook the Spiritual Exercises worked out by St Ignatius Loyola, the Founder of the Society of Jesus, persuaded him to enter the Jesuit novitiate in 1575. In 1578 he was ordained priest, and in 1580 he was put in charge of the Jesuit party sent to England.

Edmund Campion was a graduate of St John's College, Oxford, who established a reputation as a brilliant tutor and orator, and gained the patronage of both Cecil and Robert Dudley, Earl of Leicester, who were always eager to support scholars likely to be of service to church and state. Although he was made a deacon in 1568 he had doubts about the Church of England and he was reluctant to proceed to ordination. His Catholic inclinations led him to Douai where he spent two years. From there he went on foot to Rome to join the Society of Jesus. He was sent to Prague where he became Professor of Rhetoric in 1574. He was recalled to Rome in 1579 to go on the mission to England.

Parsons and Campion arrived in England in disguise. They travelled to different parts of the country, from Gloucestershire and Berkshire up to Lancashire and Yorkshire, encouraging Catholics and fortifying them in their faith. They went from one Catholic household to another, always in imminent danger of being caught. Parsons even managed to acquire a secret printing-press and was able to produce and circulate pamphlets written by him and his companion. The government knew of their presence, but, despite intensive and extensive searching for them it was a year before Campion was found and arrested. He was brutally tortured, and after a manifestly unfair trial he was hung, drawn and quartered. And yet he remained brave and resolute to the end.

Each year new contingents of priests arrived from the continent. They also travelled from house to house, often spending long periods in cleverly constructed 'priest's holes' while government agents searched the building in which they were hiding. Some were captured, of whom a considerable number were imprisoned, tortured, executed or banished. By the end of the reign nearly two hundred of them suffered martyrdom. Most of those caught remained firm and unyielding under their ordeals, although there were a few who abjured or who weakened after conferences with Anglican clergy. The severity of the government policy varied, being most pronounced at times of national crisis such as 1587 or 1588.

Because the arrival of Parsons and Campion in England coincided with the papal encouragement of rebellion in Ireland and with government awareness that Catholicism was not dying out but rather undergoing a resurgence, there was a prompt enactment of legislation against papists. An act of 1581 made the saying of mass a felony punishable with death and imposed far more severe penalties on recusants. In addition, a series of questions, the famous 'Bloody Questions', was devised, for use in cases of priests and others whom the government was considering putting on trial for treason. The questions made it necessary for those interrogated to declare that the Pope did not have power to depose Elizabeth and that they would in no circumstances support attempts to enforce her deposition. There was a deliberate attempt to identify Catholicism in general and the work of the missionaries in particular with efforts to overthrow the government by force. And, indeed, it was difficult, if not impossible, to disentangle the religious and the political in all these matters. The individual, pious, non-political, Catholic was unavoidably caught up in a European-wide political scene in which there was a complex relationship between Catholic and Protestant countries, a persecution of minorities and the machinations of powerful individuals, including the Pope.

This international political cauldron of activity increasingly impinged upon the domestic religious affairs of England throughout the 1580s. Events moved almost inexorably towards an attempt at invasion. In 1583 Francis Throckmorton, a young Catholic gentleman, was arrested by Sir Francis Walsingham, and revealed under torture many details about the invasion plans of the Duke of Guise. In the following year William of Orange was assassinated. At home the Bond of Association was drawn up in which the signatories swore to pursue to the death anyone who should attempt anything harmful to the Queen. And in the background Mary, Queen of Scots, was a continual menace as a potential focus for a Catholic uprising. In the summer of 1586 a further plot was discovered. John Ballard, a Jesuit priest, arrived from France to arrange a Catholic rising. He worked closely with Bernardino de Mendoza, Philip of Spain's ambassador, and he received the approval of Philip himself for what he was doing. He recruited a young English gentleman, Anthony Babington. The question of the possible assassination of Elizabeth was raised, and even agreed. Mary was informed of the plan and replied in terms which revealed her cognizance. Ballard, Babington and others were executed. Elizabeth was brought face to face once more with the question of what to do with Mary, an issue which she had repeatedly shirked, and at length she signed the death-warrant. Mary was beheaded on 8 February 1587.

In the mid-1580s the international situation deteriorated rapidly and, for complicated reasons which it is not appropriate to consider in the present work, Philip 11 of Spain ponderously decided to launch a direct attack on England. Pope Sixtus V was pessimistic about the chance of success, but agreed to provide financial assistance if the Spanish landed. He also made it plain that the Armada was putting into effect the papal bull of excommunication, and he issued a declaration in which he released all the Queen's subjects from obedience to her and asked them to support the invading Catholic army. Rewards were offered to any person who captured the Queen or any of her entourage, and a plenary indulgence was to be granted to those 'being penitent' who assisted in the deposition and punishment of Elizabeth and those who aided her. Cardinal William Allen strongly attacked the Queen and, without due knowledge of the actual situation which was far different from what he imagined, assured Philip II that the English Catholics were longing for his coming.

The Armada at long last set sail on 31 May 1588, but by the end of July the battered and depleted fleet was floundering in the North Sea and trying desperately to return to Spain. The crisis was over for the moment. But the government remained vigilant and did not relax its drive against the papists. The international situation continued to be full of danger and uncertainty, and England was on the alert for further difficulties and even another invasion. Nonetheless, the defeat of the Armada was of historic importance not only in the religious history of the country, but in its general evolution. It greatly enhanced national pride, national identity and the sense of national destiny.

Entrenched but divided

In the last decade and a half of Elizabeth's reign it was clear that no amount of government action or antipathy in the population as a whole would ever eradicate Catholicism completely. Throughout the country there were families prepared to endure huge fines, imprisonment and public disapproval rather than renounce their faith; there were priests

who were willing to sustain the faithful despite the awesome consequences which might follow if they were apprehended; and there
were whole tracts of the country, most noticeably in the north, where it
was hardly possible to enforce the recusancy laws systematically. It was
increasingly realized that the majority of Catholics were loyal subjects
who would never rise in rebellion against their monarch or take up arms
in support of a foreign invasion even if its success would mean the re-
establishment of Catholicism. The Catholic gentry could never have felt
secure with a government which was alert for any sign of trouble, but
in fact the 1590s saw no further anti-Catholic legislation, and there was
a less rigorous execution of existing laws.

Ironically, however, as the pressures upon them lessened, the
Catholics experienced a serious split within their own ranks. On one
side were the clergy who had taken special vows as members of some
monastic order. They, and the Jesuits in particular, were identified with
an aggressive campaign to oust Elizabeth and establish Catholicism as
the official faith of the country, if necessary by foreign invasion, and it
mattered little that many of them, and perhaps the majority, did not
approve of such a confrontational policy. Such an identification became
especially obnoxious to the population of England as a whole after the
abortive invasion of 1588, as the Armada had made explicit the willingness of some to hand the country over to the national enemy. On the
other side were many of the secular clergy, supported by many of the
laity, who resented the forceful presence of the Jesuits and the papal and
foreign aggression which they were seen to represent. The publication in
1594 of a book by Robert Parsons entitled *A Conference on the Next
Succession*, in which he examined the qualifications of all possible
claimants to succeed Elizabeth and reached the conclusion that the only
one with a valid claim was Philip's daughter, the Infanta Isabella, did
not help to endear the Allen-Parsons party to their fellow English
Catholics in the second of the two groupings just mentioned.

The contention among the Catholics, which became known as the
Archpriest Controversy, first became public in 1594–5 in the affair
known as 'the Wisbech Stirs'. Wisbech castle had been used since 1580
as an internment centre for about thirty important priests, both secular
and Jesuit. The prisoners appear to have enjoyed a good deal of freedom, and in their artificial, enclosed community dissensions arose over
the leadership of the group. One faction wanted a Jesuit, Father William
Weston, while others wanted either a secular priest or no leader at all. A
quarrel which must be considered quite trivial soon became common

knowledge among English Catholics both in England and on the continent.

Hard on the heels of this were disagreements in the English College in Rome. The students rejected the authority of the Jesuits who administered it; and at the death of Allen in October 1594 there was no obvious successor as the effective leader of the English Catholics abroad, except possibly Parsons, and he was not only a Jesuit but had very recently attracted opprobrium by the views he had expressed in *A Conference on the Next Succession*. The news of the dispute spread among English Catholics everywhere and served to increase suspicion of Jesuits, and impatience with what was seen as their intransigent refusal to even consider any compromise with the Elizabethan administration.

It is clear that not all the Catholic priesthood in England was divided over these issues. For example, Henry Garnet, the Jesuit Superior, generally speaking did his best to avoid conflict and to lower the temperature when relationships became heated. Nonetheless, the controversies in the 1590s raised the question of the organization and leadership of the Catholics within England itself. With the death of Allen it became increasingly apparent that there was a need to provide some form of effective ecclesiastical government. English Catholics had been without bishops since 1559 and their needs were not adequately met by a Cardinal Protector resident abroad. It was unfortunate that, without any prior consultation with the secular clergy, Rome appointed an archpriest with limited authority over the secular clergy working in England and Scotland, who was ordered to seek advice from the Jesuit Provincial in England before deciding upon any important matter. It was also regrettable that the appointee, George Blackwell, was a secular priest who had close links with the Jesuits. The arrangement seemed to identify English Catholics as a whole with the policy of non-cooperation with the government, and non-negotiation about possible toleration. It appeared to associate English Catholicism as a whole with the visionary schemes of Parsons about the succession. In their frustration some of the leaders of the secular clergy independently signed a declaration in 1603 in which they asserted their belief in the spiritual supremacy of the papacy, but also professed their complete allegiance to the Queen, and their willingness to disobey any papal dictate which commanded them to take up arms against her or to help an invader. The number of signatories was small, about thirteen, but it was an action which clearly revealed the deep split among English Catholics at the end of the Elizabethan era.

5

The Reign of James I

When Elizabeth died on 24 March 1603 a dynasty died with her. But a new sovereign and a new dynasty succeeded her without opposition. In certain respects James I was a welcome change. As an adult man with two sons and a daughter he conformed more closely than Elizabeth to the general perception of kingship, and he put an end to the protracted agonies and speculation about the succession. The character of James has been a matter of some dispute, and not infrequently there have been contrasting assessments. It is not easy to weigh what appear to be conflicting traits.

His early life had been full of experiences which could hardly have produced a simple, uncomplicated world view. After his father had been murdered, his mother had married the murderer and he saw her for the last time before he was one year old. His childhood was a weird blend of 'flattery and Presbyterian sermons, self-indulgence and the terror of being kidnapped or assassinated. He was a precocious child, apt at languages, with a retentive memory, intelligent far above the average; he became a learned man, shrewd and pedantic rather than original.'[1]

As far as his ecclesiastical policy is concerned, it seems to belie the characteristics which were, until quite recently, portrayed by many historians: indecision and inconsistent dilettantism. He was sagacious and calculating, and he applied his theological expertise to good account in governing the English church.[2] James I, like his illustrious predecessor Elizabeth, was primarily concerned with the pursuit of traditional conformist aims – order, uniformity and obedience. He identified two groups which at least potentially could thwart these objectives, and challenge his authority: the Puritans and the Catholics. And 'towards each he developed a similar policy of detaching moderate from radical elements'.[3] Perhaps his finest achievement was the establishment of a religious *détente*, something which had eluded Elizabeth. He displayed a flexibility which was unusual for his day and generation; and he was able to yield or to stand firm according to the demands of the circumstances, and to enforce the rules or bend them, all in order to achieve his overall objective.[4] He quite frequently voiced his strident denunciation of Puritanism and Puritan practices, and he declared unyielding opposition to what he defined in political terms as Anabaptists, sectaries and rigid Presbyterians, but this hostility did not extend to all Dissenters, many of whom were obedient subjects. This is made clear in a key statement of royal intent, the revised preface to the 1603 edition of *Basilikon Doron*:

> I protest upon mine honour, I mean it not generally of all preachers or others, that like better of the single form of policy in our Church [of Scotland], than of the many ceremonies in the Church of England; that are persuaded that their bishops smell of a papal supremacy, that the surplice, the cornered cap and such like are the outward badges of popish errors. No, I am so far from being contentious in these things (which for my own part I ever esteemed as indifferent) as I do equally love and honour the learned and grave men of either of these opinions.[5]

James I and his son Charles I had more in common in their ecclesiastical policies, and, indeed, in their central ideals and prejudices, than has often been recognized. They both considered monarchy and episcopacy as divinely-ordained and as complementary offices intended to promote true religion and punish sin. Each sought unity by a policy which they proclaimed as a *via media* between popery and Puritanism, and each was resolute in resisting the political dangers inherent in both of these religious traditions. They also shared a greater degree of tolerance towards Rome and English Catholics than was usual for many of their Protestant subjects. Thus there was continuity as well as change as we pass from one reign to another, although we will discover that the era of Charles I was recognizably different from the Jacobean and, for various reasons which we will explore, took to greater lengths policies which are to be seen only in embryo during the monarchy of James I.

The Millenary Petition and the Hampton Court Conference

The Puritans had high hopes that they would fare better under James than under Elizabeth, and that the reforms they favoured for the Church of England would be promoted by a King who had been brought up in the Presbyterian Church of Scotland, one of the best reformed churches. And they were prompt in making their requests known. Even while he was on his journey from Scotland to London to claim his English throne, they presented him with the Millenary Petition, ostensibly signed by a thousand ministers, as its title implies. It was a restrained document, with requests for moderate changes. They wrote not as 'factious men affecting a popular parity in the church nor as schismatics aiming at the dissolution of the state ecclesiastical, but as the faithful servants of Christ and loyal subjects of your Majesty, desiring and longing for the redress of divers abuses of the church . . . '[6]

The petitioners asked among other things for the removal of the sign of the cross in baptism; for baptism not to be administered by women; for the cap and surplice not to be required; that the communion service should be accompanied by a sermon; that the ring in marriage should be abolished; that church songs and music should be moderated; that the Lord's day should not be profaned; that unity of doctrine should be prescribed; that no popish opinion should be taught or defended; that no ministers should be charged to teach their people to bow at the name of Jesus; and that the canonical scriptures only should be read in the church. They urged that only 'able and sufficient' men should be admitted into the ministry, and that they should preach diligently, especially on the Lord's day; that existing ministers who could not preach might either be removed with provision for 'their relief', or be required, according to the value of their livings, to maintain preachers; that non-residency should not be permitted; that the Edwardian statute authorizing the marriage of ministers should be revived; that ministers should not be urged to subscribe except to the articles of religion and the King's supremacy; and that pluralism should be abolished. They asked that discipline and excommunication might be administered according to Christ's own institution, or at least 'that enormities might be redressed'; that men should not be excommunicated 'for trifles and twelve-penny matters', and none be excommunicated without the consent of his pastor; that the oath ex officio, whereby men were forced to accuse themselves, should be more sparingly used; and that licences for marriage without banns asked should be more cautiously granted. They said that these, and 'other abuses yet remaining and practised in the Church of England', some of which they had left unnamed, they were able 'to show not to be agreeable to the Scriptures', if the King would listen to them. They professed to desire 'not a disorderly innovation, but a due and godly reformation'.[7]

Although there were implied radical reforms in the petition, such as those which related to discipline, which, if granted, would have had profound and far reaching consequences for the whole structure of church government, it was quite conservative. And therein lay its strength and its tactical skill and success. Much to the alarm of the bishops the King was impressed with its restraint: he was prepared to give the Puritans a hearing and to examine their case. He had a personal interest in theological matters and considerable theological knowledge, and possibly relished the prospect of presiding over a theological debate. He wanted to establish unity in the church; he considered that a *prima facie* case had been made out that abuses existed within the church; and he ardently supported the call for a learned and preaching ministry.

But the initial success of the petition encouraged the more radical Puritans, such as Henry Jacob and Stephen Egerton, to agitate for further concessions, even prior to the conference, and thereby the advantage gained was rapidly lost. In reaction to the perturbation, Archbishop Whitgift arranged for nationwide information on the number and qualifications of the preachers, and for statistics about communicants, recusants, pluralists, non-residents and impropriators (laymen receiving the profit from ecclesiastical property) to be obtained. The Millenary Petition was condemned by the universities of Oxford and Cambridge. The fear of Presbyterianism was openly expressed. But Puritan agitation continued, with an ever-increasing number of petitions being organized. On 24 October 1603 James was prevailed upon to issue a proclamation against 'such as seditiously seek reformation in Church matters', in which he unambiguously stated that 'since we have understood the form and frame (of the Church of England), we are per-suaded that both the constitution and doctrine thereof is agreeable to God's word and near to the condition of the primitive Church'.[8] By their forthrightness, by the methods they had adopted and by disclosing their more extreme demands prematurely, it seems that the Puritans had damaged their cause.

The conference called by James to discuss the issues raised by the Millenary Petition was held at Hampton Court in January 1604. It is not easy to determine exactly what happened at it. The main con-temporary source of information is the account by William Barlow; and this probably misrepresents the debate. Barlow was a member of the extreme wing of the church establishment, and he was biased against the reformers, for whom he had little sympathy. In fact his portrayal of the conference was propagandist.

Those attending the conference were selected by the Council and were 'neither extremists nor sharply divided into two parties'.[9] John

Reynolds, the chief Puritan spokesman, believed, like his pupil Hooker, in a Grindalian system of moderate episcopacy, with assistance being given by a council of ministers. 'Lawrence Chaderton, Master of Emmanuel, though convinced in his opinions, was exceptionally gentle in temper; Thomas Sparke kept silence; only John Knewstubs, a man of sixty and one of the Cartwright school, had more than his share of impetuous and fiery speech.'[10] Four of the representative bishops opposed some of the ceremonies, and perhaps sympathized more with the Puritans than with Bancroft, their senior episcopal colleague. It was in fact Bancroft who appears to have caused some consternation by his brusque Lancastrian manner and somewhat hasty temper, and he was rebuked by the King on more than one occasion for his interruptions.

The conference seems to have remained fairly amicable almost throughout. There was at least one, much quoted, moment of tension, when James showed considerable annoyance because Reynolds used the word 'presbyter', but his anger was mild and brief, especially as Reynolds was referring to 'a bishop and his presbyters', and a system of limited episcopacy to which James had no particular objection. Indeed, he introduced such a system into Scotland two years later with considerable success.

The main conclusions of the conference[11] seem to have been that the apocrypha should not be read; the jurisdiction of the bishops should be somewhat curtailed; excommunication as practiced should be replaced by a new chancery writ; Ireland, Wales and the borders of Scotland should be supplied with schools and preachers as soon as possible, and learned ministers should be provided and financed in places where there was a particular need for them. It was also agreed that there should be a reduction in the number of double-beneficed men and pluralities in general; those who had double benefices should be required to maintain preachers, and efforts should be made to insure that in the event of any double benefices the livings should be as near to one another as possible. It was resolved that there should be one uniform translation of the Bible made, which would then be the sole one used in the churches of England; there should be one catechism made and used in all places; the Articles of Religion should be explained and enlarged, and no man should teach or pronounce against any of them; communion should be received at least once a year; a restriction should be placed on the availability and distribution of popish books; and the High Commission should be reformed and reconstituted. Despite all these agreements, historians over the years have concurred that the only permanent achievement of the conference was the Authorized Version of the Bible, which was completed in 1611. But what of the less easily discernable matter of the place of the conference in the history of Puritanism, and the development of a *via media*? Here we once more encounter a somewhat complex historiography.

The classic accounts of S.R. Gardiner and R.G. Usher[12] assume that the conference was a failure for the Puritan cause. Gardiner asserts that it was largely due to the pedantry and prejudices of James that the opportunity to effect a reconciliation between the Puritans and the established church was missed. He 'had sealed his own fate and the fate of England for ever. The trial had come, and he had broken down . . . The essential littleness of the man was at once revealed.'[13] Usher maintained that James, in ignorance of the factional struggles within the church and yielding egotistically to the temptation to display his theological learning, erred in agreeing to meet the Puritans in the first place. By acceding to the Millenary Petitioners he gave the Puritan ministers an equal status with the bishops, and raised hopes which he had neither the intention nor the power to fulfil. By such unwise moves he created conditions for future bitterness and frustration.

Recent historians have favoured an interpretation which is far more complimentary to James, and emphasizes the moderation and equilibrium which he helped to inject into the deliberations, in the face of real and serious criticisms. Peter White asserts that the 'foundations of the Jacobean *via media* were laid at the Hampton Court Conference'.[14] There were two sides at the conference, he maintains, but they are not as readily identifiable as might appear. There is no reference in contemporary records to the 'Calvinists' and 'Arminians' of modern historiography. The disagreement was between the 'prelates' who were unwilling to contemplate even moderate reforms, and the 'Puritans' who were self-styled zealots and reformers with one eye upon model, reformed, continental churches. Francis Bacon wrote: 'The truth is, here be two extremes: some few, would have no change; no, not reformation. Some many, would have much change, even with perturbation.' And Carleton observed 'these two companies as they differ in opinions so do they in fashions, for one side marches in gowns and rochets, and th'other in cloaks and night-caps'.[15] According to White and Kenneth Fincham, James granted concessions which were intended to entice 'moderate' Puritans to remain within the national church, and he thereby isolated their 'radical' brethren, who were subsequently ejected from their ministry. In return the King demanded that all clergymen should acknowledge his temporal and spiritual supremacy, the scriptural warrant for the Prayer Book, the degrees of bishop, priest and deacon, and the Articles of Religion. This was in effect subscription to Archbishop Whitgift's Three Articles of 1583, which were shortly afterwards to be adopted as Canon 36 of 1604.[16] The extent of James's sympathy for the Puritans has been a matter of some debate.

The conference may not have been regarded as a failure if James had been less administratively lazy, and if the various commissions appointed to implement its conclusions had undertaken their tasks whole-heartedly, and with determination. Whether it was a result of lack of application or by design, the work was only half done. The revised liturgy did not include all of the agreed changes, and the procedure of the church courts went on unchanged. And there, at centre stage, was Richard Bancroft. It would have needed a forthright and determined stance to have impressed him, and to have pressurized him into undertaking Puritan reforms. For the decision from which the Puritans suffered most was taken a few months after the conference when, at the death of Whitgift, and after some delay, James chose Bancroft as his new Archbishop of Canterbury.

Richard Bancroft (1544–1610)

Bancroft had spent much of his adult life speaking, writing or acting against the Puritans. During his teaching career at Cambridge he had been an outspoken anti-Puritan. He became a member of Whitgift's High Commission. He denounced the 'Martinists' in 1589 in a savage sermon at Paul's Cross and he helped in the detection of the printers of the Marprelate tracts. After being made chaplain to Whitgift in 1592, he rapidly became the Archbishop's right-hand man. As Bishop of London from 1597 he exercised great influence, and it was no surprise when he succeeded Whitgift in 1604. In his encounters with Puritans, as well as during his time as Whitgift's chief lieutenant in all his campaigns, his understanding of Puritanism had not become as deep as his knowledge. He suspected that all Puritans tended either to Presbyterianism or Separatism; but in either case they were enemies of the Church of England.

Bancroft began his archiepiscopate with a vigorous campaign for subscription which revived the atmosphere of 1584. It found expression in the Canons of 1604 which were as clear as they were forthright in threatening excommunication *ipso facto* for any who affirmed that the

Church of England by law established was not a true and an apostoli-cal church, teaching and maintaining the doctrine of the apostles; for any who affirmed that the form of God's worship in the Church of England, established by law and contained in the Book of Common Prayer and administration of sacraments, was corrupt, superstitious or unlawful worship of God or contained anything in it that was repugnant to the scriptures. The Canons also held out the prospect of excommunication for any who affirmed that any of the Thirty-Nine Articles were in any part superstitious or erroneous or such as they might not with a good conscience subscribe unto; for any who affirmed that the rites and ceremonies of the Church of England by law estab-lished were wicked, anti-Christian or superstitious, or such as, being commanded by lawful authority, men who were zealously and godly affected might not with any good conscience approve, use, or subscribe unto; and for any who affirmed that the government of the Church of England under his Majesty by archbishops, bishops, deans, archdeacons and the rest that bear office, was anti-Christian or repugnant to the word of God. The risk of excommunication was extended to cover any who separated themselves from the communion of saints, as it was approved in the Church of England, and combined themselves together in a new brotherhood; to any who affirmed or maintained that there were within the realm other meetings, assemblies or congregations of the King's subjects than such as were allowed by the laws of the land, which might rightly be considered true and lawful churches; and to any who affirmed that it was lawful for any sort of minister or layman to join together with others and make rules, orders or constitutions in causes ecclesiastical, without the King's authority, and who submitted themselves to be ruled and governed by them. It was a comprehensive catalogue of conditions for what was deemed as conforming to the established church.

Although Bancroft's campaign for subscription to these Canons was less drastic than it seemed possible at one stage, it did lead to the silenc-ing of about ninety ministers. An ominous portent for the future was the response of Sir Francis Hastings and others in Parliament who petitioned for some time, without success, on behalf of the affronted ministers. In the short term Bancroft had successfully checked clerical Puritanism. But in so doing he had effectively stimulated the growth of lay Puritanism in the House of Commons. And that was a far more dangerous force, as Laud was to discover.

The tightening of control made possible by the Canons also entailed a widespread use of the consistory courts and the High Commission. This in turn involved a conflict between the ecclesiastical authorities and the lawyers, not because of the exercise of spiritual discipline as such, but because of the imposition of secular penalties by courts outside the framework of the common law. And the lawyers were among the chief spokesmen in the debates in Westminster. Thus, in various ways, the Canons, and Bancroft's policy in general, stored up considerable trouble for the future.

Although he had built his career on anti-Puritanism, Bancroft was not an anti-Calvinist. He was, indeed, suspicious of several early Arminians, including Richard Butler and John Howson. He was rather 'an Elizabethan conformist protestant, whose views were closer to his predecessor Whitgift than to either of his successors, Abbott and Laud'.[17]

From the death of Bancroft to the end of the reign of James

The appointment of George Abbot to the archbishopric of Canterbury in 1611 on the death of Bancroft did not result in any radical change of direction in the affairs of the church. Abbott's religious opinions were firmly, though moderately, Puritan, and he was anti-Catholic, anti-Arminian and anti-Spanish, in contrast to the very pronounced anti-Puritanism of Bancroft; and it was also not easy to come after the disciplinarian regime of Bancroft, or to serve under such a king as James. But Abbott did not dramatically depart from the church policy he had inherited, and in his own way had just as much firmness as his predecessor. For example, Sir Edward Coke had for years been a thorn in the flesh of Bancroft as he fought for the right of the Court of Common Pleas or the King's Bench to forbid the church courts to continue the hearing of a case until the common law courts had decided whether it came under the jurisdiction of the ecclesiastical courts. And by 1610 the issue was not resolved. But Abbott continued resolutely to resist any attempt to weaken the church courts, and if anything the Court of High Commission became even stricter in its treatment of all offenders except Puritans. Abbott also exhibited his toughness when, after a mere two years as archbishop, he co-operated with James in the examination of Bartholomew Legate, a heretic who was burnt for denying the divinity of Christ. Legate, and another man, Edward Wightman, who was examined by Richard Neile, the Bishop of Lichfield, and his chaplain William Laud, shared the dubious distinction of being the last men to be burnt for heresy in England. In part this action was deliberately designed by James to convince Europe of his orthodoxy in religion.

Soon after this Abbot started on his decline from favour, and his exclusion from any effective say in the affairs of either state or church. His pro-French views brought him into conflict with Robert Carr, Earl of Somerset, and with the powerful Howard faction. Then there was the more important cause of disfavour as a consequence of his attitude over the Essex divorce. Lady Frances Howard sought to divorce her husband, the Earl of Essex, on the grounds of his special impotence due to witchcraft, so that she might marry the royal favourite, Somerset. Her case was dubious in the extreme, and on the commission appointed to examine the evidence Abbott and one other bishop resisted all the efforts of James to persuade them to vote for the divorce. Four other bishops, including Lancelot Andrewes and Richard Neile, were more compliant and the commission granted the divorce by a slender majority vote. The fall of Somerset and the meteoric rise to power of George Villiers, Duke of Buckingham, did nothing to rescue Abbot.

In 1618, he seems to have opposed the King over the *Book of Sports*, a declaration which encouraged games on Sundays after morning service, and which James ordered to be read from their pulpits by all the clergy of England. The determined opposition of many of the clergy, and possibly of Abbott, resulted in the King prudently withdrawing his order; but Abbott's attitude and actions must have angered a King who was already not well disposed towards his Archbishop.

Then came a bitter stroke of misfortune. In 1621, while out hunting, Abbot aimed his crossbow at a buck but shot and killed Lord Zouch's gamekeeper instead. The King excused him, but his enemies seized the opportunity to attack him, and a group of bishops-elect, among whom was Laud, declined to be consecrated by a homicidal prelate. The doubt about his position under canon law resulted in his temporary suspension, and after he was restored he remained somewhat ineffectual for the remainder of his twelve years of office. The dominant figures in the counsels of the church were Lancelot Andrewes, Bishop of Winchester, John Williams, Bishop of Lincoln and William Laud, successively Bishop of St David's, Bath and Wells and London, who was to succeed Abbott as Archbishop of Canterbury.

How can we best summarize the life and work of Abbot?[18] Two conflicting images emerge out of early Stuart historiography. The first, represented by Lord Clarendon and Lord Dacre, is of an indolent primate who, because of his indulgence towards Puritan non-conformists, fatally undermined the discipline of the English church, so that his successor Laud was unable to reimpose ceremonial conformity, and in the effort to do so provoked a Puritan backlash after 1640.[19] The alternative view presents Abbott as a conciliatory figure, who, by his lenient treatment of nonconformists typified Calvinist episcopalianism in the reign of James I.[20] On this view, anti-Calvinists and not Puritans were the innovators and disturbers of the peace in the Church of England. This is an interpretation which has commanded widespread endorsement among historians, but has been a cause of much historical debate.[21]

I believe that there was a general Elizabethan and Jacobean theological consensus in the English church, which was represented by a core of dogmatic Calvinists and a more general, and diffused Calvinistic orientation, but that the majority of the ordinary churchmen were theologically unsophisticated, and indeed indifferent to the niceties of theology. Abbott was one of those core members, and his theology was broadly representative of advanced Protestant thought. He derived his historical and eschatological views from Foxe and Bale, so that he was fiercely opposed to popery. He regarded the Pope as antiChrist, and used violent and immoderate language to express his detestation of the Pope and his followers. In his primacy he set before himself four priorities: to propagate the gospel, to protect the doctrinal purity of English Calvinism, rigorously to persecute English Catholics and to defend the foreign reformed churches from Catholic ambitions for world domination. In these objectives he was largely supported by the King. But James disagreed with his Archbishop in the stress placed on the danger from Catholicism, and the lack of danger from Puritanism, and adopted a more even-handed approach. Abbott realized that his influence with the King turned on his ability to manipulate royal fears of a Catholic conspiracy.

Abbot had a passion for evangelism, and believed that the effective propagation of the gospel was jeopardized by too vigorous an enforcement of ceremonial conformity, since nonconformists were often the most committed evangelists, and the most zealous preachers. He was prepared to exercise a degree of leniency towards those nonconformists who did not threaten ecclesiastical order and stability. In this there was at least an ostensible coincidence with the royal policy of distinguishing between 'moderate' and 'radical' Puritans. And it was some of the latter who were to emerge as early English Dissenters. However, before we turn to consider these it will help to keep a right sense of balance if I attempt a brief sketch of the workaday life of the Church of England at all levels, lest we forget that the events so far discussed were but the more public and dramatic aspects of a worshipping, witnessing and working church which was dependent for its nationwide and local life upon ordinary people set amidst the trials and joys of ordinary life.

The national, diocesan and parochial life of the church

Of the sixty-six men who sat on the episcopal bench in the reign of James I, twenty-six were Elizabethan appointees, and over half the Jacobean nominees had been born in the first ten years of the Elizabethan era, so that they were among the first generation to grow up in a settled Protestant church.[22] It is significant that they were mostly recruited from the middle and lower tiers of society. A few were sons of the gentry, but a larger number were from the more prosperous professional and urban families, including sons of merchants, clergy and burgesses. A quite sizeable group came from very humble social backgrounds, with fathers who were tradesmen or artisans.

Combined with this range of social background was a higher overall level of academic qualification and experience of administration compared with their Elizabethan counterparts. By the beginning of James's reign it was becoming usual for a bishop to posses at least a BD, and all but one of the forty bishops who were consecrated between 1603 and 1625 already had a doctorate in divinity. This compares with the early Elizabethan period when many of the bishops only had MAs. The administrative experience included headships of Oxbridge colleges, deanships of cathedral churches and archdeaconships. It is also impressive that, with the exceptions of George Abbott and James Montagu, the whole bench of bishops had held benefices earlier in their careers. Although bishops as a whole returned to the centre of power after 1603, and there was an increase in the still small core of them who resided at court and regularly attended court, most of them lived in their sees and confined their involvement in national politics to sessions of Parliament and Convocation. The court episcopate fulfilled a number of important roles as ecclesiastical politicians, judges and household officers to the Crown; and bishops played a leading part in the business of the Lords. But, to an extent not typical of the Elizabethan episcopate, the focus for most of the bishops was their own diocese.

Within their diocese most people encountered their bishop not so much as a spiritual guide, judge or preacher, but as a landlord, magistrate or royal commissioner. He was expected to provide hospitality, patronage or political support as much as pastoral direction and help. And throughout the Jacobean years the episcopate grew in stature in the localities.

As for the clergy, they were not predominantly graduates, although things had improved since the early years of the Elizabethan era in that most had been to a university, whether or not they had taken a degree.[23] There were regional variations, with the southern and eastern dioceses close to the universities enjoying an 80–100% graduate intake in the 1620s.[24] In the next band, geographically outward, including Bath and Wells, Coventry and Lichfield, Exeter and Gloucester, the figure was 60–70%, and in the sees even further away from the centres of higher education, such as Carlisle, Durham and Bangor, it dropped to less than 50%.

The economic situation of the clergy also seems to have been very variable, although, in this case from parish to parish rather than from area to area. For a great number of the livings the average income of stipendiary and assistant curates was between £4 and £10 a year. In the first part of the seventeenth century there appears to have been an amelioration of the living standards of at least many of the provincial urban clergy, and this may have been part of a more general revitalization of the clerical estate which James I helped to promote.[25]

And what of the life of the parishes in which the clergy ministered? Again, we have to recognize vast differences from one parish to another. Not all parish priests were like the learned Puritan divine Richard Greenham, who spent most of his life ministering to the poor and unrewarding parishioners of Dry Drayton in Cambridgeshire. It has to be acknowledged that all too often 'there was justification in the puritan complaint that good livings were filled by men who had neither the capacity nor the interest to perform the cure of souls and instruct the people'.[26]

In a number of the parishes throughout the country there was religious and cultural friction as a consequence of the beliefs and lifestyle of a vociferous minority of 'godly' Puritans. Although the Puritans shared many of the prevailing contemporary values, some of their most cherished dogmas did divide them from their less 'godly' neighbours. They did not challenge the accept norms of that fundamental social unit, the family, although they made of it a more introverted, intense, 'little commonwealth', which was a medium for religious instruction, with the husband exercising considerable authority, and the wife having greater responsibility for the spiritual education of the children than was normal for the time, but they did have an ideal for the community which was very different from the traditional one. 'Their determination to reshape their world provoked in the England of James I a cultural and religious conflict.'[27] This was most potently manifested in the Puritan resistance to revels and to the increased sexual freedom accorded to women, as, for example, in the vogue of mixed dancing, and their campaign against certain ancient feasts and popular recreations. The note of reformist indignation is sounded by the biographer of the Cheshire Puritan, John Bruen:

> Popery and profaneness, two sisters in evil, had consented and con-spired in this parish [Tarvin], as in other places, to advance their idols against the ark of God, and to celebrate their solemn feasts of their popish saints . . . by their wakes and vigils, kept in commemoration and honour of them; in all riot and excess of eating and drinking, dalliance and dancing, sporting and gaming, and other abominable impieties and idolatries.[28]

I have previously discussed the degree of congruity between Puritanism and social and educational standing in Elizabethan England, and I concluded that although there was some correlation, it was far from total. The same is true as we move into the seventeenth century. Although 'it is premature simply to equate the godly elite of early Stuart England with a social elite, or even with the broad band lying across the middle rungs of the social ladder',[29] a high proportion of the 'godly' were literate, and they tended to be strongly represented among arti-sans, small tradesmen and people of influence in local life. This meant that 'the campaign against traditional culture reflected prevailing social divisions. It also intensified them, ranging the Puritan clergy and their converts among the parish elites against much of the rest of the population'.[30] Nonetheless, 'the rest of the population' remained in the majority in most communities, and for them 'Anglicanism' was increas-ingly part of their mostly routine and unsensational lives.

At the heart of early seventeenth-century Anglicanism was the Book of Common Prayer, which even by then was establishing itself as part of the English way of life for most of the population. 'This liturgy embodied many Anglican principles: the perceived need for set forms of prayer and worship in the vernacular and the due administration of approved sacraments; the focus on Scripture in the set rota of Bible readings; psalms and canticles, "comfortable words" and other scriptural texts which punctuated its services; and the repeated use of the Creeds which linked Anglicanism to the first centuries of Christianity.'[31] The liturgy and the rites of passage provided the core of parish Anglicanism; and there still remained such potent visual images as the wall panels inscribed with the Apostles' Creed, the Ten Commandments and the Lord's Prayer which everyone was expected to learn in the catechism. These, and other tangible objects within the churches of the land, reflected Anglican priorities. The remodelled mediaeval churches of the country were constant reminders of continuity with the past, and of an Anglicanism which effectively blended the new and the old. Familiarity did not breed contempt for most Englishmen in Stuart England.

The ethos and the message of Anglicanism was also reinforced by a surge in the output of catechisms, tracts, manuals and devotional aids from the early seventeenth century onwards. 'In the simplest of these – basic oral instruction by question and answer, broadsheets with a religious message, dialogues combining entertainment with instruction, simple sermons published in a cheap format, and samplers with approved texts or moral precepts – official beliefs were distilled to their essence, and presented in ways calculated to have the greatest impact on those parishioners with a few or no reading skills.'[32]

By the early seventeenth century the social and spiritual expectations of parishioners had shifted markedly from a half century before. There was a widespread interest in expository preaching and, especially in areas of the country greatly influenced by Puritanism, this was seen as the key part of the minister's activity. Yet this co-existed with the older concept of the clergyman as part of the community, providing the rites of passage and faithfully ensuring regular prayer and Sunday worship. He was still required to perform such customary socio-economic duties as the provision of hospitality, care of the poor, and the upkeep of the fabric of the church. As with so much of the church life of the day, the new and the traditional were intermingled. But for some there was such dissatisfaction with what appeared to them as the limited extent to which the new had been introduced that they could not, with a clear conscience, remain within a church that was prepared to tolerate the unacceptable. They were the Dissenters.

The General Baptists

As we have seen, there were Separatists in the Elizabethan era. But by the middle of the reign of James I most of the survivors of this tradition lived in exile. Not only were they isolated geographically from their country of origin and the church of their birth but, more significantly, they had cut themselves off from their conformist fellow Puritans who were mostly hostile to them. Many of the Separatists in the first quarter of the seventeenth century had an ambivalent relationship with the Puritan members of the established church. This was most signally demonstrated in the church of Henry Jacob. But before we consider his distinctive contribution to the Separatist tradition we will turn our attention to other important events in the Dissenting history of the period.

The failure of the Hampton Court Conference, disillusionment with James and the severe conformist provisions of the 1604 Canons together provided a powerful stimulus to Dissent. A good illustration of this was to be found in the lower Trent valley. In 1606 a group of Puritans living in that region seceded from the established church and 'as the Lord's free people joined themselves (by a covenant of the Lord) into a church estate'.[33] The membership included William Brewster, the postmaster of Scrooby and bailiff of the Archbishop of York; Richard Clifton, who, the year before, had been deprived of his living as rector of Babworth; Hugh Bromhead, a curate of North Wheatley; Thomas Helwys, who was a landed gentleman of Broxtowe Hall near Nottingham; and William Bradford, the seventeen-year-old son of an Austerfield farmer who was later to be Governor of the Plymouth colony in New England. Their leaders were John Robinson, a former Fellow of Corpus Christi College, Cambridge, who, that year, had been deprived of his living in Norwich for refusing to conform to the Canons, and had then returned to his native Sturton-le-Steeple in Nottinghamshire, and John Smyth, a Fellow of Christ's College, Cambridge.

For whatever reasons, and they are not clear, by 1608 these Separatists had split into two groups. One of them was based on Gainsborough and included Helwys and Bromhead. This fellowship chose John Smyth as their pastor while they were still in England, and then accompanied him to Amsterdam in 1608. The other group was located at Scrooby and included Brewster and Bradford. They also emigrated to the Netherlands in 1608, and either in England or in exile elected Robinson as their leader.

In Amsterdam Smyth was soon in controversy with the 'Ancient' Separatist church of Francis Johnson, which we have previously encountered, and with John Robinson and his group. The first dispute concerned the use of the scriptures in public worship. Smyth objected to the reading of English or other translations of the Bible in worship. He asserted that the scriptures were inspired only in their original tongue. The person undertaking teaching in the congregation should bring with him the original Hebrew and Greek and out of them translate by voice. To read them in translation was to introduce an element of formalism into worship and to impede the working of the Holy Spirit. Because of their divergent views on these matters Smyth's followers broke off communion with Johnson's church and styled themselves 'the brethren of the Separation of the second English church at Amsterdam'.[34]

Smyth also objected to the singing of psalms from a book, and maintained that the collection for church expenses was an act of worship to which outsiders should not be allowed to contribute. But of greater significance, and the cause of additional contention between the two fellowships, was the dispute concerning church government. During his time in Gainsborough Smyth had published his *Principles and inferences concerning the visible Church*, in which he had contended that in a true visible church the officers were, bishops, who in the New Testament are also called elders or presbyters, and deacons. They should be received into office by election, approbation and ordination. Election should be by the majority of the votes of the members in full communion. 'Approbation is the examining and finding the officer elect to be according to the rules of his office . . . In approbation every member is bound to object what he can, especially they that denied their votes.'[35] Ordination should be performed with fasting and prayer and the laying on of hands. It was the Lord, by and through the church, who gave the officer power to administer. The power of binding and loosing was declared to be given by Christ not to the Pope or the bishops or the elders, but 'to the body of the Church, even to two or three faithful people joined together in covenant'.[36] While he conceded that pastors and elders had 'a leading, directing, and overseeing power . . . the last definitive determining sentence is in the body of the church whereto the eldership is bound to yield'. Though 'the church may do any lawful act without the elders . . . the elders can do nothing without the approbation of the body or contrary to the body'. Smyth provided the clearest of all Separatist expositions of democracy in the church. This was a direct challenge to the contrasting practice in Francis Johnson's church.

Johnson was influenced by his former Presbyterianism; and he was concerned to restrain the petty quarrels which were fomented by the disciplining of members in full church meetings. He therefore attempted to keep the discipline in the hands of himself and the church's elders. But Henry Ainsworth, the teacher in Johnson's church, saw the force of Smyth's argument and, together with others, seceded from their church in 1610. When Johnson died seven years later some of the remaining members of his church joined Ainsworth. The rest left for Virginia, but tragically died aboard an over-crowded and disease-infested ship.[37]

The most significant of all Smyth's departures was, however, his rejection of infant baptism. The Separatists had long been uncomfortable on the question of baptism. They had left the Church of England because they asserted that it was not a true church and yet they did not repudiate their baptism at the hands of that Church, and they shrank from the logical conclusion of a second baptism. As a discentive there was the memory of the Anabaptist excesses of Munster in 1534–5 with the rejection of the contemporary social and political order.[38] But Smyth was determined to build his church on what he saw as the New Testament model, and he was convinced that there was no support in the New Testament for the concept and practice of infant baptism. New Testament baptism was subsequent to a profession of repentance towards God and faith in Christ. It is baptism of the Spirit, and it must be accompanied by confession of the mouth. Infants have no knowledge of sin and cannot therefore be washed by the Spirit; and they cannot repent or confess their repentance by mouth. Thus, the baptism which he and his congregation had received in the parish churches of England was null and void. But more than that, while they had been attempting to set up a church on the New Testament model, they had failed to observe the New Testament conditions of entry. They had constituted their church on the basis of a covenant between its members, but they needed to reconstitute it on the basis of the baptism of all professed believers. Smyth baptized first himself, then Helwys, then the rest of the company.

In this manner, in 1609, the first English Baptist Church was founded though not on English soil. It was a church of baptized believers but they were not baptized by immersion but by affusion. The water used was contained in a basin. The person officiating took a handful of water from the basin and poured it on the head of the person he was baptizing. Probably the water was also applied to the forehead by gentle rubbing to symbolize the idea of cleansing.[39]

The action taken by Smyth and his church intensified the controversy between him and the other Separatist leaders in Amsterdam. Smyth was much criticized for baptizing himself, and he was dubbed the Se-Baptist, or Self-baptizer. It was Richard Clifton, who had been converted to Separatism by Smyth many years before, and was by now 'a grave and fatherly old man, with 'a great white beard', whose response was most effective. He attached himself to Johnson's church and made a case against Smyth's self-baptism which was not easy to refute. If Smyth could baptize himself, Clifton said, then any man could follow his example, and thus churches could be established of solitary men, which would be absurd. Other critics accused Smyth of doing more than Christ himself would have done. In response, he at first vigorously defended his actions. When he averred that there was no other church that he and his fellow church members could join, and from which they could with a good conscience receive baptism, his attention was drawn to a Mennonite church of Dutch people known as the Waterlanders. They practised believers' baptism, tracing their spiritual descent through Menno Simons to the Anabaptists of the early sixteenth century. Smyth decided to apply for membership of the Waterlanders and, if necessary, a third baptism. This time he did not carry all his people with him. Although the majority concurred with what he proposed, Thomas Helwys and about ten others held out. They had serious misgivings about the christology of the Mennonites, which, they claimed, was dictated too much by the unacceptable views of the sixteenth-century Anabaptist, Melchior Hofmann. It also appeared to them that Smyth was imperilling their resistance to the idea of a succession of ministers, to which the Mennonites attached great importance. Helwys asserted that if elders only could baptize, it was tantamount to going back to an apostolic succession. It contradicted the liberty of the gospel, which was free for all men, and at all times. The Helwys group excommunicated Smyth, and proclaimed themselves the true church.

Smyth died in 1612. The same year Helwys and his small band returned to England having decided that it was better to 'lay down their lives in their own country for Christ' than to flee from persecution. The church they founded at Spitalfields can be regarded as the first General Baptist church on English soil. It was also in 1612 that Helwys addressed to James I an appeal, not only for liberty for all Christians, which was what Smyth had pleaded for, but for the toleration of all men. James does not seem to have been convinced. By the following year one of Helwys' companions, John Murton, was in prison. It is possible that Helwys suffered likewise, and certain that by 1616 he was dead.

The theological innovations of Smyth and Helwys were repudiated by those other Separatists from the lower Trent valley who had arrived in Amsterdam in 1608, and whose chosen pastor was John Robinson. They were so incensed at the dissensions in Johnson's church and the radicalism of Smyth's, and so attracted to the prospect of living and worshipping in a university town, that they moved to Leyden in 1609. The church they established attracted a growing number of English exiles and reached a total of 300, which included immigrants from Norfolk, Essex, London and Kent. Robinson excelled as a pastor, and it is a tribute to his moderation and the love and respect he evoked from his church members that, as long as he lived, it alone among all the churches in exile 'was neither troubled by internal strife nor rent by secession'.[40] In 1620 a section of his church, under the leadership of William Brewster, sailed to the New World, and were subsequently renowned as the Pilgrim Fathers. This was not a break-away move, for the band of pioneers remained in communion with the Leyden church and they were sad that Robinson, who died in 1625, was never able to join them.

Smyth's ideas and actions produced a conservative reaction among the other English Separatists. In repudiating the need for a second baptism Johnson maintained that the Church of England, and even the Church of Rome, though 'a notorious harlot and idolatress', was a church of God 'and under his covenant',[41] while Robinson showed himself sympathetic to the distinctive views expressed by Henry Jacob.

Henry Jacob and the 'Jacobites'

There were other, different types, of Separatist sects in Jacobean England. There is evidence of widespread and endemic Separatism in Kent and other areas well before the Civil War. 'By the end of the [sixteenth] century Separatist or semi-Separatist meetings had spread across much of the Kentish countryside.'[42] It is known, or it can be inferred, that there were alternative churches in several other places, including Norwich, Yarmouth and Colchester; and it is most likely that Separatist congregations existed elsewhere. 'It would be foolish to deny the presence of Separatist sects in Jacobean England.'[43] Some of these derived from the leadership of Henry Barrow round about 1590, and were regarded as the 'ancient' churches of the separation, while others, as we have seen, were among the newly emergent Baptists. But there was a still further category associated with the teaching and practice of Henry Jacob.

Jacob was an Oxford graduate and former precentor of Corpus Christi College. He was a Puritan, and he had played a major part in organizing the Millenary Petition. He had visited Francis Johnson in prison in an effort to convince him of his ignorance and error in separating from the established church, and had expounded his case against Johnson in *A Defence of the Churches and Ministry of England* (1599). But some of Johnson's arguments penetrated his thinking and resulted in him finally adopting a view midway between that of the Separatists and the conforming Puritans. He set this forth in 1604 in a work entitled *Reasons taken out of God's Word . . . proving a necessitie for reforming our Church in England,* for which he was imprisoned for eight months. He concurred with Johnson in his belief that a universal, national, provincial, or diocesan church did not represent a true church. He declared that only 'a particular, ordinary, constant congregation of Christians . . . is reckoned a visible church', and such a church should be 'constituted and gathered . . . by a free mutual consent of believers joining and covenanting to live as members of a holy society'.

But Jacob's distinctive belief was that a gathered church need not renounce communion with the parish churches of England. In effect, by organizing a congregation outside the established church and yet continuing to communicate with the established church he was practising a form of occasional conformity. He did not deny the magistrate's authority over the church, but he emphasized the kingly office of Christ as the immediate head of each individual congregation.[44] Church government must be exercised with the people's free consent. Membership was voluntary, whereas in the territorial parish church it was involuntary. Later such teaching, and such practices, would have guaranteed his status as a Dissenter, but in the early seventeenth century neither he nor the undeniable Separatists recognized him and his congregation as Separatist. Jacob's system has been designated as 'Independent Puritanism', 'non-separatist Congregationalism', 'semi-Separatistism' or 'moderate Separatistism'. Contemporaries used the term 'Jacobite'. Prominent among these early 'Jacobites' were William

Bradshaw, who had been deprived of his lectureship at Chatham in 1602, Paul Baynes, who had been suspended from his lectureship at St Andrew's, Cambridge, in 1604, Robert Parker, vicar of Stanton St Bernard in Wiltshire, and William Ames, Fellow of Christ's College, Cambridge, who fled to the Netherlands in 1610 and became the leading theologian of the group.[45]

The church founded by Jacob in London in 1616 was the 'most successful of all separate churches in England before the revolution' and 'for twenty-five years served as a recruiting agency and training school for some of the most important sectarian leaders of the coming revolutionary period'.[46] The church harboured within its membership ordinary Independents, those who had doubts about their baptism but who had not then adopted Anabaptist beliefs, and, of course, those who wanted to combine the merits and advantages of 'separatism' with continued fellowship with the established church. But, while many of Jacob's followers agreed with him in not regarding themselves as wholly separated from the godlier parish churches of London, others were rigid Separatists, 'and the internal debates over this issue and other developments gave rise to a little cluster of separated and semi-separated churches, a small but variegated religious underground. In this underworld the groundwork of future denominations was being laid: congregationalists, more than one kind of baptist, and the seekers and other progenitors of the quakers'.[47]

Some general characteristics of Jacobean Puritanism

It is arguable that from 1603 to 1625 the Church of England, as in the time of Elizabeth, was kept broad enough to contain all but the most extreme radicals, and that as a result nonconformity remained a relatively insignificant force.[48] English Presbyterianism continued to reel from the attacks made upon it at the end of the sixteenth century. Although there was much activity, and many seeds were sown which were to bear fruit in years to come, Separatism made little headway in terms of conversions. The total membership of the Separatist congregations during the reign of James I was never more than a few hundred, they were scattered and by definition independent and uncoordinated, and they had little impact on the life of the nation. While the leaders and theorists of the movement were often individuals from a landed background who had attended one of the universities, the congregations as a whole appear to have been largely independent craftsmen and their families, who rejected all formalism and ceremonialism, and practised a simplified form of worship, within which extempore prayer, free discussion of scripture and preaching predominated. These Separatists were part of a total Puritan tradition which, even by then, was displaying definite characteristics.

There was first of all the centrality of preaching. The steady, unspectacular growth of Puritan preaching both within the established church and among the Separatists was a most important element in forming the character of conformist and nonconformist Puritanism. The godly were enthusiastic to hear the word; and if they were deprived of faithful preaching in their own parishes, they frequently disregarded their statutory obligation to attend their own church and looked elsewhere for spiritual refreshment. 'Gadding to sermons' became a common feature in the religious life of Puritan laymen. A Lancashire-born London preacher, George Walker, described in vivid language how the godly people of his native county

> are ready and willing to run many miles to hear sermons when they have them not at home, and lay aside all care of profit, leaving their labour and work on weekdays to frequent public meetings for prophecy and expounding of God's word, and hardly can a preacher travel through their towns and lodge there on any day in the week but they will by importunity obtain a public sermon from him and in great troupes suddenly and upon short warning assembled they will gladly and cheerfully hear him with all reverence and attention.[49]

In such preaching, the Bible was the source of authority and of all teaching. 'To the Puritan the Bible was in truth the most precious possession that the world affords. His deepest conviction was that reverence for God means reverence for Scripture, and serving God means obeying Scripture.' For him, there could be no truer act of homage than to prize the Bible and pore over it, and then to live out and give out its teaching. 'Intense veneration for Scripture, as the living word of the living God, and a devoted concern to know and do all that it prescribes, was Puritanism's hallmark.'[50] Such an emphasis on the written word was facilitated by the educational progress of the sixteenth and early seventeenth centuries. But love of the Bible, and an intimate knowledge of it, was not confined to the literate. For example, one of John Bruen's servants, Robert Pasfield, was

> a man utterly unlearned, being unable to read a sentence or write a

syllable, yet he was so taught of God that by his own industry and God's blessing upon his mind and memory he grew in grace as he did in years and became ripe in understanding and mighty in the Scriptures. He was so well acquainted with the history of the Bible, and the sum and substance of every book and chapter, that hardly could any ask him where such a saying or sentence were, but he would with very little ado tell them in what book and chapter they might find it.[51]

The Bible was for Puritans of unique importance among all literary works; but it was supplemented by the development of a distinctive corpus of Puritan literature. William Perkins, a gifted scholar, who had a remarkable flair for clarity and simplicity, was a pioneer in providing literature which was distinguished by the Puritan emphasis on homiletical, biblical, and more particularly Calvinist, teaching on matters of faith and practice, and which was both evangelistic and pastoral. In 1589 he had started a series of popular books written in sermon style to promote Puritan piety. These included *A treatise tending unto a declaration, whether a man be in a state of damnation, or in the estate of grace* (1589); *A Golden Chain* (1590), which was a presentation of the Calvinistic conception of salvation; *Spiritual Desertions* (1591); *A Case of Conscience . . . how a man may know whether he be the child of God, or no* (1592); *Two treatises: of the nature and practice of repentance; of the conflict of the flesh and spirit* (1593); and many more. Others followed the lead of Perkins. Richard Rogers produced a large work, *Seven Treatise . . . leading and guiding to true happiness, both in this life, and in the life to come . . . the practice of Christianity . . . in the which, more particularly Christians may learn how to lead a godly and comfortable life every day* (1603). John Downame wrote a folio, *The Christian Warfare* (1604); and John Dod and Robert Cleaver published *The Ten Commandments* in 1603. Writing for the layman, these and other pastors in these and a host of other works were able to capture a large readership, 'and the influence of their published works in the first half of the seventeenth century was far-reaching and profound'.[52]

Puritans believed in the permanent and paramount authority and sufficiency of scripture in all matters of church life. The innovation of the conformist Puritans was the 'idea that direct biblical warrant, in the form of precept or precedent, is required to sanction every substantive item included in the public worship of God . . . no justification of non-biblical rites and ceremonies in worship as convenient means to biblically prescribed ends could in the nature of the case be valid . . . all ceremonies must have direct biblical warrant, or they were impious intrusions'.[53] The same principle was also applied to church government.

All biblical teaching and precepts were important for Puritans, but they emphasized certain doctrines. These may be taken as summarized in the 'five points of Calvinism' which were pronounced at the Synod of Dort as counter-affirmations to Arminianism. They stemmed from what the Puritans saw as the biblical principle that 'salvation is of the Lord'. In brief, they asserted that '(1) Fallen man in his natural state lacks all power to believe the gospel, just as he lacks all power to believe the law, despite all external inducements that may be extended to him. (2) God's election is a free, sovereign, unconditional choice of sinners, as sinners, to be redeemed by Christ, given faith and brought to glory. (3) The redeeming work of Christ had as its end and goal the salvation of the elect. (4) The work of the Holy Spirit in bringing men to faith never fails to achieve its object. (5) Believers are kept in faith and grace by the unconquerable power of God till they come to glory.'[54]

The characteristics of Puritanism were not confined to these essentially biblical and theological features. Puritanism was a total way of life. Theology had to be translated into action. Puritans had a distinctive life-style. It began in the home. The Puritans extolled the virtues of marriage, in conscious contradiction of the mediaeval belief and teaching that celibacy as practised by clergy, monks and nuns was more virtuous, more Christlike and more pleasing to God than marriage, procreation, and family life. And the home of a godly family was to be sanctified to the honour, worship and service of God. In 1653 Thomas Taylor instructed all Protestants in what should be the Christian family pattern. 'Let every master of a family', he wrote, 'see to what he is called, namely to make his house a little church, to instruct every one of his family in the fear of God, to contain every one of them under holy discipline, to pray with them and for them.'[55] Unlike almost all other Protestants, the Puritans carried out this instruction to the letter. In the typical Puritan household there were prayers each day, often twice daily and on Sundays three times, there was Bible reading, and children and servants were catechized.

And the family was expected to treat Sunday as a very special day which was dedicated to the worship of God; to a specially rigorous regime of prayer, meditation and church services, with attendance at church a particular obligation. It was common for Puritans to attend three sermons, to take notes, and to meet afterwards with other 'godly' people to discuss the content of the sermons.

It is arguable that the Puritans created the English Christian Sunday, that is, the conception and the observance of the first day of the week as the one day in the week on which both business and organized recreations should be in abeyance, so that the whole time was left free for worship, fellowship and good works. Such an ideal was never generally accepted by continental Protestants. At the end of the six-teenth century, and well into the seventeenth century, it was the custom of Englishmen after church was over to pass the rest of Sunday in attending plays, participating in games, church-ales, feasts and wakes, in piping, dancing, dicing, carding, bowling, tennis-playing, in bear-baiting, cock-fighting, hawking, hunting and such like, and markets and fairs were common. James I's *Declaration of Sports* of 1618 endorsed such conduct, laying it down that apart from bull-baiting, bear-baiting and bowls, all the popular games of the day might be played on Sundays after church; and, as we have previously observed, Charles I republished it in 1633. But Puritan teaching had its effect. The Long Parliament and its successors passed a series of ordinances forbidding games, trading and travel on Sunday. And, perhaps somewhat remarkably, in 1677, when Puritans were out of power, despised and in disgrace, a violently anti-Puritan Parliament passed the Sunday Observance Act, which repeated, and confirmed, Commonwealth legislation on the subject. The Puritan teaching appears to have created a climate of opinion, not to say a national conscience on the subject; despite the persistent opposition of the Caroline divines to the Puritans and their theology. Perhaps the old Calvinist and Arminian concurrence on the morally binding nature of the sabbath, to which we have previously alluded, reasserted itself after Puritanism had passed its peak, indicating that it had left its indelible mark on the collective conscience not only of Church of England and nonconformist members but of the population of the country as a whole.

All that has been discussed so far regarding the Caroline Puritans relates to their own beliefs and conduct, but they were also evangelists. This concern for evangelism was within the context of belief in pre-destination. The Puritan type of evangelism was 'the consistent expres-sion in practice of the Puritan's conviction that *the conversion of a sinner is a gracious sovereign work of divine power*'.[56] In effect this meant that evangelism was seen as being undertaken when the pastor preached the full counsel of God on a regular basis over a considerable period of time. The pastors taught and applied the gospel to their church congregations in a church-community-friendship-centred manner which was oriented to worship. Such evangelism we will later see exemplified in the ministry of Richard Baxter at Kidderminster.

In all their evangelism, as in every aspect of life, the Puritans looked for the hand of God; and they saw God at work. In all events and circumstances of their daily round they were alert to discerning the goodness and mercy of God, but also the judgment of God on the ungodly. To the Puritan artisan Nehemiah Wallington, described by Paul Seaver, sudden death seemed 'an all too common occurrence, frequently as a consequence of an all too sudden vengeance of a God who would not be mocked with impunity'. It was reported that a certain Danbury drover, when he was warned not to drive his cattle on a sabbath, challenged God by replying, 'Let me see who dare stay me.' He had scarcely got out of town before he fell off his horse and died soon after. 'So', was the comment, 'you may see that the great Lord of the Sabbath stayed him with his vengeance.' One of Wallington's own apprentices was said to have ignored frequent warnings of the grim fate of Sabbath breakers, and was persuaded by another to go out to the fields on a Sunday to wrestle. His opponent 'fell upon him and bruised his stomach', so that a 'short time after he died of it.' An appropriately spectacular death was reserved for some who mocked God in particularly heinous ways. In Salisbury

> a jolly fellow brewed strong ale to maintain sport on the Lord's Day, and in the month of May would have a maypole set up on the Lord's Day, and on the night before he and his jovial crew went in despite of the Puritans to cut the tree, and on the Lord's Day in the morning he driving his three horses down the hill a little beyond Salisbury . . . the tree not being tied fast . . . turned round by reason of one wheel going higher than another . . . [and] so fell over [that it] beat out the fellow's brains upon the ground.[57]

Although theology was important for Puritans, it was this total experiential life-style and world view which was most distinctive. Puritanism was 'dynamic, a process of experience and experiment rather than a mere sediment of common belief and practice.'[58] It needs to be seen holistically; it was subject to tensions, ambiguities and change, but retained certain fixed points. Conformist Puritanism bridged the gulf between conventional conformity and the various forms of Dissent.

'Some of the Episcopalians within the Established church, all the Presbyterians and Independents in it before 1662, most of the Separatists and sectarian leaders outside it, and the founders of Nonconformity after 1662, are thus all spiritually nearer to one another than is any of them to the Roman Catholic Church or to the Laudian party within the Church of England. They have their own internal differences, some of them sharp . . . but in a large sense they have much in common, and for this faith and experience which they share . . . there is no other name than Puritan.'[59]

Such forms of intense seventeenth-century Puritanism were not evenly distributed throughout the land. There were very considerable variations from one region to another and, within regions, from one town or locality to another. There has been some disagreement about the overall pattern of distribution. Thus, David Underdown has posited that Jacobean Puritanism struck strong roots in the western clothing region, so that in the following generation it was to be the towns and rural clothing parishes that most obstinately resisted conformity to Laudian ritual. On the other hand, he perceived considerable hostility to Puritanism in the chalk downlands of Dorset and Wiltshire, and other arable regions such as the Cotswold fringe.[60] But this analysis has been questioned.[61] Less questionable is the undoubted concentration of Puritanism in certain towns such as Gloucester, Salisbury and Dorchester. 'By the 1620s Dorchester was in the grip of an authoritarian Puritan regime which regulated the most minute details of its residents' lives with fanatical rigour. Swearing, tippling, sexual irregularities, "night walking", absence from church, feasting and merry-making, and general idleness: these were the common targets of reformers everywhere. Under the stern eye of John White and his supporters they were pursued with an intensity bordering on a state of "moral panic". Of all the towns in the western counties, Dorchester was the one in which Puritan reformation was most systematically imposed.'[62]

It was quite common, and possibly universally the case, that there was very considerable variation within diocesan borders. To take but one example. Of the twenty deaneries of the large and unwieldy diocese of Chester, the four most remote ones showed no evidence of Puritanism; Puritanism was weak in most of the northern and western deaneries, and never developed sufficiently to become a problem; but it flourished in Liverpool, in Lancashire south of the Ribble and in Cheshire – the main territory of the archdeaconry of Chester.[63]

Even when the Puritans were in a minority they often exercised a disproportionate influence because of their commitment and fervour. According to the findings of Ogbu Uke Kalu, if Puritanism is defined as overt opposition to some feature of the established ritual, then Puritans were active in fewer than one-third of Essex parishes between 1600 and 1628. Nonetheless they did some extraordinary work, and achieved much. They attracted allies among a number of the gentry families; the number of parishes where there were cases of lay nonconformity – opposition to the churching of women, gadding to sermons, refusal to kneel at the sacrament, and the like – more than doubled from thirty-four during the period 1602 to 1610 to seventy-one between 1611 and 1619; and, perhaps most importantly, there was an increase in the number of lecturers active in these years, of whom many were Puritans, and the increase continued into the reign of Charles I.[64]

Minority groups of Puritans were influential partly because they represented Protestantism in its more extreme, they would have said 'pure', form, at a time when the country was undergoing a process of protestantization. But as Protestantism increasingly flourished, so Roman Catholicism continued to decline.

The Roman Catholics

By 1603 it had become only too obvious to most Roman Catholics that there was no longer any prospect of the restoration of Roman Catholicism in England, and that the most they could hope for was some measure of toleration. The possibility of greater acceptance was enhanced with the accession of the new monarch. Not only were hopes aroused by what were believed to be his views, but the English Catholics were at last released from the embarrassing situation of having a ruler who had been excommunicated by the Pope. Nonetheless, under James they were to experience mixed fortunes as the government varied its policy regarding the enforcement of the penal laws.

Even as the new King moved south to assume the throne of England, an English priest named Hill presented him at York with a petition asking for the full revocation of the penal laws, which was allegedly drawn up in the name of the Catholics of England. James had Hill arrested. When the King arrived in London he was presented with a much more tactful petition which requested freedom of religion 'if not in public churches at least in privatehouses, if not with approbation yet with toleration, without molestation'.[65] Copies of the petition were also distributed, and provoked some aggressive replies.

James appears to have taken note of the dangers of a 'soft' policy towards the Catholics, and one of his earliest proclamations, in May 1603, was for the continued exaction of recusancy fines. Fears of Roman Catholicism were then fuelled by the Main and Bye Plots. Three priests, William Watson, who had been prominent in the Archpriest Controversy, and two others named Clarke and Copley, together with a number of Catholic gentry, were in varying degrees involved in a scheme to seize the King and force him to grant toleration to Catholics. Fortunately for Catholics, the plot was condemned by both secular priests and Jesuits, and information about it was given to the government by a secular priest, so that Watson and Clarke were apprehended and executed. James was both horrified at the plot, and pleased at the loyalty of his Catholic subjects who were prepared to give information against fellow Catholics engaged in treason. He encouraged the 1604 session of Parliament to enact legislation against Jesuit priests, although he and the government were otherwise quite lenient, especially as far as laymen were concerned. Suddenly, however, in February 1605 there was a change of policy. James expressed in forceful language 'his utter detestation' of the 'superstitious religion' of the papists. He was, he said, so far from favouring it that 'if he thought his son and heir after him would give any toleration thereunto, he would wish him fairly buried before his eyes'.[66] The bishops and judges were instructed to enforce the recusancy laws, and over 5,500 papists were convicted of various offenses.

Then in the same year came the Gunpowder Plot. Mystery surrounds the whole event, not least concerning the motives of the conspirators. It is not clear if Cecil and the government knew about the plot and allowed it to progress in order to implicate some prominent Catholics; and there is the associated question concerning the truth of the government's official account of the events. The most probable explanation is that the conspirators were Catholics who were despondent at the fact that Spain had made peace with England, and angry that there was renewed persecution of Catholics. Jenny Wormald has suggested a further factor came into play. She is convinced that for the high hopes of the Catholics at the beginning of the reign to have turned so sour that such a devastating plot was concocted and so nearly executed needs a stronger motive than is usually attributed to the conspirators; and this additional element was James' Scottish origins and links. 'James might have all the advantages of being adult, male, and Protestant. He had, in English eyes, the irredeemable deformity of being a Scot . . . Antipathy to the Scots did not make men extremists, nor did it make them killers. But there can be little doubt that it was an extra spur to those who were already extremists, driven to embark on wholesale slaughter for the sake of their faith.'[67] But whatever the explanation, it is sufficient for our purposes to know that there was a plot, that it failed, that the whole affair was widely publicized and, above all else, that it planted even more firmly in the minds of many Englishmen the conviction that Catholicism was to be identified with treason, and that Jesuits were arch-conspirators. It was seen as irrelevant that Henry Garnet, the Jesuit Superior in England, had known of the plot under the seal of confession and had done all in his power to stop the conspirators. The government used to the full and with great adroitness the splendid propaganda opportunity with which it was presented.

The outlook for papists seemed black indeed. After twenty years of skilfully directing the operations of the Jesuits in England, Henry Garnet was taken and made the central figure in a trial designed to show that the Jesuits were implicated in the plot, and to discredit them. Parliament passed two severe measures against popish recusants. One of them added new disabilities in order to lessen the possibility of future dangers. It included a clause prohibiting Catholic recusants from educating their own children, another preventing convicted recusants from practising law and medicine, serving in the army or navy, or holding minor political offices, and a third which allowed them to keep necessary weapons for self-defence, but required them to surrender any gunpowder they possessed. But the most important enactment was that in the second recusancy statute which directed Catholic recusants to take not only the Oath of Supremacy of 1559 but also a new Oath of Allegiance. In 1610 this requirement was extended by Parliament to all subjects over eighteen years of age. The Oath obliged Catholic recusants to declare 'without any equivocation or mental reservation whatsoever' that the Pope did not have any power to depose the King, to dispose of his dominions, to invade his realm, to discharge his subjects of their allegiance and obedience, or to give license to anyone to bear arms, to raise tumults, or to bring harm against His Majesty's 'Royal Person'. The Commons rubbed salt in the wound by inserting a clause in the oath which required Catholic recusants to swear that they did 'abhor, detest, and abjure' such doctrines as 'impious and heretical'.[68]

The situation for the Catholic recusants was perhaps not as grave as it might appear, as it seems that the draconian statutes were not rigorously enforced: perhaps James' lack of administrative drive, his vacillation concerning toleration, the onset of a period of quiescence in religious controversy, the distraction of other affairs and the desire not to upset Spain all had a part to play in this inertia. Priests and those who assisted them were still punished, and twenty-five died on the scaffold under James I, but after 1618 there were no executions until 1628. The protracted negotiations which gave England a Catholic Queen in 1625 helped to ensure a considerable measure of toleration for papists in spite of the penal laws. But the fortunes of Catholics varied from one group and one place to another.

It has been estimated that in 1600 about 1.5% of the population was committed to or sympathetic to Catholicism; it had a hold on some 25% of the gentry, and was beginning to penetrate the families of a few peers.[69] Catholicism was especially strong in the north of England. There was possibly a hard core of about 1500 recusants in Yorkshire, 2000 or more in Lancashire and Cheshire and 600 in the remoter north. In a few restricted rural areas, for example around Northallerton and in Nidderdale in Yorkshire, and in some coastal areas of Lancashire, the majority of the local landed gentry families contained Catholic members. No other single area in England and Wales compared with the north in either the number or concentration of Catholics. Nonetheless, the same community structure and vigour existed fairly widely in South Wales, Staffordshire and Herefordshire, and in mainly small pockets in the midlands and the south. This geographical and social pattern appears to have remained little changed at least through-out the reign of James I.

The Catholic community continued to be firmly based upon the gentry until well into the seventeenth century, and arguably until the late eighteenth century. Indeed the list of leading gentry families in the period 1603 to 1660 is impressive: Bedingfield, Jerningham, Paston, Walpole, Arundell, Gifford, Heneage, Meynell, Mannock, Preston, Blundell, Anderton, Walmesley, Towneley, Sherburne, Clifton, Trafford, Plowden, Huddleston, Haggerston, Ratcliffe, Sheldon, Tempest, Gascoigne, Vavasour, Constable, Pudsey, Riddell, Fleming, Gage, Shelly, Thimbleby, Thorold, Monson, Eyre, Burlacy, Carey, Turberville, Pole, Trevilion, Morgan, Biddulph. Catholicism was not noticably strong in other socio-economic groups. It was insignificant and amorphous among the rural lower classes other than for the house-hold servants and farm tenants who sheltered under the wing of the papist gentry; but even the papist gentry commonly had mostly Protestant servants and tenants. With the exception of a few scattered small farmers, weavers and miners in some moorland villages and hamlets who were Catholics but not under the protection of any papist gentry, there were few non-gentry Catholics to be found in the country-side outside the north of England. Likewise, the towns contained very little working-class Catholicism, with the exception of London and Westminster, where there was 'a rabbit-warren hiding a very shifting population of country immigrants who sometimes brought their Catholicism with them'.[70]

With the organization and policies of the English Catholics remaining firmly in the hands of the papist peers and gentry, the clergy, both secular priests and religious, suffered as their status and influence was diminished. Throughout the early seventeenth century, and until at least the 1660s, the secular priests fought hard to save themselves from a sub-servient and rather ineffectual role, but they were particularly hampered by the fact that as yet there was no really solid parochial structure. During this time there was a sharp increase in the number of religious: the number of clerical students grew rapidly as did the number of those entering the Society of Jesus (the Jesuits). But the seculars slightly out-numbered the religious, and by weight of numbers as well as by strenuous efforts they probably increased their hold on the mission structure by 1660. The strife between the religious and the secular con-tinued during these eventful decades in the religious life of England, and this did not help the cause to which both were committed.

The ramifications of life among the English Catholics, and the squabbles among the Catholic clergy were matters about which contemporary Protestants, and the population as a whole cared, and, indeed, knew, little. But the affairs of court were more public, and aroused more passion. Between 1603 and 1625 there was an advance in the Catholic presence and influence at court. Peerages were for sale, and ambitious papists were prepared to accept the necessary measure of con-formism involved, and to indulge in the required servility and bribery. In 1603 there were eight or nine papist peers and in 1625 there were eighteen. Catholics received a variety of offices and favours, including offices hitherto jealously guarded by Protestants. A clear, if slackly con-formist and notoriously corrupt, papist, Emmanuel Scrope, Earl of Sunderland, held the Presidency of the North for many years. Henry Spiller, a papist with a recusant wife, was appointed Exchequer Receiver of Recusancy Fines; Sir Edward Sherburne, a prominent papist, was given the Mastership of the Ordinance Office at the Tower of London. The great architect Inigo Jones, the papist son of a London

Catholic recusant tradesman, received the Mastership of the King's Works. That doyen of royal musicians, William Byrd, remained a very definite papist until his death in 1622. His distinguished colleague, the papist John Bull, became a practising Catholic in 1614. Indeed the whole tone of Jacobean court music became distinctly Italian, with an evident Catholic tinge, as did court literature. Charles I inherited a court which was recognized as very much open to Catholic influences, and this was to prove a significant factor in his religious outlook and policy, which itself was an essential element in the growth of Arminianism.

6

Arminianism and the Emergence of High Churchmanship

There is no simple definition of Arminianism. Contemporaries in the first half of the seventeenth century were as unclear about what it was in content and character as subsequent commentators have been. The most readily comprehensible definition was that given by someone at the time who, when asked what the Arminians held, replied 'all the best bishoprics and deaneries in England'. It is clear that Arminianism, in the sense of an identifiable group of people all holding the same set of beliefs in common, did not exist. The so-called Arminians of the 1620s and 1630s were not united doctrinally. The one doctrine which they may be said to have held in common was a negative one: they rejected predestination, and were anti-Calvinist. They exhibited this characteristic in the last decade of the sixteenth century, before the major works of the Dutch theologian Jacobus Arminius were published. But his refutation of Calvinism was so systematic that he gave his name to the anti-Calvinist movement generally; and from 1612 onwards the English Arminians had, in Arminius' posthumously published *Examen* of the teaching of William Perkins on predestination, what has been authoritatively described as 'the basic document of Arminianism'. In that work the theology of grace as propounded by Arminius received its most detailed exposition. In opposition to Perkins, Arminius argued that 'God truly wills the salvation of all men, on the condition that they believe', for God does not forcibly convert men but rather moves them 'by mild and sweet persuasion'.[1]

In order to place Jacobean Arminianism in context it is necessary to go back a few years into the sixteenth century. In the mid-1590s a doctrinal dispute among the scholars of Cambridge resulted in an attempt to impose a rigid Calvinist theology.[2] The loose Calvinism of the Church of England, as reflected in the Thirty-Nine Articles, was challenged by a new Protestant scholasticism. It had its roots in the theology of Peter Martyr and Calvin's disciple Theodore Beza, and it featured double predestination with its forceful emphasis upon reprobation, limited atonement, and the indefectibility of the elect. It was promoted by an impressive array of theologians, including William Perkins, Fellow of Christ's College, William Whitaker, the Regius Professor of Divinity, and Lawrence Chaderton, Whitaker's brother-in-law; and it was endorsed by some of the heads of the colleges. The new teaching appeared unassailable. But it did not go unchallenged. Paradoxically the dominance of such views, so much in the ascendant at the time, and so vehemently and ably propagated, helped to arouse anti-Calvinist sentiment. The most prominent and distinguished opponents were John Overall, Fellow of Trinity College, and Peter Baro, Lady Margaret Professor of Divinity.

At Cambridge it is possible to date the time very precisely when direct confrontation on these issues was instigated and made public. On 29 April 1595 William Barrett, a chaplain of Gonville and Caius College, preached a university sermon in which he criticized at length the deterministic teaching of the Cambridge Calvinists. The anti-Calvinists were heavily outnumbered in the upper echelons of the university, but Barrett was probably of the opinion that if they allowed the Calvinists to continue unchallenged much longer he and those of like mind associated with him would find themselves confronted by a fait accompli, their case defeated without a hearing.

Barrett was greatly influenced by Peter Baro, who privately held that 'God has predestined such as he from all eternity foreknew would believe on Christ' and 'hath likewise from all eternity reprobated all rebels, and such as contumaciously continue in sin'.[3] Thus, according to Baro, election and reprobation are conditional; God 'foreknew' rather than 'fore-ordained', and salvation was for those who 'would believe on Christ'. Baro and Barrett declared that Christ died for all men, and that human free will had a role to play in salvation. In a sermon at the time Baro also declared that the elect could lose their faith totally but not finally, and that no man could be so certain of faith that he could be assured of salvation.

Although Barrett was called before the Cambridge Consistory Court on account of his sermon, and forced to recant, he appealed to Archbishop Whitgift, and the ensuing discussions culminated in the Lambeth Articles which we have previously considered. But this was a mixed blessing for the anti-Calvinists, or Arminians, as they were to be known, as the Articles proved in certain ways to be anathema to them during the 1620s. William Whitaker, the man who, through the medium of a sermon in which he had attacked the advocates of universal grace, had been the one to goad Barrett into his momentous sermon, was largely involved in drafting them, and in their final form they erred more in a Calvinist than Arminian direction.

The Lambeth Articles brought Baro himself into the public debate. In yet another sermon, on 12 January 1596, he concentrated the main thrust of his criticism against those articles which limited the benefit of Christ's death to the elect. Baro was not made to recant, but in 1596 he failed to be re-elected to his professorship.

Outwardly Oxford University was more uniformly Calvinist until 1607, when Humphrey Leech, a chaplain of Christ Church, appeared as a protagonist for anti-Calvinism. He, like Barrett and Baro, used sermons to communicate his views, and so did John Howson, a canon of Christ Church, in 1612. But, as I will consider in some detail in a few moments, it was William Laud who most effectively took an anti-Calvinist initiative and helped to direct an influential section of the Church of England in ways which were new and strange within the prevailing general Calvinist orientation.

One of the most crucial episodes in the rise of English Arminianism during the first quarter of the seventeenth century was the Synod of Dort in 1618. It is something of a mystery to know why James used all his influence to secure the summoning of a synod so that the Arminian doctrine could be officially condemned. And the Synod of Dort was thorough in doing that. The conference was divided between Remonstrant Arminians and Contra-Remonstrant Calvinists. The Arminian Remonstrance, which became the basis of theological discussion at Dort, contained five principles of Arminianism. Through his foreknowledge God conditionally elected those who would believe through his grace in Jesus Christ and persevere in faith and obedience, and rejected the unconverted and unbelievers who were condemned to eternal damnation. Christ died for every person, but none but the faithful should enjoy this pardon of sin. It was impossible for man to obtain saving faith by himself or by the strength of his own free will, but he needed God's cooperating grace. The grace of God is not irresistible. And, finally, true believers might fall away from God totally and finally.

The Arminians who were present at the Synod were treated throughout 'not as participants in the debate but as defendants in the dock'.[4] Strict predestinarianism was declared to be the orthodoxy of the Dutch church, and nonconformists were treated with severity, in which there was no respecting of persons. Johan van Oldenbarnevelt, the Advocate of Holland, who had used his great influence in Europe to preach Arminianism, which he saw as the means of ending schism in the Christian Church, was condemned to death as a traitor and judicially murdered. Hugo Grotius, the distinguished disciple of Erasmus, was sentenced to life imprisonment, and confined in the castle of Loevestein. 'Arminianism' in its original home, had, for a time, been totally crushed. Calvinism, in its most rigid form, had emerged triumphant.

The Synod of Dort was 'of the greatest importance for the Reformed Churches – almost as great, in the short run, as the Council of Trent for the Roman Catholic Church. It shut the door against the liberal tendencies which had been at work in Holland and England.'[5] It 'polarized the parties in the English Church and thereby so weakened the comfortable consensus of Elizabethan and Jacobean Protestantism that it never could be restored'.[6] It 'acted as a catalyst on the English religious thought of the early seventeenth century'. Differences among English theologians became more explicit and were more readily articulated. 'Dissenters from Calvinism came increasingly to be identified as a group, and they in turn felt obliged to seek out allies in defence of a common cause. Indeed the Synod of Dort was, to an extent, responsible for the creation of an Arminian party in England.'[7]

It was at this stage that the religious unity which James had so carefully fostered was threatened, if not shattered, by the impact of the Thirty Years' War.[8] This devastating event raised perplexing issues, and complicated the English domestic scene. Such was its magnitude, religious divisiveness and Europe-wide ramifications that many Protestants, including Archbishop Abbott, interpreted the conflict as an apocalyptic struggle between the forces of good and those of Antichrist. There were pleas that England should not stand aloof, but intervene on behalf of the beleaguered Protestants abroad. James resolutely rejected such a view and policy. He disclaimed any Stuart dynastic responsibility which compelled him to support the claim of his son-in-law Frederick V to the throne of Bohemia. He also denied that the conflict was a confessional strife. He was not inactive, but sought a diplomatic solution by means of negotiation, and by an intensive pursuit of a match between Prince Charles and the Spanish Infanta, which he hoped would bring the two sides together. But the approach was not successful, and its failure, combined with the Protestant defeats abroad and the prospects of the Spanish match at home, seemed to many English Protestants to represent an ominous shift in a Catholic direction. James tried to quieten the hostile criticism of his policy from both pulpit and press by proclamations, confinement of offenders and, in 1622, a set of Directions to Preachers to avoid matters of state. But it was to little avail, especially as much of the adverse comment came from senior figures in the church, including Abbott, the Archbishop of Canterbury.

The situation aroused James' latent fears of Puritanism. The turn of events had cruelly exposed the contradiction between his domestic ecclesiastical policy of trying to hold various religious traditions together in one national church by means of subscription, and an appeal to the moderates, and his foreign policy. Both policies were based on his cherished image of *Rex Pacificus*; but they were now seen to be mutually exclusive. The virulent antipapal English Protestants remained, and the arm of the anti-Calvinist divines was strengthened the more they could heighten the fear of a Puritan threat in the mind of the King. For these and no doubt other reasons which are not clear James soon started to waver in his anti-Arminianism. He moved in an Arminian direction.

By 1624 he was giving support to the doctrines elaborated in Richard Montagu's *A New Gagg for an Old Goose* (1624). Montagu was an able scholar, and a lucid and witty expositer. He seems to have devoted himself to controversy, and he cherished the hope of standing in the breach between Puritanism and popery. His teaching on the Church of England position was based on the thought of Lancelot Andrewes, but his manner was provocative; 'very sharp the nib of his pen', commented Thomas Fuller, 'and much gall in his ink'.[9] *A New Gagg for an Old Goose* in which he enunciated his views caused such a stir that the House of Commons committed it to the attention of Abbott. But meanwhile Montagu took the initiative, amplified his views in a new publication, *Appello Caesarem* (1625), and appealed to the Crown over the heads of the Archbishop and Parliament alike. The House of Commons, incensed at this contempt of authority, summoned him before them in plague-stricken Westminster and committed him to the custody of the Serjeant at Arms. By now Charles I was on the throne and tried to protect him by announcing that he was a royal chaplain and that he, the King, was displeased with the action of his Commons, a statement which did nothing to ease the situation. After a period on bail, Montagu was sick, and the plea of illness was accepted as a reason not to attend a hearing on his case at Oxford. The whole matter was left in abeyance. It had all served to show at an early stage in the reign of the new King the actual or potential dangers of a divide between the views and actions of the monarch and those of the Commons. It also indicated where the religious sympathies of Charles lay: he favoured a radical departure from Calvinist orthodoxy.

By the end of the reign of James I, the Arminians had made remarkable progress in a relatively short time. From the 1590s, when their views were only represented by a few isolated voices, and while still remaining a small minority, they had, within thirty years, strengthened their position at court, in the church, and in the universities, and with a change of ruler they could contemplate enlarged influence and power. Nevertheless, it was clear that they would probably face increasing resistance. What was not so evident at the time was the way they would be embroiled in political developments, and how the interaction of theology, politics, and social and economic factors would produce such an explosive mixture in the second quarter of the century.

Historiography of the 'rise of Arminianism'

As we stand on the verge of the Caroline era, of Laud and Laudianism, and of the series of events leading ultimately to the Civil War, and before we move on from this consideration of Arminianism, it is perhaps the right time to stand back a little and consider the whole sweep of theological thinking and ecclesiology from the late sixteenth century to the mid-seventeenth century, and more particularly the extended historiographical debate over 'the rise of Arminianism'.[10]

Let us take the 1970s as a starting point, for it was then that the 'revisionist' debate began. For those who posited a 'rise of Arminianism', Arminianism, and more especially Laud, was cast as the villain of the piece. The conflict was to do with the Calvinist doctrine of predestination. Society was steeped in Calvinist theology in the late Elizabethan and the Jacobean years, and the Arminian assertion of 'the free will of all men to obtain salvation' was revolutionary, and set in motion trends and events, particularly surrounding the life, career and teaching of Laud, which made religion an issue, if not the issue, in the causes of the Civil War.[11] With Calvinist predestinarian ideas providing a good measure of theological consensus, differences over rites and ceremonies or over church government had not been too divisive. Under Elizabeth, and even more so under James I, such theology provided 'a common and ameliorating bond'; the majority of the clergy and probably most of the educated laity were convinced predestinarians. But, unfortunately, this Calvinist heritage was overthrown in the 1620s by Arminianism. A small group of clergy, consisting of Richard Neile,

Lancelot Andrewes, John Buckeridge and John Overall, with William Laud in the background, captured the mind of the senile King, and then of Buckingham and the heir to the throne. The new King became the architect of a revolution, as doctrinal Calvinists were excluded from royal counsels and from ecclesiastical preferment, the Court was isolated from Calvinist opinion, and an aggressive Arminianist policy during the period of the personal rule of Charles I finally drove previously law-abiding episcopalian Calvinists into counter-resistance to the King and the church hierarchy. It was unquestionably the King and Laud who were the innovators, and the Puritans were the reactionaries.

Peter White criticized this interpretation, and gave an alternative explanation for the course of events. He contended that there was no 'rise of Arminianism' in early seventeenth century England. To endorse such an argument is to be a dupe of Puritan propaganda. Within the Elizabethan church there was 'a spectrum of views on the doctrine of predestination'. Intermittent debate on such theological matters was only occasionally acrimonious, but it was generally acknowledged that these were abstruse questions which were not fit for public debate. It is improper to describe either the Elizabethan or Jacobean church as Calvinist. A '*via media* between extremes' remained the intrinsic characteristic of English theology from the Elizabethan Settlement onwards, and the 'outlook was essentially patristic, irenic, comprehensive and if necessary properly agnostic'. Theological tensions within the Church of England had to do with Rome and not Calvinism, and were between those who regarded the papists and all their works as Antichrist, and those who opposed Rome but acknowledged the force of Counter-Reformation apologetic. Both responses could normally be accommodated within the church. Even Richard Montagu was not 'a genuine Arminian', and it is a myth to think that James I ever held Calvinist beliefs. It was only the strains of war, and especially the war against Spain, that temporarily made predestination a contentious issue, because it exposed the English to 'the theological debate in the Low Countries and their role as representatives of international Protestantism against Spain'. With the return to mainstream Jacobean foreign policy after 1629 'the theological consensus was re-established'. Predestination and Arminianism were not issues in the Civil War crisis.[12]

In connection with this discussion there has been some, albeit mild, cautionary warning that, while 'a certain labelling of historiographical positions sometimes serves a useful and even necessary purpose in the teaching and writing of history, name-calling and the polemical division of scholarly opinion into revisionist and anti-revisionist camps can only have a negative effect on the analysis of often complex problems'.[13] To assert, as Patrick Collinson does, that 'Calvinism can be regarded as the theological cement of the Jacobean Church'[14] does not preclude acceptance of much that White maintains. It is tenable to argue 'both for the heterogeneity of "Puritanism" and the revolutionary implications of the impact of Arminianism'.[15] Puritans can be regarded as but the most self-consciously godly elements within a Calvinist consensus. If Puritanism is defined in personal pietistic terms it can be denied any direct political significance until it was collectively provoked by an aggressive Arminianism, thus creating a politically assertive Puritanism where there had been none before. White had given particular consideration to the rise of Arminianism up to 1629, when Charles I began his personal rule, but such a cut-off point cannot be accepted for the consideration of, say, the origins of the Civil War. 'Let us suppose that the rise of Arminianism up to 1629 was innocent of ideological calculation, and let us even suppose that the imposed truce between 1629 and 1640 was as even-handed as White seems to imply. It would not follow that the sincere (if mistaken) perception, in the minds of Laud's opponents, of a doctrinal counter-revolution was a factor to be discounted by historians explaining the origins of the Civil War.'[16]

Whether Laud and the Laudians, whom we will be considering in the next chapter, were simply attempting to maintain good order against forces which threatened unity and harmony in the Church of England, or whether they were a prominent part of an Arminian or anti-Calvinist movement which was a destabilizing force in early seventeenth-century England, is an unresolved issue. Perhaps it is helpful to think in terms of ideal-type models. 'The bishop as preaching pastor or custodian of order represents two enduring views of the proper priorities of the order which came into conflict in the reign of James I.'[17] There was a preponderance of Calvinists on the bench, but these were increasingly challenged by a minority of Arminian bishops who stressed the disciplinarian concern of the office. Not every Calvinist or Arminian prelate conformed to one of these two models, and it would be inaccurate to talk about two monolithic factions, but 'it is clear that the division between Arminian and Calvinist was not confined to academic argument at court or in the universities, but extended to episcopal practice in the dioceses'.[18] There were 'two rival visions of the English Church'.[19]

The High Church party

The latter part of the sixteenth century and the first twenty-five years of the seventeenth century witnessed the emergence and initial growth within the Church of England of a strain of thought, theology, liturgical practice and ecclesiology which, although as yet somewhat ill-defined, represented the birth of a High Church party.[20] What had been seen in embryo in the early manifestations of Arminianism and in the teaching of John Jewel, a theologian who had contributed to a nascent High Churchmanship despite his definite Protestant leanings, Richard Field and, most notably, Richard Hooker, was more precisely adumbrated, and was expressed in action by church leaders such as Lancelot Andrewes, Richard Neile, John Buckeridge, John Cosin, Richard Montagu and, above all, William Laud.

Such High Churchmen as we are considering are to be recognized by a general cluster of attitudes and actions which they had in common. These include not only an acceptance of the main tenets of Arminianism as a theological orientation, but stress upon the sacraments as sources of grace with an accompanying caution about placing too much importance upon preaching at the expense of the sacraments; considerable reservation about the personal interpretation of scripture by the laity; emphasis upon the central importance in the life of the church of the divinely instituted episcopate, and upon the clergy as constituting God's appointed order for ministering and mediating the divinely ordered means of grace; a stress upon the divine sanction which lay behind royal authority and an emphasis on the duty of all subjects to obey monarchs without question. There was also an acceptance of errors and abuses within Roman Catholicism, but a denial that the Pope was Antichrist and that it was impossible for Catholics to attain salvation; dislike of the asceticism and astringency of Calvinism, and a desire to return to what Laud called 'the beauty of holiness', by means of well ordered churches, and conformity in church furnishings and liturgy.[21]

The Jacobean bishops who subscribed to this cluster of beliefs and practices were in a minority on the bench. They applauded James I's general support for church interests, but they were alarmed at what they saw as the 'fateful brew of Calvinist divinity, puritan practices and lay rapacity', which had, they claimed, 'produced false teaching, irreverence and clerical poverty'. And they also 'looked for the restoration of the revenues and political authority of the clerical estate'.[22] Although Buckeridge conceded that James preferred a policy of tolerance, and the encouragement of unity, rather than confrontation, he pleaded for the enforcement of ceremonial order. He feared that the English Reformation had replaced superstition with profanity, and that royal policy had not checked the Puritan advance. John Cosin believed that false teaching and irreverence thrived as the episcopate ignored cere-monial conformity and concentrated too exclusively on a form of evangelism which reduced the Christian faith to salvation by means of knowledge of the catechism and the teaching of sermons. He declared that government and discipline, as opposed to preaching, should be the prime concern of the episcopate.

In retrospect it is possible to see the promotion of Richard Neile to Durham in 1617 as 'a blow at the dominant position of Calvinism with-in the English Church', especially as it was followed by the advancement of Lancelot Andrewes to Winchester in 1618 and George Montaigne to London in 1621. Such moves represented a gradual shift in favour of Arminianism, and a major phase in the establishment of a pronounced High Church tradition.[23] Neile was especially influential as a con-sequence of the high offices he held and because of his determination to promote his particular churchmanship. In a quite remarkable episcopal and geographical coverage, he was successively Bishop of Rochester, Coventry and Lichfield, Lincoln, Durham, Winchester and York. He early became identified in the minds of Puritans as a bishop 'whom all the pious, as well as ministers', thought 'would do the most mischief'.[24] In 1608 he became William Laud's 'patron', and as Bishop of Lincoln between 1614 and 1617 he had Laud first as his chaplain, and then as Archdeacon of Huntingdon. Several other of Neile's chaplains were to serve the church with distinction, most notably John Cosin, Augustine Lindsell and Thomas Jackson. He came into greatest prominence as an Arminian patron as Bishop of Durham between 1617 and 1628. His influence was also extended by the group he drew around him, known as the Durham House circle. Many of its members, although able, were excluded from the highest ecclesiastical positions during the reign of James I because of their theology, but they seem to have addressed themselves to some extent to long-term planning on the expectation of a new sovereign who would be more sympathetic to their views.

The essence of Jacobean High Churchmanship can perhaps best be understood if we examine in some detail the life, work and especially the teaching of perhaps its most distinguished representative, Lancelot Andrewes, being aware that in the wings, with his most important time still to come, was William Laud.

Lancelot Andrewes (1555–1626)

The life of Lancelot Andrewes almost exactly spans the period we have so far considered in the present work.[25] He was born in 1555, the year when the Protestant martyrs suffered in the Marian persecution; it was during his impressionable youth that the Elizabethan Settlement was being applied, and he was a schoolboy when Elizabeth was excommunicated; at Cambridge he was confronted with the ferment over Presbyterian Puritanism, and was involved in the predestination controversy; after his ordination he was engaged in disputation with both recusants and Separatists, and later became the leading apologist against Rome; he was present at the Hampton Court Conference; he was one of the translators of the Authorized Version of the Bible; and he contributed to the new school of theology which was providing a firm theological basis for the Church of England.

Andrewes entered Pembroke Hall, Cambridge in 1571. He was an able and diligent student who had an immense capacity for learning languages. He was elected a Fellow of his college in 1576. After experience as a vicar in London, as Master of Pembroke Hall and as chaplain to Archbishop Whitgift and to Queen Elizabeth, in 1601 he became Dean of Westminster. But then, 'at the age of 50 a new life began for Andrewes'.[26] He occupied successively the episcopal sees of Chichester (1605–9), Ely (1609–19) and Winchester and, from 1605 until the end of the reign of James I, he was a court preacher. He was the most popular and admired preacher of the time, with the King as one of his main devotees. He was deeply involved in general in the affairs of the country, and he was engaged in various national debates and controversies.

Andrewes was a man of prayer. Bishop Buckeridge said of him that his 'life was a life of prayer'. He spent about five hours every day in prayer and devotion to God. His *Preces Privatae* became the most popular and widely read of all Anglican devotional works, and in it we glimpse something of the wide range and detail of his prayer, the breadth of sympathy and interest in his intercessions, and the discipline which lay behind his prayer life, with its method, system and order. It can be seen how he wove scripture into almost every prayer he uttered, and yet how he drew 'freely upon the ancient Liturgies, Eastern and Western, upon several of the Primers, upon the Prayers of the Synagogue, the Rabbinical writers, the Fathers, the Mediaeval authors, and even pagan sources. It is indeed a liturgical and theological form of private prayer, and succeeds – in Dean Church's words – in bringing the spirit of the Prayer Book "from the Church to the closet".[27] He had many weaknesses, such as his frequent absences from his dioceses, his condemnation of pluralism and yet his practice of it, his use of patronage for the benefit of his family and his failure to speak out for truth and justice on Commissions, in the Privy Council and in the House of Lords, but he had a quality of character, and an aura of genuine, attractive godliness which is impressive. S.R. Gardiner presents such a picture of him. 'Going in and out as he did amongst the frivolous and grasping courtiers who gathered round the King, he seemed to live in a peculiar atmosphere of holiness.'[28]

Andrewes' sermons to a large extent arose out of his devotional life. The same faith that is summed up in the *Preces Privatae* underlies the sermons. They reveal a man who was possessed of a deep spirituality and understanding of fellow human beings, who had the ability to move the hearts of his audiences. 'They convey the personality of one who would seem to have had first-hand experience of the mysteries of the faith he talked of and who was concerned that understanding of the Christian doctrines should never be separated from the leading of the Christian life. Here is manifest a character which is grave, learned, dignified, possessed of a certain sense of humour and of a humility before great mysteries.'[29] Andrewes tried to allow his sermons to be part of a consistent, integrated life. 'He preached what he did his utmost to live: union with God in prayer, fasting, repentance, and continual conversion, the hearing of the Word and participation in the Sacrament.'[30]

Nonetheless, he never sought to live his life, or to seek a relationship with God, as primarily an individual experience outside the context of the church. His personal prayer, and the sermons that were an expression of his personal experience, were set within a conscious awareness of communion at once with his contemporaries and with the church visible and invisible. 'He prays in the communion of saints, with the heavenly powers, the Fathers, the departed, the living. It is thus also in this profound sense that his prayer is liturgical. The same approach characterizes his preaching: it is the expression of the faith of community and is strongly marked by the sense of the tradition which it seeks to make alive for the hearers of his time.'[31]

Although this is not to be gainsaid, it is questionable whether it is the whole truth. The inconsistencies in the life of Andrewes which we have already mentioned are to be found in his preaching also. All that has been said applies to the majority of his sermons, but a different approach, and a different spirit, animated those special sermons he preached on the anniversaries of the Gunpowder Plot and the Gowrie Conspiracy. Then the words uttered display 'a severity, a harshness, a polemic, a lack of charity and understanding, which, though characteristic of the age, assort oddly with the temper of his other sermons'.[32]

The most striking feature of Andrewes' theology is the extremely important place occupied by the incarnation. He proclaimed it as the central event in the history of humanity, and indeed of the whole cosmos, and an event of revolutionary character. 'Christ, in becoming Incarnate, inaugurates a new relationship between man and God, thanks to which the relationships of men and women with one another and of mankind with the whole creation become new.'[33] The incarnation was omnipresent in the preaching of Andrewes not solely because of the paradox of God made man, or because of the doctrine in itself, but because of the place it occupied in his conception of the salvation of the world. Supremely, he wanted to bring to birth a personal relationship between his hearers and Christ, the God-man; to help them to grasp the reality of this union and its implications. Eternal salvation is only to be found in the person of Christ, and Andrewes never tired of inviting his congregation to life in Christ. All else beside this pressing invitation was secondary to him, and all else that he taught was arranged around that vital appeal. Salvation can, and indeed must, be experienced in the here-and-now, although it only attains its fullness at the end, when God will be 'all in all'. Eschatology for Andrewes was both present and future: an existing reality and participation in the risen life of Christ in tension with the full consummation that remains to come.

The theology of Andrewes was christocentric, but the role of the Holy Spirit in the economy of salvation was also accorded considerable importance. It was not seen as inferior to that of Christ. Andrewes insisted that the two persons were inseparable, distinct and equal. All that Christ does, he does in and by the Spirit. The redemptive action of Christ is authenticated by the Holy Spirit, and he affixes the seal that thus actualizes the work of salvation for man. He reveals Christ, he by dwelling in the heart of man makes it possible for him to be incorporated into Christ, and to become a member of the Body of Christ, which is, *par excellence*, the bearer of the Spirit. But this work is accomplished only in collaboration with the free will of man. Even in his fallen state, with his nature vitiated by sin, man remains as created in the image of God, and there subsists in him at least a trace of the

Holy Spirit. 'Man, by his free will, can desire to turn away from sin and, immediately helped by the Holy Spirit, enters on the way of repentance, of conversion of heart.'[34] Andrewes was careful to avoid even the possible impression of any subordination or minimization of the Holy Spirit, and constantly reminded his congregations that the Holy Spirit is a divine person in the fullest sense, in total equality with the Father and the Son. 'The accent placed on the role of the Holy Spirit in the economy of salvation is without doubt the most distinctive characteristic of the theology of Lancelot Andrewes.'[35]

Andrewes also stressed the indispensability of the body of Christ. He repudiated individualism. The possession of the Holy Spirit implied communion with all the other members within the unity of the body of Christ, and one can only become a unique and responsible person within the unity of the body whose head is Christ. He denounced the pretence to interpret the scriptures in the light of individual conscience. The revealed truths, and the holy scriptures in particular, can only be interpreted in the church, which is to say within the unity of the Spirit who is the same throughout the ages, in accordance with all the confessors of the catholic and apostolic faith.

Andrewes made frequent mention of the Fathers and of the councils of the first five centuries. But he did not view them as infallible. They were human beings with their limitations and weaknesses. He acknowledged them, where appropriate, as champions of dogmatic purity and witnesses to the apostolic faith, and this it was that gave them the status of Fathers of the church; it was not because they lived in a supposedly privileged period of Christian history.

Andrewes had a high view of episcopacy, regarding the bishops as successors of the apostles, and of the ordained ministry in general, holding, for example, that the power of absolution was left to clergy. He also had a high doctrine of the eucharist, emphasizing the real presence of Christ in the sacrament, and stressing that in the sacrament we receive the true body and blood of Christ. He repeatedly used sacrificial language to describe the rite. And he yearned for the Church of England to express its worship consistently in a decent and ordered ceremonial. In his own chapel he used the mixed chalice, incense and altar lights. It seemed natural to Andrewes and to others of his reverent type of mind, that the three bows with which the courtier approached the King should be used by the celebrant, aware as he was of the presence of God at the holy table. Other ceremonial enhancements were taken from the early church or from the customs of the East, and were regarded at the time

as less open to misunderstanding than old English or Western ceremonies. They included the practice of turning to the East for the creed
at the daily prayer and eucharist and the use of the credence table.
Nonetheless, despite some innovations, old customs were not neglected:
the use of copes and wafer-bread, the washing of the priest's hands
before he prepared the elements, the mingling of water with wine in the
chalice, and the use of incense were among a variety of customs which
were resuscitated or carefully preserved. It seems that Andrewes was not
a zealous introducer and propagator of high ceremonial, but the
practices he adopted in his own chapel increasingly commended themselves to others and became the model for other cathedrals besides
Winchester, and his modest and unobtrusive example exercised a great
and widespread influence.[36]

It has been claimed, rightly, that Andrewes was 'the first great
preacher of the English Catholic Church'.[37] His most lasting contribution to the English church lay, however, first in the realm of devotion
and piety and, secondly, in that of theology and history. To the *via
media* of the English Church, Andrewes, together, one must say, with
others, and especially with Hooker, 'brought theological and historical
enrichment, investing it with a positive apologia based on Scripture and
the Fathers and delivering it from a predominantly negative defence
against Rome or a too close alliance with Calvinism. He demonstrated
the fact that Anglicanism had its own body of theology and its own
historical continuity, and thus established its claim to be a true and real
part of the Church Catholic of all ages.'[38]

7

The Reign of Charles I to 1642

Historiography

The Whig historians of the reign of Charles I worked within a liberal tradition which can be traced back, in its modern phase, to S.R. Gardiner's monumental *History of England* in ten volumes (1883–84). Such an interpretation discerned a constitutional and political struggle between an authoritarian, arbitrary monarchy, and the rule of law, the property rights and the liberties of individuals, all represented by an opposition based in the House of Commons. As part of this, a staunch English Protestantism was seen as pitched against the superstitious, unpatriotic, and near popish religion espoused by Charles I. The picture painted is of a sort of historical inevitability as the forces of good defeat the forces of evil. It was an unstoppable process of progress.[1]

Marxist accounts worked within this general framework, but the 'superstructure' was firmly related to the nature of economic developments and class relationships as they developed in England in this period. 'The Civil War thus becomes in some sense a "bourgeois revolution", a crucial step in England's transition from a traditional "feudal" to a modern "capitalist" society.'[2] The first modern presentation of such a view was by R.H. Tawney in 1941 in an article on 'The Rise of the Gentry'.[3] H.R. Trevor-Roper replied to Tawney's argument in an article on the decline of the gentry.[4] When Christopher Hill wrote his influential work *Economic Problems of the Church from Archbishop Whitgift to the Long Parliament* in 1956 he explored the links between Puritanism and capitalism.[5] He built upon studies of the relationship between 'the spirit of capitalism' and the 'Protestant ethic' which are particularly associated with the thoughts and theories of Max Weber, Ernst Troeltsch and R.H. Tawney, and which ultimately go back to Karl Marx.[6] The Weber-Tawney analysis had put the ideas of the Puritans in the forefront of any explanation of the great social changes which took place in Caroline England.

In the 1970s there was a challenge to the whig-Marxist received orthodoxy. Historians began to think that it was, indeed, time 'to question those assumptions which nineteenth-century Whig and early twentieth-century Marxist historians have in common.'[7] Conrad Russell suggested that the Civil War was accidental, arising out of 'a state of chronic misunderstanding, terror and distrust'. Such a view crucially influenced the work of such 'revisionists' as John Morrill and Kevin Sharpe, and helped to centre analysis on the long-term structural problems of the English state, including the financial weaknesses of the Crown. Explanations for the chain of events leading to the Civil War were sought among the specific political and constitutional situations of the years concerned, and the impact upon events of the main contemporary actors in the historic drama which was unfolding. The new approach rejected the idea of insuperable dilemmas which could only have been resolved through war, or of profound and deeply-rooted cleavages over religious and political principles which irresistibly resulted in confrontation. Revisionists replaced the whig and Marxist notions of inevitable and progressive developments with a portrayal of particular problems in the conduct of high politics; crises provoked by the aggressive promotion of change, and the mistakes of Charles I. Armed conflict was not inevitable. In the memorable phrase of G. R. Elton, there was no 'high road' to civil war.[8]

In many respects the work of the revisionist historians since the 1970s, with all its valuable re-appraisals and intensive, detailed study, has caused confusion about a range of matters, including the causes of the Civil War, the role of religion in the affairs of the nation in the two decades before the outbreak of war, and the life, career, character, religious beliefs and policy of William Laud. It is not that the desire for some fixed points and an accepted framework should result in an unquestioning acceptance of broad 'whig' or other interpretations, and there is always scope for revision. But the multiplication of conflicting ideas can be counter-productive, and there is a need at times to seek a way through the competing perceptions and complicated array of short-term causes, with the stress on personalities, faction and accidents, to a more coherent interpretation.[9] We are now at the stage when historians are able to take a 'post-revisionist' view which can combine some of the findings of the revisionists with an acceptance of some long-term factors. The Marxist interpretation is based on an unacceptable ideological presupposition. However, there were long-term factors as well as immediate precipitating causes which helped to bring about the Civil War; it is not a case of 'either or'. The most important underlying forces leading towards conflict were the processes of protestantization and religious pluralism, to which I have already drawn attention, and an unfolding political and religious 'democratization'. These can be traced back to the early years of the Reformation, and they contained inherent tensions and conflicts of interest which could at any time assume various local and national forms of expression. Within this wider context, the particular ideologies, policies and characters of individuals, and especially those of the King, Stafford and William Laud, played their part, and helped to bring into the open political, constitutional, economic, social and religious differences which, without their influence, might have remained dormant, or at least might have found some form of resolution which was less public, dramatic, disastrous and nationwide in extent. As with most historical situations, chains of events, and causes and effects, there was a subtle, and sometimes elusive or difficult to discern and interpret, interplay of underlying forces, key incidents and important individuals. We will see all these as we review the dramatic years covered by this chapter.

The accession of Charles I marks a definite turning point in the history of the 1620s in general, and in its religious history in particular. The Arminian clergy had experienced greater security in the favour of James in the last years of his life than they had ever known before. But with Charles they had expectations of a constancy of such favour which they had never obtained from his father. In his religion Charles had grown up as an unswerving Arminian Anglican. In his political beliefs he inherited in full from his father the belief in Divine Right, saying in 1628, 'I must avow that I owe the account of my actions to God alone.'[10] In the first half of the seventeenth century, when religious and political beliefs were inseparable, this was a logical stance. But, from the very start, it set him against a powerful and growing group of his subjects, 'those members of the landed and mercantile class who were adopting Puritan opinions and who made clear in his father's reign their intention of using the House of Commons to press their policies'.[11] Also, contact between Parliament and court became increasingly tenuous and fraught. Although many members of Parliament, including the Puritans, retained contact with the court, ever hopeful of court office and patronage, parliamentary leaders found it harder and harder as the reign progressed to co-operate with royal ministers. Not only were the King's own religious views at variance with those of the majority of members of Parliament, but his personality and the perception he had of his role as King were, in many respects, disastrous. He may well have displayed in adult life characteristics which were attributable to an unhappy childhood, but whatever the causes, his shyness and inarticulateness made him unapproachable and uncommunicative, especially in Parliament, where his intentions and actions often went unexplained. There was 'a fatal combination of superficially contradictory elements' in his make-up, which manifested itself in his seemingly irresistible capacity to be 'an authoritarian meddler who could be obsessively concerned with the details of his politics while blithely unaware of the realities of the broader political context'.[12] Whatever else divides the revisionist historians and their critics, most of them have inclined to concur that 'however serious the problems of the early Stuarts and their relations with parliaments, they were made a great deal worse by Charles I than by his father'.[13] The work of late twentieth-century historians has tended to rehabilitate James I, and very much to raise his stature, and this has focussed attention on the period after 1625, and on the inadequacies of his son. Such personality and policy defects were compounded by the shortcomings of the most influential man in court and government circles, George Villiers, Duke of Buckingham. A favourite of James, during whose reign he had experienced quite phenomenally rapid promotion to high office, Buckingham's position at court became even more dominant under Charles. He was disliked by the old nobility as a parvenu, and generally regarded as an upstart. He also prevented other councillors from getting close to the King.

There was trouble early on in the reign. Charles called his first Parliament in 1625 for the granting of money, and it offered about one-seventh of what was needed, proposed to grant tonnage and poundage for one year only, instead of for life, as was customary, and, most pertinently from our point of view, attacked the writings of that leading Arminian whom we have already met, Dr Richard Montagu. It also criticized foreign policy, and began to oppose Buckingham. Charles dissolved it. It was not an auspicious start for the new King; and within months of his accession he further aggravated the situation by giving ominous support to the few clerical Arminians, and most notably to Montagu. The alarm aroused by the evident religious trends drove two leading Calvinist peers, the Earl of Warwick and Viscount Saye and Sele, to attempt to clarify matters, and at their request Buckingham called a theological debate at his London residence, York House, in February 1626.

The subject of the meetings was the published views of Montagu. 'Up to this point Buckingham's ecclesiastical and political patronage had spanned the whole theological spectrum, doubtless as an insurance against every possible eventuality. But knowing which way the wind from the throne was blowing, at York House the favourite leaned decisively against the Calvinists.'[14] When opening the conference he affirmed his 'good opinion' of Montagu, whose 'soundness in religion' had been certified by 'divers learned prelates'.[15] He did not cite any names, but the bishops involved were Lancelot Andrewes, John Buckeridge, William Laud, George Montaigne and Richard Neile, Arminian sympathizers to a man. The signs were there for all intelligent observers to see. For over a year William Laud, at that time Bishop of St David's, had been the chief religious adviser to the Duke, and, within ten days of James' death, had submitted to Buckingham a schedule of leading clergy, tabulated on the basis of 'O[rthodox]' and 'P[uritan]', for perusal by the new monarch. And it was the information which that list contained which probably lay behind the virtual exclusion of Calvinists from various episcopal committees appointed in the succeeding months, and the more long term dwindling promotion prospects for Calvinist bishops. It was also significant that Laud was appointed to preach at the opening of Parliament in 1625 and in 1626, and in October 1626 was promised the archbishopric of Canterbury. In the context of the growth of Arminianism, which we have previously traced, and in the light of the early religious indicators under the rule of Charles, to which I have alluded in this chapter, the York House Conference 'can be seen as poised between two worlds. Calvinist England was soon to be transformed into a country of overtly competing sects and churches and Calvinist bishops were about to be overtaken by the fate of prehistoric animals, unable to survive in a changed climate. If in the long term such a development was inevitable, the York House meeting hastened the process. The conference also marked the approximate point at which the circle of clerics patronized by Bishop Neile of Durham emerged as the effective spokesmen of the English Church.'[16]

The Durham circle included such men as Augustine Lindsell, Bishop of Hereford, Thomas Jackson, President of Corpus Christi College, Oxford, and Dean of Peterborough, John Cosin, Bishop of Lichfield, Dr Benjamin Lang, Master of Queens' College, Cambridge, and Dean of Rochester, William Juxon of St John's College, Oxford, Robert Newell, Prebend of Westminster, Gabriel Clarke, Archdeacon of Durham, Eleazer Duncan, Prebend of Durham, Richard Montagu, Bishop of Chichester, and William Robinson, Laud's elder half-brother, who was made Archdeacon of Nottingham by Neile.

In 1628 Charles appointed one of their members, Richard Montagu, as Bishop of Chichester, and thus gave the Calvinists further concern about the effect of his religious sympathies and his provocativeness. In the same year Buckingham was assassinated, but although the 'grievance of grievances' was thus removed, the breach between court and Parliament was not healed. The King was embittered at the popular rejoicing which greeted the news of the murder. The Commons of the third Parliament was elected amid an outburst of feeling against the court, and it compelled Charles to accept the Petition of Right which condemned unparliamentary taxation, arbitrary imprisonment, marital law and billeting. In the second session there was a vociferous attack on the appointment of Arminians to high places in the church. The session ended with the dramatic episode in which the Speaker was held down in his chair to forestall Charles' intended adjournment of the House, and the Commons passed the Three Resolutions against those who introduced religious innovations 'or by favour or countenance seem to extend or introduce Popery or Arminianism' and against those who paid 'the subsidies of tonnange and poundage, not being granted by Parliament'.[17] This was revolutionary talk and action. The Commons were in effect demanding an extension of their power into spheres hitherto denied them, most notably foreign policy, the church, and the appointment of ministers. Although Charles was on strong constitutional grounds, his economic and political situation was very precarious; yet he showed no inclination to be conciliatory, and he consistently and persistently underrated his opponents. It is of little surprise that in 1629 he determined to cope without calling Parliament. But it was an unfortunate decision, with dire and sad consequences, for it inaugurated the eleven years of personal rule, which was followed by one disaster after another.

Laud and Laudianism

Church affairs in the 1630s were dominated by William Laud.[18] Because of the high offices he held, and his belief in using power and authority to achieve his goals, he was able to adopt a course of action which had not been possible for his 'High Church' predecessors. Laud, and Laudianism, united with the insensitive, assertive and single-minded ambitions of Charles, inevitably resulted in conflict, although few would have anticipated such a fearful and devastating outcome as the violence, divisiveness and trauma of the Civil War, the execution of Strafford,

Charles and Laud, the Protectorate, the Commonwealth and the Restoration. What Laud was and what he believed is therefore crucial not only to an understanding of the 1630s, but as one important clue to the appreciation of the events of the succeeding twenty years. Indeed, he has left his indelible mark on the history of the nation and of the church in particular.

He was born in Reading in 1573, the only son of a Reading clothier. He matriculated as a Commoner of St John's College, Oxford, in 1589, after an undergraduate career in which he established his academic work on the foundation of the Fathers and early councils. Little is known about his religious views in his youth and early manhood. Although he came into contact with Arminianism in Oxford, it is far from certain that he immediately and enthusiastically embraced it. He emphatically agreed with the Arminian rejection of predestination, but he did not accept the Arminian emphasis on toleration. Nonetheless, over a period of some years he increasingly and with resolution opposed the dominant Calvinism of the university. Together with John Buckeridge and William Juxon he started to spread High Church doctrines in his college, which was somewhat liberal in its traditions, and in Oxford generally. He was later to disseminate the same dogma throughout England.

Laud was made a deacon in 1601 and held a divinity lecturership in 1602. In 1603 he became a proctor and was appointed chaplain to the Earl of Devon. He was a strenuous opponent of the Millenary Petition. From 1607 to 1611 he was an incumbent, and in 1608 he proceeded to his Doctorate of Divinity. He secured the patronage of Dr Richard Neile, Bishop of Rochester, who was to be of immense help in his career. From Neile he received several of his preferments, and it was also through Neile that he came to the attention of the King.

In 1611 he was elected President of St John's. Immediately his Catholic, anti-Puritan, views aroused the indignation of many, and especially Robert Abbot, Master of Balliol, the elder brother of the Archbishop of Canterbury, who was Regius Professor of Divinity from 1612 onwards. But his forceful character, his determination and his persistence prevailed in establishing the college as the stronghold of Arminianism in Oxford. His wider influence was enhanced by his appointment as one of the chaplains to the King. He also helped to transform the college from a poor and struggling foundation, which owed its presidents to the favour of Christ Church and its continued existence to chance benefactions, to a position of prominence, if not pre-eminence, in the university.

Laud was able to translate his ecclesiastical convictions into action, and to demonstrate publicly his determination to introduce ecclesiastical, liturgical and disciplinary reforms, when he was appointed Dean of Gloucester in 1616. He signalled his arrival by having the communion table removed from its former place in the body of the cathedral and fixed altarwise in the chancel, and by ordering those who entered the cathedral to bow to it. Such action was viewed by most people as symptomatic of doctrinal belief, especially if it was accompanied by the railing off of the communion table. It must have seemed, as it did to the Root and Branch petitioners of 1640, to be 'a plain device to usher in the Mass'.[19] The communion table was seen as having been transformed into an altar, and the elements to have become the body and blood of Christ, transmuted by the divine power delegated to the priest.

It was at the accession of Charles that Laud started on that part of his career when he was embroiled in the political, social and economic, as well as the religious, life of the country. He was a prominent member of the court of a new King who had distinctive and strong political and religious opinions, and on whose favour he was to depend for his continued power and influence; a King who was prepared to uphold his particular concept of the Church Catholic against a predominantly Calvinist Parliament. The gulf between court and Commons widened as the court continued to be crowded with papists or crypto-papists, and Puritans were treated with distrust and fear. Laud did not approve of all of the King's ideals, nor admire and approve of the many time-servers who surrounded the monarch. But it was essential that he should preserve his influence with the King and Buckingham if he was to retain and increase his authority, and enhance his power to promote High Church beliefs and practices. If he was to be deprived of court favour he had no power base of his own as a second line of defence.

Laud was an idealist with a clear vision of the kind of church he thought was required. He was a reactionary who sought to restore the Church of England to what he regarded as its mediaeval power and status, subject only to the authority of King instead of Pope. He was a champion of conservatism, and chief persecutor of the Puritans. He was concerned to make the church a great social institution. He sought to recover the property of the church which had been alienated during the reign of Henry VIII. He shared with Lord Wentworth a concern to restore social harmony, justice, stability and communal responsibility by a restoration of the former rights of the Crown, of the people and of the church, even at the expense of material progress. Such a grand design and stupendous task of reconstruction was, unfortunately, frequently carried out in a narrow, intolerant spirit and gradually gave way to destructive conservatism, but the ideal remained. Both he and Wentworth were by temperament authoritarian men of action, and they shared an attitude towards government to which they gave the name 'Thorough', signifying an unsparing emphasis on loyalty to the Crown and individual responsibility among the servants of the King, combined with a relentless inquiry into abuses and a merciless crushing of opponents.[20] The Laudian programme of reform and purification was resisted by the strongest forces in the country: the pioneers of the remarkable Elizabethan and Jacobean material and intellectual revolution who found in Puritanism a sanctification for their aims and an ally in their cause. It was a clash of giants, and a titanic struggle was inevitable.

At the very heart of Laud's master plan was a reformed church, purified in doctrine, in discipline, in worship and in conduct. His translation to the bishopric of London in 1628, and to the archbishopric of Canterbury in 1633, gave him new and elevated platforms for influence and action, as did his election as Chancellor of Oxford University in 1630. And there was undoubtedly need for discipline and order to be restored in the church as a whole and in many of the parishes. There was widespread clerical nonconformity at parochial level, with much failure to catechize, major shortcomings in the way services were conducted, and inadequate preaching. In the diocese of Chester in the year Laud was translated to Canterbury Archbishop Neile gloomily reported that

> the Book of Common Prayer is so neglected and abused in most places by chopping, changing, altering, omitting and adding at the ministers' own pleasure, as if they are not bound to the form prescribed. In sundry places the Book of Common Prayer was so disregarded that many knew not how to read the service according to the Book.[21]

Machinery already existed as an aid to the achieving of his purposes. It merely needed to be re-activated. There were episcopal courts, the Star Chamber, the Council of the North and the Court of High Commission, which had been used effectively by Abbot and others before Laud, but which he used more fully, much to the annoyance of his opponents who, incapacitated and inarticulate at the national level because of the dissolution of Parliament, could only vent their frustration and anger at the local level by such acts of sabotage as church-wardens thwarting their vicars. Laud had joined the Privy Council in 1627, and he was prominent in the Star Chamber as well as in its ecclesiastical counterpart, the High Commission.

It was during his archiepiscopate that Laud fully launched into the twin policies which, perhaps above all else, caused controversy and opposition: his restraint of preaching, and his 'campaign to remove the "Protestant" communion table from the nave and rail it off in the chancel as a "popish" altar'.[22]

Charles I was not hostile to all preaching, but he 'had little sympathy for the relative freedom of religious expression found within the Jacobean church, and anathematized evangelical Puritanism as a move-ment which subverted all forms of authority and hierarchy'.[23] He was averse to the lectures, which had persisted since the time of Elizabeth, and would only contemplate their continuance if they were circum-scribed in the most rigid fashion. In 1629 he issued Instructions which consituted a severe programme for binding preaching to the liturgy and discipline of the church. For Laud preaching was subordinate to prayer and the sacraments in public worship, and he was concerned through-out the 1630s to redress what he considered had become an inbalance in favour of preaching. So he was at one with the King in attempting to favour liturgy over preaching. The decline in preaching, as perceived by contemporaries, was

> relative to the increased importance attached to the liturgy and the sacraments, rather than absolute. Not without reason, this appeared to many as a frontal attack on the preaching of the gospel. Had Charles I and his bishops gone out of their way to encourage preach-ing, while at the same time reinvesting the catholic life of the Church, they might have been more cushioned against the crisis of 1640 and preserved the unity of Anglicanism.[24]

The altar policy of Laud aroused as much if not more indignation than his restraint of preaching. By 1630 England was thoroughly imbued with all the values associated with Protestantism. The popula-tion as a whole accepted the Protestant status of the country as axio-matic. The fundamental doctrines and practices of Protestantism were woven into the very fabric of society, and Englishmen were jealous of their Protestant traditions. And with this went hostility to all that smacked of Roman Catholicism. It was therefore totally predictable that when Laud attempted to remove the communion tables of churches to the east end, to change them from an east-west axis to a north-south axis, to erect rails to separate them from the main body of the church, and to require communicants to receive communion at the rail, there was widespread and often fierce opposition. For Laud and his fellow sympathizers, it was part of a high sacramentalism. It was an expression of a deeply-felt sacerdotalism. 'Thus the table was withdrawn from the "midst of the people" into the relative seclusion of the presbytery, where only the priest held sway. The table of communion had become not a table of free access, but, as John Milton perceived, "a table of separation".'[25] As Bishop of London, and as Archbishop of Canterbury, Laud greatly respected various parish conventions, and he moved with caution in his attempt to introduce what he appreciated were radical and controversial measures. Indeed, although he was instrumental in implementing the full altar policy just described, he personally was among a minority of bishops who, in his own diocese, attempted to enforce the east-end position and the rail, but not the north-south, altar-wise position, or receiving at the rail; and he started court proceedings later than almost all other bishops of the Southern Province. The severe, uncompromising nature of the full altar policy may well have owed more to the King and the hawkish Matthew Wren, the Bishop first of Norwich then of Ely, than to Laud, and may have taken some at least of its main features from the example of Bishop Lancelot Andrewes. Nonetheless, it was launched and implemented in Laud's name, and associated with him more than with any other single person.

And it was resisted with vigour and determination in many parishes. Few parishes appear to have wholeheartedly welcomed it. Some complied reluctantly, with much grumbling from churchwardens; others were less accommodating. Opposition was at its greatest in those parishes which had been most noted for their Puritanism, and 'among the middling sort, the parish oligarchies of yeomen and clothiers who had for so long been struggling to impose their notions of godly discipline upon the disorderly poor'. In countless parishes they and others from lower socio-economic groups went 'gadding to sermons, attended conventicles and flocked to hear itinerant preachers'.[26]

It was inevitable that the implementation of such widely unpopular policies, and the singleminded exercise of such power as Laud wielded, would rapidly make enemies. Laud and all he stood for was seen as a threat by various groups. Landowners saw their right to tithes and control over advowsons in danger. Those prosecuted by the Court of High Commission, without any regard for social distinctions, and those men and women, great and small, who were hauled before the ecclesi-astical courts for a wide range of misdemeanours, were aggrieved and angry. And there was widespread resentment at the growing inter-ference of clerics in secular affairs. All those who suffered or were grossly inconvenienced by the new regime which confronted them, identified the system with Arminianism and High Churchmanship.

Then, clearly, there were the Puritans. Accompanying the Laudian emphasis upon the church, and upon church discipline to enforce the particular code of behaviour thought appropriate, there was the high valuation placed upon bishops and priests. And still further, as a con-sequence of the increased importance attached to the succession of grace, functions related to benediction received greater prominence: 'the consecration of the elements, the sign of the cross at baptism, the con-secration of church structures and objects, the blessing after the marriage and at the end of the service, the confirmation of the young, churching after childbirth, and hearing confession, and of course the ordination of priests and deacons'.[27] Much of this was anathema to the Puritans. But there was more to cause them anguish.

The Puritans were also at loggerheads with Laud over his attitude to the lay use of Sunday. Laud's accession as archbishop coincided with the re-publication by Charles of his father's *Declaration of Sports*. And Laud was at one with Charles in denouncing sabbatarianism, and in commending such Sunday recreations as dancing, maypoles, ales and archery. The Puritans found this obnoxious, impious and unacceptable, for they wished to enforce strict limits on what was permissable on Sundays. Both Laud and the Puritans were agreed about the need for the church to be an ascetic and austere body, and this embraced the right use of Sunday. Where they differed was on the definition of the church. To Laud and other High Churchmen it was a separate, visible entity, represented by the clergy who were a class quite distinct from the laity whom they directed; whereas, to the Puritans, minister and congrega-tion were all one, and the asceticism which the Anglican Catholic confined to the clergy was demanded of all the godly.

The difference in attitude to the lay use of Sunday sprang also from the Laudian insistence that the church, and that of course meant the Church of England, had the power to create holy times. Laudians con-sidered the Puritan approach to be simple-minded scripturalism, in which Sunday observance was based on the premise that the fourth com-mandment was part of the moral law and that Christians under the New Testament as well as Jews under the Old were bound to devote one day in seven to the worship of God, and to rest for the whole day from all secular business and recreation. In effect the Laudians were saying that the Puritans had transferred the sabbath from Saturday to Sunday and, what is more, that they had, by elevating the Lord's day, as they insisted on calling it, to a uniquely scriptural status, belittled the other holy days of the church, in a number of cases explicitly condemning them as merely human, indeed popish, superstitions. This was seen by the Laudians as an attempt to restrict the power of the English church to order the details of its own public worship, and thereby deprive it of one of its important means of inculcating piety and reverence in the laity.

In contrast to the Puritans, the Laudians construed the fourth commandment as partly moral and partly ceremonial. The ceremonial part had been abrogated by Christ, and as a consequence there was no obligation to give a whole day to divine worship, and to refrain for the whole day from secular activities. The moral part, which was still fully in force, simply required that a due and convenient time should be given to the worship of God, and it was laid upon the church and the Christian magistrate to determine what this meant in practice. The Laudians thought that the Puritan sabbatarianism was an admixture of superstition and Jewish servitude, and that it undermined the authority of the church which should include the ability to define and demarcate holy places, objects and times. And it was this insistence on the power and authority of the church which was central to the Puritan opposition to Laudianism.

It has been powerfully argued that despite their open conflict in Parliament, court, and the church, there was general agreement on the sabbath doctrine among Calvinists and Arminians; both traditions accepting the morally binding nature of the sabbath as a point of orthodoxy. On this interpretation, Laud's opponents were 'justified in their charge of innovation in doctrine and practice'. A fraudulent anti-sabbatarian tradition was promoted by the Laudians, and this 'confirmed the fears and suspicions of many, and provided a focus for the polarization of religious and political attitudes throughout the nation'. If this is so, the 'assumption that this doctrine was a unique characteristic of Puritanism must be revised, for sabbatarianism did not become a "puritan *cause célèbre*" until a few Laudians made it so'.[28] It is certainly strange that such a fundamental issue as the attitude to Sunday should only have become a matter of fierce controversy in the 1630s, with the implementation of Laudian policy.

It was in large part because of the stance taken on the topics just discussed that a contemporary caricature of Arminianism, and of Laud and Laudianism, emerged, in which all the reforms introduced were portrayed as signs of encroaching Catholicism. They were viewed as inextricably bound up with the 'popery, painting and playacting' of the court,[29] where open favour was shown to Catholics by Henrietta Maria, and where, for instance, the papal agents Gregorio Panzani and George Con were received. The contrasting savage Star Chamber punishment in 1637 of the three authors of anti-episcopal pamphlets, William Prynne, Henry Burton and John Bastwick, only helped to stress this seeming trend away from Protestantism and towards Roman Catholicism. These and others endured the indignity of the pillory, the agony of having their ears cropped or removed, or of being branded, and the extended suffering of imprisonment in the foul prisons of the age. Laud has been particularly criticized for the way he used the Star Chamber as an instrument of dire punishment in the quest to achieve his goal, but he viewed actions by that daunting body as a means of penalizing expressions of opinion which were subversive of the social order; and his attitude towards those who were judged offenders was not personal or vindictive. It was all of one piece with his conservatism, and with his consistent policy in church and state of upholding tradition and order, and of fostering religious and social stability.

The judgment of history and of historians on Laud has been remarkable for its variety and degree of intensity. At one extreme there are those who, for various, and often different, reasons, extol his virtues, and give him a place of great honour and eminence among the Christian leaders of the post-Reformation church, while some consider that he and his followers were a disaster for the church and for the country. He can be described by one historian as deserving 'to rank among the greatest archbishops of Canterbury since the Reformation',[30] and yet another can state 'that it is almost impossible to overestimate the damage caused by the Laudians'.[31]

Laud should be seen, and his life and work evaluated, in the context of the protestantization of the country; a theme which we pick up from our consideration of the Elizabethan and Jacobean church. The intense focus in recent historiography on Puritanism and the 'rise of Arminianism' has perhaps diverted attention from this more basic process which was taking place nationally, and at a local level in the parishes of the land. It may not be so relevant in understanding the history of the Church of England in the latter half of the sixteenth century and the first half of the seventeenth century to know if there was a growing Calvinist consensus around the turn of the century which was shattered by the destabilizing force of Arminianism, as to appreciate that there was a growing and, by the 1630s, seemingly almost indestructible, Protestant consensus, of which the Puritans were the most extreme and vehement representatives. It was a multi-faceted religious tradition. A distinctive theology was important, but it was only one aspect of a maturing and increasingly pervasive cluster of beliefs and behavioural patterns, liberally mixed with folk religion in various forms, which was subsumed under the umbrella designation of Protestantism. By the 1630s such a popular, comprehensive, national faith, which comprised both positive Protestant elements and a great deal of anti-Catholicism, was well entrenched at all levels of society. Seen in a wider historical context, we are witnessing the process which would result in 'Britishness' being identified with Protestantism; a fundamental feature of eighteenth- and nineteenth-century British history. Such Protestantism could accommodate Puritanism, which was but its most 'pure' and radical expression, but it reacted against anything which savoured of Catholicism. Hence the generally antagonistic response to Laud and Laudianism. This does not imply that there was a widespread, popular, reaction, although there is evidence of local opposition. Most people were content to live their lives within the confines of a known and accepted routine, and were not unduly troubled about the Laudian beliefs and practices. But traditional Catholicism, which, as we have seen, was still precious to many, and influential throughout the country until well into the sixteenth century, and lingered on as a diminishing but important aspect of national life until after the end of the century, had been well and truly replaced by Protestantism, and Laud raised fears of a return to the old, now generally alien, hated and despised religion.

Also, and this introduces another of the themes of this book, the Church of England had become the national embodiment of the Protestant 'faith of the people'. It was comprehensive within the limits laid down by the Articles of Religion, and the liturgical boundaries established by the Prayer Book, but it did not allow for beliefs or liturgical practices which strayed too far in a Catholic direction.

I conclude that Laud made a genuine attempt to promote godliness, orderliness and the beauty of holiness, but that he unconsciously offended against a by then deeply established Protestantism, and so he was, tragically, a destabilizing influence, when what he sought was the opposite outcome.

Caroline High Church spirituality

Caroline Anglican High Church spirituality was a complex phenomenon which was not represented in total by Laudianism. As we have seen, Laudianism was closely linked to the total policies of the King, and it was inextricably entwined with the political ambitions of the monarch. There were many churchmen who fully endorsed the core elements of Laud's sacramentalism and sacerdotalism, but who were not happy with the policies on preaching, on the altar and on the use of Sunday which were an integral part of Laudianism, and were uncomfortable with other measures which were taken in the name of High Churchmanship. They, like Laud, were heirs of a distinctive spiritual and ecclesiological tradition, but it was the spiritual orientation of that tradition which was of consuming concern to them – the sacraments, the liturgy, the 'beauty of holiness', and the life of prayer and contemplation. The flavour of such churchmanship is encapsulated in the career and beliefs of Nicholas Ferrar and the life of the Little Gidding community which he founded and lead, and in the life and works of George Herbert and Jeremy Taylor. John Donne also contributed to a broader intellectual and literary climate of opinion which was sympathetic to this distinctive spirituality.

Nicholas Ferrar was born on 22 February 1592, within the sound of Bow Bells.[32] He was one of five children. His father was a prosperous East India merchant. The family were habitual worshippers at the local parish church, and the children were brought up in a strict and pious household.

Having completed his degree, Nicholas had to spend more than five years travelling in Europe, under doctor's orders, in an attempt to improve his poor health, which was so grave that it threatened a premature death. After his return to England, he took his father's place in the Virginia Company, and for the next five years was intimately involved in the direction of its affairs, for the latter part of the time as a Deputy of the Company. It was at that stage of his career that he was elected as a Member of Parliament. He was offered a choice between two important posts in government service. He refused them both, for his eyes were now fixed on another goal.

Since early childhood Nicholas had displayed a serious, but that is not say sombre, disposition. At college he was known for his remarkable knowledge of the scriptures, and for the discipline and the depth of his devotional life. It was his faith which gave direction to all his actions, and he had now decided after much thought and prayer that he would lead his family in a life of corporate retirement from the world, where they would seek complete self-dedication to God.

In 1625 the deed of purchase was sealed and signed for the manor house of Little Gidding, a tiny hamlet on the borders of Huntingdonshire not important enough to be marked on any maps. The property consisted of the dilapidated manor house with the adjacent little church which had been converted into a hay barn. The parish was depopulated, save for a few shepherds. The house itself stood on a low ridge with a fine view to the south-west. In this isolated spot Nicholas and members of the family set about the strenuous work of repairing and renovating the church, the house and the estate, and then of establishing the only Anglican religious community to be founded between the time of the Henrician dissolution of the monasteries and the mid-nineteenth century.

The number of people living at Little Gidding varied from time to time, as there was continuous coming and going of friends and relations, some of whom stayed for considerable periods. Some visitors came as paying guests, and there were children who were sent by their parents for part of their education. The core of the community consisted of members of the family, but even these were occasionally away from Little Gidding on private visits, and Nicholas himself usually made at least one annual excursion to London to attend to matters of family business.

Little Gidding was maligned as an Arminian nunnery, but it was in no sense monastic, and Nicholas had no intention that it should be. It could hardly be so, with the endless variations in the membership of both sexes and the inclusion of children. But its members did exercise corporate and individual discipline in the conduct of their affairs, and for this purpose they had a code of behaviour. In many of its points the rule was the practical expression of the ideals and beliefs of Nicholas himself. It mirrored his

> wide knowledge of history and theology; his veneration for the lives and writings of the Christian Fathers; his precision and accuracy of thought; his respect for order and punctuality in all things; his profound reverence for the Scriptures, and more particularly for the gospels and the Psalter; his belief in the great value of memory-training; his carelessness of his own comfort and his constant thoughtfulness of others; his moderation and common sense; his

shrewd judgement in practical matters; his love of the Anglican liturgy; his hatred of idleness in any form; his belief that a man should not work for long stretches at any one occupation.[33]

The fully developed pattern of life, with its ordering of the day's tasks and duties, took time to become established and it was only followed completely in the last few years of Nicholas' life. It did not come easily, but after much effort, experiment and modification.

When it was finally formulated, the Sunday schedule involved rising at 4 a.m. in summer and 5 a.m. in winter, and it was then well regimented until 8 p.m. when the day closed with a hymn and prayers. Weekdays began at the same time, but they were punctuated by a short office which was said each hour from 6 a.m. onwards until 8 p.m. During the day there was never a moment's idleness, but there was also no feverish activity. All was perfectly ordered and unhurried. The timetable did not, as it might appear, place excessive demands upon the members of the household. It was strict, but even quite young children could join in fully; the Sunday services in church were short and the daily family prayers did not usually last more than a quarter of an hour at a time. The rule also provided for a proper night's rest for everybody. There were no unnecessary comforts, and luxuries were shunned, but the food, although plain, was wholesome and plentiful. The house was always well warmed in winter, and throughout the year regular times were allotted for outdoor exercise. In fact, under this bracing regime children developed healthily and sturdily. Some of the household embraced a stricter, but entirely voluntary, discipline which included fasting and night watches.

The disciplined activity of the community was not dissipated in a fruitless and undirected way, but was channelled into varied and imaginative enterprises. The Ferrars were an extremely talented and cultured family, extraordinarily well-read, and with a high sense of both the dignity of learning and of its place in a full Christian life. The 'Little Academy' which they established was a forum for the consideration of various topics, such as the life of a saint, a homily on one of the Christian virtues or a tale from classical antiquity. One person acted as story-teller, with stories which, for the most part, emphasized the varied lessons of the church's year and illustrated some aspect of Christian living.

Nicholas's brother John devoted much time to a translation of a book by the Spaniard Juan Valdez entitled *Divine Considerations*, which was a call to purity and simplicity of heart and life, and a protest against the belief that the devout life was the vocation of only a few chosen people. He also translated two other devotional works. In addition, he was busily engaged in arranging and superintending the rebuilding of George Herbert's church at Leighton Bromswold which was in a sorry state, with its roof having fallen in and the fabric generally having reached a pathetic level of disrepair. It was excellently and thoroughly restored.

In 1633 Charles I visited the community, and he was so impressed with the worship of the household that he borrowed the great Concordance of the Gospels from which the readings were taken and studied it for an hour each day for many months. He then arranged for it to be returned with an apology for having retained it for so long and for having written so freely in the margins, but asked for a personal copy. The work had been put together with exquisite craftsmanship by the members of the community, and this request started them on the production of other equally fine, superbly bound volumes.

The story of Little Gidding does not end with the death of Nicholas in 1637, although of course this was a shattering blow to its members. The life of the community continued under the impetus of his inspiration with its accustomed way of devotion and good works, spreading its own distinctive aroma of sanctity in the midst of a turbulent national religious scene until the death of John Ferrar and Mrs Collett in 1657. Thereafter the real Little Gidding was no more. The short but remarkable story of that intimate community came to an end.

George Herbert (1593–1633) undertook his duties as a country parish priest, and wrote his poetry, in a spirit which was identical to that which animated the Little Gidding fraternity. He was born at Montgomery Castle, the fifth son of Sir Richard and Lady Herbert, and he was the brother of the famous Lord Herbert of Cherbury. He was educated at Westminster School and Trinity College, Cambridge, of which he also became a Fellow. He was appointed University Public Orator in 1619, and had high hopes of a successful career in public service. But he was frustrated in such plans at an early stage by the death of potential patrons. He had for some time also been growing in his spiritual life, and he gradually made his way, despite ill health, toward his ordination in 1630. He became the incumbent of Layton Ecclesia, about two miles from Little Gidding, and in 1626 he was presented to a prebend in Huntingdonshire. It was in 1630 that he was instituted as rector of the parish of Fuggleston-cum-Bemerton, near Salisbury.

Herbert's ministry was conducted in an orderly and sensitive way, with immense pastoral concern and care for his parishioners. The focus was the church, where regular daily prayer, and services were a central feature in the life of the community. Herbert was loved by the parishioners, and the worshipping life of the church was a precious thing to them. Indeed, it seems that most of his parishioners, and many gentlemen in the neighbourhood were frequently part of the congregation which gathered twice a day.

Herbert was pacific in his whole approach to his life and ministry. His poem *The Priesthood* shows him to be a sturdy Protestant of the middle way, explaining the office of the priest as two-fold: to convey the word of God in sermons and to convey God himself in the sacrament of communion. 'His 'Parson's Church' shows a discreet love of ceremonies; Herbert urges that the church should, for example, be 'at great festivals strawed, and stuck with boughs, and perfumed with incense', and 'that there be a fitting and sightly Communion cloth of fine linen, with an handsome and seemly carpet of good and costly stuff'. 'And all this he doth, not as out of necessity, or as putting a holiness in the things, but as desiring to keep the middle way between superstition and slovenliness'.[34]

Herbert most poignantly, and famously, expressed his beliefs, and articulated the essential nature of his spirituality in his extended poem *The Temple*. It set forth something of his own spiritual struggles, and his pathway to greater holiness. When he was about to die he dispatched it to his friend Nicholas Ferrar, saying that it should only be published if he thought it would be beneficial to others, and Nicholas read and re-read it, being captivated by its tone and content, and insisted that it should be issued forthwith without any alteration.

The Temple conveyed the flavour of spirituality associated with the 'Caroline Divines'. Those who are identified with the term were not a self-conscious group; but they had enough in common to justify its use. They were a cluster of writers who, in their lives as well as in their writings, rejected the claims of Rome and yet refused to adopt the theological system of the continental reformers, and who set forth a distinctive form of High Church teaching. They included Andrewes, Laud, Anthony Sparrow, Herbert Thorndike and Thomas Ken; but Jeremy Taylor (1613–1667) was perhaps the most outstanding in that he wrote some of the most influential devotional works to emanate from the Church of England in that or any other age. He exhibited a greater beauty of style than any other of his contemporaries, and he displayed an unrivalled loyalty to the national church. In his masterpieces *Holy Living* (1650) and *Holy Dying* (1651) we see clearly his erudition, as he quarries from obscure and exotic as well as traditional mines. His distinction as a casuist, his gift as a preacher, his magnificence of style, and his subtle combination of sympathy and imagination with practicality, were all directed by a pastoral heart.[35] In his expression of tender devotion he avoided ecstasy and posturing. 'He also exhibits that sobriety and moderation which the Caroline divines thought should mark the Christian life.' He recaptures the spirit of mediaeval devotion, and, 'like the metaphysical poets and other Caroline divines, sees through a transparent world to its Creator'.[36]

John Donne (1573–1631) was arguably the most distinguished of the quartet we are considering, both in terms of his contemporary standing and reputation, and in terms of the subsequent perceptions of his place in literary history. His contribution to seventeenth-century High Church spirituality was somewhat indirect, through his literary work, and especially his poetry. Indeed, it may be reckoned that with him there 'begins a new era in the history of English lyric poetry, of English satire, and of English elegiac and religious verse'.[37] Through his mother's side of the family he inherited a link with a sister of Sir Thomas More, and he was bred in the old faith. It was an influence which never left him. After a somewhat stormy career, and a number of irregularities such as a secret marriage against the wishes of the bride's father and a period of imprisonment, he found, like George Herbert, that his secular ambitions were frustrated. He was ordained in 1615; but unlike Herbert his advancement in the church was rapid, and in 1621 he was made Dean of St Paul's. Only a few of his poetical works were published in his lifetime. In the best of his *Divine Poems* an intense spirit is seen to burn; and he displays those qualities which make him 'not only the first of the "metaphysical" love poets', but 'the first of the introspective, religious poets of the seventeenth century'.[38]

The Great Tew Circle

Another, and quite novel, aspect of Caroline churchmanship is represented by the Great Tew Circle. Here we encounter an almost liberal approach. The Circle consisted of a group of mostly young men who met together 'in a kind of continuing seminar or reading party at the Oxfordshire house of Lucius Cary, 2nd Viscount Falkland, in the 1630s, those halcyon years before the storm of the civil wars and revolution'.[39] It was a distinguished company. A fine account of the circle is given by its most famous member, and an intimate friend of Falkland, Edward Hyde, Earl of Clarendon. He relates how Falkland, in the isolation of the seventeenth-century countryside, used his time in voracious reading. Then, when his chosen friends came to stay, he turned from reading to discussion:

> . . . his whole conversation was one continued *Convivium Philosophicum*, or *Convivium Theologicum* . . . His house . . . looked like the University itself, by the company that was always found there. There were Dr Sheldon [the future Archbishop of Canterbury], Dr Morley, Dr Hammond, Dr Earles, Mr Chillingworth, and indeed all men of eminent parts and faculties in Oxford, besides those who resorted thither from London; who all found their lodgings there, as ready as in the colleges, nor did the lord of the house know of their coming or going, nor who were in his house, till he came to dinner or supper, where all still met; otherwise, there was no troublesome ceremony, or constraint to forbid men to come to the house, or to make them weary of staying there; so that many came thither to study in a better air, finding all the books they could desire in his library, and all the persons together whose company they could wish, and not find in any other society.[40]

The intellectual and theological tone was largely set by Falkland, Clarendon and Chillingworth, the latter being Falkland's closest intellectual friend. This, and the freedom allowed for the expression of diverse opinions, ensured that it was a welcome refuge from the conformity of Laudian Oxford, and that no orthodoxy reigned. The members were accused of being Socinians, but they all believed, or believed that they believed, in the Trinity. They were greatly influenced by a number of continental thinkers; largely those who were in the Erasmian humanist tradition, and most particularly the Dutch scholar, statesman and philosopher, Hugo Grotius, whom they regarded as the Erasmus of the seventeenth century. Among English thinkers, the group looked back especially to Richard Hooker. They valued the distinction Erasmus made between *fundamenta*, or essential doctrines, and *adiaphora*, on which men could agree to differ, and they appreciated Hooker's application of that principle in his insistence that the church did not consist of the 'elect' or the 'godly' only, but included all who professed and called themselves Christians. But with this tolerance went quite a measure of scepticism. Theologically, the tolerance also meant that they emphasized universal redemption and the ideal of the reunion of christendom.

During the Interregnum, when, as we will see, the Church of England survived in all its essentials intact, but in the meantime a decimated body, it was Sheldon and Hammond and certain other members of the group who most significantly upheld the Church of England principles and practices, and helped to prepare the church for the Restoration. They also sought by scholarship and controversy to establish its credentials against both its Catholic and its Puritan enemies. They worked to secure the continuity of episcopal succession and ordination, to provide a concerted policy in the face of the divisive tactics of the Puritan government, to raise money for impoverished clergy, to encourage the loyal Anglicans, and to plant chaplains in Royalist houses.

Hammond was the philosopher and theologian of the underground Church of England. His theology was 'Laudianism with a significant difference. Arminian indeed in doctrine, rational in method, ecumenical in its ultimate aims, it was also conciliatory, not authoritarian, and respectful of lay reason and lay interests.' He and those of like mind with him 'looked back from the political Arminianism of the Laudians to the intellectual Arminianism of Andrewes'.[41]

The Puritans 1625 to 1642

Although all that I have said so far about the religious situation in England in the years 1625 to 1642 has tended to illustrate the essential identity of Laudianism and High Churchmanship in general with the policy of the King, caution needs to be exercised in analysing the religious divide in the country as a whole between supporters of the King and supporters of Parliament. There were subtleties which must not be missed. Theological opinions were not always as clear cut as they are often depicted. There were, as we have seen, 'Arminians' who might have rejected predestination but who were at one with 'Puritans' in other beliefs, and this also worked in reverse. There were supporters of the King who were 'Puritan' in many of their beliefs and practices, and parliamentary men who would have subscribed to much of what was reckoned, in a fairly vague way, as belonging to 'Arminianism'. Also, 'Puritanism' in the period 1625 to 1642 embraced a variety of attitudes of mind and spirit, and was 'too volatile to be caught within the confines of Westminster'.[42] And, of course, there were divisions which were determined by economic and social considerations which cut across the religious divide. Nonetheless, in spite of these qualifications, for a variety of reasons, the 'Puritans' were to be found mainly on the side of Parliament.

Church government as established under Elizabeth and continued under James remained firmly under the control of the Crown, so that English reformers were prevented from instituting any major structural or institutional changes such as the introduction of Presbyterianism, but they were far from being completely suppressed or eliminated.[43] Puritans were not permitted to rule, but neither were they ruthlessly driven out or entirely silenced. They were granted a wide if ill-defined degree of freedom to edify the spirits of men in their own way, as long as they desisted from opposing the established church. Those who broke away were few in number or influence, and did not become numerous or important until the 1640s. Until then the main body of Puritans remained within the church, and were content to bide their time, and to move as circumstances permitted towards the fulfilment of their hopes. 'In the meantime, under Elizabeth and James and even in some measure under Charles and Laud, they were able to preach the Word, that is, to set forth in pulpit and press, not to be sure their notions for reforming Church government, but their conception of spiritual life and the code of behaviour that best expressed it.'[44]

By the early 1630s the conformist Puritans had succeeded in establishing within the church an unacknowledged and unauthorized, largely informal and unstructured, brotherhood of preachers, working to a large extent independently of, though not in direct conflict with, constituted authority. Such people were linked together by ties of kindred and friendship, as well as by conviction and interest. They tended to look mainly to Cambridge University for inspiration and intellectual leadership, and they had the support of many of the peers and gentry, merchants and lawyers, especially in East Anglia, the Midlands, London and the Home Counties. By the time that Laud came to power the London preachers and their supporters were especially well organized in a body which was well supplied with funds. Charles was compelled to take action against the Puritans if the Crown was to maintain effective control of the church. He suppressed systems for the lay impropriation of tithes; the universities were subjected to visitation by Laud; lectureships were forbidden; the writers of illicit pamphlets were prosecuted; preaching as a whole was put under restraint; and, as we have formerly noted, the canons of 1640 asserted the duty of absolute obedience to the crown, and a stricter degree of doctrinal conformity from 'all Bachelors or Doctors in Divinity', together with certain other persons of formal education.

Puritanism was 'the leading edge of the evangelical Protestant effort to proselytize the mass of the people after 1570, its theology a mere continuation of the English reformed tradition or synthesis propagated by the arbiters of orthodoxy in the church and universities; its spiritual or devotional style or timbre merely the pietistic consequence of both the successes and failures of that Protestant proselytizing effort'.[45] This is not incompatible with the assertion that there was a prevalence of Calvinistic predestinarianism among the theologically sophisticated during the reigns of both Elizabeth and James. There was a large measure of theological consensus among at least the more theologically discerning until the 1620s, and the legacy remained for many more years to come. The Puritans were the storm troopers for such theology; and they were also in the van in calling for further reformation in a Protestant direction. The subtleties and refinements which recent studies have introduced into our understanding of the various trends, ecclesiologies and theological allegiances of the late Tudor and early Stuart period do not entail all but the death of Puritanism. It remained an identifiable phenomenon until the Restoration period when, for various reasons, including its dissemination among more formalized 'denominations', as well as within the Church of England, it ceased to be so discernable. Arguably it emerged in a different form in the second quarter of the eighteenth century with the appearance of modern evangelicalism.

The Separatists

The Caroline Puritans in the years before the outbreak of Civil War were zealous reformers, like their forebears, who wanted to rid the church of what they considered to be popish ceremonies; but the great majority of them showed no desire to destroy the framework of the established church or to get rid of bishops. 'It was not until the Arminians began to have a real impact on the liturgy and practice of the Church of England in the 1630s that Puritans found themselves in serious conflict with the diocesan authorities.'[46] Although Independency and anti-episcopalianism in terms of numbers and influence were so small that they may be reckoned as negligible elements in English Protestantism, they are worthy of attention, partly because they did exist; partly because they helped to provide the ethos and to some extent the pattern for those various and varied groups which were to emerge so suddenly in the era of the Interregnum; and partly because they helped to keep alive a concept of churchmanship which was to survive all the vicissitudes of the coming half century and more, and was to form the basis of future, lasting denominations.

The most notable 'gathered church' in the first four decades of the century was that established by Henry Jacob in 1616, the origins and founding of which we have previously considered. From this one church there had by 1640 developed a number of offshoots in the City. But the total combined membership of these congregations appears to have never been more than 1,000.[47] Henry Jacob was most significant in the second quarter of the century when his teaching was adopted by some of those ministers who were forced out of their livings by Laud and his fellow bishops in the 1620s and 1630s, and who sought refuge in the Netherlands and New England. 'And once in exile the Puritan ministers' past experience of reforming their parishes at home combined with the present needs of their situation abroad to impress upon them the virtue of organizing churches which were self-governing but not separatist.'[48] There were congregations of English merchants and soldiers in the Netherlands who found difficulty in attracting conscientious conformist clergymen to serve them, and who welcomed the services of the exiled Puritans. The pastors reorganized them as gathered churches. In 1623 the English church at Middelburg chose John Drake as its pastor on the recommendation of the Jacobite theologian William Ames, who himself had recently taken up a post at the University of Franeker in Friesland. Four years later Hugh Peter was deprived of his lectureship at St Sepulchre's, Farringdon, London, because he prayed that Charles I's Catholic Queen would forsake idolatry, and he fled to the Netherlands where he also was taken under the protection of William Ames. In 1629 Peter became minister of the English congregation at Rotterdam, which he changed from its previous Presbyterian organization to a gathered church in which those who would not accept its covenant were excluded from communion. In 1633 Ames joined Peter as co-pastor, but he died shortly afterwards. All these were self-governing but not Separatist churches.

When Laud became Archbishop in 1633 he joined forces with the Dutch authorities in an effort to counter the way Puritan ministers in the Netherlands were leading their churches without reference either to the Prayer Book or to the rules of the Dutch Reformed Church. The Merchant Adventurers were required to employ only conformist ministers who were approved by the King, and as a consequence John Forbes was forced to retire from his pastorate at Delft. Pastors who ministered to state-supported English congregations in the Netherlands were warned by the Dutch Council of State that they must conform either to the Church of England or to the Dutch Reformed Church. The more extreme Puritans who were consequently deprived of their livelihood turned their eyes to New England as the last place of refuge. Thomas Hooker and John Cotton sailed there in 1633; John Lathrop, who had succeeded Henry Jacob as pastor of his Southwark church, arrived in Massachusetts in 1634; in 1635 Hugh Peter resigned his Rotterdam pastorate and started out for the colony; John Davenport succeeded Peter, but in 1637 he too sailed to New England with some of his former Coleman Street parishioners and in 1638 founded the colony of New Haven. The circle was completed when, by the end of the decade New England began to influence the old country. Thus, William Wroth, the venerable and popular rector of Llanfaches in Monmouthshire, when he was deprived of his living, founded, in 1639, a gathered church 'according to the New England pattern'.[49]

Doubt has recently been cast on the social and religious circumstances, and more particularly on the motives of those who emigrated. Professor Cressy has persuasively deconstructed the orthodox view that there was 'a mass exodus of the godly from the shores of persecution to the land of freedom where they could establish a true church and moral commonwealth'.[50] He argues that while religious conviction and escape from harassment was part of the complex web of motivations which inspired emigration, 'terms like "Puritan migration" . . . should be dropped from discussion of seventeenth-century Anglo-American history'.[51] And Kevin Sharpe has stated forthrightly that the 'history of the puritan migration, the "puritan hegira", is one of the triumphs of myth over evidence, and of nationalist historiography over research'.[52] This is not the place to weigh the evidence, but it seems that the case has been made that a good proportion of those emigrating were impelled by economic hopes and ambitions, or were convicted criminals fleeing from the wrath of the law. Nonetheless, emigration for religious reasons undoubtedly took place, and it is that group, however many of the total number of emigrants it represented, that is of interest in the church history of the period.

The Puritan exiles to the Netherlands who further emigrated to the New World in the 1630s were promptly succeeded by a second wave of like minded pastors. But the non-Separatist churches of the Netherlands and New England during these years 'always contained within them the seeds of more radical tendencies'.[53] In Rotterdam Sidrach Simpson unsuccessfully tried to persuade William Bridge's church to follow the Separatists in allowing members to prophesy and to question the minister after the sermon, and, being thwarted, he and a handful of followers seceded to form a rival church. In Southwark some members of the original Jacobite church, now under the care of John Lathrop, were provoked by the Laudian regime and persecution to reject the church's non-Separatist stance, and in 1630 seceded under John Duppa to form a Separatist church. There were further secessions in 1633. One of their number, a button-maker named Samuel Eaton, underwent a second baptism, supposedly at the hands of a cobbler named John Spilsbury. Eaton, and also possibly Spilsbury, objected to any kind of baptism received in the Church of England, as they rejected the Church of England itself as being no true church. It is not clear whether, in 1633, they rejected infant baptism or only baptism received in the parish churches. It seems that by 1638 Spilsbury was probably pastor of an antipaedobaptist church, or had risen to leadership in Eaton's church. Unlike the adherents of Smyth and Helwys, they remained orthodox Calvinists. Bearing this in mind, and in view of the fragmentary evidence regarding what church believed what and when, 'the safest thing to say is that the first Particular Baptist church was founded not earlier than 1633, and not later than 1638'.[54]

A further innovation related to the mode of baptism. A certain Richard Blunt, who had been among those who seceded with Eaton in 1633, became convinced that baptism ought to be by dipping the body into the water, resembling burial and rising again. He found no one in England who baptized by immersion. He went over to the Netherlands in 1641, and received baptism by immersion from an offshoot of the Dutch Mennonites called the Collegiants. After his return baptism by immersion was soon established as the accepted practice among both the Particular and General Baptists.

The late 1630s also saw a minor resurgence of Presbyterianism. 'The persecution of Puritanism by Laud had consequences of which he had never dreamed. It forged Puritanism into State-Presbyterianism. His Arminianism had hardened its Calvinism and his theory of the divine right of bishops had hardened its Presbyterianism.'[55] The first statement of a revived Presbyterianism came in February 1641 when five Puritan clergymen, Stephen Marshall, Edmund Calamy, Thomas Young, Matthew Newcomen and William Spurstowe published a reply to

Bishop Joseph Hall's *An Humble Remonstrance* in defence of 'the divine right of episcopacy'. They sought to show from scripture and the Church Fathers that in the early church 'bishops and presbyters were originally the same', that there 'was not one chief bishop or president, but the presidency was in many', and that there was parity among them. They argued that in the New Testament, 'bishops and presbyters are the same in name, in office, in edifying the church, in power of ordination and jurisdiction'.[56] There was to be only a short period of Presbyterian dominance during the turbulent crisis years from 1640 to 1649, as monarchy gave way to Commonwealth, but it left its mark on the history of the Church in England.

Thus, the years from 1625 to 1642 were important for conformist Puritanism and for Dissent. The pressures placed upon the Puritans, especially as a consequence of Laud's attempts to enforce uniformity to a pattern of belief and practice which was so abhorrent to them, actually gave a stimulus to both groups. A brief consideration of four of the most celebrated Puritans of those years, two of whom, William Prynne and John Bastwick, remained in the Church of England fold, and two of whom, Henry Burton and John Lilburne, were driven from Puritanism to Separatism, will help in appreciating the forces which were at work, and the devastating immediate, short term and long term effects of Laud's policy. It will help to particularize and to 'earth' some of the generalized comments which have been made on the situation. Each of these, and especially Lilburne, were influential in the period which will be considered in the next chapter, but they all had a major impact on the history of the churches in England before 1642, and their activities after that date were moulded by their experiences in the earlier period.

William Prynne (1600–1669) was the son of a gentleman farmer. He was educated at Bath Grammar School and Oriel College, Oxford, and became a member of Lincoln's Inn. He was much influenced by the sermons of John Preston. He began his career as a Puritan pamphleteer in 1626, and ultimately wrote about 200 pamphlets and books. 'A man of pedantic nature, fiery and intemperate, but deeply sincere, he denounced what he believed was immorality with unparalleled anger. In him is seen at its zenith the Puritan fear and distrust of the world and its pleasures, and the Puritan spirit of active moral reform.'[57] In *Healthe's Sickness* (1628), he depicted the prevailing wickedness of the times; in *Lame Giles his Haultings* (1631), he made a direct attack upon Laud's church policy; and in *Histriomastix* (1633), he assailed stage plays and actors, and everything associated even tenuously with the stage, such as organs, paintings in church and May-day festivities, in a work of over one thousand pages which was interpreted as an indictment of the Queen and Court. For the latter work he was brought before the Star Chamber, where he was deprived of his academic degrees, expelled from Lincoln's Inn, fined £5,000, condemned to the pillory, suffered the cropping of both his ears and was sentenced to life imprisonment. From the Tower he continued his attacks upon episcopacy in a series of pamphlets against bishops in general and Laud in particular. Once again, in 1637, he was brought before the Star Chamber, but this time in the company of John Bastwick and Henry Burton, and once again he was condemned to the loss of both ears, or what remained of them, a time in the pillory, a fine of £5,000 and life imprisonment, in addition to being branded 'SL' on his cheeks, to signify Seditious Libeller, although his own version was Stigmata Laudis. The savage treatment he received made him into a martyr: 'handkerchiefs were dipped in the blood from his ears, and his journey to imprisonment in Caernarvon Castle (whence he was later moved to Mount Orgueil in Jersey) was a triumph'.[58]

Prynne was released in 1640, to become a prosecutor for Parliament, and to conduct proceedings against Laud with malicious relish. But he seemed almost incapable of avoiding confrontation, or of undertaking any role other than that of opponent and critic, for he was soon pouring out his writings against the army, the Independents, the execution of the King, the extreme claims of the Presbyterian ministers and Oliver Cromwell. But that is to stray into our next period.

John Bastwick (1593–1654) was for a short time a student at Emmanuel College, Cambridge, served in the Dutch army, took a doctorate of medicine at Padua and then practised at Colchester. He began writing Puritan tracts in the 1630s, at first in Latin to imply that their target was merely the Church of Rome. But his treatises denounced episcopacy, and thus brought him into conflict with the authorities. The Court of High Commission excluded him from his practice of medicine, imposed a fine of £1,000, and remanded him to the Gatehouse until he retracted his opinions. In reply he published in 1636 the *Apologeticus ad Praesules Anglicanos*, which was a more provocative work than any of his previous writings.

Then, in 1637, he turned to the vernacular and wrote *The Litany of Dr John Bastwick*, his most famous production, and 'one of the most bitter and highly coloured attacks on the Bishops ever published in the

English language'.[59] In a scurrilous and sustained onslaught, he condemned the bishops as 'enemies of God, the Tail of the Beast, depicting them in a series of lurid anecdotes as gluttonous, lecherous, brutal and arrogant'.[60] Abandoning the learning and more restrained terminology of his former publications, he couched his arguments in angry and contemptuous phrases which were calculated to make a direct appeal to the emotions of the reader. It was a work which fired the enthusiasm of many, including John Lilburne, who was so impressed that he made his way to the Gatehouse and to Bastwick. But, understandably, the authorities were incensed, and his sentence by the Star Chamber was the same as that meted out to Prynne and Burton who were tried alongside him. As with his fellow sufferers, the execution of the punishment produced a wild popular demonstration of sympathy. He was freed from prison in 1640, fought on the parliamentary side in the Civil War, and wrote further tracts, but this time for the Presbyterians against the Independents.

Henry Burton appears to have been tormented throughout his life by fear of Roman Catholicism, believing it to be intent on subjugating England to 'papal thraldom and to . . . Spanish cruelty'.[61] He was educated at St John's College, Cambridge, was clerk of the closet first to Prince Henry and then to Prince Charles, and was dismissed soon after the accession of Charles for warning the new King of the popishly tainted Laud. Subsequently, while holding the living of St Matthew's, Friday Street, he issued a stream of pamphlets in which he tried to defend both the Church of England and Charles from what he perceived as the innovations of popish prelates. He was summoned before the High Commission in 1626 and the Privy Council in 1627. He was temporarily suspended in 1629, and finally, in 1637, sentenced with Bastwick and Prynne. The experience 'turned Burton from a self-appointed guardian to a bitter opponent of the Church of England'.[62] Denied ink, pen and paper on his island prison in Guernsey Castle, he improvised with his own manufactured ink and goose wing pens, so that he was able to continue his campaign against the Laudians. His writings were smuggled back to England for publication, and they show that by 1639 he had come to share with Separatists a wholesale condemnation of the Church of England as anti-Christian.

One of the first acts of the Long Parliament in 1640 was to order the release of Burton, who returned to a hero's welcome. He continued to exercise his influence in denying any claim of the Church of England to represent a true reformed Protestant religion. Burton rather declared 'that the liturgy, discipline, government, rites, and ceremonies of the Church of England are all of them so many branches of popery'. And he also continued to share many views with Separatist pioneers. For instance, as that 'a particular church or congregation rightly collected and constituted, consists of none but such as are visible living members of Christ the head'. He concluded that the Church of England was so overspread with profaneness and darkness, and had for so long been enslaved 'under the yoke of prelatical tyranny' that it would 'be very difficult, if not rather impossible, to reconstitute it . . . as is agreeable in all points to a true and visible congregation of Christ'. He therefore advocated 'the new forming of a church', by gathering all believers 'into several congregations, who are fitted and who desire to draw near unto Christ in a holy communion with him'. Godly parish ministers might 'reform their own congregations'. It was Burton who, in 1641, coined the name 'Independent' for the opponents, on the parliamentary side, of the reformation of the Church of England on Presbyterian lines.

John Lilburne was a raw apprentice of twenty-two years in 1637 when Prynne, Bastwick and Burton were arrested. As we have already observed, the forthright teaching of Bastwick appealed to the essentially nonconformist temperament of the young Lilburne who, by 1637, was a radical Separatist in the making. In December of that year he was apprehended and accused of importing 'scandalous' books from the Netherlands, and in particular Bastwick's *Letany*, and in February 1638 he was sentenced to a fine of £500, ordered to be whipped at a cart's tail from the Fleet prison to Westminster, to stand in the pillory, and to remain in the Fleet until he conformed. But he refused to toe the line. In response to the treatment he received, he moved from being a conformist Puritan to being a Separatist. And in a tract in which he described his sufferings, entitled *A Worke of the Beast*, he called on all true Christians to withdraw from the 'antichristian power and slavery' of the Church of England. He argued that the bishops were the limbs of the Beast spoken of in Revelation 13.2. He was especially fierce in his indictment of Laud. His writings were smuggled out of prison and dispatched to Amsterdam, where they were printed and distributed. After his release at the behest of the Long Parliament in 1640, he joined a Separatist congregation. When war broke out he enlisted as a captain in the regiment commanded by the Separatist sympathizer Lord Brooke, but left the army in 1645 rather than subscribe to the Covenant. For the following ten years he campaigned for what he considered his own and his country's liberties, and became a leading Leveller propagandist, as we will see in the next chapter, when I examine some of the radical sects of the Interregnum period.

The Roman Catholics

Although Protestantism in the various forms I have described was by far and away the dominant religious tradition in England during the reign of Charles I, Catholicism was by no means extinct. In fact, in the first four decades of the seventeenth century the number of English Roman Catholics grew considerably. It was partly because the Counter Reformation was taking effect in England as elsewhere, partly because of the somewhat variable Catholic sympathies of James I, and the more pronounced and consistent sympathies of Charles I, partly because of the increasing Catholic influence within the Church of England, and in part because of the effective strategy and work of the Roman Catholic Church itself. There were probably between 30,000 and 40,000 recusants, or principled absentees from the established church, in England in 1603, whereas there were about 60,000 within these categories by 1642, the end of the period presently under review.[63] These numbers relative to Protestants remained small, even in areas of particular concentration such as Yorkshire, where they represented no more than 2% of the population, but they were dedicated and prominent.

Approximately 10% of the peerage in 1642 was Catholic. Many of the major Catholic gentry had property rights over Protestant churches. They were often lay rectors of parish churches, in which capacity they had the right and duty to appoint and sustain Anglican vicars; and the average Catholic squire, whether he was a rector or not, leased the tithe rights of local Anglican incumbents. Although the great preserves of the Protestant establishment, the public and grammar schools, the universities and Inns of Court, the leading professions and government offices, were ostensibly barred to papists, in practice, they were all quite extensively infiltrated by them by the 1640s. The majority of Catholics in these Caroline years must have belonged to the categories of mere or poor gentry and better-off yeomen and tenant farmers, from which social background a great deal of talent, including Oliver Cromwell and Isaac Newton, originally came, and about which there was nothing aristocratic.

During the reign of Charles, up to 1642, there was an ever growing number and influence of Catholics at court. At his accession in 1625 Charles inherited a court which was distinguished by its openness to

Catholic influence. Between 1625 and 1642 that influence increased dramatically, and in the eyes of some Protestants, alarmingly. In the royal family itself this was due chiefly to the character of the new Queen, Henrietta Maria, and to the insensitive and unwise complaisance of Charles. 'Henrietta Maria, sallow, plain, *petite*, but vivacious and always exquisitely dressed, was a devout Catholic of an unintelligent sort. Her religion found its stay in pretty devotions, to our Lady of Liesse, the three Kings of Cologne, relics of saints and scapulars.'[64] Many factors combined to make her formidable. After the assassination of Buckingham in 1628, the King became passionately attached to her. He would hardly leave her side, and he allowed himself to be persuaded by her to grant ever more sweeping concessions to Catholics, despite the fact that he was repelled from Catholicism by her devotions. She became the centre for a household which was distinguished by its exquisite French taste, and it became an artistic and literary salon which attracted the best poets, artists and wits, both Protestant and Catholic. Strategically placed in the Queen's household were Catholic ladies and priests, and such successful lay proselytizers as Endymion Porter, gentleman-in-waiting to the King, and his wife Olivia, lady-in-waiting to the Queen. There were a number of notable successes, such as the dramatic reconversion of the lapsed Catholic celebrity, Sir Kenelm Digby; and it was said that Mrs Porter had persuaded her old father, Lord Boteler, to become a Catholic on his deathbed, that she had converted her relation, Viscount Purbeck, the Marchioness of Hamilton, the Countess of Newport and Sir Robert Howard. The Catholic influence at court was also enhanced by what was probably the Queen's important part in the choice of Ministers of State, some of whom were married to Catholics or themselves had known Catholic sympathies. Despite the emotions which court Catholicism aroused, it is not easy to assess the extent of its influence. It combined menace and fragility in so confusing a way that the soberest observers found it difficult to gauge its real strength, but it was undoubtedly considerable.

Lastly, as an indicator of the growth of Catholicism in these years, there was a massive increase in the number of priests and of Catholic institutions. The number of priests soared from 250 in 1603 to over 700 in the 1630s, and the much feared Jesuits quadrupled. There was an equally impressive growth in the number of English Catholic establishments on the continent. From no more than ten in 1600, they underwent a dramatic ten-fold increase by the 1660s; a number made the more remarkable if we add the forty or more Irish Catholic and the dozen Scottish Catholic institutions. Nonetheless, this is somewhat deceptive as, despite their vigour and increasing numbers, the real control of the English Catholic community, its organization and policies, remained firmly in the hands of the papist peers and gentry.

Arrayed against the various segments of the Caroline Catholic community were a variety of attitudinal and legal responses from the Protestant majority. The Catholic peerage suffered from ostracism by the establishment rather than outright legal persecution. Likewise, the major papist gentry, as a consequence of their wealth and involvement with the establishment, shared this relative immunity from persecution. It was the middling and poorer gentry who were largely unprotected; and the anti-Catholic legislation was particularly directed against this category of Catholic laymen. Since 1603 the rather haphazard penal laws had been reshaped and co-ordinated into a large, coherent body of law with a number of components. There were the capital offences, which applied to anyone convicted of being a Catholic priest who had been ordained abroad and had come into England, and to laity convicted of giving aid of any kind or shelter to such a priest; both were subject to the horrific punishment of being hung, drawn and quartered, with the additional refinement for laity of having all their property confiscated. Then there were the fines imposed for recusancy which were complex and applied with varying degrees of strictness. They were supplemented by a variety of other rigorous measures, including the power of local authorities to exact on the spot an extra fine of one shilling per person for every single wilful absence from the parish church on a Sunday or weekday holiday of obligation. The tremendous accumulation of penal laws were such that, had they been consistently executed, the practice of Catholicism would have become impossible for the vast majority of Catholics. In fact they were not so applied. It was considered by the government and high society that the menace of Catholicism could be adequately met by the threat of punishment and an actual policy of ostracism and discrimination. It was a practical *modus operandi* which was arrived at by both Protestants and Catholics, excluding an extremist minority on both sides.

The coming of Civil War

During the years 1637 to 1640 there was a surge of events which hastened the drift towards Civil War. Despite the growing opposition to his financial and religious policies, at the beginning of 1637 it was not obvious that the end of the personal rule without Parliament which Charles had sustained for eight years was in sight. The immediate precipitating cause of the collapse of the personal rule was the outbreak of rebellion in Scotland, for which Charles himself must largely take the blame. He handled the Scots in an inept and insensitive way, and showed lamentable ignorance of Scottish opinion. His policies for Scotland were misdirected and misunderstood, and his greatest blunder was in promoting Arminianism in the country, thereby upsetting the ecclesiastical *modus vivendi* developed by his father. James had skilfully erected a system of church government for Scotland which combined features of episcopacy and Presbyterianism, and thus made episcopacy acceptable to the majority of the people. By identifying Scottish bishops with Arminian policies Charles generated radical opposition among those who might, if rightly handled, have continued in their support of episcopacy. By increasing the secular power of bishops Charles and Laud together strengthened the anti-episcopal movement in Scotland as they had done in England.

The particular matter which focussed opposition was the attempt to introduce into Scotland a revised Scottish Prayer Book, based on English models and Scottish liturgical practice. Laud had urged Charles to take such action as early as 1629, but a definite and fatal decision to do so does not seem to have been made until the King's visit to Scotland in 1633. The 'most inflammatory thing about the book was not its contents, but the manner of its imposition'.[65] No attempt was made to consult Scottish opinion, apart from the bishops, and all protests from Scotland were ignored or suppressed. In 1634 Lord Balmerino was sentenced to death for possessing a copy of a petition stating religious grievances. By such heavy handed, insensitive conduct and attitude this specifically religious issue, and others associated with it, widened in significance, and a strong anti-English element was infused into the opposition. But Charles and Laud would not be diverted one iota from the course they had set before them. In 1636 new Canons were issued which were based on the English Canons of 1604, and the Scottish Privy Council was ordered to command the use of the new Prayer Book when it was ready in 1637. The continued uncompromising attitude drove Scottish moderates into an unlikely alliance with such radical heirs of a long apocalyptic tradition as Archibald Johnson Laird of Wariston. A further provocation was the fresh effort to effect the Act of Revocation. The scene was set for a major disaster.

The venue for the first dramatic confrontation was St Giles Cathedral in Edinburgh. The occasion was the first use of the new Prayer Book on 23 July 1637. 'As the bishop stood, in obedience to the provisions of the new service book, facing the holy table, members of the congregation, apparently from among the meaner sort, clamoured that the mass was come amongst them.'[66] Active resistance had needed something violent to set it in motion, and here it was. It appears that about thirty or forty women, with one accord, started railing, cursing and scolding, and that a stool was aimed at the bishop. 'From that moment all the strands of Scottish animosities seemed to wind together – patriotism, protestantism, property and privilege.'[67] But it was religion which was the binding force. Although the nobility in general had never displayed any remarkable enthusiasm for Presbyterianism, many of them now hastened to put themselves in the van of a movement which, with a certain amount of prodding and encouragement, sprang up to embrace people of all classes under the plausible claim of being a national crusade.

Such defiance only strengthened Charles' determination to remain uncompromising, and he made it clear that he would continue with his policy although it was evidently impractical. Faced with such an unyielding stance, in February 1638 a National Covenant was drawn up which denounced the Canons and the Prayer Book. Even at that stage there was support for limited episcopacy, as shown, for example, by the fact that the Covenant did not mention bishops. But the persistent stubbornness and insincerity of Charles during the next ten months cut the ground from beneath the moderates. The Glasgow Assembly which met in November 1638 abolished episcopacy. It heralded the beginning of the 'Scottish revolution', and both sides girded themselves for war.

Charles, Laud and England in general were in a parlous state. Back in England there was a widespread lack of enthusiasm for war against the Scots, which was a measure of the deep unpopularity of Charles and Laud and their policies. 'Laud had achieved the impossible: to make himself more hated in English eyes than the Scots.'[68] Charles went north in an aggressive move, but his 'military movements, aimless and dilatory, merely exposed the rawness and "untowardness" of his troops and soon dribbled to a stop.'[69] He had little choice but to negotiate, and he concluded a truce at Berwick in which he agreed to a meeting of the Scottish Assembly and Parliament, and the disbandment of both armies.

The truce settled nothing, and Charles was resolved to resume the war. But he needed money. He called a Parliament which met in April

1640. It proved to be a recalcitrant body which resisted the granting of any subsidies for the purpose of prosecuting the war. There were clear signs of possible rebellion. Charles thwarted any such intentions. After it had sat for a bare three weeks, he abruptly dissolved the Short Parliament. The country was rapidly heading for a serious constitutional crisis. But Charles relentlessly proceeded on his way. With no regard for fostering any possible remaining chance of co-operation, he arrested the Earl of Warwick, Lord Brook and Viscount Say and Sele, who were among the leading parliamentary spokesmen in the Lords. Ignoring Laud's advice to be conciliatory, he ordered the continuation of Convocation. A set of far-reaching Canons were framed which embodied the Laudian innovations of the 1630s, and which have been well described as 'the high-water mark of Laudian Anglicanism'.[70]

Events were now moving fast. The Scottish Parliament met in June, without a royal Commissioner, and declared that its resolutions could become acts even without the King's assent, which was an example followed within two years in England. Soon after this a covenanting army, with little resistance from Charles's demoralized troops, moved over the border and invested Newcastle-upon-Tyne. Charles had little option but to accept humiliating conditions as the basis for a truce with the Scots. It was agreed to pay them £850 a day pending a permanent settlement. He was compelled to call a new Parliament; and this one he could not discard after less than one month.

In the Long Parliament it was apparent that control would pass to those with the ability and boldness to grasp it. Without hesitation John Pym, with the backing in the Lords of men like the Earl of Bedford and Lord Brooke, and with the support in the lower House of Denzil Holles, John Hampden, Oliver St John, Walter Erle and, at that stage, essentially moderate men such as Benjamin Rudyard and Edward Hyde, took it. He was the outstanding Parliamentarian in the Commons, and he exercised diplomatic and political skills of a high order in the pursuit of his objectives.

The radical Puritans who had made their mark some years before came back on the scene. The 'prison gates creaked open. William Prynne, his grim features split by a grin stretching from ear-stump to ear-stump, made a triumphant entry into London, his way strewn with flowers. Lilburne, Burton and the other victims of "Thorough" found November warm with affection. But there was no drop in the prison population, merely a change in personnel. Laud, Stafford and many others were arrested and "caged" on the orders of parliament.'[71]

But the sudden redisposition of power within and without Parliament tended to produce disagreements and disunity rather than a solid front against the King, and it was church matters which most potently demonstrated this. 'After Laud and Laudianism were swept away there was little agreement on what to put in their place.'[72] There were radical groups that called for a 'godly reformation' and an end to all bishops. Anti-episcopalianism was most vividly and poignantly expressed in the London Root and Branch Petition of 11 December 1640 which catalogued the alleged evils of bishops and demanded that 'the said government [of bishops] with all its dependencies, root and branches, may be abolished'.[73] But in the debates on this Petition in the Commons in February 1641 there was much support expressed among Members of Parliament for the retention of bishops, and all realized the need to ensure that the new Parliament did not go the way of the last. This gave them a common, if somewhat negative, purpose. 'The presence of the Covenanters in the north made that goal easy to attain.'[74]

Outside Parliament there was a rash of rioting which encouraged the belief that a greater measure of religious freedom equalled social disorder. This was only partially justified. Much of the disturbance had nothing to do with religious matters. But some of it did, and it was largely associated with a widespread fund of anti-Catholic prejudice. As we have seen, suspicion of Catholics was one of the most common constituents of popular politics, and it was easily generated in times of crisis.

A steady drumbeat of accusation and innuendo, assiduously encouraged by John Pym and other leaders in Parliament, aroused widespread fears of a vaguely defined yet profoundly threatening popish conspiracy by courtiers, army officers, and Laudian bishops against the liberties of Protestant England. The riots that erupted in London after the dissolution of the Short Parliament were directed against the Queen's household, the Catholic peers, the Papal agent – and Archbishop Laud. The 'great fear' of Catholic conspiracy, fed by rumours of Army plots fomented by the Queen to put an end to Parliament altogether, steadily intensified during the following year.[75]

But these panics were dwarfed by the ones that followed hard on the heels of the Irish Rebellion in the autumn of 1641. Soon there was a rumour-laden atmosphere in which horrific tales of the murder of English settlers by Catholics mingled with cries of alarm that the Irish rebels were coming. The revolt had an immediate and marked impact

upon parliamentary politics. The Commons were regaled almost weekly
with accounts of plot and massacre and this played into the hands of
Pym, and undermined the credibility of Charles. Public awareness of the
revolt doomed any lingering hopes the King may have harboured of a
return to normality. The need to suppress the revolt also raised with
new immediacy the question of the trustworthiness of Charles. Many
were disinclined to risk giving him authority over the troops. 'The
rebels' not entirely empty claim to be acting in the King's name lent
credibility and urgency to the opposition's charges that Charles was the
tool of a Catholic conspiracy.'[76] He desperately needed money to fund
the suppression of the revolt, but Parliament was not prepared to vote
him such funds to cut their own throats.

Clearly King and Parliament were locked in a fierce and seemingly
insoluble conflict. The stage had been prepared for one of the great
melodramas of English parliamentary history. On 3 January 1642 the
King sent to the Lords charges for an impeachment for treason against
Viscount Mandeville and against the 'five members', John Pym, John
Hampden, Sir Arthur Haselrig, Denzil Holles and William Strode.
Charles went to the House with armed men at his back, set upon arrest-
ing them. But both Houses had been forewarned of the King's intended
action, and the five members had adjourned to the safety of the City.
When Charles tried to fetch them from their refuge, angry crowds lined
the way. In fear of mob assaults, on 10 January Charles left Whitehall,
'never to return until he was brought back in 1648 to face trial and
execution. He had lost London in more ways than one'.[77] He retreated
to Hampton Court, and on the following day the five Members of
Parliament returned in triumph to Westminster.

The attempted coup strengthened the determination of the parliamentary leadership 'to carry out the radical programme which had
emerged during the last few months: press for the removal of 'evil
councillors' round the King, secure parliamentary approval of the commanders of the militia, forts, and the Tower, and force an Exclusion Bill
preventing bishops sitting in the House of Lords through the Upper
House'.[78] A Militia Ordinance was approved which required local
gentlemen to choose whether or not to obey the orders sent to them
to secure the local militia for Parliament. The issue was sharpened
from June when the King began to send out Commissions of Array
appointing his own local army commanders. Local conflict was almost
inevitable, as when the King tried unsuccessfully to seize control of the
garrison at Hull from Sir John Hotham. Over a period of months there

was a slide into civil war. It became official when Charles raised his standard at Nottingham on 22 August 1642.

Although historians are largely agreed that this sequence of events in the years preceeding the outbreak of the First Civil War was the immediate precipitating 'cause' of that war, there has been much debate about underlying, long-term 'causes'. As we have previously noted, for a considerable period up to the 1970s historical attention had been largely directed to the interraction of various political, economic and social factors which were at work in the first four decades of the seventeenth century, and which helped to explain the way the history of the country developed during that period; but the religious element was to a great extent marginalized.[79] John Morrill and others are helping to bring it back into the equation.[80] They do not discount the 'explanations' of such historians as Christopher Hill. The work of Hill and others, and the kind of explanatory hypotheses they had offered had 'played a fundamental role in breaking "religious" history and especially the history of religious ideas free from "denominational" history'; had drawn attention to 'literary' texts as historical documents; and had 'set the *nature* of the English revolution at the heart of the historical agenda'.[81] But Morrill and his 'co-revisionists' were concerned to go beyond an examination of Puritanism, and to provide a more balanced assessment of other groups; and they studiously avoided any preconceived ideological notion of *necessary* historical processes.

Morrill considers that 'what England suffered in the 1640s was its delayed, or deferred, wars of religion'.[82] Elizabeth had managed to stave off any major conflict by the establishment of a hybrid church, and James had successfully continued to hold the religious centre together. The crisis came because of the insensitive religious policy of Charles I which allowed the ever-present religious tensions to develop into open conflict. Charles I was all too generally seen by contemporaries as frog-marching the Church of England in a Romewards direction. 'Together with his abandonment of the political latitudinarianism essential to stable government, his reckless authoritarianism and his corruption of justice, England fully experienced its reformation crisis.'[83]

This interpretation seems to be consistent with the present knowledge of English history from the Reformation to the mid-seventeenth century. It is not claiming 'that the crisis of the 1640s was "only" about religion.' But perhaps 'religious poles are the ones around which most other discontents formed'.[84]

Popular religion and local church life

Although the trends, attitudes and events I have described dominated the national public life of the church in England in these pre-Civil War years, and have therefore inevitably and rightly commanded the attention of historians, they were not the most important features in the religious life of ordinary people as they went about their daily tasks. Before leaving the world of Caroline church life, therefore, it is well to turn the focus of attention on what the Christian faith meant to most people in the towns and villages of England.

First, there were those parishes, in the minority, where the 'godly' were dominant or exercised great influence. Both Separatists and non-Separatists agreed that the Church of England was composed of what was false and what was true; of hypocrites and Christians only in name, as well as sincere and true believers. It was the price paid for being a territorial church rather than a gathered church. 'The promiscuous membership of the public assemblies had always been the nub of the separatist indictment of any churchmanship less dramatically exclusive than their own.'[85] This meant that in many of the parishes of the land the 'godly' constituted a distinct group, a church within the church. In some cases this godly core of parishioners resolutly set themselves against any form of schism. In other parishes, where there were exceptionally favourable conditions, a form of covenant was imposed on entire parochial congregations, as at Dorchester under the commanding patriarchical ministry of John White in the 1630s, where a schedule of ten vows was made the condition of receiving the communion. When there was an alliance of the local squire and the minister to achieve such rigid conformity to a strict code this was made even more effective in promoting godliness, at least in outward form, as at Ketton in Suffolk, where Sir Nathaniel Barnardiston and his minister Samuel Fairclough co-operated in a 'design to exclude from the Lord's table the "visibly prophane"'. Barnardiston set the example in requiring all those wishing to communicate to first make a personal reaffirmation of their baptismal covenant. Once consituted, this body of communicants promised to undergo regular admonition where there was an obvious breach of the covenant. In such parishes 'the tables were fenced, but this was not a separation of the godly but a forcible separation of the ungodly'.[86]

Throughout the first four decades of the century a cultural conflict developed at various levels of society, and it was bound up with differences of religious belief and practice. This has been finely described and analysed by David Underdown:

> At the elite level the conflict ranged the Protestant country gentry and middling sort – the 'Country' – against what they perceived as the corrupt and popish extravagance of the Court and its hangers-on. At the popular level it ranged many of the gentry, the Puritan clergy and their allies among the respectable parish notables against the bulk of their social inferiors and the poor. Elements of the elite such as the Laudian clergy and conservative laymen such as Robert Dover attempted to rescue and preserve the older festive customs because the values they expressed were closer to their own. The two cultural positions reflected the two conceptions of society . . . one stressing tradition, custom, and co-operative, harmonious, 'vertical' community; the other moral reformation, individualism, the ethic of work, and personal responsibility.[87]

But, in addition to these ideological, theological and social divides, there was the first appearance of systematic post-Reformation English rationalism. The rationalists were few in number; and rationalism was ill-defined until the Age of Reason, but the seeds were being sown. Two theologian-philosophers were especially influential and effective in this seed-sowing operation: Edward Herbert, First Baron Herbert of Cherbury, and William Chillingworth. Herbert expounded his understanding of the rationally discernible character of authentic religious belief in three works: *De Veritate* (1624), *De Religione Laici* (1645) and *De Religione Gentilium* (1663). Reason, he said, was the ultimate arbiter in religious matters. He argued that 'by using reason (aided by prayer) an individual can decide between the faiths that compete for allegiance. The one that is to be accepted is the one that most closely conforms to the common notions – a religion summed up . . . as "love and fear of God, charity towards one's neighbour, repentance, and hope of a better life" . . . Doctrines allegedly imparted by revelation, transmitted by tradition and taught by priests are to be accepted only if they are in accordance with what reason perceives.'[88]

William Chillingworth placed supreme reliance on the decision of the individual according to what reason taught him. He repudiated any higher authority than reason. People could not be expected to believe with assurance that which the evidence did not justify. Reason was the faculty given by God to enable us to discern between truth and falsehood, and it was the final court of appeal.

Rationalism was not to blossom in full until the advent of the Cambridge Platonists, the publication of Hobbes's *Leviathan* (1651) and the emergence of the Deists at the end of the seventeenth century, but Herbert and Chillingworth paved the way. It is impossible to gauge the extent to which such philosophies percolated downwards in the first forty years of the century, although there is some evidence of religious indifference and of scepticism at parochial level in these years.[89]

But for the bulk of the population religion was an important component in their lives, and religion meant the established church as represented in the parish church which they knew so well, especially if they were among the majority of the population who lived in small, rural communities. Here they were instructed in the main tenets of the faith; here was the liturgy, familiar to them from the cradle to the grave; here they experienced the rites of passage; and here they found the focus of individual and corporate life. It was the mostly ordinary clergy and catechists, with no pretentions to 'Puritanism', who inculcated the essentials of the faith in a way which unlettered men, women and children could grasp: who taught 'the Apostles' Creed (a summary of theology), the Decalogue (a rule of duty), the Lord's Prayer (a model of prayer) and an explanation of the sacraments (as tokens of faith and signs and channels of God's grace to us)'.[90] The short catechism, which was printed in the first Edwardian Prayer Book, extended in 1601 and somewhat modified in 1661, was widely used, and exercised a profound and lasting influence in the lives of countless people, rich and poor, renowned and unknown, educated and ignorant. Basic, orthodox Church of England teaching was also available in two little works printed in tens of thousands of copies throughout the Jacobean and Caroline period: *The ABC with the Catechism* and *The Primer and Catechism*.[91]

Even the most untutored churchman regarded prayer as a daily duty, and accepted the obligation to master the Lord's Prayer, the Creed and the Decalogue. Devotional aids were available in abundance, and they mostly repeated the fundamental teaching of the Anglican Church. Here, in this daily, weekly, monthly, yearly, and life-long reiteration of elementary truths, with the integration of teaching into the routines of life, was to be found the type of Christianity which the multitude understood and practiced. Certainly, it would be false to paint an idyllic picture of unsullied faith and morality. The reality was far from that, for there was much which was sub-Christian in belief and in conduct, and there was an ample measure of impiety and immorality among the 'multitude'. But, for most of the population, the faith and life portrayed in the Ten Commandments, the Sermon on the Mount, the Lord's Prayer and the Creeds was seen as normative; and anything which was a denial of such standards, or over-enthusiastic was regarded as the abnormal, and was unacceptable. The 'multitude' was mostly conservative in its views, its beliefs and its mode of life. It was therefore a shock when war, with its accompanying political and religious radicalism, came so suddenly and traumatically upon them.

8

The Civil War and the Interregnum

The course of events

Although there has been a wide divergence of opinion among historians about the extent to which religion played a part in the long or short-term causes of the English Civil War, there is virtually no disagreement that religion loomed large in the life of the country during the Interregnum. It is an overstatement to call the mid-seventeenth century crisis 'England's wars of religion', but religion was central in both the causes and course of those epoch-making events. The national struggle was 'diffracted into a series of unique patterns in each region', but 'the beam of light entering the prism was essentially religious in character'.[1] It was also a time when the 'lower and middle sort of people entered the political [and one should add 'religious'] arena to an extent which no one could possibly have anticipated'.[2] The assault upon the Church of England was severe. A religious laboratory was created; and in it religious experiments were conducted of a type and diversity which has not been seen at any other time in the history of the country.

Indeed, few short periods in the whole history of England can compare in complexity and the pace and drama of events with the eighteen years from the opening of the Civil War in 1642 to the Restoration in 1660. This pivotal era witnessed a concentration of religious activity which was of considerable importance not only in terms of the contemporary history of the country, but as a breeding ground for developments of major significance in the future. As the political, constitutional, economic and social context for the story of the churches in these years is crucial, and complicated, we need to start by describing, unravelling and analysing what took place.

'In the autumn of 1642 the majority of England's leading citizens appear to have been surprised, not to say dismayed and incredulous, to find themselves at war.'[3] This reaction probably filtered down to all levels of society. Even in the King's camp at Nottingham there was a strong body of feeling which favoured negotiation rather than war.

At Westminster war was far from the minds of most of the Parliamentarians, for the threat of war had only been a means of forcing Charles to come to a political settlement. At worst, the expectation was that a single decisive victory might be sufficient to ensure a satisfactory negotiated settlement. This reticence to take military action was even greater among leaders in the counties. 'It is probable that the commonest reaction in most counties to the coming of the war and the war itself was non-commitment, neutralism, and that the activists for the royalists and parliamentary causes were few.'[4] But this raises the unresolved question of 'the ecology of allegiance in the civil wars' which has been a matter of considerable scholarly debate.

There is little sign of a marked and serious social divide in 1642 between the Royalists and the Parliamentarians. As the war developed, allegiances became more pronounced, and there emerged a 'popular Royalism' as well as neutralism and 'popular Parliamentarianism'. It also appears that 'contrasts in popular allegiance had a regional basis, and were related to local differences in social structure, economic development and culture'.[5] It has been asserted that the division of the English body politic which erupted into civil war was in essence between two groups.

> On the one side stood those who put their trust in the traditional conception of the harmonious, vertically-integrated society – a society in which the old bonds of paternalism, deference, and good-neighbourliness were expressed in familiar religious and communal rituals – and wished to preserve it. On the other stood those – mostly among the gentry and middling sort of the new parish elites – who wished to emphasize the moral and cultural distinctions which marked them off from their poorer, less disciplined neighbours, and to use their power to reform society according to their own principles of order and godliness. These two socio-cultural constellations can be observed in all parts of England, but in varied strengths in different geographical areas: the former more conspicuously in arable regions, the latter in the cloth-making wood-pasture districts.[6]

Critiques of this thesis have been offered.[7] The notion that Puritanism had a particular appeal to the middling sort has a strong pedigree.[8] Lucy Hutchinson observed that 'most of the Gentry of the country [i.e. the county of Nottingham] were disaffected to the Parliament. Most of the middle sort, the able substantial free holders, and the other Commons, who had not their dependence upon the malignant nobility and gentry, adhered to the Parliament.'⁹ This has been the substantial conclusion of modern research, and has been found to be widely applicable throughout England.

Given the initial prevailing neutralism and lack of enthusiasm for war, and also the general inexperience of both the generals and the rank and file in each of the opposing armies, it is not surprising that the early military engagements of the war, like the battle of Edgehill on 23 October 1642, were inconclusive. The failure of either side to win a decisive battle in these first few weeks and months of the conflict gave force to the growing peace movement, especially in the House of Lords among people like the Earls of Pembroke, Holland and Northumberland. In late 1642 both houses agreed, the Commons after some pressure from opinion in the City and the country, that negotiations should open with the King. This resulted in the Oxford 'treaty' and the peace petitions and neutrality pacts of 1642 and early 1643, the collapse of which marked the definite end of the first phase in the war.

Hopes for peace were destroyed because of the military successes of the King. In the spring and summer of 1643 the royalist armies threatened to carry all before them and thus held out the prospect to Charles of being able to defy the Long Parliament and the reforms it was demanding. In fact there was no nationwide strategy by either side until 1645, although it seemed that Charles had achieved one and was implementing it in 1643. But quite rapidly reality asserted itself and a stalemate ensued. The contending parties were faced with the possibility of a long-drawn-out war. In such a situation Pym and his friends saw only one way to swing things in their direction, without handing over control of the army to people radical enough to drive some of their supporters over to the King, and they negotiated an agreement with the Scots. A Solemn League and Covenant was signed at Edinburgh. In return for Scottish military assistance, Scottish troops were paid by the English Parliament. In addition, the English agreed to reform their church according to the example of the best reformed churches and according to the word of God, which was a loophole considering the previous requirement for the introduction of Presbyterianism into England. The reform of the church was referred to the Westminster Assembly.

As a counter move, Charles arranged an armistice with the Irish rebels, enabling him to bring over some English regiments from Ireland. This did some good for Charles from a military point of view, but it was diplomatically disastrous as it raised the spectre of invasion by the 'barbarous Irish', and the move only helped to confirm many people in their fear that Charles was dangerously pro-Catholic.

In 1644 the balance of the war was tilted in favour of the Parliamentary forces. The Scots made their presence felt militarily for the first time at the biggest battle of the war, Marston Moor on 2 July 1644. This was also the occasion when the first major contribution was made by the man who was later to become the Scot's greatest enemy, Oliver Cromwell. At that time he was commander of the cavalry of the Eastern Association. The victory gained by the Parliamentarians compelled the King's northern army to turn round to face the Scots, and it reopened the London coal trade. Although the battle gave Parliament the control of the north, it did not settle the war. A Highland army under the Marquis of Montrose distracted the Scots from the war in England by winning victories over the Covenanters in Scotland. The Earl of Essex allowed his army to be surrounded in Cornwall, escaped and left his infantry to surrender. Then, in the autumn, there was another indecisive battle at Newbury, so that at the end of 1644 the war seemed no nearer a conclusion than when it had begun.

From 1643 onwards there were strong differences of opinion in Parliament on how the war should be conducted. On the one side was the peace party which regretted the war, and was constantly looking for the first convenient means of getting out of it. As in 1642, it was Denzil Holles who was the most vocal advocate of a settlement with the King at almost any price, although even he would probably have balked at the return of Laudianism. But he and the rest of the 'peace party' were so fearful of the social and religious radicalism which had surfaced as a result of the war, and which we will be examining later, that they were willing to trust Charles to maintain the legislation of 1641 without any safeguards. Pending any such settlement, they advocated a purely defensive war policy. On the other side were the 'war party' who were less explicit about their long-term religious and political aims. They were very clear in recommending an offensive strategy which sought total military victory, prior to which there should be no negotiations with the King. Between these two extremes there was a 'middle party' led by John Pym until his death in December 1643 and thereafter by Oliver St John. It combined the 'war party' requirement of military victory before negotiation with Charles with a commitment to an eventual constitutional settlement of the traditional sort, but grafted on to this the novel features of the 1641 legislation.

Given this Parliamentary disunity, and the military deadlock at the end of 1644, the Parliamentary victory in the Civil War came remarkably quickly. The New Model Army and the genius of Cromwell played their part in what proved to be decisive battles at Naseby and Langport in the summer of 1645, and in the spring of the following year Charles gave up the military struggle.

In the immediate post-Civil War period there were no clear cut party divisions in Parliament, although the three policies to which I have just referred to a certain extent held good. At one extreme were those who were prepared to accept the King's return with minimal conditions, while at the other extreme were the hardliners who demanded cast-iron limitations on his power before they would condone the disbandment of the army. It was in this sense that the terms 'political Presbyterians' and 'political Independents' were used of the two poles of political opinion among Parliamentarians in the late 1640s. Although the groups do not appear to have corresponded to any rigid theological divide, the split in the Parliamentary ranks deepened from 1645 onwards and, for the first time since 1640–1, the issue of religion started to assume a central place at Westminster.

In 1645 Parliament approved the abolition of the Prayer Book and its replacement by the Presbyterian Directory of Worship. The Ordinance establishing Presbyterianism in England, which was finally approved in 1646, disregarded the Westminster Assembly recommendation that the Scottish system should be adopted, whereby churches were given the power of appointing ministers and elders, and instead gave Parliament the supreme voice in church affairs. The most controversial issue was the extent to which the state should be involved in determining the doctrinal and liturgical practices of individual congregations, for the establishment of independent gathered churches had already begun.

In the meantime, dramatic events were unfolding. The details of the capture and escape of Charles I, the onset of the second Civil War, the purge of Parliament in December 1648, and the trial and execution of the King in January 1649, need not detain us, as the story has been often and fully told, and it is not particularly relevant to the history of the churches in these years, which I am soon to recount and examine. The important thing to note, from the particular perspective of the church historian, is 'the unique revolutionary nature of the abolition of episcopacy, monarchy, and the House of Lords, the involvement in politics of masses of people from outside the normal political sphere, and the ventilation of radical ideas of universal importance in the late 1640s. What was done was not as wide-ranging as the Russian Revolution or as permanent as the French Revolution, but if there ever has been an English Revolution it surely took place from December 1648 to January 1649.'[10]

After such a period of war and revolution the need which was universally acknowledged was for an extended period of peace and stability. At the same time, it was necessary to adopt policies which would satisfy the demands of the army and the sects for further reform. First the Commonwealth governments of the Rump Parliament from 1649 to April 1653, then the Barebones Parliament of July to December 1653, then the Cromwellian Protectorate from December 1653 until Cromwell's death in September 1658, struggled to achieve 'a permanent political-constitutional framework which would comprehend revolutionary radicalism and conservative traditionalism'.[11] Although each attempt failed, the regimes of the 1650s came nearer than is often realized to reaching this very difficult goal. And, of course, Oliver Cromwell played a dominant part in this 'quest for settlement'.

Oliver Cromwell (1599–1658)

Great caution needs to be exercised even in giving a brief outline of the early life of Cromwell, because of the considerable re-appraisal of the evidence which has been a feature of Cromwellian studies in the last quarter of the twentieth century. And the evidence is thin. 'For the first forty of his fifty-eight years, Oliver Cromwell lived in obscurity.'[12]

Cromwell's father was the younger son of a knight, but his inheritance was quite meagre, and he had seven daughters as well as Oliver to provide for. In 1631 he sold up all but seventeen acres of his land, and in that same year Oliver moved from Huntingdon, his place of birth, to St Ives. Although he says of himself that he 'was by birth a gentleman, living neither in any considerable height nor yet in obscurity', his standing in St Ives was that of a yeoman, a working farmer. He was a member of the 'middling sort'. In 1620 he had married Elizabeth, the daughter of the city merchant Sir John Bouchier, in what was to prove a happy match. In 1636 he inherited land near Ely from an uncle which substantially increased his wealth, so that by 1641 his status was improving.

Nothing is known of Cromwell's role in the government of Huntingdon in the 1620s, but in 1628 he was elected as Member for the town in Charles's third Parliament. His one speech was delivered in 1629 in the Committee for Religion. He witnessed the holding down of the Speaker, and the dramatic dissolution of Parliament. In 1640 he was elected Member of Parliament for Cambridge and sat in both the Short and the Long Parliaments.

It is evident that he regarded his religious development as by far the most important aspect of his life. He may well have experienced much and prolonged spiritual agony and searching, which may have been especially acute in the years 1629 to 1631, when he seems to have passed through a dark night of the soul. But he found release. Using language which was characteristic of the preaching in hundreds of pulpits throughout the land, he was able by 1638 to declare: 'I hated godliness, yet God had mercy on me . . . my soul is with the congregation of the first-born, my body rests in hope, and if here I may honour God either by doing or by suffering, I shall be most glad.'[13] His faith was rooted in Calvinism, although it was wider, more tolerant and more tender than that of many of his contemporaries. But we have to acknowledge that we know little of his personal beliefs and religious practices. His 'private religious thinking and devotion are sparsely documented'.[14] We have to rely almost entirely on public utterances, and these reveal something of his public, rather than his personal, spirituality.

Cromwell viewed the contemporary scene from a religious perspective. He had an image of God presiding over the national destiny, and accomplishing his purposes through varying, but chosen, agents. He knew that God had a 'special and surpassing purpose in the civil wars'.[15] The Lord 'hath been pleased to make choice of these islands wherein to manifest many great and glorious things', 'such things amongst us as have not been known in the world these thousand years'.[16] Within such a context Cromwell saw himself as a weak instrument raised up by God for a particular purpose. His personal concern was to remain a true servant of providence, to help promote national as well as personal godliness, to be aware of the prospect of a coming millennium, to create an environment of liberty of conscience for all people who were honest, godly and conscientious, and who pursued Christianity in substance and not merely for form's sake, to promote a Christianity of substance, of the heart and spirit, and to achieve his own salvation.[17] As we will see, there was a strange paradox at the heart of these objectives. He longed for the creation of a godly nation, 'yet he placed his faith in a Church structure that was wholly non-didactic and non-directive'.[18] In fact his sincere attachment to liberty was, without his awareness or intention, helping to pave the way for the religious plurality and the denominationalism of the modern state. He was unconsciously fostering that process of departure from a single national church to a variety of sects, denominations and churches which was identified at the beginning of this work as one of the themes running through the period covered.

Cromwell took his public spirituality into his political life. But it took time for this to develop and mature. In Parliament he was initially not a distinguished speaker, but he made it clear that he was a radical who favoured the Parliamentarians against the King, supported the abolition of episcopacy, and was committed to the defeat of the King and the pursuit of a full programme of reform. At a somewhat later stage, when he was within sight of achieving national power and authority 'he felt himself charged with the divine responsibility of framing a peaceable religious settlement for God's distracted Englishmen'.[19]

As an army officer he showed his own 'Independent' religious views, and, for example, encouraged the troop of horse which he raised in 1642 to form themselves into a 'gathered' church. Early on in his political career he showed that he was hostile to the Presbyterian beliefs of the majority in the Commons. But the instinctive conservatism which asserted itself despite his radical stance on so many issues, made him fearful of indiscipline and anarchy. It made him distrustful of the agitators in the army who favoured a democratic settlement, and who pressed for strong action against a Parliament bent on imposing Presbyterianism. He sought a church 'system' which would provide order and stability, and a measure of uniformity, but at the same time would allow for tolerance and flexibility. When he reached the pinnacle of his power as Lord Protector from 1653 until his death five years later, he remained tolerant, without his religious vision for the country being dimmed. But in practice the religious policy adopted for England was, in many ways, at variance with his ideals. There was the same conflict of principles and aims to which reference has already been made. He wanted to protect and fulfil the hopes of the godly, and also to found the republican government upon consent instead of force; but these objectives were contradictory, for the godly were a minority.

The Puritan church settlement took the form of Presbyterianism but without coercion, and most of the sectaries could worship freely. The use of the Church of England Prayer Book was forbidden, Catholics were persecuted, and there were some savage attacks upon Quakers. Nonetheless, because of his innate tolerance, the law, which appeared in certain respects as intolerant, was slackly enforced. Certainly the whole period from 1642 to 1660 provided sufficient toleration to allow many new sects to appear, and already established ones to burgeon.

The Westminster Assembly and the revival of Presbyterianism

When the government abolished episcopacy and showed reluctance to enforce the law against Dissent, it did not thereby intend to undermine the established church, or encourage the proliferation of Separatism and the mushrooming of sects. It was emphatic 'that there should be throughout the whole realm a conformity to that order which the laws enjoin according to the word of God', and for the drafting of such laws it proposed the calling of 'a general synod of the most grave, pious, learned and judicious divines of this island'.[20] Charles vetoed the proposal, but the opening of the Civil War removed the necessity for his assent, and the Westminster Assembly met on 1 July 1643. The conference consisted of 151 nominated members, 121 of whom were divines and 30 of whom were lay assessors. The laymen included such notable persons as John Pym, John Selden, Bulstrode Whitelock and Sir Henry Vane. The ordained members were carefully selected to reflect a great diversity of views. The episcopalians were represented by four bishops, R. Brownrigg of Exeter, J. Prideaux of Worcester, J. Ussher of Armagh and T. Westfield of Bristol, and five Doctors of Divinity, D. Featley, H. Hammond, R. Holdsworth, G. Morley and R. Sanderson. The Presbyterians, who were much the largest group, included E. Calamy, E. Reynolds, later Bishop of Norwich, A. Tuckney, W. Twisse and R. Vines. And there was a small group of Independents of disproportionate influence because of the favour of Oliver Cromwell and the army which they enjoyed, among whom were Thomas Goodwin and Philip Nye. The Assembly met 1163 times between 1 July 1643 and 22 February 1649. It continued meeting until 1653, under the Commonwealth, but its gatherings were irregular and mainly for the trial of ministers. It was never formally dissolved. Out of loyalty to the King the episcopalians very seldom attended the sessions.

Although the Assembly set out to revise the Thirty-Nine Articles, its distinctive contribution to English theology and its prime influence on English church history came with the preparation of the Directory of Public Worship, the two Westminster Catechisms and, above all, with the celebrated Westminster Confession. As the Confession 'embodies Puritan theology in its classical form',[21] shows the world view of Puritans at that time and has been of such influence and importance subsequently, we will examine its main tenets.

In 33 chapters, the Confession expounded all the leading articles of the Christian faith from an emphatically Calvinistic perspective, although it recognized freedom of the will and 'the liberty or contingency of second causes' in the divine decrees. On the ground of justification it declared:

> Those whom God effectually calleth He also freely justifieth; not by infusing righteousness into them, but by pardoning their sins, and by accounting and accepting their persons as righteous; not for anything wrought in them, or done by them, but for Christ's sake alone; not by imputing faith itself, the act of believing, or any other evangelical obedience, to them as their righteousness; but by imputing the obedience and satisfaction of Christ unto them, they receiving and resting on Him and His righteousness by faith; which faith they have not of themselves; it is the gift of God.[22]

The drafters of the Confession reflected in their Confession the Puritan 'covenant theology'. They defined the gospel as declaring:

> the Covenant of Grace; whereby [God] freely offereth unto sinners life and salvation by Jesus Christ, requiring of them faith in him, that they may be saved; and promising to give unto all those that are ordained unto life his Holy Spirit, to make them willing and able to believe.[23]

And it is constantly stressed that the conversion of a sinner is a gracious sovereign work of divine power:

> All those whom God hath predestinated unto life, and those only he is pleased, in his appointed and accepted time, effectually to call, by his Word and Spirit, out of that state of sin and death in which they are by nature, to grace and salvation by Jesus Christ.[24]

The Confession addressed the question of antinomianism, and stressed that the moral law still binds believers, as expressing God's will for his adopted children, and that the Father-son relationship with believers is spoiled if his will is ignored or defied:

> God doth continue to forgive the sins of those that are justified: and although they can never fall from the state of justification, yet they may by their sins fall under God's fatherly displeasure, and not have the light of His countenance restored unto them, until they humble themselves, confess their sins, beg pardon, and renew their faith and repentance.[25]

The Confession upheld the distinction between the visible and the invisible church. However, the strong emphasis upon predestination lead naturally to the concept of a gathered church which, at least in the eyes of the formulators of the Westminster Confession and those of similar views, made the coincidence of the visible and the invisible more complete than, for instance, would be so with the church as expounded by Hooker.

In the Confession great stress was laid on the identification of the Jewish Sabbath with the Christian Sunday, and the consequent required observance of the Sabbath rest:

> As it is the law of nature that, in general, a due proportion of time be set apart for the worship of God; so, in his Word, by a positive, moral, and perpetual commandment binding all men in all ages, he hath particularly appointed one day in seven, for a Sabbath, to be kept holy unto him: which, from the beginning of the world to the resurrection of Christ, was the last day of the week; and, from the resurrection of Christ, was changed into the first day of the week, which, in Scripture, is called the Lord's Day, and is to be continued to the end of the world, as the Christian Sabbath.[26]

As the Presbyterians dominated the Westminster Assembly, the Confession, together with the 'Larger' and the 'Shorter' Westminster Catechisms, which in essence were popular restatements of the teaching of the Confession, and the Directory of Public Worship, which was designed on Presbyterian principles, represented both an expression of a revived Presbyterianism and a boost to that revival.

For forty years English Presbyterianism had been a lost cause, which had been kept alive virtually single-handed, and at a distance, by John Paget, who had been pastor of the English Reformed Church in Amsterdam for thirty years from 1607. The dominance of Presbyterianism on the Parliamentary side in the early years of the Civil War was due to 'the fear of the Puritan clergy and the propertied laity of the anarchy that would follow any relaxation of ecclesiastical discipline, and to the necessity imposed on Parliament, by the plight of its arms, of seeking an alliance with the Scots'.[27]

The Directory of Public Worship was Presbyterian in that it did not prescribe a set liturgy, like the Book of Common Prayer, nor leave it entirely to the individual minister or congregation to regulate its own worship at will, as with the Independents and Quakers, but was a manual of general guidance. In any case, Puritan worship continued to focus to a considerable extent on preaching. The Puritan tradition in preaching had been created at the turn of the sixteenth and seventeenth centuries by people like William Perkins, Paul Baynes, Richard Sibbes, John Cotton, John Preston and Thomas Goodwin. What they had in common was a theological outlook, not a programme of ecclesiastical reform, for on that they were not agreed. Perkins and Baynes advocated the Presbyterianizing of the establishment on the lines previously championed by Cartwright; Cotton and Goodwin became Independents; Preston was a nonconforming Anglican; and Sibbes remained a conformist. Their Puritanism was of the deep Calvinistic type which I have previously described. Their principles in preaching were first formulated by Perkins in his *Arte of Prophecying*, but they found their most balanced expression in the Directory of Public Worship. So, in this respect, the Directory was not specifically Presbyterian but of relevance to Puritans as a whole.

What were these principles of preaching which the Presbyterian, Independent and other Puritans held in common? As preaching was at the heart of Puritanism in its various forms in the years I am reviewing, I will allow the Directory itself to delineate what its authors perceived as the correct spirit and manner in which preaching should be undertaken, before I turn our attention to the main rivals of the Presbyterians, the Independents:

> Preaching of the Word, being the power of God unto salvation, and one of the greatest and most excellent works belonging to the ministry of the gospel, should be so performed, that the workman may not be ashamed, but may save himself and those who hear him . . . The servant of Christ is to perform his whole ministry: 1. Painfully [ie, taking pains], not doing the work of the Lord negligently. 2. Plainly, that the meanest may understand; delivering the truth not in the enticing words of man's wisdom, but in demonstration of the Spirit and of power, lest the cross of Christ should be made of none effect; abstaining also from an unprofitable use of unknown tongues, strange phrases, and cadences of sounds and words; sparingly citing sentences of ecclesiastical or other human writers, ancient or modern, be they never so elegant. 3. Faithfully, looking at the honour of Christ, the conversion, edification, and salvation of the people, not at his own gain or glory; keeping nothing back which may promote these holy ends, giving to every one his own portion, and bearing indifferent [equal] respect to all, without neglecting the meanest, or sparing the greatest, in their sins. 4. Wisely, framing all his doctrines,

exhortations, and especially his reproofs, in such a manner as may be most likely to prevail; showing all due respect to each man's person and place, and not mixing his own passions or bitterness. 5. Gravely, as becometh the Word of God, shunning all such gesture, voice, and expression, as may occasion the corruptions of men to despise him and his ministry. 6. With loving affection, that the people may see all coming from his godly zeal, and hearty desire to do them good. 7. As taught by God, and persuaded in his own heart, that all he teacheth is the truth of Christ, and walking before his flock, as an example to them in it; earnestly, both in private and public, recommending his labours to the blessing of God, and watchfully looking to himself, and the flock whereof the Lord hath made him overseer. So shall the doctrine of truth be preserved incorrupt, many souls converted and built up, and himself receive manifold comforts of his labours even in his life, and afterward the crown of glory laid up for him in the world to come.[28]

The Independents and the Baptists

It is impossible to identify the 'Independents' with any precision, or to know in detail how those so identified related on the one hand to the Separatists who preceded them, and on the other hand to the Congregationalists who emerged in the 1640s. It seems legitimate to use the term to embrace both of these groups. They were at one 'in asserting the independence of the local congregation from any higher ecclesiastical authority'.[29] They believed in the gathered church of true believers, who were bound together by covenant, and they agreed in placing power in the hands of such Christians, rather than in giving authority over the church to any secular magistrate or other agent. All the members, it was claimed, being Christians, were 'priests unto God'.

Although the Presbyterians were the dominant religious group in the affairs of central government from 1640 to 1648, the machinery of the new Presbyterian system was not popular, and it had been established in only a few counties. Cromwell was concerned to evolve some order out of chaos. He was not concerned about dogmatic niceties, and it meant little or nothing to him whether a man was ordained episcopally, by the Presbyterian method or in no recognized official way. He was personally an Independent in the broad sense of the term. Nonetheless, with his overriding concern for tolerance and order, he maintained the established church, but in a much modified form. In the ministry of the state church he did not scruple to include Presbyterians, Independents and Baptists, and to accept non-royalist Anglicans, provided they did not use the Book of Common Prayer. At the same time, he resisted any tendency for one particular religious group to impose its will upon other Christians. In order to achieve these objectives, a general commission, the Triers, was set up in March 1654, based on London, for the approbation of ministers, to ascertain whether persons nominated by patrons were intellectually, morally and spiritually competent. But, once appointed, the new incumbent might organize his congregation on Presbyterian or Independent lines, if he gained their consent. Individuals who objected to the state church were at liberty to form separate congregations at their own discretion, provided 'they abuse not their liberty to the civil injury of others, and to the actual disturbance of the public peace'.[30] Cromwell 'had come to believe that religious toleration was the most precious fruit of civil war and its retention was to be his constant preoccupation'.[31]

With the outbreak of Civil War and the abolition of the ecclesiastical courts, the Baptists, as well as the Presbyterians, and the Independents were given an opportunity for the free expression of their opinions. The censorship of the press, which Laud had exercised for many years, was also removed, in consequence of which there was a spate of pamphlets which discussed various issues, and especially the validity of infant baptism. Public disputation was also a feature of these years, and there were frequent open debates between Baptists and Quakers, as well as between Baptists and a variety of other opponents of their baptismal views. As a result there were not a few who were converted to Baptist opinions, including some men of standing. There were others, notably the poet John Milton and Colonel John Hutchinson, who appear to have accepted Baptist principles without committing themselves to the Baptist Church.

During the period of Presbyterian dominance Baptists were sharply attacked by the Presbyterian divines, and no Baptist was included in the Westminster Assembly of Divines. The Baptists were in fact so maligned that the Particular Baptists of seven London churches decided in 1644 to publish their first Confession of Faith, which created some surprise by its orthodoxy and moderation. This helped their cause, as did the fact that their power was growing in the army. It is true that the Independents were prominent in the army, but the 'use of the term "Independent" to designate the religious texture of the Army as distinct from the "Presbyterian" has obscured the fact that the New Model Army was largely recruited and officered from Baptists'.[32] At the outbreak of the Civil War they had ranged themselves on the side of Parliament and had joined the army in droves. Promotion was often rapid, with troopers sometimes becoming colonels or even generals. And Baptists in the army were commonly not afraid to make the prayer-meeting rather than the ale-house their favourite relaxation. They also declared their distinctive beliefs with boldness and with remarkable success.

There is evidence that in the 1640s and 1650s there was a growing sense of denominational coherence and exclusiveness among the Baptists, as well as among other bodies. Both the Particular and General Baptists demonstrated their distinctiveness by adopting the dramatic ritual of baptism by total immersion. Henceforth their opponents referred to them as Dippers as well as Anabaptists, and in doing so they did not generally distinguish between the General and the Particular Baptists. But in fact the differences, particularly over redemption, so outweighed common rites of church entry 'that co-operation, even friendly communication between the two sorts of Baptists, was practically impossible during the Revolution'.[33] The Particular Baptists outrightly condemned general redemption as heresy, whereas the General Baptists tended to consider that doctrine, rather than believers' baptism, as the foundation of their faith. In 1651 thirty General Baptist churches in the Midlands came together to draw up a confession of faith; and three years later General Baptist representatives from 'several parts of the nation' met in London in their first national assembly. In various parts of the British Isles representatives of the Particular Baptists met together in periodic 'general meetings' or associations throughout the 1650s. And these associations communicated with each other by personal contacts and by correspondence.

As the individual Baptist churches viewed themselves as gatherings of those whom the Lord had sanctified by his grace, and called out to be his chosen fellowship of believers, they understandably considered themselves to be an egalitarian, democratic and consensus society.[34] No distinction was made between clergy and laity, and in the vast majority of Baptist congregations the ruling ministry consisted of lay elders supported by deacons, with elders chosen by the congregation and then ordained by their fellow elders. The typical congregation consisted mainly of small craftsmen and tradesmen of the 'middling sort', such as weavers, shoemakers, tailors, ironmongers, bakers, glovers and button-makers, with a far more limited number of prosperous bourgeoisie, radical gentry and members of the 'professions'. By 1660 there were more than 250 such churches, about 60% of which were Particular Baptist, although there is some evidence that the General Baptist congregations were usually larger. The total Baptist strength may generously be estimated as 25,000, in congregations which ranged in size from 18 to 261.

The Independents had neither the regional associations of the Particular Baptists nor a national gathering to compare with that of the General Baptists, until, in 1658, representatives from over a hundred Congregational churches met at the Savoy palace in London. During the Interregnum, before 1658, it seems that there was a complicated nexus of ties by which Congregational churches 'exchanged advice on, and gave approbation to, the drawing up of church covenants, practised intercommunion and gave and received the right hand of fellowship, sent representatives to each others' churches on the ordination of pastors, and transferred members from one church to another'.[35] The individual churches were often small gatherings. 'Those who formed the church at Broadmead, Bristol, numbered five; those who signed the first covenant at Bury St Edmunds numbered eight, and those who two years later signed a second covenant numbered ten; at Cockermouth there were seven signatories; at Axminster about a dozen.'[36] Even if these early churches were generally small, they were also numerous and widely scattered, and there was characteristically a great sense among them of the divine initiative and call to holiness and evangelism.

The Independents also had one of the most distinguished Christian thinkers and leaders of the age in the person of John Owen. Owen was born in 1616. He entered The Queen's College, Oxford, at the age of twelve, and he took his MA in 1635. He experienced a spiritual struggle in his early twenties, from which he emerged with the kind of lively faith and trust which typified the Puritans of his day. In 1637 he left the university as a result of conscientious objections to Chancellor Laud's statutes. After Laud's fall, under the Long Parliament, he rose rapidly. In 1651 he was made Dean of Christ Church, and the following year he became Vice-Chancellor of the university. After use as the headquarters for the Royalists during the Civil War, the university had been left bankrupt and in chaos, and Owen reorganized it with conspicuous success. During the bitter years of persecution after the Restoration, he led the Independents, and remained in the country to fulfil this task despite the offer of the presidency of Harvard, and during years of suffering from asthma and gallstones. He was 'one of the greatest of all English theologians',[37] and has been widely regarded as 'the prince of the Puritans. At every point he speaks for the entire school of Puritan pastoral theologians, differing from others only in the weight and wisdom with which he formulates their common certainties'.[38]

Owen placed considerable emphasis in his teaching upon the kingdom of God, but he constantly stressed that this was essentially a spiritual concept, not a political one, and he would have nothing to do with the teaching of the Fifth Monarchists and others who sought to prepare the way for an approaching millennium by political measures.

The Fifth Monarchists, the Levellers and the Diggers

The groups about to be considered well illustrate the sociological characteristics of sects which were delineated in the Introduction. Here we will encounter the intense, personal religious experience, the centrality of the charismatic figure, the absence of structure and organization and the formal definition of beliefs, the radicalism and rejection of the worldly standards around them combined with a sense of the distinctiveness and exclusiveness of their own beliefs and moral stance, which have always and everywhere distinguished sects from other corporate religious bodies. Although it is, once more, part of that theme of development from sect, via denomination, to church, in all these cases bar one, the process stopped short at the sect stage.

We can identify a chronology for the main radical sects. The Levellers dominated the 1640s, to be replaced by the Fifth Monarchists of the early 1650s, until they were eclipsed in the mid-1650s by the Quakers. The Diggers came briefly into the scene in 1659–60.

But before we consider the Fifth Monarchists, the Levellers, the Diggers and a number of the other sects which in their different ways were expressions of the reforming and radical ideas which flourished in the ideal climate of the 1640s and 1650s, it is well that we attempt to place them in a wide religious context.[39] People in seventeenth-century England were still very much aware of the spiritual, and one might also say, the magical dimension of life. God and the devil were reckoned to intervene daily and in detail in their lives, and witches, fairies and charms were present realities to most of the population. In the long run Protestantism worked against magic in its various guises and manifestations, but the process was not so well advanced by the 1640s that ordinary men and women were freed from either a magical outlook or deep-seated superstition. Even so, 'most orthodox members of the Church of England assumed that the Reformation had brought an end to miracles', but 'they were less certain about the status of religious prophecy'.[40] Indeed, it has been argued that the 'Reformation for all its hostility to magic, had stimulated the spirit of prophecy. The abolition of mediators, the stress on the individual conscience, left God speaking direct to his elect. It was incumbent on them to make public his message.'[41] The Reformation also made the scriptures generally accessible, and drew greater attention than in former times to the prophetic parts of Daniel and Revelation; and this, together with the encouragement given by Puritan preachers to eschatology, cultivated a widespread and intense interest in millenarianism. Such interest operated at different levels; at the popular level in the often highly-charged atmosphere of the local congregation, and at the scholarly level, whereby Milton could speak of Christ as 'shortly-expected King'.[42]

With the onset of Civil War there was a multiplication of messianic figures. Roland (or Reynold) Bateman, a labourer, was imprisoned in London in 1644 after his declaration that he was Abel the Righteous, who had been slain and had risen again. William Franklin, a London ropemaker, attracted many followers when he claimed to be the messiah, but was crestfallen when he was brought before the Winchester assizes in 1650, and recanted. Other episodes in the same tradition included the unsuccessful attempt by three Newbury Anabaptists to ascend to heaven in 1647; a claim by Thomas Tany to be God's high priest, who had been sent to gather in the Jews; a claim by Mary Adams, that she had conceived a child by the Holy Ghost; the appearance of a number of other would-be messiahs; and the crucifiction of an elderly woman at Pocklington by a couple who, it was said, had persuaded her that she would rise again on the third day. In addition, there were many people who boasted of direct revelation from heaven, among whom the most well-known was the self-styled prophet Lady Eleanor Davis (or Douglas), the daughter of the Earl of Castlehaven, who first married Sir John Davis and then Sir Archibald Douglas, and who for a period of twenty-seven years 'had a continuous career of prophetic utterances, interrupted only by consequential periods of imprisonment'.[43] It is of note that women were to the fore in this surge of religious prophecy. It is of more significance that the overwhelming majority of those who laid claim to divine inspiration as the source of their utterances were seeking authority for a political or social programme. The two most prominent examples of the association of prophecy with radicalism were the Fifth Monarchists and the Levellers.

'It is difficult to exaggerate the extent and strength of millenarian expectations among ordinary people in the 1640s and early 50s.'[44] Why this should have been so during the Interregnum is difficult to say, although it may well have been associated with the apocalyptic sense generated by an awareness of living in a time of unprecedented political change and uncertainty. Perhaps the casting down of such bastions of the old order as bishops, the House of Lords, monarchy, and Parliament itself, and the general disruption of the age, led many people to think that they might be experiencing the upheavals foretold in scripture which were said to herald the world's end or its transformation.[45] The vision of England remoulded in the biblical pattern was common to all millenarians of that period, but the scriptural concept was sufficiently vague and flexible to allow for a variety of interpretations and hopes. The New Jerusalem might essentially be an ordered moral common-wealth; it could be a Geneva writ large; it could stand for a social revolution; or it might imply an arcadian world of peace and plenty. And it was even more complex than this. 'The cheap tracts, newspapers, and almanacs which popularized millennial ideas brought still greater diversity by incorporating astrological predictions and other prophetic material from the Roman sibyls to Merlin and Mother Shipton. In some popular writings there was little distinction between the millennium and the golden age, or between Antichrist and the Norman Yoke.'[46] And this millenarianism was to be found at the top and centre of society as well as among the lower socio-economic strata. 'Cromwell's letters and speeches are suffused with scriptural allusions to the millennium.'[47] The millenarian exhilaration and sense of triumphant expectation coloured the Baptists, Congregationalists, Ranters, Diggers and Quakers, but it most markedly enthused the Fifth Monarchists.

This activist group was fired by the prospect that the Four Monarchies of Daniel's vision (Babylon, Persia, Greece and Rome) might now be followed by the rule of the saints. In order to attain the millennium, this association of preachers, soldiers and urban lower classes, with, it seems, a particular concentration of cloth workers, was prepared to resort to political action and, in the case of a minority, even violence. The rule of the saints was to be marked by the abolition of tithes, reform of the law, the raising of the humble, and the pulling down of the great. There would be no painful labour, no premature death, no famine: 'there is no creature comfort, no outward blessing, which the saints shall then want'.[48] In the millennium political power would be assumed by Christ. But the Fifth Monarchists had a clear present political agenda and, as an instance of this, were strongly in favour of war with the Dutch, possibly, as one of their leading preachers said, because the Dutch tolerated Arminianism and allowed Henrietta Maria to import arms to England during the Civil War, but also, no doubt, because it suited the economic interest of the high proportion of their most influential members who were small traders and craftsmen. Fifth Monarchism was a pressure group rather than a religious sect, despite its millennialism, and as such it drew support from a variety of Congregationalist and Baptist churches.[49] The Levellers were even more active in the political and social affairs of their time than the Fifth Monarchists.

It was Cromwell and his son-in-law Henry Ireton who, in 1648, came into conflict with a group of men on whom they bestowed the name of 'Leveller'. Those so named consistently repudiated the title with its implication of seeking to reduce all men to a common plane. But they did constitute the left wing of the Parliamentary forces in the Civil War. They represented those artisans and small masters who felt that their economic situation was threatened by the growth of monopolies, dis-contented or apprehensive soldiers, and sectaries who were fearful that Parliament might attempt to curtail their liberty after the freedom of the Civil War. And they had a radical list of demands, which included 'an extension of the franchise, at very least to all men who were not servants, wage-earners, or in receipt of poor relief; a more equitable division of Parliamentary constituencies; the removal from Parliament's jurisdiction of power to compel men's religion or to impress them to serve in the armed forces; the replacement of the excise by a propor-tionate tax on property; the abolition of tithes and monopolies; and the end of imprisonment for debt and of capital punishment for any crime except murder'.[50]

Although the Levellers were largely intent upon political change they did have a religious aspect as they frequently claimed to derive their political, economic and social beliefs from what they understood as general biblical principles, and they are most relevant to the upsurge of more specifically religious sects at that time. There were three leading Leveller propagandists, John Lilburne, Richard Overton and William Walwyn, of whom the first two were at some time members of Separatist churches and the latter was an eloquent advocate of tolera-tion for Separatists. They, like the Levellers as a whole, believed that the essential points of religion were simple and within the grasp of all men. People could discover for themselves all they needed to know. They did not need to depend on the teaching of the clergy or the judgments of learned men. And what was true of religion was likewise true of the laws of the land, which should be translated into English, reduced in number and simplified, with the legal proceedings made easier, so that ordinary people would be able to understand them, and would be in a position to conduct their own cases.

The Levellers held that the foundation of true religion was 'doing good'. It was radical indeed, in the midst of the dominant Puritanism of the age, with its emphasis upon doctrine, to attach greater value to works than to faith, and thus to stress human effort and the capacity of men to choose to do good. It has been called 'Arminianism of the left', as it involved the rejection of the prevailing Calvinism of the Parliamentary party, but also rejection of the 'Arminianism of the right', which assumed that salvation was possible only through the church and its ceremonies.[51] The religious beliefs of the Levellers were linked to political action by the 'golden rule', 'to do unto others as you would have them do unto you'. It was, for example, central to Lilburne's personal religious experience. It made them profoundly distressed at the plight of the poor. They were indignant about the extremes of wealth and poverty, and blamed the rich for the state of the poor, and indeed for the existence and continuance of poverty, which they pronounced to be the greatest evil of their society. But their condemnations remained somewhat generalized and theoretical, as they did not set forth any comprehensive practical programme for the amelioration, let alone the elimination of poverty. They looked mainly to a change of heart on the part of the rich, and conversion to what they declared to be the true religion of 'practical Christianity' as the only way to solve the problem of poverty. 'The religion of the leaders of the Levellers led them to be sympathetic towards the poor, but it did not provide them with an ideology of social change. It operated within the traditional notions of good neighbourliness held by the people they represented – the small producers (craftsmen and peasants). There was a tension between their concern for the poor and their position as representatives of the small property owners. They defended private property and accepted inequalities of wealth. They could not advocate confiscation of property or compulsory redistribution of wealth and so confined their hope for the abolition of poverty to urging the rich to give voluntarily more of their wealth to the poor.'[52]

Of central importance in the Leveller programme was the demand for religious liberty. They believed that each individual should be free to hold whatever religious opinions his reason convinced him were true and to worship God in the way his conscience told him was right. This did not mean unlimited freedom for the individual, for the distinction was made between 'things natural', which came under the jurisdiction of the civil government, and 'things supernatural', which came under the jurisdiction only of God. The exact dividing line between the two became the main issue of debate between the Levellers and those in authority. In the exposition of their concept of liberty, and in their critique of society, they avoided exclusive dependence on religion by adopting and developing the myth of the Norman Yoke.

Another group, the Diggers, called themselves the True Levellers. Their history is closely bound up with the personal history of Gerrard Winstanley. Born in 1609, Winstanley was a Lancashire man, the son of a mercer who, it seems, was on the edge of the gentry class. His parents had, before his birth, been in some trouble with the local church authorities for attending conventicles. He was apprenticed to a London merchant-tailor, and he may thereafter have been a tradesman or merchant for a time. In about 1643 he moved to Surrey where his wife's family had property, and he was apparently reduced to being a herdsman for them or someone else. Then came the few concentrated years from 1648 to 1652, that is from the time of the second Civil War to the last years of the Commonwealth under the rule of the Rump Parliament, when, with his writings and activities, almost 'everything of any consequence connected with him belongs'.[53]

From his earliest published works Winstanley was consistent and distinctive in what he taught. He accepted that the world and the human race were created by God, but his use of biblical texts was loose, and often symbolic, figurative or metaphorical. He believed in the Fall, but interpreted it not as some kind of a genetic defect, but as the defeat of good by evil, which is repeated in all people, or at least all adults. Few people have won the battle, but with the help of Jesus Christ and the Holy Spirit within, the potential for victory is there for all human beings. He rejected the concept of a chosen, preordained elect who alone would be saved, but proclaimed the hope of universal salvation, 'in which the poor, the humble, and the downtrodden might well lead the way'.[54] Winstanley used millenarian images and well-chosen scriptural texts to convey his sense of immediacy, urgency and crisis. He was vehemently and unwaveringly anticlerical. He was opposed to any form of ecclesiastical organization and to academic systems or institutions of any kind, although he was not anti-intellectual. He declared the 'saints' to be those individuals in whom the Beast had been overthrown, and they were pathfinders or examples set before us. His most revolutionary concept was 'that of the earth as a "common treasury" for all mankind, a passionate conviction that private ownership and inheritance, the payment of rent, the buying and selling of the land and its products, and the system of hired labour must all be brought to an end in the process of spiritual regeneration and self-fulfilment within individuals'.[55]

Winstanley was convinced that to him had been revealed the time, place and means whereby he and a few others were to demonstrate what his beliefs meant in practice. The time was 1 April 1649, the place was the common at St George's Hill in the parish of Walton-on-Thames, and the means was to dig, manure and plant for the good of all. The number of Diggers grew, although it never reached more than forty or fifty. Despite some fear that such activity represented a threat to property and the social order, no decisive action was taken by the army or the central government to curtail the demonstration. But the local landlords, and possibly some lesser freeholders also, began to use force against them. They embarked on a campaign of sustained and systematic harassment. They trampled down the crops and drove off the Diggers' animals; they pulled down their huts and severely beat individuals. They were aided by some of the infantry soldiers stationed locally who behaved with needless brutality, but seemingly on orders from headquarters. The Diggers moved their main site to another common in the neighbouring parish of Cobham. Other groups appeared in Northamptonshire and Buckinghamshire.

Until the 1970s Winstanley was either perceived as a forerunner of nineteenth and twentieth-century socialism, with little importance being attached to his theology, or he was regarded primarily as a religious thinker whose communistic ideas arose out of a mystical experience and the study of the Bible, and whose digging was symbolic rather than political. Christopher Hill suggests that 'the Norman Yoke, radical theology and his theory of communism came to be indissolubly linked'; and that he was 'groping his way towards a humanist and materialist philosophy, in which there were no outward Saviours, no heaven or hell or afterlife, but only men and women living in society'. But other views of the theology, and, indeed, of the very identification, of Gerrard Winstanley, have subsequentyly been voiced.[56]

The Muggletonians, the Family of Love, the Grindletonians, the Ranters and the Seekers

The millenarian ideal of a 'godly reformation' was most commonly and variously expressed in religious terms, rather than in quasi-religious, but largely political or social terms, as in the sects we have just been considering. And there was an astounding proliferation of millenarian sects in the 1640s and 1650s. I will take a few of them to illustrate something of the religious climate, and its often bizarre expression, in these unique years of religious activity in England. All of them are different in what they taught and in the life-style which resulted from such teaching, but they have in common the belief that God works through the individual. Although the Protestant Reformation had challenged the long established Catholic notion that the interpretation of the word of God in the Bible was the preserve of the priesthood, the radical religious sects of the mid-seventeenth century took the further step of claiming that 'a poor plain countryman by the spirit which he hath received, is better able to judge of truth and error touching the things of God than the greatest philosopher, scholar or doctor in the world that is destitute of it'.[57] The inner spirit of the individual was of prime importance, so there was no place for a national, uniform church imposed on the individual by the state, and such an emphasis also required a drastic reduction in the power of the clergy over the individual, if not its elimination altogether. In response to the argument that the individual interpretation of the scriptures and congregational autonomy would lead to religious anarchy, the religious radicals were able to retort that the inner light is one, and that it can be recognized by the children of light. John Milton, in his *Areopagitica* assumed that, given freedom of debate, then sooner or later men's reason must naturally lead them to recognize the same truths. This is not to say that the various sects we are now to consider were not frequently in strong competition to win the hearts and minds of the people of England.

'The Fifth Monarchy men were the political zealots of Puritanism, but their extravagance appears sobriety compared with the obscurantist convictions of the Muggletonians, who nourished their faith out of the Apocalypse.'[58] Ludowicke Muggleton was a London tailor who became a dedicated Puritan much in fear of hell-fire, and punctilious about such matters as listening only to Puritan ministers with short-cut hair. In the year after the execution of the King he was greatly influenced by two men who claimed to be greater than the several prophets in London:

John Tannye, who declared himself the Lord's High Priest who was to gather the Jews out of all nations, and John Robins, who claimed to be God Almighty and to raise the prophets from the dead. Soon after this Muggleton and his cousin, John Reeve, began to have revelations of their own. In 1652 they announced that they were the two witnesses of Revelation 11 sent, they said, to seal the elect and the reprobate with the eternal seals of life and death, after which Jesus would appear in power and glory. They added, 'with an earnestness insensible to humour', that 'if any of the elect desire to speak with us . . . they may hear of us in Great Trinity Lane, at a Chandler's shop, against one Mr Millis, a Brown Baker, near the lower end of Bow Lane'.[59] The way they spoke with the utmost self-confidence, and with assurance pronounced curses against those who rejected them, enabled them to found a sect which became known in their day, and which apparently lingered into the nineteenth century.

When we come to the Ranters we are drawn into an historical debate of considerable duration and intensity. Until J. C. Davis stirred the pot, there was a generally accepted perception of what and who they were. They were seen as an identifiable group which gave supreme importance to personal revelation, and in fact represented in its most extreme expression the revolt against authority; they were on the far left wing of the sects which came into existence at that time, both theologically and politically.[60] What the inner spirit led people to think and to do overrode all considerations of law, conventional morality or religion. The Ranters believed that they were on the threshold of the third dispensation prophesied by the twelfth-century Cistercian abbot Joachim of Fiore, the Age of the Spirit in which men and women would be directly inspired by God and would attain perfection. The revolutionary events of the 1640s inspired them with a sense of liberation; they coupled this with a mystical pantheism, and took the teachings of the antinomians to what they regarded as their logical conclusions. The man who acknowledged the fact that God was in him could not sin. Lawrence Clarkson, who had reached a Ranter position after experiences of Presbyterianism, Independency and Anabaptism, said that there was 'no such act as drunkenness, adultery and theft in God . . . Sin hath its conception only in the imagination . . . What act soever is done by thee in light and love, is light and lovely, though it be that act called adultery . . . No matter what Scripture, saints or churches say, if that within thee do not condemn thee, thou shalt not be condemned.'[61]

According to the widely-accepted view, the Ranters, of whom the most clearly identifiable were Jacob Bauthumley, Joseph Salmon, Lawrence Clarkson and Abiezer Coppe, flourished for only two brief years, but in that time they confirmed the worst fears of those who had been incredulous at the earlier assurances that their doctrines would not lead to licentiousness. Between 1648 and 1650, in order to demonstrate that they were rid of sin, the Ranters proceeded shamelessly to flout the moral code of the Puritans. Clarkson went on a preaching tour of South-East England, and had brief sexual relations with a succession of women while counting it to his credit that he continued to give financial assistance to his wife; saying that 'only my body was given to other women'. Abiezer Coppe, a former Baptist, was reputed to spend much time 'in belching forth imprecations, curses and other such like stuff' and to lie 'in bed with two women at a time'. And a certain Thomas Webb, also a former Baptist, who in 1649 obtained the living of Langley Burrell in Wiltshire, was said to have a 'man wife' and to argue that a man could sleep with any woman except his mother.

The so-called Blasphemy Act of 1650 was occasioned by the activities of the Ranter prophets, and brought them to a speedy end. Only a tiny minority of those who embraced antinomian doctrines used their beliefs to justify indulgence in Ranter-like excesses; and the antinomian doctrines 'were not such as would inspire martyrs', so that 'a few months in prison were sufficient to dampen the ardour of the most fervent Ranter'.[62] Coppe recanted and returned to the Baptists, Webb was ejected from his rectory, Clarkson repudiated his Ranter beliefs and ended his days as a Muggletonian. But even if it was but a passing thing, like the much more famous and lastingly influential events at Munster over a century before, it left an indelible reminder of the dangers inherent in any movement which allowed the doctrine of the 'Free Spirit' to go unchecked.

But much of this reading of the history of the Ranters has been questioned, especially by J. C. Davis. In 1986, in *Fear, Myth and History: the Ranters and the Historians*, he argued that the Ranters 'were not so much a real religious movement, sect or group, made up of real men and women identifying themselves with particular beliefs and practices, but existed rather as a projection of the fears and anxieties of a broader society. They were closer to the image of "folk devils" projected in a "moral panic" which reached its climax in the wake of the revolution of 1648–9. That image was made up of mythic materials readily to hand and used in ways which were virtually traditional.'[63] The cat was among the academic pigeons. In short, Gerald Aylmer concludes that 'the burden of probability lies somewhere in between [Hill, who aligned himself with the prevailing pre-Davis view, and Davis], but nearer to Hill than to Davis'. J. F. McGregor concludes 'that there were advocates of practical antinomianism called "Ranters" in England during the Interregnum. The myth is Davis's own creation.'[64] Bernard Capp has decided that the 'Ranters were not a sect but a number of groups, some loosely linked, with related and alarming ideas on the nature of God and on sin', and their emergence 'galvanized the Rump into a rare display of speedy, determined and effective action'.[65] Others supported Davis, at least in his questioning of the use of the word 'Ranter' to refer to any specific group of radicals, as it was a title which was rejected by many of them, and 'its indiscriminate application by contemporaries and historians alike has led to widespread confusion'.[66] It is consistent with the evidence available to say that the term was applied to a disparate number of Sectarians, and not necessarily, but also not improbably, a coherent group which recognized itself as a distinctive and separate entity, or was perceived as such, who took antinomian theology, and the practices which accompanied it, to its limits. There were extremists of this type, and it is more important to recognize this than to argue over nomenclature.

And so we move on to yet another radical group which was active in the years of the Interregnum. The Familists, or Family of Love, traced their origins to the time of the Munster Anabaptists, and to Henry Nicholas. They believed that men and women might recapture on earth the state of innocence which had existed before the Fall. Nicholas had enunciated eight stages of religious development which, he said, could lead to a state of sinless perfection and mystical union with God:

> The true Light is the everlasting life itself and . . . shows itself through illuminated, i.e. *godded* men, for through such persons the Most High is *manned* [incarnated]. The true Light therefore consists not in knowing this or that, but in receiving and partaking of the true being of the Eternal Life, by the renewing of the mind and spirit and by an incorporation of the inward man into this true Life and Light so that the person henceforth lives and walks in the Light in all love.[67]

The Familists asserted that only the Spirit of God within the believer can properly understand scripture. And they largely turned the Bible into allegories. In the 1640s and 1650s they were greatly influenced by the availability in England of the translated works of continental mystics. They were radical in some of their social beliefs, and held their property in common.

Akin to the Familists were the Grindletonians, 'the only English sect which takes its name from a place rather than a person or a set of beliefs'.[68] The movement probably antedates Roger Brearley, curate of Grindleton in Yorkshire from 1615 to 1622, but he was important in its history. Their beliefs can be seen from some of the fifty charges brought against them in 1617:

> (1) a motion rising from the spirit is more to be rested in than the Word itself; (2) it is a sin to believe the Word . . . without a motion of the spirit; (3) the child of God in the power of grace doth perform every duty so well, that to ask pardon for failing in matter or manner is a sin; (7) the Christian assured can never commit a gross sin; (14) a soul sanctified must so aim at God's glory, as he must never think of salvation; (33) a man having the spirit may read, pray or preach without any other calling whatsoever; (38) neither the preacher nor they pray for the King . . . They know not whether he be elected or not; (46) they cannot have more joy in heaven than they have in this life by the spirit.[69]

Brearley spoke of mastering sin in order to set believers free from hell and death, and, as we have already seen, belief in the priority of the Spirit over the word of the Bible, denial of the relevance of ordination, the possibility of sinless living and of attaining heaven in this life were themes which were common among most of the sects of the twenty years from 1640 to 1660, and they were a grave challenge to traditional Calvinism.

The Grindletonians emerged before the Interregnum. They are mentioned in the context of the Interregnum sects because they were of a similar type to those sects which were to succeed them, and in a sense prefigured the later sects in their main characteristics.

With the multiplication of sects, controversies over church government and over baptism, a confusion of claims and counter claims about a host of matters, endless conscientious scruples and ceaseless bickerings, it is hardly surprising that there was widespread confusion, and 'that men and women, faced with an unprecedented freedom of choice, passed rapidly from sect to sect, trying all things, finding all of them wanting'.[70] All the leading protagonists for a variety of religious causes seemed equally certain of the truth for which they were contending, and all appeared to have authority and backing from the Bible or from the witness of the spirit within. In such a situation many people concluded by questioning the value of all ordinances, of all outward forms, and even of all churches or religious sects. And such an outlook was reinforced by the strong prevailing millenarianism: if the end of the world was probably near at hand, a resigned withdrawal from sectarian controversy appeared to be a valid solution in the religious quest, or, indeed, a rejection of all sects and all forms of organized religion. Those who adopted such a view were called Seekers. But they did not only represent a somewhat negative amalgam of disdain and disillusionment. They had at least some fixed points in the endless religious debates of their day. They asserted that the 'true church was defunct, all ordinances and rituals invalid. The sign of the visible church of Christ was its possession of the grace given to the apostles and demonstrated through miracles. Since none of the Puritan churches claimed such charismatic gifts the Seeker could only withdraw from them and patiently await a new divine dispensation.'[71]

William Erbery most ably and articulately championed the Seekers. He had been ejected from his living in Cardiff in 1638 for refusing to read the *Book of Sports*, and he was a convinced supporter of Parliament during the Civil War. He was an army chaplain, and was to the fore in criticizing Presbyterian ministers, tithes and persecution. He proclaimed that 'the fullness of the Godhead shall be manifested in the flesh of the saints', as in Christ's flesh. Christ 'is still suffering till he shall rise in us'. Men therefore should 'sit still, in submission and silence, waiting for the Lord to come and reveal himself to them'. 'And at last, yea within a little, we shall be led forth out of this confusion and Babylon, where we yet are, not clearly knowing truth nor error, day nor night: but in the evening there shall be light.'[72] The essence of the Seeker position was the belief that there had been such a corruption and destruction by the Church of Rome of the powers and authority granted to the apostles in the New Testament that no true church could be constituted until God raised up a new race of apostles. And for this Erbery and the other Seekers waited. They met together not to pray or to preach, but to wait in a silence which was only occasionally broken when 'anything arose in any of their minds, that they thought savoured of a divine spring'.[73] Like so many of that day and generation, the Seekers looked back to the first, exuberant, Spirit-filled Apostolic Age, when 'all was administered under the anointing of the Spirit, clearly, certainly, infallibly'. To be a Seeker was to have adopted a particular view and attitude of mind, rather than to have joined a recognizable radical group. Because this was so, the label 'Seeker' has been applied to such diverse individuals as the Leveller William Walwyn, the poet John Milton, and even Oliver Cromwell.[74] Many people went from the various sects to join the Seekers, including ministers. Thus, it was these 'Seekers or Waiters, who felt the insufficiency of the current doctrinal and external religion, and were not yet brought into a deeper soul-satisfying experience', who 'afforded the most receptive soil in England' for the message of George Fox.[75]

The beginnings of Quakerism

In the midst of the plethora of newly emergent sects, Quakerism arose as the only new religious group which stood the test of time and developed into a worldwide denomination. It sprang directly from the vital and vitalizing experience of its founder, George Fox.[76]

George Fox was born in July 1624, at Drayton-in-the-Clay in Leicestershire, the son of a weaver, and apparently godly parents. He was, according to his own account, serious and God-fearing in his youth, and his relations considered him a possible candidate for the priesthood. In fact he was apprenticed to a shoemaker. His piety and concern for a high standard of moral behaviour set him apart from his fellows, but he was not able to find a spiritual home in any particular church. In 1643 he began his solitary religious quest in earnest. In response to what he believed to be the command of God, he left his relations and friends and for four years he moved about from place to place, mostly shunning any intimate intercourse with either those who were indifferent or hostile to religion, or 'professors', that is those who declared themselves as of a particular religious persuasion. He discussed spiritual matters with a number of priests, but found them wanting in what they could offer. He then describes how he found light:

> And when all my hopes in them and in all men were gone, so that I had nothing outwardly to help me, nor could tell what to do, then, Oh then, I heard a voice which said, 'There is one, even Christ Jesus, that can speak to thy condition', and when I heard it my heart did leap for joy. Then the Lord did let me see why there was none upon the earth that could speak to my condition, namely, that I might give him all the glory; for all are concluded under sin, and shut up in unbelief as I had been, that Jesus Christ might have the pre-eminence, who enlightens, and gives grace, and faith, and power. Thus, when

God doth work who shall let [prevent] it ? And this I knew experimentally. My desires after the Lord grew stronger, and zeal in the pure knowledge of God and of Christ alone, without the help of any man, book, or writing. For though I read the Scriptures that spoke of Christ and of God, yet I knew him not but by revelation, as he who hath the key did open, and as the Father of life drew me to his Son by his spirit . . . I had not fellowship with any people, priests, or professors, nor any sort of separated people, but with Christ, who hath the key, and opened the door of light and life to me.[77]

Fox soon acquired a reputation as a young man with a discerning spirit. And he had what he describes as openings, and prophecies, so that he was able to speak to people who came to him 'of the things of God'. As he toured around Derbyshire, Leicestershire and Nottinghamshire he attracted some disciples, and there were the first meetings of 'Friends'. He emphasized, as he did in the account of his own awakening, 'that every man was enlightened by the divine light of Christ, and that they who believed came out of condemnation and came to the light of life and became the children of it'.[78] He saw himself as having been sent to turn people from darkness to the light that they might receive Christ Jesus.

In these early years of the Friends, Fox also records how, in his view, God forbade him to put off his hat to any, high or low; and how he was required to address all men and women as 'thee' and 'thou', without any respect for rich or poor, great or small. He was not to bid people 'good morrow' or 'good evening', nor was he to bow or scrape to any. He also boldly spoke and wrote to judges and justices to urge them to do justly, warned keepers of public houses not to allow over-drinking, and testified against wakes and feasts, May-games, sports, plays and shows, which, he thought, trained people to be vain and undisciplined, and led them from the fear of God. He spoke out at fairs and markets about deceitful trading, warning those concerned to deal justly, to speak the truth in simplicity and directness and to do unto others as they would have others do unto them. He forewarned them of the great and terrible Day of Judgment which would come upon all of them. He also cried out against all sorts of music, and against the stage. He suffered abuse many times, violence on occasions and quite frequent imprisonment. His account of a visit to Lichfield in 1651 captures the spirit of his extraordinary, charismatic personality, and the force of his fearless ministry:

. . . I came within a mile of Lichfield. When I came into a great field where there were shepherds keeping their sheep, I was commanded of the Lord to pull off my shoes of a sudden; and I stood still, and the word of the Lord was like a fire in me; and being winter, I untied my shoes and put them off; and when I had done I was commanded to give them to the shepherds . . . And the poor shepherds trembled and were astonished . . . as soon as I came within the town the word of the Lord came unto me again to cry, 'Woe unto the bloody city of Lichfield !'; so I went up and down the streets crying, 'Woe unto the bloody city of Lichfield !' Being market day I went into the market place and went up and down in several places of it and made stands, crying, 'Woe unto the bloody city of Lichfield !', and no one touched me nor laid hands on me. As I went down the town there ran like a channel of blood down the streets, and the market place was like a pool of blood . . . so when I had declared what was upon me and cleared myself, I came out of the town in peace about a mile to the shepherds: and there I went to them and took my shoes and gave them some money, but the fire of the Lord was so in my feet and all over me that I did not matter to put my shoes on any more and was at a stand whether I should or no till I felt freedom from the Lord to do so.[79]

In a public ministry which spanned more than forty years, Fox's missionary journeys, in which he tried to convince all the people that he heralded a new apostolic dispensation, were to take him five times round England, to Wales, Scotland, Ireland, the Netherlands, Germany and America, and to nine different prisons. He lived simply, wearing plain leather breeches and white hat, and wore his hair long, much to the disgust of the Puritans. He was temperate, eating and sleeping little. He was almost totally lacking in humour, and he often used violent, and sometimes vulgar, language in order to lambast his opponents. But, with his outstanding personal qualities, his powerful voice, and his singleness of purpose, he achieved much, even by the end of the Interregnum.

In the early years, as throughout his ministry, Fox stressed that which he had experienced himself, and which he believed was lacking in the teaching of the various Christian groups in the country. Of central importance was his 'great affirmation that every man had received from the Lord a measure of light which, if followed, would lead him to the Light of Life'.[80] This was in conflict with the current Puritan conceptions of the nature of God and of human nature, and the dealings of God with man. The doctrines of election and reprobation were to the fore in Puritanism, the line was drawn sharply between the human and the divine, and there was little emphasis on doctrines which related to the universal Fatherhood of God. The 'opening' which came to Fox resulted in a different focus, as he declared

> . . . that every man was enlightened by the divine light of Christ, and I saw it shine through all, and that they that believed in it came out of condemnation and came to the light of life, and became the children of it; but they that hated it, and did not believe in it, were condemned by it, though they made a profession of Christ. This I saw in the pure openings of the Light, without the help of any man, neither did I then know where to find it in the Scriptures, though afterwards, searching the Scriptures, I found it.[81]

Fox saw his mission largely in terms of light. He regarded himself as sent to turn people from darkness to the light that they might receive Christ. He also saw that mission in terms of the Spirit, for he considered himself charged with the task of directing people 'to the Spirit that gave forth the Scriptures, by which they might be led into all Truth, and so up to Christ and God, as they had been who gave them forth'.[82] And he regarded himself as sent to turn people to the grace of God which was open to all mankind. He declared that he 'was to bring people off from all the world's religions, which are vain, that they might know the pure religion'.[83]

Fox found the most fruitful soil for his message in the various communities of Baptists and Seekers dispersed throughout the land. For example, very early on he encountered a long-established Baptist community in Nottingham which, before he arrived, 'had lost its spiritual life and become scattered and broken'.[84] He was attracted to them, and found them a 'tender people'. They seem to have accepted his message, and they formed a new association together under the appropriate name of 'Children of the Light'. It was the earliest name by which the Friends were known.

In June 1652 an important move forward for the new movement was made in Westmorland:

> This crowded fortnight was the creative moment in the history of Quakerism. In the freshness of his powers and of his experience Fox had a living message, which he uttered with prophetic authority,

and both the message and the prophetic messenger answered the yearnings and the hopes of a strong community of earnest-hearted Seekers. Under the influence of half-a-dozen powerful meetings and of the personal intercourse with Fox enjoyed by his hosts and their friends, a great company was gathered in. Many of these became the heroic pioneers of the new movement, overcoming the buffetings of opposers and persecutors by their invincible faith . . . It is evident that the accession to Quakerism of this vigorous community of Seekers greatly enriched the intellectual and spiritual forces of the movement, and made possible its further extension on a large scale.[85]

It was also in 1652 that Swarthmore Hall, near Ulverston, with its fervent mistress, Margaret Fell, who was to become Fox's wife, and its large-hearted master, Judge Thomas Fell, first assumed a significant place in the movement. It soon became both a shelter and a family-hearth for Quakerism. Margaret and some of the household received Fox as almost a new messiah, although Judge Fell was more sanguine in his reactions. These developments helped to make the northern counties the prime centre of strength for Quakerism in these early formative years. During the 1650s, the movement also spread to the south of England and made inroads into Scotland, Wales and Ireland.

The life and practice of the new communities was characterized by intensity of conviction and separation from other religious groups, features which were common in other sects of the time. The claims of the Inward Light resulted in a separation from all that was outward in religion, and no place was found for such ceremonies as baptism and the Lord's Supper. In this incipient stage of Quakerism the stress was laid upon securing times of religious fellowship and efficient spiritual leadership. Typically, the local group met once or more a week, and there was a General Meeting for Friends in the district once in two or three weeks. In addition to Fox, other leaders in these first few years included Richard Farnsworth, William Dewsbury and James Nayler. These apostles of the movement were supplemented by a band of what became known as Publishers of Truth, who also exercised leadership according to their gifts.

In this first period the fellowship experienced internal difficulties which were also similar to those in other sects. In 1652 the infant community in Furness was seriously compromised by one of its members, James Milner, a tailor, who, after a fourteen days' fast, uttered various prophesies, including the prediction that Wednesday 1 December would be the Day of Judgment, and Thursday 2 December would be the first day of the new creation, when a four-cornered sheet would come down from heaven with a sheep in it. A number of Friends went about naked or in sackcloth on occasions, to signify spiritual or moral nakedness, or impending doom. A certain William Simpson went for some time naked and in sackcloth as a sign to the priests that God would strip them of their power, and that they should be stripped of their benefices. Such conduct was initially condoned by Fox, although it was soon disowned by him and the other Quaker leaders.

The outstanding example of bizarre behaviour, and the most public scandal for the nascent movement, was the outlandish conduct of James Nayler.[86] Nayler had served with some distinction in the Parliamentary army, in which he was noted as an Independent preacher. He became a convinced Quaker in 1651 as a direct result of the ministry of Fox, and from the outset he was second only to Fox in the leadership of the movement. In 1652 he preached widely in the north of England and was imprisoned at Appleby. From mid-1655 to mid-1656 he was in sole charge of the flourishing London Society. About that time he came under the influence of a group of Ranters led by a certain Martha Simmonds. Soon they were regarding his Inner Light as indicative of absolute unity with God, and they tried to worship him as Christ. In the late summer of 1656 he was imprisoned in Exeter gaol. On the eve of his release in October of the same year, he received a letter from a fellow Quaker, Hannah Stranger, styling him 'the fairest of ten thousand' and 'only begotten Son of God', with a postscript from her husband John, a London comb-maker, which contained the words, 'Thy name shall be no more James Nayler, but Jesus.' Nayler afterwards confessed that the letter struck him with fear, but he put it in his pocket intending no one to see it, as he repudiated its contents.

Released from prison, Nayler set out with a company of Friends for London. As the party approached Bristol a young man led Nayler's horse, another walked in front, two men followed on horseback, each with a woman behind him, and some of the party walked on the raised causeway. As they went along, they sang 'Holy, holy, holy, Lord God of Sabbaoth'. It was between two and three in the afternoon, it was raining heavily, and two women, who by now were leading Nayler's horse, had to plough their way through the mud, but they trudged along, singing 'Holy, holy, holy, Lord God of Israel', and the women spread their garments before Nayler. So the sorry procession made its way to Broad Street, followed by a crowd, for much of the city was aroused by the strange spectacle. When they were soon afterwards summoned before the magistrates, they were still singing 'Holy, holy, holy'. All were clapped into prison.

The case was examined by a Committee of the second Protectorate Parliament and then referred to Parliament. A proposal to bring in a Bill to provide a death penalty for Nayler's offence was defeated by a narrow margin, but the punishment inflicted upon him was savage enough. He was pilloried, whipped through the streets, had his tongue bored through with a hot iron and his forehead branded with the letter B. He was taken to Bristol, where he was carried through the city on horseback, bare-ridged, with his face backwards, and was whipped on the market-day. And, lastly, he was imprisoned in Bridewell, in solitary confinement, with hard labour, without the use of pen, ink and paper, until Parliament agreed to release him.

Perhaps the happiest sequel to this whole unfortunate affair was Nayler's repentance:

> . . . with what strength of mind, when the delusion he had fallen into, which they stigmatized for blasphemy, had given way to clearer thoughts, he could renounce his error, in a strain of beautifullest humility, yet keep his first grounds, and be a Quaker still! – so different from the practice of your common converts from enthusiasm, who, when they apostatize, *apostatize all*, and think they can never get far enough from the society of their former errors, even to the renunciation of some saving truths, with which they had been mingled, not implicated.[87]

Nayler was released from prison by the Long Parliament in 1657. And his story has a reasonably happy ending. For he was not only repentant, and restored to his former beliefs, but he regained acceptance, and indeed popularity, among the Friends and, after four years of estrangement, he found reconciliation with Fox.

Some Quakers made the ultimate sacrifice for what they regarded as the true Quaker witness. The 1650s saw the first of the Quaker martyrs. In 1656 a young man named James Parnell died as a consequence of the harsh treatment he endured in prison; and the barbarous exposure for seventeen hours in the stocks, without the provision of a seat, on a freezing November night in 1657, occasioned the sickness and death of Margaret Newby. Violence and suffering at the hands of the mob or the authorities became the common lot of the leaders of the movement and of the Publishers of Truth.

But the movement flourished; and its early success was impressive. Within a decade there were certainly 35,000 to 40,000 Quakers, including men, women and children.[88] It seems that the new sect mainly drew its membership from the by now familiar middling sort of people, such as wholesale and retail traders, artisans, yeomen and husbandmen.

Quakerism was devoid of any coherent and identifiable political philosophy, but it was regarded with apprehension by those in authority. Edward Butler, Member of Parliament for Poole, fervently believed that Quaker 'principles and practices are diametrically opposite both to magistracy and ministry; such principles as will level the foundation of all government into a bog of confusion'.[89] Throughout the ensuing centuries this gloomy prediction was not fulfilled, but in the fullness of time the Quakers were to exercise a quite remarkable social, and indeed political, influence.

The Church of England 1642 to 1660

The Church of England survived the Interregnum, despite the abolition of episcopacy, the banning of the Book of Common Prayer, and the chaos of sects, and in spite of widespread and often fierce antagonism directed against it. The loyal Church of England divines throughout these years were stigmatized as 'Prayer Book men' by their opponents and the authorities. Although the Book of Common Prayer was banned it supplied the 'prayers' in many churches, and several churches were able to continue Common Prayer services.

'In 1641, when the English Parliament began to dismantle the regime of Charles I, the most systematic and ferocious attack was not upon the political and legal agents of Stuart tyranny, but upon the Church of England.'[90] At first the Parliamentarians were enthusiastic to reform the church, but this soon gave way to ad hoc purges of the clergy, and to the piecemeal demolition of what was increasingly regarded as a largely irrelevant institution.[91] Between 1641 and 1646 Laudian doctrinal, governmental, disciplinary and liturgical innovations were overturned, and ecclesiastical jurisdiction was emasculated by the Acts abolishing the Court of High Commission, and excluding those in holy orders from holding secular offices. Orders were issued for the reversal of recent radical changes in church furnishing, which included most notably an abandonment of the railing of altars. Bishops were imprisoned, exiled or had retired, and the last consecration of a bishop took place in 1644. Laud went to the scaffold in January 1645. Then the execution of

Charles seemed to be the final act to signify the end of the Church of England: by the inexorable march of events it seemed that it had come to 'No King, no Bishops'. The outlook was gloomy. 'With Charles died any hope that the Church of England, in however attenuated a form, might be negotiated back into existence; "the church here will never rise again, though the kingdom should", concluded William Sancroft. In less than a decade the Church of England had been deprived of her nursing father the King, her bishops, her liturgy, her cathedrals and chapters, her courts and her revenues.'[92] As we have seen, the Prayer Book was abolished and replaced in 1645 by the Directory of Public Worship; and in the same year the doctrinal formularies of the Church of England were abrogated, and no replacement definition of orthodoxy was ever forthcoming, as the Large Catechism, small one, and Confession of Faith of the Westminster Assembly were never approved by the Houses and thus never published by authority. There was an attack on the Anglican calendar, which was later augmented by a comprehensive ordinance which banned the observance of Christmas, Easter, Whit, Holy Days and Saints Days and the perambulations of parish bounds at Rogationtide. It was a devastating assault. It left the parish system with such traditional officers as churchwardens and overseers, select and general vestries, lay impropriation, and the responsibility of all to pay tithes; and nothing was expressly done to challenge the basis of the Elizabethan Acts of Supremacy and Uniformity. But the damage inflicted was severe. In 1641 pro-bishop petitions flooded into Parliament, and this stiffened the opposition of Members of Parliament to root and branch reform. Nonetheless, the position was dire for the previous national church.

Despite the unprecedented severity of the attack upon the Church of England as an established church, the parish and the parochial ministry survived. But, if Richard Baxter's account is to be believed, it was a precarious situation, and the quality of the clergy remaining was not high. 'For you must understand,' he explained,

> that when the Parliament purged the ministry, they cast out the grosser sort of insufficient and scandalous ones, as gross drunkards, and such like; and also some few civil men that had assisted in the wars against the Parliament, or set up bowing to altars, and such innovations: but they had left in near one half the ministers, that were not good enough to do much service, nor bad enough to be cast out as utterly intolerable: these were a company of poor weak preachers,

that had no great skill in divinity, nor zeal for godliness; but preached weakly that which is true, and lived in no gross notorious sin: these men were not cast out, but yet their people greatly needed help; for their dark sleepy preaching did but little good.[93]

Be that as it may, the parochial structure did weather the storms of the Civil War and the Interregnum and that was to a large extent due to the protection of the landed classes. There had been an increase over many years in the authority exercised by the local gentry over the parishes of the land, their officers and their affairs as a whole, and this was reinforced during the 1640s. In the 1650s they were reluctant to accept any reduction in their control.

Also, the evidence suggests that there was no mass desertion from the established church. Although there was no obligation to attend the parish church, 'perhaps only 5% of the English attended other religious assemblies between 1643 and 1654'.[94] Sectarianism only posed a challenge to the parochial system once, when the radical Members of the Barebone's Parliament prepared for the abolition of tithes in 1653, and then the forces of conservatism immediately rallied at Westminster and in the shires.

Many of the clergy maintained at least a measure of continuity for the Church of England by keeping up worship according to the Book of Common Prayer, and by reading the Common Prayer privately in aristocratic and gentry households up and down the land, and even in the metropolis.

A large proportion of the lower clergy, and almost certainly a substantial majority, sympathized with the King during the Civil War, and there were frequent charges of royalism levelled against them. Pluralists, non-residents, and those who for various reasons were considered incapable of adequately performing their pastoral duties, understandably attracted the criticism of the authorities throughout the Interregnum. There were nearly 3,000 ministers who were ejected or suffered from some form of serious harassment during this period, representing about 34% of the 8,600 parish clergy in England. Many were summarily dismissed or put under great pressure to resign from their livings, while others were imprisoned or compelled to pay substantial composition fines for giving support to the royalist cause. But Richard Baxter seems to have erred in his assessment of the number and proportion of deprivations, for even of these 3,000, over 1,000 remained beneficed clergy; about 400 of those ejected were later appointed to another parish, approximately 200 pluralists retained one of their parishes, and another 270 or so managed to cling on to their parishes despite the active hostility of the authorities. Such men had mainly been ordained during the primacy of Laud's predecessor, George Abbot, and shared the firm attachment of many of the laity to the doctrines and liturgy of the traditional, pre-Laudian church.[95] Perhaps 70% or even 75% of all parish ministers were left in possession of their benefices until their death or until the Restoration. It has been estimated that 60% of English parishes had the same minister in 1649 as they had at the beginning of the Civil War, and frequently the attempt to oust a minister led to resistance from parishioners.[96] Nonetheless, in spite of all that has been said, at no time during the Interregnum did the Church of England enjoy widespread popularity or the devoted allegiance of a majority of the population. It probably only attracted the regular worship of a minority of the people, and it was but one of many corporate expressions of the Christian faith. It was maimed and emaciated, but it did continue its life of worship. 'The authorities of the Interregnum effectively turned a blind eye to the continued use of Common Prayer while it posed no political threat.'[97]

The survival of the Church of England owed much to a group of divines of the pre-1640 generation, which included Henry Hammond, John Bramhall, Jeremy Taylor, Robert Sanderson and Matthew Wren, who were geographically isolated from one another, but 'kept up a correspondence, sharing ideas and knowledge, swopping titbits of academic and royalist gossip, and encouraging each other in the service of "our distressed mother the church"'.[98]

Thus, some of the gentry and many of the clergy strove to maintain the Church of England; but what of the ordinary parishioners? In addition to the evidence that the prohibited Prayer Book was widely valued and used, there is the more striking evidence of the continued observance of holy communion. Despite variation from one diocese to another, the general practice before 1643 was for communion to be held on the three great feasts of Christmas, Easter and Whit. 'By 1650 the pattern of holy communion at Easter and (less frequently) at other major feasts was observed in 43% of the parishes. In almost every case the amount spent on bread and wine was comparable with the sums spent before the civil war.'[99] Evidence from churchwardens' accounts indicates that such liturgical conservatism was in fact a manifestation of long-established loyalties, rather than a reaction against Parliamentary interference. But perhaps the best evidence of commitment to the old ways is afforded by the reinstatement of ejected ministers in their parsonages and pulpits by their old parishioners. There were so many examples of such successful lobbying by parishes that local communities often decided not to enforce planned ejections. It appears that many people cared for the Church of England, and 'that after eighty years of maturation, a hybrid church, thoroughly if murkily reformed in its doctrines, unreformed in its government, a mish-mash in its liturgy, had achieved not only an intellectual self-confidence but a rhythm of worship, piety, practice, that earthed itself into the Englishman's consciousness and had sunk deep roots in popular culture'.[100]

The Roman Catholics

'The tolerance of even a Cromwell or a Milton did not extend to Papists.'[101] Papists were regarded as politically dangerous. They were perceived as agents of a foreign power, and hostile in intent. In any case, they had solidly supported Charles in the Civil War, and the plan of the King to invoke Irish intervention on his behalf, which was revealed when his papers were captured at Naseby, only reinforced the image of Catholics as set on the overthrow of the Parliamentary cause. As a consequence of this anti-papalism, repressive measures were adopted against the Catholics, and a fierce policy of military subjugation was carried out in Ireland.

During the first war Parliament had decreed that those who had supported the Royalist cause by military action or with money, and who were designated delinquents, were to be classified into categories. Royalists who were deemed to be traitors were liable to the death penalty or transportation, while lesser offenders were liable to gaol sentences. All were to suffer the confiscation of their entire goods and real estate. The more general term papist was applied to those who rejected a long and explicitly anti-Catholic Oath of Abjuration, and the punishment for papism was confiscation of two-thirds of all property. Moreover the pre-war principle of double-taxation of papists was retained, with ordinary taxation rates being by then far higher, and the money far more efficiently exacted. In practice only a small number of Catholics were reckoned to be traitors, and they were ruined. The Catholic non-traitor delinquents often took the Oath of Abjuration with private mental reservations, which had long been the custom for many in such circumstances. Others, who insisted on remaining publicly professed Royalists, tried by various legal and quasi-legal methods to escape disaster. As the Interregnum progressed, the extent of tolerance towards Catholics in England increased. Indeed, the Catholics 'were better off during the Protectorate than they had ever been under James or Charles I'.[102] But in Ireland the situation and the policy of Cromwell was different.

Cromwell and his associates were motivated by military and political concerns, as well as by religious antagonism in their ruthless policy against the Irish Catholics. They were angered by the lead which the priesthood and the papacy itself had undoubtedly given in the Irish revolt. They were also concerned that whereas the 1640s had, rather to the surprise of Puritans and Parliamentarians, shown up the political weakness of popery in England, and its lack of effective foreign contacts, the same ten years had demonstrated the complete failure of the previous eighty years of proscription to uproot Catholicism in Ireland or to sever its strong links with Rome. This fear of a political threat posed by Irish Catholicism, which had ceased to apply to Catholicism in England, helps to explain, although it in no way justifies, Cromwell's dreadful sacking of Drogheda and Wexford, and his hanging of priests and shooting of officers.

In England, although by the time of Cromwell's death the sun was beginning to shine a little brighter on non-royalist Catholics, despite the absence of full agreement on a *modus vivendi*, between his death in September 1658 and the arrival of Charles II in May 1660, the possibilities of some form of co-existence were abruptly terminated, and the Catholics were faced with an uncertain future. 'Timid Catholics fled abroad or went to ground in remote places. The Catholic lobby broke up.'[103] In general the Catholics played only a small part in the ensuing quick succession of events as the army generals quarrelled, as General Monck intervened, and as the Convention Parliament issued its invitation to Charles II. The Parliament contained some Catholics, and here and there some local Catholic gentry who had particular links with local politics played a very minor part in this turn of events, but overall Catholic Royalists were perforce largely spectators to moves which baffled them, as they did most people.

As Charles II stepped cheerfully ashore on the quay at Dover the most thoughtful Catholics could not make head or tail of the wildly contradictory features of their situation. Numbers of gentry recusants had slithered down, financially, in social standing and status, and in the rights they enjoyed, from the level of the 1630s. The political world was sprinkled with ex-Catholics. The colleges and religious houses were heavily in debt, largely because the gentry had for years been unable to keep up their contributions. The clergy were infested by the general wave of scepticism and restlessness, as were younger Catholics. It seemed that, with the restoration of the King, there would be a scramble for Establishment jobs and Catholic Royalists and neutrals alike would be elbowed aside: the Royalist minority were too few and already too much on the shelf to make good claims for compensation for their sufferings; and the neutral Catholic majority would be victimized for their support of the Republic. There were pious or pessimistic Jesuits and Old Catholic gentlemen who foresaw a long bleak age for the Catholic community.

Yet there were other Catholics, lay and clerical – including Jesuits – who saw the restoration of the Stuart monarchy as a second wind for the community, a golden chance to achieve through court Catholicism real freedom and even real power which they had sought but failed to get in the 1630s and again in 1654–8.

The mixed feelings and the uncertainty which permeated the Catholic community as it contemplated the prospect of a return to monarchial rule was typical of the Church of England and the various Christian denominations and sects which had proliferated during the 1640s and 1650s. No one knew what to expect, and the reign of Charles II was to spring some surprises as well as confirm some fears and gratify some expectations.

Religious indifference, agnosticism and atheism

It is exceptionally difficult to rediscover the beliefs, or absence of belief, of ordinary people two-and-a-half centuries ago who mostly lived in small, scattered communities of whose history we have no record. But historians have started to undertake the task, and the main contours of a religious map are beginning to emerge.[104] Until at least the middle of the seventeenth century belief in God was considered to be axiomatic, and it would have been difficult to find an Englishman who advocated atheism in intellectual terms.[105] But the critique of the established church made by many sectaries and others during the Interregnum was so radically anti-clerical and condemnatory of existing religious beliefs and practices that it was often virtually secularist in content. The breakdown of the longstanding structures and features of the established church after 1640, the prevalence of antinomianism, the materialist pantheism which emerged in the teaching of some of the radicals, doubts engendered by the popularization of science, and especially the impact of Copernican astronomy, and the consequences of greater religious toleration combined with a greater freedom of the press, all helped to promote scepticism, or to bring into the open a scepticism which already lurked not so far beneath the surface in the lives of many citizens. There were telling signs that there was a good deal, if not of atheism, then at least of positive irreligion in the 1640s and 1650s. In the minor classic of the Interregnum, *Gangraena*, the author, Thomas Edwards, not only attacked the sectarians but drew attention to the irreligion which an anarchic religious situation encouraged:

> In September last, Die 25, being at a merchant's house in London, there came in one Mr Y who related that in his family there were but four persons, himself, his wife, a man and a maid servant, and saith he, we are of several churches and ways; I am of the Church of England, my wife was of one Mr Jessey's church; but she is fallen off from that church (as many others have) and is now of none, doubting whether there be any church or no upon the earth; my maid-servant is of Paul Hobson's; my man belongs to a company of which there are some twenty or more young men, who meet together to exercise, but sing no psalms, abominate the hearing of our minister, keep none of our days of fasting nor thanksgiving.[106]

Then, into this situation, in 1651, came Thomas Hobbes' *Leviathan*. It immediately aroused strong feelings. The book was an affront even to people who had formerly admired Hobbes and his philosophical writings. Henry Hammond described it later that same year as a 'farrago of Christian Atheism'.[107] It appeared to justify submission to the new Republic and abandonment of the Church of England, and it sent shock waves through the Royalist and Anglican fraternity.

Hobbes shared with Decartes the sceptics' argument that it is not possible to have any direct and truthful experience of the external world. All we can perceive is the internal activity of our own brain. He also rejected the scholastic idea that words might refer to abstract 'essences' or 'universals'. He was a kind of 'nominalist' and 'relativist'. And his relativism was applied to ethics. There were no facts in ethics. The only possibility in ethical matters was to uncover some principle or set of principles on which all men would spontaneously agree. He believed that independency of judgment about the world would only lead to conflict. Independent judgment about matters of fact should therefore be eliminated. Individual judgment in matters of uncertainty should be transferred to a common decision-maker, a sovereign. In the process Hobbes 'handed the sovereign unlimited ideological authority, over morality and religion as well as day-to-day politics, and it is this power which has most alarmed his readers . . . Christianity became merely another socially sanctioned way of expressing the feelings of natural religion, and the sovereign could interpret Scripture or determine doctrine without paying any attention to ordained clergymen'.[108] Contemporaries not unreasonably inferred that if the sovereign had the power to determine any religious dogmas, including those of Christianity, and if natural religion had very little of a personal God in it, then conventional theism had disappeared from Hobbes' writings, and accusations of atheism were justified.

And such accusations were heaped upon Hobbes. If the detractors could have foreseen his long-term influence in promoting or abetting scepticism and even atheism, they might have been even more indignant and alarmed.

9

The Restoration and the Reign of Charles II

Historiography

It will have been evident from the last chapter how our knowledge of the Interregnum in general, and of religion in that period in particular, has been immeasurably increased during the last twenty years by major works, monographs, articles and unpublished theses. There has been a voluminous literature, and on a number of topics there has been fierce, and at times even bitter, historiographical controversy. In marked contrast there has been less research on the Restoration era, and much greater agreement among scholars on the correct interpretation of Restoration history. It must be said that such comparative lack of animated discussion has in part been a consequence of less interest in the reigns of Charles II and James II compared with the periods on either side of them. It is a time which 'has scarcely begun to shake off its reputation as an unconstructive episode in English history, an era marking time between the climacteric of the Puritan revolution and the apparently enduring resolution of a century's problems in the Glorious Revolution'.[1] Perhaps the landmarks of Restoration history have been regarded as too few and familiar, and there has been too little imaginative historical exploration of its potentially rich soil. Nevertheless, there have been signs of new initiatives, and new thinking by historians of the period.

J. R. Jones holds a widely acknowledged place of honour among the pioneers of recent Restoration studies, especially for his work on the first Whig party, first published in 1961, which provided an authoritative account of exclusionist politics.[2] Then, for further groundwork on the politics of the period, there are the fine biographies of the first Earl of Shaftesbury by K. H. D. Haley, of the second Earl of Sunderland by J. P. Kenyon, and of James II by John Miller. The latter author has also provided an excellent study of the key issue of popery and politics.[3]

During the 1950s, 1960s and 1970s there were important works on the nature and course of Anglican history during the Restoration

period, notably by R.S. Bosher, A. Whiteman, G.R. Abernathy and
I.M. Green; and in these post-Second World War years significant
studies of Puritanism by W.R. Cragg, of Dissenting politics by D.R.
Lacey, and of Restoration Dissent in general in a series of essays edited
by G.F. Nuttall and O. Chadwick, as well as the more all-embracing
survey of Dissent by M.R. Watts. Mention should also be made of the
scholarship of G.V. Bennett and G. Every. The outstanding publications
by N. Sykes come from the inter-war years. They have some relevance
to the Restoration period, although they mainly relate to the later
seventeenth century and the eighteenth century.[4]

Since the 1970s there has been a new generation of scholars asking
new questions, probing new areas and questioning the received
wisdom.[5] In spite of this, the understanding of the period remains very
incomplete, although there is much current study in the form of unpublished theses and monographs which is beginning to percolate through
into the mainstream of historical ideas and interpretations. There is
healthy disagreement about particular issues, and indeed about the
general perspective on the period, but there is a widespread consensus
on the need to challenge three previously well-entrenched basic historiographical preoccupations and preconceptions: the view that 1660 marks
a fundamental watershed; the assertion that after 1660 religion ceased
to be so important, as politics became increasingly secularized; and the
undue focus upon high politics, or politics from above. The new stress
is largely upon continuity with the previous period; and an important
contribution to the awareness of continuity in the life of the nation as a
whole, and of its religion in particular, is John Spurr, *The Restoration
Church of England, 1646–1689* (1991). The attempt to break away
from the dominant concern with central high politics has been fostered
by local studies, the more significant of which will be encountered as we
examine the 'church of the people'.

On 4 April 1660, on the advice of Edward Hyde, the First Earl of
Clarendon, Charles II issued the Declaration of Breda. In it he expressed
his concern to contribute to the binding up of those wounds which had
for so many years together kept bleeding as a result of the general distraction and confusion throughout the whole kingdom. He articulated
his desire, when restored to the throne, to allow his subjects to enjoy
what by law was theirs, 'by a full and entire administration of justice
throughout the land, and by extending our mercy where it is wanted
and deserved'. He offered a general pardon to all who would declare
their loyalty and obedience to the new regime:

And because the passions and uncharitableness of the times have produced several opinions in religion, by which men are engaged in parties and animosities against each other (which, when they shall hereafter unite in a freedom of conversation, will be composed or better understood), we do declare a liberty to tender consciences, and that no man shall be disquieted or called in question for differences of opinion in matter of religion, which do not disturb the peace of the kingdom; and that we shall be ready to consent to such an Act of Parliament, as, upon mature deliberation, shall be offered to us, for the full granting of indulgence.[6]

In the first twelve months after his return to England Charles II 'did all that he could to bring about a compromise settlement of the church'.[7] During the summer of 1660, in keeping with the Declaration of Breda, he nurtured the spirit of reconciliation, and as a consequence for a brief time the Protestants of different persuasions were brought closer together than they had been for decades. Then, in October of that year, he issued a declaration on ecclesiastical affairs which proposed that the Church of England should be governed by a form of limited episcopacy. There was considerable resistance to such a policy. 'There were those both to the right and the left of the moderates who scorned such a settlement. To the right there were the more extreme supporters of episcopacy who did not wish to see its powers reduced, and to the left the Independents and the covenanting Presbyterians who did not wish to see its re-appearance in any shape or form.'[8] Also, although an important element in uniting the country was the support of the army, the submission of the Cromwellian army to the Restoration was an act of necessity rather than willingness; it did not mean that it had suddenly become a strong supporter of monarchy, let alone episcopacy.

It was claimed by Robert Bosher that at the Restoration 'the Laudian party emerged as the dominant force on the religious scene',[9] and that it was they who were directing the Church of England revival. Ian Green countered this with the suggestion that the church's clerical leaders were relatively impotent, and that if anyone was responsible for restoring the church it was the backwoods country gentry – men who were as antagonistic towards Dissenters in the shires and parishes as, he alleged, were their representatives in Parliament. They recognized that they shared with the Church of England an interest in the maintenance of order and hierarchy, and in the preservation of a whole range of privileged economic relationships, and this fusing of affection and duty with self-interest obliged them to support the church to the full. Much subsequent research has produced little evidence that such an identity of interest, if it existed, had much effect in practice. It has tended to show that the 're-establishment of the church, and its defence against the threat of nonconformity was not, in fact, principally due to any single group, be it "Laudian" hierarchy, the government or the gentry'.[10] The strength and importance of popular Anglicanism is being discovered.[11] But historians are cautious about placing too much importance on any spontaneous support as the sole explanation. A multi-faceted approach is now favoured, in which popular survivalism, influential leaders such as Gilbert Sheldon, country gentry, city elites and others all played their part in the Restoration settlement. This accords with the evidence available.

It was perhaps inevitable that Charles should press initially for a compromise. He not only inherited a fraught and highly charged religious situation, in which every shade of religious predilection was represented, and in which any extremism would invite division and antagonism, but in 1660 he was perhaps more interested in political, social and religious harmony than in the promotion of any particular religious tradition.[12] His reactions in 1660 and during his reign were also inevitably determined to a great extent by his drama-filled, complicated personal history, and the complex character this had helped to produce. He had been brought up as an Anglican rather than a Roman Catholic. He had seen the dire consequences of a distinctive politico-religious policy when his father had been executed and his whole regime had been discarded. In order to win Scottish support in 1650 he accepted a Covenant in which he did not believe. His enforced exile brought him into contact with a wide range of religious traditions, and when in 1660 he started to negotiate for a return to England he dealt largely with Presbyterians. He had long demonstrated a considerable capacity for self-indulgence, and this remained a dominant trait in his character throughout his life. He had a great many mistresses, and he was reckoned to have had fourteen illegitimate children. He was wary, cynical and unprincipled, and he was a realist. There is little evidence that he pursued any consistent policy, or maintained any distinctive principle for any length of time if it did not serve his short-term interests. If a compromise religious settlement would best meet the need of the hour, so be it. In his own private life, he ostentatiously, if carelessly, practised as an Anglican. He showed little sign of religious devotion to Anglicanism at any stage of his life, but was very aware of the importance of adherence to it. He made little secret of his acquaintance with Catholic beliefs and practices or of his idea that Catholicism was the proper religion for gentlemen.

Whatever his defects of character, and they were legion, they were not known to many, and most Englishmen were overjoyed at his return as King. 'A Munsterian anarchy' had been averted by the return of a lawful monarchy; the tyranny was 'over-past' and a new dawn had arrived for a nation purged by affliction: 'it was the Lord's doing, *et mirabile in oculis nostris*'.[13] The restoration of the Stuarts was widely seen as the work of the Lord, and was therefore not to be disputed. Confusion and chaos were about to be dissipated, and a new age of new openings, new dawnings of liberty and new possibilities was at hand. It was important that the nation should make the most of its God-given opportunity. But there was apprehension. If 'the Restoration was at all felt as a "triumph" by cavalier Prayer Book loyalists, that feeling was constantly mixed with anxiety and foreboding. The fear was less that monarchy would again be violently overthrown, than that the monarch would overthrow them, his "natural" constituency'.[14]

The attempted settlements

The Convention Parliament which met on 25 April 1660 was split on religious lines between the Anglicans, Presbyterians and Independents, and the political divisions were sharpened by the bitterness of civil war and regicide. In the country at large there was a desire to establish a comprehensive church, and this was clearly expressed by a number of Members of Parliament. Some churchmen and some moderate Presbyterians resurrected Archbishop Ussher's scheme of the early 1640s for a modified episcopacy. Charles appeared to favour such an effort to reconcile opposing Protestant factions, and in this he was supported by Clarendon. As a gesture in the direction of comprehension and toleration a few non-Anglican Protestants, such as Richard Baxter, Edmund Calamy, Simeon Ashe and Edward Reynolds, were appointed royal chaplains. It was very widely accepted that Royalist clergy, like all other Royalists, should resume the positions from which they had been ejected. Any remaining obdurate republicans should be removed from positions of influence in London and in the provinces. Such ends were accomplished by an act passed at the end of the first session which confirmed the security of all parish clergy who were not Baptists, who had not preached against the King and who did not occupy the livings of Royalists requiring restoration. The majority of the clergy ejected as a consequence of this measure suffered because of their suspect political attitudes rather than because of their questionable title to benefice. Nonetheless, there is evidence from individual case-studies that parishioners and patrons not infrequently took advantage of the situation to get rid of unwanted incumbents on false pretences.[15]

During the parliamentary recess Charles and Clarendon made a determined effort to forge an agreement between the Anglicans and the Presbyterians, in a series of meetings at Clarendon's residence, Worcester House. The outcome was the Worcester House Declaration of 25 October 1660 in which Charles reiterated the principles of toleration of the Breda Declaration, expressed abhorrence at his past dalliance with the Scottish Covenant, and promised 'to promote the power of godliness', to appoint a clerical commission to review the Prayer Book, and to refer the question of ceremonial uniformity to a national synod. On the vital matter of church government, the Declaration outlined a form of reduced episcopacy, in which bishops would only exercise their powers, including ordination, with the assistance of a body of grave and learned clergy drawn from the cathedral chapter and the diocesan clergy.[16]

The sincerity of both Charles and Clarendon in seemingly searching after comprehension has been questioned. The evidence is inconclusive. In addition to the negotiations and proposals emerging from Worcester House, leading Presbyterians were offered bishoprics, but all such actions and expressions of good intent could as well be interpreted either as political expediency or as genuine attempts to accommodate varying Protestant points of view. What is certain is that within a few months this moderate conciliatory 'settlement' had collapsed, to be replaced by a narrower Act of Uniformity.

One reason for this change may have been the more rapid than expected recovery of the Church of England, and the restoration of a reasonably healthy parish life in a large number of the parishes of the land. As we have noted, parish life had in any case continued with some vigour in many areas during the Interregnum, and it seems to have survived in a form which could respond quickly to the changed, more favourable, circumstances of the Restoration. Another factor was the influence of the government, which wanted to postpone decisions on such explosive, divisive issues as the shape and liturgy of the Restoration church until the new regime was more firmly established. The recovery of the Anglican Church went on apace as, during the winter of 1660–61, Anglican ministers who had been ejected in the 1640s returned in considerable numbers to livings under the patronage of Anglican gentry patrons. Anti-Puritanism was becoming prevalent, as was reflected in 'harsh, popular satirical plays and broadsheets directed against Presbyterians, Baptists and Quakers with titles like *The Lecherous Anabaptist* or *The Dipper Dipped*. Ben Johnson's *Bartholomew Fair* was revived and Samuel Butler produced his popular anti-Puritan diatribe, *Hudibras*, between 1662 and 1678.'[17]

But the future was still unclear.

Although two decades of Puritan political supremacy had come to an end with the Restoration of Charles II, this momentous development was obscured at the time because political power was so nearly balanced in the Convention Parliament. At the beginning of 1661 it would have been difficult to foretell with any certainty whether the impetus of the complex developments that had brought the Restoration would add to the strength of the Anglican royalists in the coming elections, or whether there would be a resurgence of Puritan power.[18]

It was unfortunate that in such a delicate and sensitive situation there was a rising of London Fifth Monarchists, under the wine cooper Thomas Venner. For three days he and some fifty followers terrorized the city of London, killing twenty-two people, until they were put to flight by the train-bands and lifeguards. The affair reinforced in people's minds the association of religious nonconformity with political sedition, and 'appeared to confirm the Cavalier view that the "Good Old Cause" was not dead but only slumbering in Dissenting conventicles'.[19] It was in vain that the Baptists dissociated themselves from Venner's actions and drew up a declaration of loyalty to the King, renouncing on their own behalf and that of Quakers all forms of strife, fightings and the use of weapons for any end or under any pretence whatsoever. The rising was rapidly followed by a royal proclamation which forbade all meetings of Anabaptists, Quakers or Fifth Monarchy men, and within a few weeks 4,230 Quakers were in prison.[20] Baptist homes were raided, the pastor of a London Sabbatarian Baptist church was arrested and sentenced to be hanged, drawn, and quartered, and by the end of 1662 Newgate contained '289 Anabaptists and others taken at unlawful meetings'.[21] Alarm was also caused by the election in March 1661 of four fiercely anti-episcopalian Members of Parliament, to the cry of 'No Bishops! No Lord Bishops!'

It was on 15 April, in the midst of such inauspicious events, that representatives of the episcopal and Presbyterian clergy met at the Savoy under a royal commission to discuss what revisions and additions were necessary to the Prayer Book. Ostensibly the purpose of the conference was to find common ground between Presbyterians and Anglicans, but 'Baxter and the other leaders of the Puritan clergy soon realized their weakness, finding themselves little more than suppliants before the supremely confident Anglican churchmen: before the Cavalier Parliament even met the Church of England had in all essentials already been restored in its old form'.[22] The negative tone of the conference was set from the very start, when Gilbert Sheldon, at that time Bishop of London, but later Archbishop of Canterbury, insisted that the Puritans should draw up a list of their exceptions to the existing liturgy, thus stressing differences, not the hope of accord. In response ninety-nine points were enumerated, of which only seventeen were eventually conceded by the bishops. They covered all sorts of matters, including the observance of saints' days, the choice of lessons, clerical nomenclature, and disputed points of ceremonial, but they also revealed fundamental theological differences, a divergence of opinion in regard to the nature of the priesthood as well as an utter lack of mutual understanding. The Conference was the death knell to goodwill and fraternity between the Church of England and the various forms of Christian Dissent at the time; and in the meanwhile the King was crowned, the new Parliament assembled and a Convocation of the clergy gathered in the vestry of St Paul's.

The Cavalier Parliament which met on 8 May 1661 contained a few Members who were sympathetic to the Protestant Dissenters, but a majority who were determined to crush religious and political nonconformity. Within ten days of its first meeting bishops had been restored to the House of Lords, and the House of Commons had voted by 228 to 103 that the public hangman should burn the Solemn League and Covenant, and that all Members of Parliament should receive the sacrament according to the Prayer Book rite. Two months later, on 9 July, the Bill of Uniformity was passed. It was a return to the situation and to the laws which had existed before the Civil War. And as by that time the Savoy Conference was hopelessly deadlocked, it was the bishops and Convocation who decided exactly what form the revised Prayer Book should take.

The process of revision was completed by December 1661, and accepted by Parliament in April 1662. The revised Book was as obnoxious to many Dissenters as the Elizabethan Prayer Book, but the changes introduced were far from partisan or extreme. The suggestions of 'Laudians' like John Cosin and Matthew Wren were not adopted, except in the case of the Ordinal, and the 600, mostly minor, revisions, in many ways leaned towards meeting the Puritan objections. In as far as this was so, it might reflect the role of the moderates, Robert Sanderson and Edward Reynolds, in the revision process. Reynolds contributed the first draft of the General Thanksgiving.

The Act of Uniformity and the ejection

The new Prayer Book was attached to the Act of Uniformity, which received the royal assent on 19 May, and came into force, with devastating consequences, on St Bartholomew's Day, 24 August 1662. The overwhelming majority of the English parish clergy endured the changes introduced in 1660–2 as they had those of the previous decades; but between 1660 and 1663 about 1,760 priests were forced to leave their parishes. The 1660 Act for Settling Ministers 'indiscriminately affected both those whose religious and political convictions prevented their absorbtion into a revived national church and those who had no more commitment to the Puritan Revolution than the fact that they had served in the place of a sequestered divine';[23] and it resulted in the ejection of 695 parish ministers. This meant that a large proportion of the irreconcilable Puritan clergy, including many of the incumbents who were Independents or Baptists, had left the Church of England before the hammer blow of 1662. There were also leading Puritan divines, such as John Owen, Peter Sterry and Increase Mather, who had not occupied any living at the Restoration from which to be ejected.

The bulk of the 936 ministers ejected in 1662 'were men who could have accepted some sort of diluted uniformity, perhaps along the lines of the Worcester House Declaration, but who jibbed at the requirements of 1662'.[24] There were four specific difficulties to the scrupulous:

> to qualify for a clerical living it was necessary to give 'unfeigned assent and consent to all and everything contained and prescribed in and by' the Book of Common Prayer, including the sacraments and ceremonies, psalter and ordinal; to subscribe to the Thirty-nine articles, of which three concerned church government; to renounce the obligation of the Solemn League and Covenant for themselves and all others, and to forswear 'to endeavour any change or alteration of

government either in church or state'; and, finally, to have received ordination from the hands of a bishop.[25]

Most of those who were ejected made it plain that they were constrained by their consciences to depart, and they went with a sense of sadness and yet of divine imperative, rather than with anger and bitterness. Sunday 17 August 1662, one week before the Feast of Bartholomew, ' was a day of farewells to crowded congregations, in the churches of those who could not conform'.[26] Dr William Bates, preaching at St Dunstan's, London, declared:

It is neither fancy, faction nor humour that makes me not conform, but merely for offending God: and if after the best means used for my illumination, as prayer to God, discourse and study, I am not able to be satisfied concerning the lawfulness of what is required; if it be my unhappiness to be in error, surely men will have no reason to be angry with me in this world, and I hope God will pardon me in the next.

Dr Thomas Jacomb, of St Martin's, Ludgate, expressed similar thoughts:

Be good in bad times; be patterns of good works to those that shall behold you . . . Walk as becometh the Gospel . . . Let me require this of you, to pass a charitable interpretation upon our laying down the exercise of our ministry . . . I censure none that differ from me, as though they displease God; but yet as to myself, should I do thus and thus, I should certainly violate the peace of my own conscience and offend God, which I must not do, no, not to secure my ministry, though that is, or ought to be, dearer to me than my very life; and how dear it is, God only knoweth.

Thomas Lye, Rector of All Hallows, declared:

Let the God of Heaven do what he will with me. If I could have subscribed with a good conscience I would: I would do anything to keep myself in the work of God, but to sin against my God, I dare not do it.

Robert Atkins, of St John's, Exeter, spoke in the same tones:

I beg that you will not interpret our nonconformity to be an act of unpeaceableness and disloyalty. We will do anything for His Majesty but sin. We will hazard anything for him but our souls. We hope we could die for him, only we dare not be damned for him. We make no question however we may be accounted of him; we shall be found loyal and obedient subjects at our appearance before God's tribunal.

A high proportion of the ejected resolved to exercise their ministry as opportunity should afford, often in private houses. Richard Baxter indicates how they attempted to continue some form of ministry:

> The greatest part of them forbore all public preaching and only taught some few in private at such hours as hindered not the public assemblies, and many of them lived as private men . . . Those that live where they find small need of their preaching, or else have no call or opportunity and cannot remove their dwellings do hold no assemblies, but as other men content themselves to be auditors. Those that live where are godly and peaceable ministers in public, who yet need help, do lead the people constantly to the parish church, and teach them themselves at other hours and help them from house to house. This is ordinary in the counties, and even in London with many ministers . . . that were ejected out of city parish churches.[27]

But most of the ejected had to find some other type of employment, even if they managed to fulfil some form of preaching or pastoral ministry as well. About one hundred kept schools, including nine who ran academies for the training of ministers. Some acted as tutors to the sons of families who readily recognized the academic qualifications which the ministers possessed. Some of them took to farming, and others became tradesmen. Nearly sixty are recorded as practising medicine, and almost fifty others held chaplaincies or domestic posts in the households of the nobility. Between thirty and forty of the ejected ministers went to Scotland, Ireland or America, although some of these returned to their native land at a later date. In general, although there were cases of severe distress, and many more where it was less acute, but nevertheless real, it would seem that the suffering was not as intense as might be thought, although it was to be increased under the penal Acts which followed the Act of Uniformity, as we will see in a moment. Certainly, the loss to the Church of England of so many godly men, a large proportion of whom had received university education, and in some instances had attained to considerable scholarship, was profound.

The Act of Uniformity also marked the consolidation of Dissent. From thenceforth there was no prospect of incorporating all the sects and denominations into a comprehensive national church, and Dissent was recognized as a permanent factor in national life. In fact the Act made a clear-cut legal distinction between the orthodox and the rest. No matter that it classed the sober and scrupulous nonconforming clergyman with the inspired sectarian fanatic, all were equally beyond the pale, equally worthy of severity. And severity is what was meted out to them in the so-called Clarendon Code.

In October 1663 there was an abortive rising in Yorkshire which involved several Presbyterians as well as sectaries, and this only helped to vindicate the arguments of churchmen about the treasonableness of Dissent, and to give substance to the rumours of Nonconformist risings, of arms stockpiled at conventicles, and of plotters in league with the Scots and the Dutch, which abounded in the early 1660s. Churchmen, and especially Gilbert Sheldon, were in the fore in demanding the imposition of restraints on Nonconformists. 'Conscience was the one thing Gilbert Sheldon, Archbishop of Canterbury, would not allow to nonconformists. It is his name, rather than Clarendon's, which should be attached to the penal legislation, for, whereas Clarendon had worked to mitigate the severity of the Act of Uniformity and had promoted Charles's policy of toleration, Sheldon was an inveterate opponent of both toleration and comprehension and an implacable pursuer of nonconformists.'[28]

In May 1664, frightened backbench Members of Parliament passed the First Conventicle Act, which aimed at completely crushing all centres of sedition. It recognized the Act of Elizabeth as still in force, but supplemented it with a provision that no person of sixteen or upwards should be present at any assembly of five or more which was under pretence of religion, 'in other manner than is allowed by the liturgy', if they were not members of the household in which the service was conducted. For the first offence of breaching this law the offender was to be imprisoned for up to six months, or to be fined five pounds; for the second offence an imprisonment was again to be imposed of not more than six months or a fine of ten pounds; and for the third the offender was to be transported. JPs were empowered to break into houses if they were informed that a conventicle was taking place. The Act was directed mainly at lay people. The next measure was aimed at Nonconformist ministers.

The Five Mile Act of October 1665 required all persons 'in holy orders or pretending to be', who had not taken the oath and made the declaration under the Act of Uniformity, to swear that it was not lawful upon any pretence to take up arms against the King or at any time to endeavour any alteration of government either in church or state. All ministers who failed to take this oath were forbidden to go within five miles of any corporate town or any place where they had been accustomed to officiate, except as travellers.

The fall of Clarendon in December 1667, and the expiry of the First Conventicle Act on 1 March 1669, brought some relaxation in the purge of Dissenters, but the relief was short-lived. In early 1670 a second Conventicle Act passed into law. Its penal demands were less severe than those in the first act, but provisions were made for the second act to be more stringently applied. It was a determined effort to suppress conventicles 'in the most effectual manner possible'. It was described by Andrew Marvell, in a phrase which achieved fame, as the 'quintessence of arbitrary malice'. In the year following the passing of the act the Dissenters suffered as perhaps never before, although a large proportion of the gentry had no stomach for enforcing uniformity by means of the Clarendon Code.

Throughout this period of persecution, the King was uncomfortable, and there were those about the Court who were urging him to exercise his prerogative in the direction of toleration. The Declaration of Indulgence was issued by the King on 15 March 1672. It suspended 'the execution of all and all manner of penal laws in matters ecclesiastical, against whatsoever sorts of nonconformists or recusants'. Nonconformists were permitted freedom of public worship provided that their ministers and their meeting places were licensed, and Roman Catholics were allowed to worship in private. 'This reversal of the religious policy of a decade was sprung on an unsuspecting nation.'[29] Petitions for licences poured in rapidly from all parts of the realm. The result of the Declaration was 'to give a sharper definition to Nonconformity, to encourage the *rapprochement* of Presbyterian and Congregationalist wings, and to give a fillip to the Nonconformist ministry which had been declining in numbers during the preceding decade'.[30]

Try as he may, the purposes of the King were defeated. He was in desperate need of cash from Parliament, and most of its members opposed his tolerant policy. So, on 7 March 1673 the Declaration was cancelled. But in any case the years 1672–3 witnessed a considerable shift in public opinion. Fear of popery, of France and of arbitrary government started to replace fear of Dissent.

A period of intense anti-Catholicism

The year 1673 saw 'the greatest outburst of anti-popery since the early 1640s'.[31] It was intensified, if not immediately caused, by the widespread suspicion regarding the royal intention in issuing the Declaration and seeking a closer alliance with France, and, secondly by the dawning realization that James, Duke of York, brother to the King and heir to the throne, was a Catholic. During the 1660s the Duke moved from High Anglicanism to Catholicism, and by 1676 he had been received into the Catholic Church and had ceased to attend Anglican services. His Catholicism was made very public in 1673 when, to the amazement and horror of Protestants, he resigned his office as Lord Admiral rather than take the 'test' stipulated by the Test Act. This one act, set against a background of prolonged, and at times violent, anti-Catholicism, was enough to make popery the dominant issue of English politics.

The Test Act of 1673 insisted that the holder of any civil or military office must take the Oath of Allegiance and Supremacy, must receive communion according to the rites of the Church of England, and must make a declaration against the Catholic doctrine of the mass. Under pressure from Parliament, Charles ordered the enforcement of the penal laws against Roman Catholics throughout 1674 and 1675. Catholic houses were searched for arms and papist assemblies were investigated. In London especially, the fear of popery, which had not been far from the surface for a century and more, was resurrected and reinstated as a central theme of popular politics by preachers. It was expressed in pope-burnings, and fuelled by rumours of popish plots.

Two figures loomed large in the ensuing years of escalating anti-Roman Catholicism, and were, in their different spheres of activity, focusses for this nationwide mood: Sir Thomas Osborne, First Earl of Danby, the key figure in the central government of the country, and Titus Oates who was a charismatic leader among the people at large.

Danby's father had been Vice-President of the Council of the North under Wentworth and a Royalist in the Civil War, and he himself rose rapidly in his own political career. He was evidently chief minister by 1675 and although, like everyone else, he could never be certain of the continued support of Charles, he remained as the foremost minister and political influence in Parliament for the next two or three crucial years at least. He wanted a strong monarchy based upon traditional Cavalier loyalty and uncompromising Anglicanism, and this entailed the firm enforcement of the penal laws against both Dissenters and Catholics.

'Here at last was the prospect of real political power if only the church would grasp it; Danby's ministry offered the church the chance to give substance to the shadowy Anglican ascendancy.'[32]

Churchmen were obsessed with the dangers facing the church from factious Dissent, from subversive popery and from irreligion. The bishops informed the King that despite all efforts

> atheism and profaneness daily abound more and more, and defections are frequently made on the one side to the superstitious and idolatrous practices and usurpations of Rome, on the other to the pernicious and destructive novelties of the various sects raised in the worst of times . . . nothing is more necessary than the suppressing of atheism, profaneness and open and professed wickedness . . . [33]

Danby was not wholly unsuccessful in curbing Dissent and Roman Catholicism, and he co-operated with the embattled Church of England in an attempt to tackle irreligion.

But it was Catholicism, and anti-Catholicism, which was taking centre stage. For some time there had been a growing tension between Parliament and Court over the issue of Catholicism. There was a widespread fear that the army which was being raised supposedly to fight the French would be used against Parliament in an attempt to establish absolutism and popery. Then came to so-called Popish Plot. And this brings Titus Oates into the scene.

Titus Oates (1648–1705) was the son of a parson who had become an Anabaptist. He was expelled in his first year at Merchant Taylors School. He subsequently attended two Cambridge colleges, Caius and St John's, without attaining a degree, but still managed to get himself ordained. In 1674 he became curate to his father, who by then had reverted to Anglicanism and held a living at Hastings. It was not long before they were both in gaol for perjury, for bringing false charges against a local schoolmaster. Titus escaped from Dover prison, and spent several months as a naval chaplain before becoming chaplain to the Protestant members of the Duke of Norfolk's household at Arundel. He then joined forces with Israel Tonge, a London vicar, in seeking fame and fortune by discovering or, failing that, inventing, Catholic, and preferably Jesuit, plots. He haunted coffee houses where Catholics met, and frequented the Queen's Chapel in Somerset House in an effort to pick up any information or gossip which might promote his cause. He even managed to deceive the Catholics into thinking that he wished to be reconciled to Rome, and in 1677 he was admitted to the Jesuit college at Valladolid in Spain. Expelled after five months, he left Spain claiming a bogus degree as Doctor of Divinity of Salamanca. Despite such a record, he was able to gain acceptance to the English Catholic seminary at St Omer, in the Netherlands, but was again expelled, this time after six months.

On his return to England he and Tonge concocted the celebrated 'Popish Plot'. 'Most of the details of a conspiracy masterminded by the Jesuits to assassinate the King had their origins in the twisted minds of Titus Oates and Israel Tonge.' The elaborate plot was said to include not only the intended murder of the King and the entire Council, but a French invasion of Ireland, a general massacre of Protestants, and the installation of the Duke of York on the throne; and it was all a tissue of absurdities and lies. But it filled London with terror in 1678–9. Although the examination of the allegations by the Privy Council exposed Oates as a liar on certain details, and showed up manifest inconsistencies, the Cavalier Parliament recorded its unanimous conviction 'that there hath been and still is a damnable and hellish plot contrived and carried on by the popish recusants', and anyone who dared to cast doubts on the authenticity of this assertion was in danger of his life.[34] That such patently false accusations were believed is testimony to the long-established, and deep-rooted anti-Catholicism which prevailed in the population as a whole. The wave of anti-Catholic hysteria which news of this non-existent plot aroused was shortlived, even in London, but there were several state trials, as a result of which it has been estimated that some thirty-five men were judicially murdered, and the whole affair contributed to the legacy of anti-Catholicism out of which it had grown, and on which it had fed for its success.

With English Catholics making up only 2% of the population, historians have struggled to explain the apparently disproportionate impact of the Popish Plot crisis upon leaders, and upon the population of the country as a whole. Kenyon draws attention to a number of possible explanatory factors.[35] There was the fear of foreign invasion, and especially the deteriorating position of European Protestantism in the seventeenth century with the Catholics steadily gaining ground. There was the assumption of many Englishmen that Catholicism was always to be identified with absolute monarchy. Kenyon maintains that the robust faith of the English gave them confidence that they could beat off attacks from abroad, but they remained on their guard lest their Protestant citadel was captured from within.

The masterminds behind any plotting and conspiracy for a Catholic take-over of the country were widely seen as the priests, and especially the Jesuits. And Englishmen were in no doubt about the consequences if Catholics seized control: all good Protestants would burn, as was clear from the reign of Mary I and the lurid details of Foxe's *Acts and Monuments*. And pamphleteers fanned the flames of this paranoiac fear of Catholicism:

> Casting your eye towards Smithfield, imagine you see your father, or your mother, or some of your nearest and dearest relations, tied to a stake in the midst of flames, when with eyes lifted to heaven, they scream and cry out to that God for whose cause they die, which was a frequent spectacle the last time popery reigned amongst us.[36]

Despite the propaganda there was little official persecution of Catholics. There were certainly enough anti-Catholic laws on the statute books, with an abundance of severe, even draconian, penalties. But these laws were never stringently enforced except, in part, at times of crisis and panic, such as between 1605 and 1612 in the wake of the Gunpowder Plot, under the personal rule of Charles I between 1629 and 1637, and in the 1640s when the Long Parliament passed several new and stern edicts against papists. Many heads of Catholic families were 'church-papists', and Catholics were generally well integrated into society. Indeed, 'outside the period of the Civil Wars it is difficult to find any Catholic family against whom the penal laws were enforced vigorously and consistently'.[37] But the widespread anti-Catholicism at all levels of society persisted.

Kenyon points to two specific matters which had reinforced the prevailing anti-Catholicism. First, the Great Fire of 1666, which 'took its place in the mythology of ultra-Protestantism'. For 'it confirmed the belief of the credulous and fearful that the Church of Rome was an organ of international conspiracy, and that the Jesuits were a secret society employing fire, poison and gunpowder for the conversion of England'.[38] Then the fervent fear of the English Protestants had been exacerbated by the uncertain religion of their monarchs: none of whom, since Elizabeth 1, had been able to convince a suspicious public that he was a fully convinced and committed Protestant.

In his important work, *Popery and Politics in England, 1660–88* (1973), John Miller argues that the Roman Catholic minority had owed its survival after the Reformation to the firm faith of the Catholic nobility and gentry, and that this situation prevailed until the massive

Irish immigrations of the late eighteenth and nineteenth centuries. This primarily aristocratic and rural Catholicism depended on priests trained in seminaries abroad. Like Kenyon, he stresses that although there were fearsome laws in force against all aspects of Catholic life, they were only implemented in times of crisis, and the norm was for Protestant magistrates to show considerable tolerance in dealing with their Catholic neighbours. In such a setting Miller maintains that the often violent and hysterical anti-Catholicism during the reign of Charles II, which lay behind the reaction to the Popish Plot, could only be explained in terms of 'the religious policies of Charles II and even more in the conversion to Catholicism of James'.[39] There was a latent English anti-Catholicism which was far from dead, for Englishmen were tolerant of their Catholic neighbours while retaining a vigorous fear and hatred of 'popery', and more particularly 'popery' at the royal court or among those in positions of power. This helps to make clear the 'exclusion crisis' after the Duke of York's conversion became known, and the subsequent colouring of the attitudes of James's subjects to him when he became King. Jonathan Scott has disputed this explanation. He attributes more to religious fears, and less to political causation than Miller, and more to religious dangers created by the policies of Charles II than to apprehensions about the future.[40] England, Scott affirms, in the words of a seventeenth century contemporary of the plot, now felt itself to be the last 'bulwark of liberty, protestantism, and Christian faith in general, throughout the world; the main bank, that hinders the see of Rome from overwhelming all Christian nations with an universal inundation of tyranny and superstition'.[41] Mark Goldie concedes that unquestionably 'an overwhelming fear of popery bloomed in the 1670s, and certainly the bills to exclude James from the succession became the parliamentary focus of those fears'. But he cautions against an undue stress upon the 'popish plot' and the 'exclusion crisis', which throw the weight of emphasis upon Protestant fears of Catholicism. For 'what is liable to go missing, or become inexplicable, in any account dominated by those terms, is the clamorous language of "presbyterian" and "church" interests, of "prelacy" and its enemies, of uniformity versus reconciliation in church affairs'.[42]

What seems clear is that, for the reasons just mentioned, the protestantization process had established a deep suspicion and fear in the minds of many Englishmen, and had produced a near hysterical dread of popery among a small number of the population. The unwise action of any public person simply triggered such apprehension and readily resulted in aggressive language and behaviour, as in the reigns of Charles II and James II.

The Roman Catholics

Although anti-Roman Catholic feeling ran high on a number of occasions during the reign of Charles II, in certain respects the Catholics gained in strength at that time. Indeed, this may have been one of many causes of the strong opposition to Catholicism in that period. And the growth in influence and in confidence of the Catholics was in no place more evident than at the very heart of national affairs, the court.

'Before the civil wars court Catholicism had been an alien, minor, contemptuously tolerated influence in a confidently Anglican court. After its return to Westminster in 1660 its ramifications and influence rapidly grew so much that court Anglicanism was put on the defensive.'[43] It was not that the number of practising or latent Catholics at court showed a great numerical increase, for they did not. The Protestant establishment still controlled almost all the main seats of power. Nonetheless, there developed a myth among Anglicans, which was well established in the 1670s, that Catholicism, albeit in a very hidden and insidious way, was close to capturing power. Charles himself, despite his at least outward support for a vacillating policy towards Catholics during his reign, according to what at any particular time seemed politically most advisable, was known to be well acquainted with, and highly to respect, their beliefs and practices. In fact he kept Protestants guessing about his real religious opinions all his life. He can, perhaps best be described as a true church papist who was prepared to countenance a policy at certain times which was antipathetic to Catholics if this paid political dividends. Whatever his personal views, he inherited and followed his families policies of drawing the sting of Catholicism by receiving Catholics at court, by forging Catholic connections through family marriages, and by forming alliances with Catholic powers. He could adopt such policies, and carry them quite far, without arousing too much suspicion about his motives or about the sincerity of his adherence to Anglicanism.

Catholicism was also strong in the royal family. As we have previously seen, the Queen Mother, Henrietta Maria, had, as the wife of Charles I, exercised a considerable influence at court by her vivaciousness, her penchant for dances, masques and music, her circle of literary celebrities, supplemented by young officers and elegant courtiers, and, above all, her Romanism. Under Charles II she was allowed an official Catholic Household and palace, St James's, in London, until her death in 1669. She had a chapel and priests to attend on her. Although she was often absent in France, had little opportunity to re-establish the political and social ties of her pre-Civil War days, and was rather discredited by her mysterious close association with Harry Jermyn, the old *roué* who had danced attendance on her since the 1630s, and who was now a Catholic and Earl of Dover, her presence, her past reputation, her status, and her chapel and priests, helped in the promotion of court Catholicism.

Then there was the King's brother, and the heir to the throne, James, Duke of York. He went through a period of genuine Anglicanism, and married an Englishwomen who was a strict High Anglican. But, as we have seen, they underwent a very long and painful process of conversion to Catholicism, which caused widespread concern, immensely increased the extent and intensity of anti-Catholicism, and resulted in the Exclusion Crisis of 1679–81.

During the reign of Charles II there was an increase in the number of Catholic peers to about forty-five. There were six Dukes and Duchesses, two Marquises, eleven Earls, six Viscounts and over twenty Barons. Despite the fact that, as before the wars, their Catholicism was for the most part fragile and unimpressive, it was a factor of importance in the general nationwide presence and influence of Catholicism. Although the leading Catholic peer, the first Duke of Norfolk, was a lunatic confined in an Italian asylum, and the Catholicism of the Howards was sometimes thin, and the Catholic Earl of Bristol, who came after the Howards in political importance, was an eccentric who professed his Catholicism in the House of Lords but periodically attended Anglican services, and Earl Rivers and Lord Mounteagle, like many of the other peers, considered themselves to be Catholics although they had not been seen at mass within living memory, they represented a residue of Catholicism which had an impact among Catholic gentry throughout the land. There was less of a gulf between court and country Catholics than before the wars, and increasing numbers of squires pushed forward to get their sons and daughters into posts in the Catholic royal households and to acquire commissions in the forces. 'Up and down the country and in London there were frequent meetings where papist squires respectfully met papist peers and toasted the Duke of York.'[44] The activist Catholic country gentry were sharply declining in numbers, and they were spurred on to maintain and extend contacts with their

Catholic social superiors by a sense that a victory of court Catholicism and the furtherance of royal Catholicism was their only hope of breaking into an establishment which was resolutely excluding them from office in their own counties.

In the Restoration governments Catholic influences seem to have been more covert and yet more widespread than in pre-war years. The Earl of Arlington was ostensibly a Protestant, but appears to have harboured Catholic beliefs and to have sent for a Catholic priest on his deathbed. The Earl of Danby, although himself a solid Anglican, had a devoutly Catholic mother and relations. The raffish second Duke of Buckingham had an indiscreetly Catholic mother, but had such veiled religious beliefs himself that both the local vicar and a Catholic priest were summoned at the time of his death. Lord Clifford went through agonies of conscience before he finally declared his conversion to Catholicism in 1672, and resigned his office as Treasurer. Others who were church papists, ex-Catholics with considerable sympathy for Catholicism, or at least leanings towards Catholicism, included the second Earl of Portland, the Earl of Arlisle, the Earl of Scarborough and the Earl of Fauconberg.

The rules excluded Catholic recusants from being civil servants, and they appear to have been adhered to more strictly than before the wars. 'But, concealed (or half-concealed) behind this Anglican facade and behind the undoubted current of religious scepticism amongst civil servants, Catholic influences seemed to lurk more widely than ever.'[45] There was a sprinkling of those who at the very least favoured Catholicism, and a number of declared church papists.

In the fashionable London world, amongst artists, musicians, writers, mathematicians and scientists, it was the opinion of those reckoned as good judges that Catholicism was as muted and yet as diffused as elsewhere at court.

In the country at large it is difficult to assess the number of Catholics, and even more difficult to estimate their strength and influence. The Compton Census of 1676, which was the most thorough of the attempts at the time by leaders of the Church of England to assess the number of their adversaries, estimated that Roman Catholics represented less than 1% of the population of most dioceses, compared with less than 5% of Nonconformists. Roman Catholics were quite easily identified by their recusancy and their tendency to gather around an eminent Catholic family. In the early 1670s, when anti-popery was at a peak, English Catholicism as a whole was quiescent. 'The Roman Catholic com-

-munity was introspective, gentry dominated and politically loyal, its numbers remained stable at about 60,000, and the mission which served it was only just beginning to revive under the influence of the secular clergy.'[46]

For the most part Catholic secular clergy and religious spent at least the first ten years of the Restoration period recovering from the grave dislocations of their organization which had been inflicted during the troubled years from 1642 to 1660. Much energy was expended by the most able among them in rebuilding the shaky finances of the colleges and monasteries, and in recruiting young men and women to fill their depleted ranks. They carefully avoided offending the Catholic peers and gentry on whose sympathy and active support they so much depended by not reviving the pre-war idealistic clericalism.

And so matters proceeded until 1685, when even the wisest of Catholics could not discern the future of the community.

> Meanwhile Charles II was dying. The Duke of York conferred with him. When the King was sure there was no hope, he consented to receive a Catholic priest. As the Anglican clergy were ushered out of the bedchamber, a toothless, shabby old man, John Huddleston, carrying a stole and an oil-bottle, was hurried in through a side-door from the ante-chamber in which he had long been kept waiting. He was a Benedictine who, many years before when a secular priest missioner in Staffordshire, had helped to shelter the King fleeing after the battle of Worcester. Huddleston was probably the best-known priest in England, since, by special royal orders, his name (and those of a few of his parishioners who had helped the fugitive King) had figured in every Act of Parliament or royal Proclamation concerning Catholics: they had been protected from all prosecution and awarded pensions for life. Huddleston now received the King into the Catholic Church. The following morning the King died.[47]

The Presbyterians

At the time of the Restoration, many Presbyterians, though by no means all, desired comprehension in the new religious establishment. In August 1660, three of their leaders, Edmund Calamy, Simeon Ashe and Thomas Manton, acknowledged in a letter to their Scottish brethren that there was no hope of imposing a full-blown Presbyterian establishment and yet they expressed their fear of the liberty which toleration would afford to papists and Sectarians. They therefore concluded that 'no course seemeth likely to us to secure religion and the interest of Christ Jesus our Lord, but by making presbytery a part of the public establishment . . . by moderating and reducing episcopacy to the form of synodical government'.[48] As we have seen, the King at first seemed prepared to meet some of the Presbyterian requests, but their hopes were shattered when, after the initial discussions at Worcester House and Savoy, the 1662 Act of Uniformity confronted Presbyterian clergy with the stark choice between total submission to episcopacy or the loss of their livings. 'In the final analysis, the Presbyterians lost at the Stuart Restoration through their disunity, their numerical weakness, their indecision, their lack of a positive and consistent policy, and their unwillingness to support Charles II and Clarendon at the risk of gains for Catholics.'[49] Many of those deprived of their posts as priests, lecturers and fellows were Presbyterians. As the hopes that some entertained that the rifts of 1662 would soon be healed were never realized, within a decade some few Presbyterians, especially in London, who had large congregations and liberty and encouragement, ceased to expect a return to the Church of England. When subsequent attempts to achieve comprehension as, for example in 1666–7, 1680 and 1689, failed, those Presbyterians who were not willing to conform were driven even closer to Dissent.

The tension for Presbyterians, as in varying degrees for other religious groups, between comprehension and toleration, was well illustrated at the times when Charles II made his Declarations of Indulgence. Thus, when he issued one of these in 1672, suspending 'all manner of penal laws in matters ecclesiastical', and allowing all Dissenters to meet freely for worship provided that they had a licence for their meeting place and for their preacher, the Presbyterian response was mixed. The new provision was clearly advantageous for all Dissenters, at least in the short term, but it included the right of Roman Catholics to worship in private houses. Misgiving would have turned into outright opposition if the Presbyterians had known that the granting of toleration was part of a deal with Louis XIV in which Charles had promised to declare himself a Roman Catholic in return for French money. Also, the information that Dissenters had to supply about their meeting-places and preachers in order to obtain licences could one day be used against them. Nevertheless, of the total of 1,610 licences issued for preachers, 939 were said, not always accurately, to be for Presbyterians. 'The more conservative Presbyterians had their own reasons for disliking the

Indulgence for, as always, toleration's victory meant comprehension's defeat.'[50] There was fear expressed that the sanctioning of separate places of worship would help to overthrow the parish order, which was not the intention of most Presbyterians, and a group of Yorkshire Presbyterians were anxious to explain that in taking out licences they were not proposing to set up any distinct or separate churches in opposition to those already established, nor intending to preach at times when services were held in the parish churches.[51]

Nevertheless, despite the reservations and protestations which were voiced at the time, this particular Declaration of Indulgence gave an important stimulus to Presbyterianism, as to Dissent in general. Presbyterians formed themselves into regular churches and subscribed to a declaration of faith not unlike an Independent covenant, as, for example, at Northowram near Halifax. Presbyterian ordinations, of which only one example is recorded in the ten years before the Declaration of Indulgence, began again; and the Presbyterians of Leeds and Sowerby went as far as erecting their own meeting-house. It is therefore somewhat ironic that persecution by means of measures such as the Act of Uniformity, and tolerance, by means of such measures as the 1672 Declaration of Indulgence, had the same effect of driving Presbyterians away from conformity to Dissent, so that by the end of the reign of Charles II they were more of a Nonconformist body than they had been at the beginning of the reign. It was yet another unintended contribution to the pluralization of Protestantism.

The Independents or Congregationalists

'To Congregationalists the future must have seemed bleak in the weeks immediately following the Restoration.'[52] They first of all feared Stuart revenge. And indeed such retaliation for the ills of the previous two decades was revealed in the Act of Free and General Pardon, Indemnity and Oblivion which received the royal assent on 21 August 1660. Of the thirty-eight named persons who were exempt from the mercies of the general pardon, and of whom thirteen suffered death and twenty-five life imprisonment, several were fervid Congregationalists. But, even so, the Act had proved to be far more generous than the Independents had dared to hope. Such generosity was not displayed to nearly the same extent in the ecclesiastical settlement of the same year.

At the Restoration, those Independents who had not been involved in the execution of the King could hope for no more than that they would be permitted to worship outside the established church, and even before the Act for the Confirming and Restoring of Ministers, passed in September 1660, at least fifty Congregational ministers had voluntarily withdrawn from their livings. In fact, 'the Restoration destroyed for ever the Jacobite dream of reconciling the ideal of the gathered church with conformity to the established Church of England'.[53]

The Independents were not consulted in the long and tortuous negotiations and discussions which took place in 1660 between the representatives of Dissent, who were mainly Presbyterians, and the leaders of the Church of England. But they made their views on liturgical uniformity known in various publications, most notably Philip Nye's *Beams of Former Light*, Vavasor Powell's *Common-Prayer-Book No Divine Service*, and Dr John Owen's *A Discourse concerning Liturgies*.

> The main points made by the Congregational disputants were that Christ and his Apostles never used liturgies; that they did not command their followers to compose them; that they did not suggest that they were in any way useful and that the primitive church did not compose and use them. The present use of liturgies leads to an atrophy of spiritual powers and kills the gift of prayer. And even if these formidable objections could be overcome, it is intolerable that any liturgy should be imposed upon any Christian congregation whatsoever by a body outside itself.[54]

By the end of 1661 twelve more Congregational incumbents had joined the ranks of the ejected, at least seven of whom were either lecturers or public preachers in the established church before their ejection. By the end of that year Congregationalists also knew that, in common with other Dissenters, they would henceforth be excluded from membership of municipal corporations. In the following year Congregationalists likewise shared with other Dissenters the devastating effects of the Act of Uniformity. Of the 1,909 ejections from the Church of England between 1660 and 1662 171, or 9% of the total, were definitely known to be Congregational at the time of their ejection.[55] There was also a group of some fifty-nine ejected incumbents who were not known as Congregationalists in 1662, or who were known to be Presbyterian in their sentiments, who later became connected with Congregational churches, or adopted Congregational principles.

For a quarter of a century the Congregationalists, in common with all Dissenters, suffered from the harassment of the government and the attempt to uproot all forms of Nonconformity. It was a severe time of testing, but it was not systematic over the whole period. As we have seen, it ebbed and flowed. In certain respects it was a golden age for Independency. Shorn of the political power which they had tasted during the Interregnum, they were driven to contemplate the fundamentals of the faith they sought to defend. John Milton, who very much sympathized with the Independents, completed 'the noblest expression of the concern of seventeenth-century Puritanism with the eternal issue of Good and Evil'[56] when he published his *Paradise Lost* in 1663, and followed this with *Paradise Regained* and *Samson Agonistes* in 1671. In 1666 John Bunyan issued his *Grace Abounding to the Chief of Sinners*, and in 1678 and 1684 there followed parts one and two of *Pilgrim's Progress*. He also published *The Life and Death of Mr Badman* (1680) and *The Holy War* (1682).

Throughout the period of persecution, the Congregationalists were not deficient in leadership or action. In many ways the leaders were a remarkable company of men. The majority of those who either were Congregationalists at the time of their ejection or later became so were graduates, thirty-seven of them were Fellows of colleges, and six served as Heads of colleges. In these times of testing, with the consequences of the Clarendon Code to endure, John Owen was an outstanding man even among this distinguished array of leaders. 'His sense of the unity of the Independent churches and of the fundamental importance of their witness; his resolution not to fritter away what was essential in doubtful compromises with the Presbyterian or Anglican; his implacable opposition to the policy of coercing conscience; his uncanny ability to keep in touch with people of all kinds both within and without the circle of Congregational churches and his quiet and dignified influence upon those in authority, made him the nerve-centre of the Congregational resistence to the penal code.'[57] He also had the advantage of the counsel of Dr Thomas Goodwin, the grave and erudite President of Magdalen College, Oxford.

Despite the repressive laws the Congregationalists continued to gather together, in the open air, in woods, caves and shaded nooks, as well as in places specifically fitted out for worship. They were mostly quite small, compact societies. Their worship was of the simplest kind, with the emphasis on preaching and prayer, and with any form of written liturgy strongly proscribed. They faithfully and regularly met in fellowship in the face of possible dire consequences if they were discovered.

The persecution of Congregationalists, and of Dissenters in general, was increased at the end of the reign of Charles II as a result of the Rye House Plot. On 12 June 1683 Josiah Keeling, a Baptist oil merchant, divulged a plan to waylay the King and the Duke of York at Rye House in Hertfordshire, on their return from the Newmarket horse-races. Both men were to be assassinated, and this was to be the signal for a general insurrection which would place the Duke of Monmouth on the throne. The plot failed because Newmarket was accidently burnt down and the King had to leave ten days sooner than he anticipated. It is difficult to determine the accuracy of Keeling's information, but there is no doubt about the consequences of his disclosure. It gave the authorities around the King another 'proof' that Dissenters were a threat to the church and state, and an opportunity to crush the Whigs once for all. Some Independents were said to have been implicated in the plot. It was a period of depression and darkness for Congregationalists and Dissenters as a whole. And it was at that juncture that some of the main old leaders, whose service went back to the Cromwellian era, died. William Bridge and William Greenhill had died in 1671, Philip Nye had died in 1672, Joseph Caryl and John Loder in 1673, Ralph Venning in 1674 and Thomas Goodwin in 1680. Then, on 23 August 1683, 'the greatest Independent of his generation',[58] John Owen, died. In the midst of a period of acute persecution, on the verge of another reign, the leadership of the Congregational churches was devolving upon a new, and as yet little tested, generation.

The Baptists

Most Baptists were as ready as the majority of the population in 1660 to accept the restoration of the monarchy as the only alternative to chaos. Unfortunately for them, they continued to be identified by many as Anabaptists, and associated with the fanatical excesses of Munster. This was a particular problem when they were about to face a new regime which abhored any sign of revolutionary activity. So the General Baptists held their Assembly in London in March 1660, and issued *A Brief Confession or Declaration of Faith*, which became the standard Confession of the General Baptists, in order 'to inform all men (in these days of scandal and reproach) of an innocent belief and practice, for which we are not only resolved to suffer persecution, to the loss of our goods, but also life itself, rather than to decline the same'.[59] They affirmed their belief that the magistracy was of divine appointment, but they denied to it any jurisdiction in religious matters. They repudiated utterly any attributed intention of the Baptists to take up arms against those who differed from them in their religious opinions.

Regrettably for Baptists as a whole, there were a few of their number who were hotheads, and who were far from adopting what rapidly became the prevailing attitude of passive resistance. They wanted to foment a rebellion. Among these was the firebrand Thomas Tillam, a member of Hanserd Knollys' church and the founder of the church at Hexham, who was cast into prison in 1660 for joining with some other Baptists in plotting rebellion, and for communicating with leading regicides who had fled abroad. Plots, or supposed plots, were unearthed in various parts of the country. In addition to the insurrection led by Thomas Venner in January 1661, in November of the same year an example was made of John James, a Seventh-Day General Baptist, who had been guilty of openly preaching sedition. After his execution, 'his heart was taken out and burnt, his quarters fixed on the gates of the city, and his head set up in Whitechapel, on a pole, opposite the alley in which his meeting-house stood'.[60] The Seventh-Day Baptists were apparently in some way connected with the Fifth Monarchists. They held their services on Saturdays, maintaining that the seventh day of the week was sanctified by the Creator for all mankind (Gen. 2.2 f.); that the fourth commandment was as immutable as the others; and that there was nothing in the New Testament which justified the substitution of the first day of the week for the seventh as the sabbath. Some of the Seventh-Day Baptists were Calvinists or Particular, while others were Arminian or General, and not all those who held Seventh-Day views were Baptists.

Only nineteen Baptists suffered deprivation of their posts as clergy, lecturers and Fellows between 1660 and 1662; an indication that not many Baptists had entered Cromwell's State Church. But the Baptists felt the full force of the new legislation, and at the end of 1662 there were 289 Baptists in Newgate Prison and 18 in the Tower.[61] The enforcement of the Act of Uniformity drove them into a greater measure of separation, and helped to forge them into a more coherent, identifiable entity. Together with the Congregationalists and the so-called Presbyterian churches, the Baptists gradually formed themselves into what they styled as 'Nonconformists' or 'Nonconforming Churchmen', and what the Church of England people called 'Dissenters'.[62]

In 1672, as a provision of the Declaration of Indulgence, as many as 210 Baptists were licensed as teachers out of a total of 939 licences issued.[63] Just over 200 houses were also licenced as Baptist places of worship. But with the renewed persecution the licences were useless, and the record of them provided informers with the means of readily knowing where conventicles were held and who were the leaders. The new onslaught had one unanticipated consequence. In addition to welding the Baptists into a tighter and stronger unit it brought the Baptists and the Congregationalists nearer to the Presbyterians who, since the ejection of 1662, had defied the Conventicles Acts.

In order to make their identity with the Presbyterians and the Congregationalists explicit, the Particular Baptists issued a new Confession in 1677 to show 'our hearty agreement with them in that wholesome Protestant doctrine which . . . they have asserted'.[64] It was based on the Westminster Confession of 1648 and the Congregational revision of that declaration in 1658. Two years later the General Baptists produced *An Orthodox Creed* which was stated to be 'an essay to unite and confirm all true Protestants in the fundamental articles of the Christian religion against the errors of Rome'.[65]

The Quakers

The Quakers were probably 'the most radical of all the religious groups spawned by the Civil Wars, the most numerous, and the most offensive to episcopalians, presbyterians, and independent congregations alike. They rejected all ecclesiastical government, all rituals, all texts, and all oaths, and propagated their views with noisy public demonstrations'.[66] Their leaders had held aloof from the republican regimes and seemed to stand in judgment on almost all other corporate expressions of the Christian faith during the Interregnum. Now at the Restoration they hailed Charles as their sovereign to whom they looked for protection. Somewhat surprisingly they found an initial, and to some extent persistent, positive response from the monarch. He graciously permitted them to retain their hats in the presence of others, and he seems to have been both flattered and amused by their attitude and behaviour. He promised them that they could meet in safety, and for a short time he was true to his word, for seven hundred of them were released from prison on his orders. In this liberal approach he parted company with the overwhelming majority of those in central and local government. His ministers were visibly embarrased by his whole treatment of the Quakers, and his acquiescence in their peculiar dress, manner of speech and conduct. The Commons clamoured for radicals to pay double taxes, and the Lords pressed for the dispersal of Separatist meetings. Charles was clearly at odds with the general, prevailing climate of opinion. While to some extent he pandered to the Quakers, and sought to treat them with leniency, mobs attacked their gatherings, and across England many of the newly appointed justices ignored his policy and proceeded to lock up Quaker leaders and preachers faster than the King could free them.

The ten years of bitter persecution of Quakers from 1662 to 1672 began with the severe Quaker Act directed specifically against them. This piece of persecuting legislation imposed penalties on any person who maintained that the taking of an oath, even before a lawful magistrate, was altogether unacceptable and contrary to the word of God; and it made it an offence for Quakers to leave their homes and assemble, five or more at a time, for the declared purpose of worship. If convicted by a jury, by confession, or as a result of evidence submitted, the offender was subject to fines and imprisonments for the first two offences, and for a third was to abjure the realm or be transported to one of the British plantations overseas. With the passing of the Act a storm of persecution broke over the London Friends, and for some months their meetings were frequently raided, often with great brutality. There developed a general attempt to root out Nonconformity, in which the Friends bore the brunt of the attack. This subsided to some extent under the stress, and with the distraction, of the Plague, the Great Fire and the Dutch War. It gathered fresh strength with the Conventicle Act of 1670; and the decade of suffering ended with the signal triumph of the King's Declaration of Indulgence in 1672, and with the Great Pardon of Friends later in the same year.[67]

The attack was mainly met with fortitude, patience, non-resistance and a radiant testimony to the truth as it was perceived by those who looked to the inward light. The leaders set an example. Francis Howgill 'lay in the prison on the old bridge at Appleby till his death in January 1669, stuffed up for want of air, and at the mercy of a tyrannous gaoler'. Yet he could write from prison to his fellow-sufferers:

God by His Holy Spirit gives daily hints of His love in the inward man unto all stayed minds, and assurance of the victory, which makes me often overlook present suffering and forget the afflictions that are passed and little to heed present things though they seem to frown; because the light of God's countenance is lifted up, and His favour and love and strengthening power felt in the inward man, which balances all and weighs down the scale of present trouble and affliction.[68]

Margaret Fell endured imprisonment, and Fox himself a shorter, but harsher period of confinement. Even from his prison-cell he was shaking the country, so he was hastily moved under military escort to Scarborough, where he was incarcerated for sixteen months, and was, in his own words, 'as a man buried alive', shut off from his friends, and the butt and object of curiousity for visitors to Scarborough Spa.[69]

It was in this period, in 1667, during a lull in the persecution, that William Penn, the son of a court favourite, Admiral Sir William Penn, and the foremost champion in England of religious liberty during the following twenty years, threw in his lot with the Friends. He was rejected by his father because of his religious commitment, but the Admiral's resentment wore off. As a Quaker he exercised considerable influence both in England and in the American colonies.

From Dissent to Nonconformity

During the Restoration period we can identify a distinct phase in the transformation of Dissenting sects into Nonconformist denominations. For it was in these years that as a result of legislation and public policy from without, and changes in structure, life and dynamics from within, the main sub-divisions of Dissent underwent a process of consolidation. From being disjointed, somewhat unco-ordinated and insecure groups, whose effectiveness in uniting their adherents and in making an impact upon the society in which they were placed depended largely upon the emergence at any particular time of one or more charismatic leaders, they quite quickly assumed a more permanent and stable identity, with a defined set of beliefs and practices, and a recognizable, and in the main socially acceptable, style of life. They were increasingly perceived as a valid religious alternative to the Church of England. They were not, to anywhere near the same extent as in the recent past, largely regarded as a peculiar rabble of enthusiasts. They were assuming a distinctive shape and character, the legislation acknowledged them, and the population as a whole even if, for the main part, they did not like them, recognized their right to exist. It was a remarkable change from the Elizabethan era, when they were a despised band of dissidents.

In parallel with this, the Church of England became more established and accepted as the national church but also, for the first time, regarded as only one among many expressions of Christian belief and practice. The modern age was dawning in which no one tradition could, with any authenticity or general assent, assert its right to be the only representative of the Christian faith in the country. It was one of the most important stages in the long history of the transformation of sects into denominations, and the evolution of ever greater pluralism, first within the total Christian fold, but then, three hundred years later, embracing other religious traditions.

Varying degrees of Dissent and Nonconformity

Although the events of the 1660s which I have been discussing helped to transform Puritanism into Dissent, and Dissent into Nonconformity, many gradations of Dissent appeared among those who refused to conform completely to the restored Church of England.[70] The moderate Puritans who had striven long and hard to reform or change the national church and at last felt compelled to become Dissenters found themselves in the company of the more extreme Puritans who were Sectarian, Separatist or independent in tradition. They did not immediately become complete Nonconformists, but adopted the practice of occasional or partial conformity. Not long after the Restoration, therefore, terms such as 'conformable Nonconformist' came into use to describe these citizens of two religious worlds. There were conforming Nonconformists and nonconforming conformists, and considerable variations within and between these categories. Congregationalists were divided on the matter of occasional conformity; and a few years later the same divisions appeared among the Baptists. The practice of attending the established church to hear the sermon but not to participate in the Common Prayer or sacraments, which had been the custom of some Congregationalists prior to the Civil Wars, seems to have been revived to some extent after 1662. Strong feelings were aroused by the issue. There was a body of opinion to be found in all the major denominations of the time, which fervently objected to such conduct. Indeed, the Congregationalist minister in Yarmouth, William Bridge, appears to have been so incensed by the custom that he threatened his members with excommunication if they went to hear the Church of England clergyman.[71] But by about 1667 the practice was sufficiently common that one of their prominent ministers, Philip Nye, taught that limited conformity was not only lawful but even a duty, provided that it did not entail participation in the Common Prayer or receiving the sacrament.

As the Church of England became more secure and self-confident, occasional conformity became less acceptable as a means of gaining the benefits of Nonconformity as well as the status of the established church. It was made clear that individuals could not have the best of both worlds. The Restoration, with all its supporting legislation, ensured that partial conformity and the acceptance of the established church were not sufficient to establish a person's Anglicanism. 'In law and in the judgment of the officials of both Church and State, as well as in the conviction of Dissenters themselves, those who attended Nonconformist services or objected to Episcopalian government, or to Anglican ceremonies or doctrines, had clearly demonstrated their dissent from the Church of England.'[72] And in this process of differentiation a leading part was played by the two most prominant churchmen of the age, Gilbert Sheldon and Henry Compton.

Although the figureheads of the restored Church of England were its two archbishops, William Juxon and Accepted Frewen, the real source of power and influence from the outset was Gilbert Sheldon, the Bishop of London, and later himself Archbishop of Canterbury; the confidant of politicians. He was born in 1598 and educated at Trinity College, Oxford. In 1636 he became Fellow and Warden of All Souls. 'Oxford don, royal chaplain, friend of Edward Hyde, Sheldon was a member of Falkland's circle at Great Tew, not one who favoured or was favoured by Laud.'[73] He was evicted from All Souls in 1648 and briefly imprisoned, and throughout the Commonwealth he lived in retirement. He was reinstalled at All Souls in 1659, and made Bishop of London at the Restoration.

As we have seen, Sheldon was the dominant figure at the Savoy Conference and in the religious settlement which followed. 'The iron entered Sheldon's soul in August 1662.'[74] He saw his task as the enforcement of a strict, unyeilding conformity. Nonconformity was an ill which must be eradicated:

> Tis only a resolute execution of the law that must cure this disease, all other remedies serve and will increase it; and it's necessary that they who will not be governed as men by reason and persuasions should be governed as beasts by power and force, all other courses will be ineffectual, ever have been so, ever will be . . .[75]

For Sheldon and his like-minded Anglican brethren the issue of religious conformity was simply reduced by the Act of Uniformity to a matter of submitting to the law. Schism and sedition were almost coterminous, and it was nonsensical to speak of peaceable and loyal Dissenters. As a fervent Royalist he identified religious Dissent with political disloyalty. As archbishop from 1663, he was able more effectively to use his astute political skill and manipulative ability to good effect in promoting the supremacy of the church, and the inter-related dependence of church and state. In equating religious Dissent with political disloyalty he was playing on the social and political fears of the gentry. 'It was a commonplace of conservative lay thinking that "uniformity is the cement of both Christian and civil societies", and that neither society nor authority can stand without religious unity.'[76]

'Gilbert Sheldon, and the country gentry and city elites were both powerful influences in the creation of the Restoration settlement; to some extent they were partners; but it was only a small (if potent) minority among the latter which shared the depth of commitment of the Bishop of London.'[77] But it must not be thought that Sheldon was merely a political churchman: Royalist as he was, he had the sense of duty and the boldness to reprove Charles II for adultery; and he was a pastor as well, as was demonstrated in the plague of 1665–6 when he remained at his post at Lambeth while the court and many London clergymen fled from the capital. As an aside, it can be noted that the hasty exodus of so many parish clergy, and the contrasting courage of Dissenting pastors who ministered in their place, did considerable harm to the reputation of the Church of England, and much to increase respect for the Dissenters. The Fire of London in September 1666 was also devastating for the church, as it laid waste 89 of London's parish churches.

It was ironic that in the latter part of his archiepiscopate the Royalist Sheldon had to contend with the problem of excessive political 'loyalty' within the church from a group of divines whose enthusiasm for the royal prerogative knew no bounds. Such a politicization and polariza-tion by a band of zealots like Thomas Pierce, Lawrence Womock, Samuel Parker and James Arderne began for the first time to appear as a threat to the church's interests. They grew in significance as the 1670s progressed, and they formed an 'extravagant, ultra-Tory wing of the Church, which, in the course of the 1680s, not only grew in importance, but also repeatedly threatened to subvert the stability of the Anglican Establishment from within'.[78] Such a threat came to a climax in the reign of James II.

By the 1670s another 'political' bishop was taking centre stage in church and state affairs: Henry Compton, a successor to Sheldon as Bishop of London.[79] He was born in 1632, into a distinguished old Warwickshire family which in 1618 was honoured with the Earldom of Northampton. Until the Restoration he was for the most part abroad.

He became Bishop of Oxford in 1674, and the following year he was translated to London. It was also in 1675 that he was made Dean of the Chapels Royal, an office of considerable political importance, especially in these years, because it gave him a decisive influence in the education of the Princesses Mary and Anne, the daughters of James, Duke of York. He opposed Exclusion, but he did not attempt to disguise his fervent Protestantism. 'In fact his anti-Roman-Catholic vigour was particularly noticeable at this time.' 'He was constantly securing the suppression of Popish books, urging the dismissal of Roman Catholics from Court, receiving converts from Rome, and encouraging the writing of Protestant pamphlets.'[80] He was a close ally of the Earl of Danby, and was intimately involved in trying to disentangle the Popish Plot. He served as a member of one of a Committee of the Privy Council which interrogated Oates. His Protestant zeal persisted throughout the reign, although it did not represent an insummountable barrier between the bishop and the King, and as late as 1681 the King constituted him and William Sancroft a small committee to advise on ecclesiastical preferments.

The prominence of such a 'Protestant' bishop as Compton was symptomatic. In various ways, and not least of all in the reactions to the Popish Plot and the exclusion crisis, the population as a whole had demonstrated that Protestantism was well entrenched in the life of the country, and that the Church of England was accepted as its official expression. This was most signally manifested in the life, worship and witness of ordinary people.

Diocesan and parochial life, worship and witness

Throughout the reigns of Charles II and James II England was still a country whose population was overwhelmingly dependent for their livelihood on agriculture, and who lived mostly in hamlets, villages or small provincial towns. Industry was on a small scale, with most manufactured goods produced by small craftsmen, using local, mainly agricultural, raw materials and serving a local market. The normal unit of industrial production was the home. The whole national economy was therefore largely static, traditional, and community-based. And in these communities the parish church was centrally placed as a tangible symbol of the centrality of its worship, teaching and norms in every aspect of the lives of the inhabitants. The annual, seasonal and weekly round was to a great extent routinized around the demands of agricultural life, or the life of the country town, and was imbued with religious connotations which were at the very heart of individual and corporate living.

After the violent events, the rapid and dramatic changes of fortune, the tensions and the turbulence of the decades immediately preceding 1660, it is little wonder that the life of many parishes during the Restoration period was somewhat unsettled. The political upheavals and Puritan enthusiasms of the Commonwealth years had tautened the strained nerves of the people in many parishes, and had created dark areas of insecurity and fear which the superficial splendours of the Restoration did not dispel. Terling, in Essex, was typical of many parishes. During the reign of Charles II it was 'deeply divided in matters of religion. The long years of Puritan influence and the turmoil of the Interregnum had left their mark.'[81] Many parishes were not able to escape the divisive effect of the trend towards religious choice: religious pluralism had become a fact of life. 'When the parson of Congestone, Leicestershire, announced his intention to catechize his parishioners they "shut the church door and would not suffer him to come in, but went many of them to a conventicle held in Mr Palmer's house at Temple Hall, the pretended patron of Congeston".'[82] Quite frequently lay patrons presented partially conforming incumbents, or required conformist ministers to allow Dissenting preachers to use the church, and if parishioners had a say in appointments the situation was often worse. On the other hand some parishes apparently enjoyed a great measure of Christian unanimity. This was so with Brightwell

> through the exemplary piety and prudent conduct of that worthy gentleman, the worshipful John Stone Esq., lord of the town and the Revd. Mr Fiddes then rector of the place, and their predecessors, and the good disposition of the people themselves, [whereby] all matters both of spiritual and temporal concern, have been so effectually pressed and prudently managed, that there has not been known any such thing as an ale house, a sectary, or suit of law commenced within the whole parish (which is of a large extent) in the memory of man.[83]

The Restoration clergy were a crucial element in the attempt of the Church of England to re-establish its authority at parochial level; and in certain respects they were well equipped as the front-line forces of the church, for they were better educated than any of their forebears. Most of them were graduates, so that in Leicestershire in 1670 95% of incumbents possessed degrees.[84] There was also probably an oversupply, so that there was a measure of selection possible with employment in the church for only about half those seeking such a profession. But the usual, long-standing clerical problems remained. There was still poverty and pluralism, with the inevitable associated non-residence. The clergy continued to receive tithes, but such offerings were very frequently begrudged by the laity, and the cause of unseemly squabbles. The most oft-repeated complaints from laity related to non-residence, not exercising proper care and control over curates, not catechizing, omitting the whole or part of the services, and not administering baptism and communion.

The authority of the clergy was undermined by the plurality of religious traditions. The options which had been opened up to people in many parishes between various sects or religious groups, the parish church, or no religious attachment at all had caused confusion and encouraged indifference, or even irreligion. There was a marked lack of Christian unanimity in Restoration England. Local clergymen often found that there was a preacher or pastor of the Interregnum still living and working in their parish or neighbourhood, and ejected ministers quite often continued to be a thorn in the side of their Anglican successors. Men like William Bagshawe, known as 'the apostle of the Peak district', William Bridge of Great Yarmouth, Oliver Heywood of Halifax, Christopher Fowler of Reading, John Stalham of Terling, or Francis Holcroft of Bassingbourn and Nathaniel Bradshaw of Willingham, who were collectively reckoned as the fathers of Cambridgeshire Congregationalism, all created a virtual 'shadow ministry' in their own districts.[85] In some places the meetings of dissenting groups were held at the same time as the services of the parish church. It was difficult at the parish level for the Church of England to defend itself against the trend towards religious choice: 'this was a society which enjoyed a plural, competitive, religious culture'.[86]

The services of the Church of England after 1660 were characterized by a higher ceremonial than that to which most Englishmen had become accustomed.[87] Candlesticks were again placed on the altar, organs returned to the churches, the church year with its different seasons was celebrated, crosses and religious pictures were commonly used in the furnishings of churches, and gestures expressive of reverence were commonly seen again. But trends in the Restoration churches were not all in one direction. The Puritan influence remained. The *Westminster Directory of Public Worship* of 1644, which combined fixity and freedom in its order of worship and proposed themes for prayers without prescribing their wording, was not a dead letter. It still represented an attractive alternative to the Prayer Book to some, even within the established church, and was a permanent reminder of a tradition which so very recently had flourished and been in the ascendant. Then there was Richard Baxter's *Reformed Liturgy* of 1661, which was based on what he had practised and found to be so acceptable and effective in his Kidderminster ministry, and which was given the seal of approval by his Presbyterian colleagues.

Nonetheless, despite the pressures on the established church, and the nonconforming options available, overall there seems to have been a remarkable degree of continuity in the pattern of church life in most parishes throughout much of the seventeenth century, and indeed on into the eighteenth century. The norm seems to have been 'the performance of two services on a Sunday (one in each church in the case of a poor pluralist), and the administration of holy communion four times a year (six to twelve times in urban parishes and some late eighteenth-century rural ones), the performance of the rites of passage on demand, and a series of sessions of catechizing for part or all of the period between Lent and Michaelmas'.[88] This is not to say that anywhere near the majority of the population attended their local parish churches. In this, as in every age since the sixteenth century, there was considerable variation 'according to the size and pattern of settlement (larger parishes with scattered hamlets usually had lower attendance), the mobility of the population (parishes with higher turnovers had smaller turnouts), the inhabitants' chief occupations (pastoral workers, sailors and miners were less regular attenders than arable workers) and the attitude of the village notables (while some encouraged their servants and tenants to attend, others did not)'.[89] Although the Compton census of 1676 suggests that the majority of the population were loyal church attenders, some local studies indicate that as few as 10% partook of communion in some parishes. But what seems to have been common in all, or at least a vast majority, of the parishes of the land, was an acceptance by most of the inhabitants of the church as the legitimate representation of Christianity in their community. The other, new, religious traditions did complicate the scene, and, as we have seen, the emergence of religious pluralism was one of the prime factors in the history of the Church in England in the period 1558 to 1688, but the parish church retained its status as the place to which many of the local people resorted for baptisms, confirmations, weddings and funerals, not just out of necessity, because there was no other place where they could receive such religious services, but willingly, as being 'the right thing to do'. By 1688 parish Anglicanism was integral to the life of most Englishmen, either because they participated in its life or simply because it was a vital part of the fabric of society, and life would not have been the same without it.

And finally as we survey the diocesan and parochial life of the Church of England during this period we note a trend which was to become significant in the post-Revolutionary era – the emergence of 'latitudinarianism'. It was a pejorative term. There was no specifically 'latitudinarian' party or even outlook among Restoration churchmen. It was an expression of hostility, and an attempt 'to brand the theological repudiation of Calvinism as a deficiency of character or a lack of principle. But the renunciation of the old orthodoxy, associated as it was with the younger generation of churchmen, was fast becoming "the dominant theological school" of the day. It is this dominant temper of Restoration Anglicanism, and not the chimera of "latitudinarianism", which should claim our attention if we are to understand how England came to terms with her puritan legacy.'[90]

Richard Baxter

Having reviewed the general religious situation during the reign of Charles II, the beginning of the consolidation of Dissent into Nonconformist denominations, and the way the Church of England emerged from its trial by fire during the Interregnum, I will conclude this survey of the Restoration period with a brief consideration of the remarkable life, thought and writings of a man who stood in a unique relationship to all these Christian traditions: Richard Baxter, the 'Bishop of Nonconformity'. Above all others of his generation he was able to exercise a profound influence in the counsels of both the Church of England and the Nonconformists, as well as in the relationship between these two traditions.

Baxter was born in 1615 and came to maturity at a time when Laudianism was dominant in the Church of England, when the active Puritans were few in number and persecuted, and when Dissent was manifested in what were generally regarded as small and aberrant groups. By the time he died, in 1691, the Presbyterians, Congregationalists, Baptists and Quakers were well embedded in the national life, with their own chapels or meeting places, their own corpus of belief and their own patterns of corporate life. He was ordained deacon in 1638, but soon found 'his sympathies were moving from conventional Puritanism in the direction of Nonconformity'.[91] He was troubled by what he regarded as the indiscriminate giving of the Lord's Supper, and as an 'Assistant' at Bridgnorth he never administered the holy communion. He also refused to baptize any child with the sign of the cross, and did not wear a surplice. He made his mark as an army chaplain, where he gained a reputation as a vigorous opponent of the more extreme manifestations of Separatism, Anabaptism and antinomianism, and as the pastor of the Kidderminster church, where his ministry had an outstanding impact upon the lives of the whole local population, and resulted in many joining the ranks of the godly.

Baxter suffered greatly from physical illness, which apparently brought him close to death and resulted in much frustrating loss of ministerial time. But this did not drive him to despair or resignation. Instead, he learnt to husband every moment available, which made possible his extraordinary activity and literary output. It coloured and sharpened whatever he said or wrote.

> I Preach'd, as never sure to Preach again
> And as a dying man to dying men.

It was his abundant writings which extended his influence far and wide at a time of great religious activity, tension and flux. He delighted above all else in pastoral work and preaching, but when he was prevented later in life from undertaking these cherished roles because of his ejection from the Church of England, he concentrated on writing. Although *The Reformed Pastor* was mainly concerned with matters other than preaching, a few extracts from that work on the subject of preaching will give some insight into what he sought to do, and to be, as a preacher with evangelical passion:

> It is a fearful case to be an unsanctified Professor, but much more to be an unsanctified Preacher. Preach to your selves the Sermons that you study, before you preach them to others; [for] God never saved any man for being a Preacher; [and] many a Preacher is now in hell. All the week long is little enough to study how to speak two hours. Be much, above all, in secret prayer and meditation: [the people] will likely feel when you have been much with God. In preaching, there is intended a communion of souls, and a communication of somewhat from ours unto theirs. [Then] see that you have a constant serious-

ness; . . . especially see that there be no affectation; . . . remember that they must be wakened or damned.[92]

In his preaching as well as in the other aspects of his ministry he was concerned to use his very considerable intellect in the service of God, but in doing so to be subject to the authority of the Scriptures and to the Holy Spirit:

We must not try the Scriptures by our most spiritual apprehensions, but our apprehensions by the Scriptures . . . This trying the Spirit by the Scriptures, is not a setting of the Scriptures above the Spirit itself; but is only a trying of the Spirit by the Spirit . . .[93]

He was concerned that all public worship, whether it was preaching, prayers or praise, should be informed with intensity of devotion:

Preach with such life and awakening seriousness; Preach with such grateful holy eloquence, and with such easie method, and with such variety of wholesome matter, that the people may never be aweary of you . . . Pray with that Heavenly life and fervour as may wrap up the souls of those that joyne with you, and try then whether they will be aweary: Praise God with that joyful alacrity which beseemeth one that is ready to pass into Glory, and try whether this will not Cure the peoples weariness.[94]

Baxter was greatly concerned to promote Christian unity. He was on occasions the chief spokesman for the Presbyterians, and yet never a fully fledged Presbyterian. He was an advocate for Nonconformists, and persistently pleaded for an understanding of their case, yet he remained a moderate episcopalian. This does not imply that he was indecisive or ambiguous in his beliefs, his ecclesiology or his allegiances. Far from it. He had deep and firm convictions, and he was prepared to declare them boldly and without fear or favour. But he stood for 'Catholicism against all sects, a Catholicism not merely Roman or Greek or Anglican, but Christian, and therefore genuinely universal. He saw, as one born out of due time, the vision of a Church whose limits are coterminous only with Christianity itself'.[95] In his *Key for Catholics* (1659), he wrote:

Christianity is our religion. Protesting against Popery is our negation . . . Christianity is it that we are agreed in, and that is our religion, and nothing but that. Protestancy as such is but our wiping off the dirt . . . We still profess before men and angels that we own no religion but the Christian religion, nor any church but the Christian church, nor dream of any Catholic Church but one, containing all the true Christians in the world, united in Jesus Christ as the head.[96]

And this was a theme which was dear to his heart, and which he particularized with reference to the situation which confronted him in England:

> The most that keeps us at odds is but about the right form and order of Church-government. Is the distance so great that Presbyterian, Episcopal and Independent might not be well agreed? Were they but heartily willing and forward for peace, they might – I know they might . . . If we could not in every point agree, we might easily find out and narrow our differences and hold Communion upon our agreement in the main . . . But is this much done? It is not done. To the shame of all our faces be it spoken, it is not done. Let each party flatter themselves now as they please, it will be recorded to the shame of the ministry of England, while the gospel shall abide in the Christian world.[97]

Finally, it needs to be noted that Baxter's massive outpouring of literature in various forms was but part of a remarkably productive era of Nonconformist creativity. Historians have perhaps been 'far too conservative in their estimates of the spread of reading ability' in the latter half of the seventeenth century. It appears that 'illiteracy was everywhere face to face with literacy', that by the end of the century even popular culture was literate rather than oral and that, though 'we shall never be able to assess' the 'true size' of the late seventeenth-century reading public, it was almost certainly greater than statistics alone suggest.[98] It seems that literary rates were higher among the Nonconformists than in other sections of society. Milton, Bunyan, Baxter and others wrote copiously, confident of Nonconformist readers. Nonconformists were heirs of the educational drive of Puritanism, they were enthusiastic advocates of the benefits of literacy, and they encouraged all classes of society, and especially children, to learn to read and to write and to be diligent practitioners of these skills.

The literary culture of Nonconformity was rich and vital.[99] It was essential to the survival of Nonconformity and, faced with the adverse circumstances of the late seventeenth century, Nonconformity 'created a committed Christian literature of distinctive character. It was a literature which in its premises and procedures dissented from evolving literary canons'. It was 'creative, positive and salutary in its demotic realism, its subjective authenticity, its metaphorical richness and its sensitivity to the numinous. In these respects it anticipated a later, and greater, literary movement: its tendency is towards the work not of Pope but of Blake, Wordsworth and Coleridge, men who admired not only the genius of Milton, as the eighteenth century had done, but also that of Bunyan and Baxter, as the eighteenth century had not.'[100] This Nonconformist liturature shows little evidence of concern with literary fashions or poses. It shows great concern for 'experimental' knowledge of God.

It spoke directly to the reader with the urgent immediacy of personal conviction and with the persuasive authenticity of varied, and variously modulated, individual voices. It spoke with an honest awareness, born of personal experience, of people's imperfect natures and of the complexity of worldly affairs, but, though it toyed with no extravagant impossibilities, it spoke also with the sure confidence that the world could be overcome, that in the sufferings of Nonconformists lay the promise of final victory. Hence, as its experiential basis preserved Nonconformist writing from the escapist flights of romance, so its supernatural faith preserved it from sardonic pre-occupation with political machinations and social mores. Although this refusal to take refuge in either the ideal or the material was also a refusal to prefer either romance or realism, it denied neither: rather, it admitted both. It married the alternative worlds that literary fashions and genres tended to divorce.[101]

The Reign of James II and the Revolution

James II

James was the second son and third child of Charles I and Henrietta
Maria.[1] He was born in 1633, and his early life was clouded by political tension and crisis, by the Civil Wars, and by the execution of his
father. He was nearly captured at Edgehill, taken prisoner when Oxford
fell in 1646, and escaped to Holland in 1648. By then, he was still only
fifteen years of age.

He returned to England at the Restoration. During the reign of his
brother he was active politically, socially, and sexually. He had
numerous mistresses, who, although fewer than was the case with
Charles, were reputedly uglier. He was Lord High Admiral until 1673,
an office to which he had first been appointed at the age of four, and he
had a genuine love of the sea and an aptitude for naval command. He
readily supported reforms of the navy like those of Pepys, and he helped
to improve the system for officer training and the organization of
discipline.

When James was converted to Catholicism is not clear, although it
was some time in the 1660s. By the beginning of 1669 he was convinced
that there was no salvation outside the Catholic Church, and he was
admitted into that church early in 1672.[2] For the remainder of the reign
of Charles he epitomized the danger of popery to all anti-Catholics.
His position was made the more difficult because of the infertility of
the Queen, so that he remained the heir, and because his second wife
whom he married in 1672 was a Catholic. The potential for disaster
if he became King was therefore considerable, and caused widespread
apprehension. The fear of popery and arbitrary government was the
dominant theme of English politics for at least fifteen years from
1673. But he weathered the exclusion crisis, and in 1685 'he succeeded
to the throne in a glow of popularity, with Whigs broken, the Tory
Anglicans vowing non-resistance, London tamed and the countryside
enthusiastic'.[3]

Immediately after Charles died, James declared to the council that it was untrue that he was 'a man for arbitrary power':

> I shall make it my endeavour to preserve this government both in church and state as it is by law established. I know the principles of the Church of England are for monarchy and the members of it have shown themselves good and loyal subjects; therefore I shall always take care to defend and support it. I know too that the laws of England are sufficient to make the King as great a monarch as I can wish; and as I shall never depart from the rights and prerogatives of the crown, so I shall never invade any man's property.[4]

He made it clear that he did not want to establish Catholicism as the sole religion of the country, nor did he wish to eradicate Protestantism by force. He resisted many of the outlandish proposals of his Catholic advisers, and strove to counter the charge that he was a dupe of Louis XIV. His aims were to all appearances quite moderate and limited, for he claimed that he simply wanted to establish the rights of English Catholics to worship unmolested, and to take a full part in the political life of the country.

The reign began in a deceptively quiet and uneventful way for the Catholics. There was initially no great discontinuity. The Catholics in general enjoyed limited toleration. At court Catholicism was reconstituted and resumed the subordinate position on the fringes of the establishment which had been its status in the years before 1678. The King's household and the offices of state remained firmly in the hands of Tory Protestants, and the Anglican Chapel Royal remained the spiritual centre of the government. The sense of continuity was reinforced by the Anglican coronation service in Westminster Abbey, when the Catholic convert King and his devoutly Catholic second wife, Mary of Modena, together with some forty Catholic peers and peeresses, submitted to the unamended Anglican service, in which two anthems by the great Anglican composer Henry Purcell were sung, but the holy communion was excluded. By hereditary right, the whole ceremony was organized by the Duke of Norfolk, who was an ex-Catholic, and a few Catholic peers carried out minor duties in the service. It was the most public example of many occasions when the Catholic King conformed to the protocol of sitting through Anglican worship. In the early part of the reign the King demonstrated what was to Protestants a gratifying impartiality, with no handout of titles and offices to Catholics, only a small number of military commissions granted to Catholics, and those mostly in Ireland, and just a few papist civil servants returned to minor offices under letters of protection, who had been excluded in 1673. For the first year or so of the reign it all seemed to be hardly the coming again of the Catholic religion so long prayed for and anticipated by Catholics.

There was, however, evidence that his real purpose was the reconversion of England: that his seemingly cautious approach was but for the moment, and would be succeeded by a more determined effort to achieve his heart's desire. Whatever his hidden motives, he was naive in thinking that the mere repealing of the Corporation Act of 1661 and the Test Acts of 1673 and 1678 would accomplish even his more limited objectives. He was blind to the extent of anti-Catholicism in the country, which made the defeat of his plans inevitable. He was even more unrealistic if he believed that the English would eagerly embrace Catholicism if they were but given an opportunity to do so. The whole tenor and tone of the times, a century and a half after the first official introduction of Protestantism into the country, militated against any such transformation. The Protestant world view which had permeated to the very core of the nation, and into the very hearts of the people, made the re-conversion of England to Catholicism unthinkable. The somewhat less ambitious aim of establishing the Roman Catholic Church on an equal footing with the Church of England was also unattainable. The Catholic mission had little chance of achieving much: with little time, insufficient priests and a restricted appeal, the Romish missionaries during his reign were to reap a disappointing harvest before their whole enterprise collapsed in almost total failure, with as few as ten Anglican clergymen transferring their allegiance to Rome.

The Monmouth Rebellion

James, Duke of Monmouth (1649–1685) was the eldest son of Charles II by his Welsh mistress Lucy Walter.[5] He was born at the Hague and spent his childhood in exile. He spent his youth in the Restoration court as the pampered favourite of Charles. 'Good-looking, athletic, dashing and brainless, he was a considerable libertine and popular with the London mob.'[6] His vanity was stimulated by this, by his victory when he led a force against covenanting rebels in 1679, and by the attention given to him by the Earl of Shaftesbury and the Whig extremists, who regarded this Protestant claimant to the throne as an ideal candidate in the succession crisis which followed the Popish Plot revelations. After a series of indiscretions and actions which indicated his own self-willed political ineptitude, including an equivocal role in the Rye House Plot, in 1683 he was banished from court, and after a short-lived reconciliation with his father he fled to Holland.

He returned to England in the summer of 1685 in order to claim the throne from his uncle James II. Landing at Lyme Regis, he proceded to Taunton where he was crowned. The scene was set for a fiasco. The Rebellion was doomed to failure, largely because, at that early stage in the reign, there was a general willingness to trust the King, and the anti-Catholic sentiment had not as yet been sufficiently aroused against him to make a spontaneous uprising likely. A few of the local population rallied to the intending usurper, but soon a good proportion of them fell away. He attempted a surprise attack by night at Sedgemoor which failed miserably, and he fled from the battlefield, leaving his wretched peasant followers to be butchered. He was captured in a ditch in the New Forest and, despite his pitiful pleas to James for mercy, was executed on Tower Hill. The sequence to the Rebellion was the brutal punishment of the rebels by Lord Chief Justice Jeffries in 'the Bloody Assizes'.

As a claimant to the throne, the Duke had stood for Protestantism and constitutional monarchy. This, it was to prove, was a cause for the future, and his death was more advantageous to it than his life. His appeal did not win support from the Church of England or any of the Protestant Dissenting bodies. Some of those who joined his army came from the middle ranks of society in Somerset, West Dorset and East Devon, where Protestant Dissent flourished in cloth-making villages, and where there was considerable fear about the imposition of Catholicism and absolutism, but there was little support from the gentry, and little, if any, evidence that the type of support he sought, and to a limited extent gained, was widespread throught society nationally.

In fact, in the summer of 1685 the Church of England dutifully came to James' aid. The Bishop of Winchester, Peter Mews, actually directed the artillery at Sedgemoor, while the Bishop of Oxford, John Fell, drilled the students in preparation for possible action. On 26 July, the day of thanksgiving for Monmouth's defeat, 'the nation's churches resounded to denunciations of rebellion and to the assertions of divine right and the duty of passive obedience'.[7] But even at this early stage of the new reign, unease was growing at the impertinence of Roman Catholics and the telling signs of a possible and drastic shift towards the imposition of Catholicism in one form or another. By the time that Parliament met in November 1685 James had not disbanded his army, in which Catholic officers were employed who had been promoted by the King despite the Test Acts. When the Marquis of Halifax opposed this, and then Bishop Henry Compton of London protested about it in the Lords, claiming that he merely expressed the opinion of all the bishops, they both immediately lost their seats on the Privy Council. The King had also made known his intention to secure the repeal of the Test and Corporation Acts. Opposition to James was intensified by the identification of James and his policies with Louis XIV's cruel campaign against the French Huguenots. The Revocation of the Edict of Nantes in October 1685 resulted in a flood of French refugees to England, and they brought with them another batch of horror stories about the sufferings imposed upon Protestants by Catholics. In such an atmosphere James' moderate Catholic aims were inevitably misunderstood. 'As with his father's Arminianism in the 1630s, what people *thought* James's plans were became more important than his actual intentions. His aim of securing limited toleration and political rights for Catholics was widely seen as the beginning of a policy of Catholic-inspired repression and *dragonnades*.'[8]

Moves in a Catholic direction

During the winter of 1685–6 new alignments began to be forged at court: the Earl of Sunderland collaborated with a Catholic cabal, and certain appointments of Catholics were made which flew in the face of the requirements of the Test Acts. Sunderland was inordinately ambitious, and after his career had been shattered first by his miscalculation in supporting exclusion, and secondly by the untimely death of Charles, he fought his way back by convincing James of his zeal for his interests, and by encouraging him in his ambition to advance the interests of Catholicism. And having committed himself to that particular policy, and having convinced James that his objectives could be attained, he was trapped. When he saw that his plans were provoking a dangerous amount of distrust and resentment at home and abroad he could not confess to an error of judgment, which would have meant the end of his influence and his power.

In March 1686 the King defied the efforts of the church to ensure conformity by issuing a general pardon which annulled many legal proceedings, and gradually he began to grant personal dispensations from the penal laws to Quakers, Baptists and other Dissenters. These moves were ominous for those Protestants who were acute and sensitive enough to read the signs of the times. Not only was there an apparent encouragement of Dissent, but what was done for Dissent at that time could, on the morrow, be done for Catholicism. The clergy were becoming dispirited. Several of the bishops died that year: John Dolben of York, John Pearson of Chester and John Fell of Oxford. The choice of their successors, Thomas Cartwright for Chester and Samuel Parker for Oxford, was a blow to churchmen, as it was made despite the known dissent of Sancroft, the archbishop and other leading churchmen; and leaving the archbishopric of York vacant until the hurried appointment of Thomas Lamplugh in 1688 was even more discouraging.

It was evident throughout 1686 that James was failing to secure the support of Anglican opinion. This was epitomized and made most explicit in his public confrontation with Henry Compton, the Bishop of London. It was inevitable that such an avid Protestant as Compton would attempt to combat the King's Catholicizing policy. We have already noted his condemnation in 1685 of the King's claim to be able to dispense with the Test Act. In March 1686 James issued some Directions to Preachers in which he ordered the clergy to confine their sermons to those doctrines which could be found in the catechism, and to shun provocative topics, like attacks on Rome. When the rector of St Giles in the Fields, London, John Sharp, later to be Archbishop of York, disobeyed in May, Compton refused to comply with the royal order to suspend him. In response, the King established the Court of Ecclesiastical Commission, and its first act in September was to suspend Compton from the exercise of his episcopal functions. William Sancroft was another victim. He refused to serve on the new Commission, and he was deprived of his place on the Privy Council as a consequence.

Most contemporaries saw the Commission as a revival of the Court of High Commission abolished by Parliament in 1641, and they therefore concluded that it was illegal. It had the wide-ranging powers of a vicar-general to visit, examine and order. The most offensive aspect of the Commission was perhaps the way it was used to stop Anglican clergy from warning their flocks against the dangers of popery and to force the universities to admit non-Anglican students and teachers. It was to be the primary instrument used by the King in his attempt to achieve his ecclesiastical objectives, and as such it was the focus for much of the opposition to both the King and his policy.

For some Anglicans a disconcerting corollary of James' disillusionment with the established church was the softening of his hostility towards Protestant Dissenters. It is not clear when he finally decided to commit himself to a political alliance with the Protestant Dissenters against the Church of England, but the signs were ominous in 1686. During that year he showed considerable favour to individual Dissenters, including the Quaker Penn family. He dispensed a number from the penal legislation, and in November 1686 he established a Licensing Office where Dissenters could buy certificates of dispensation. It was to William Penn that he entrusted the mission to Holland in 1686 which attempted to pursuade William and Mary to give support for the repeal of the Test and Corporation Acts. The failure of that mission was a major factor in the decision of James to abandon the Anglican alliance. Soon after the return of Penn from his abortive mission James dismissed his two principal Anglican ministers, the Earls of Clarendon and Rochester.

The process of Catholicizing went on apace. After a long and difficult campaign, James forced a Catholic President on Magdalen College, Oxford, the symbol of the Anglican educational monopoly, but at the expense of much public discontent and the ejection of the entire college Fellowship. The developing passions both of the King and of his opponents are dramatically epitomized and captured in the action of the Fellows, who defied James to his face when he went to Oxford, and in the almost incoherent rage of the King when confronted by such defiance:

> You have not dealt with me like gentlemen. You have done very uncivilly and undutifully . . . Is this your Church of England loyalty? . . . Go home and show yourselves good members of the Church of England. Get you gone, know that I am your King. I will be obeyed and I command you to be gone. Go and admit the Bishop of Oxford head, principal, what do you call it of the college, I mean president of the college. Let them that refuse it look to it; they shall feel the weight of the sovereign's displeasure.[9]

The universities as a whole were being salted with Roman Catholics or with compliant Anglicans. The ultra-Tories of the early 1680s, such men as Samuel Parker and Thomas Cartwright, were increasingly assuming influence, and, in the view of some, were betraying the church. It is possible that by the end of 1687 the Bishops of Durham, Chester and St David's, all of whom had been appointed by James, were prepared to vote for the repeal of the Test Acts. The King was also taking advice from Nonconformists like Stephen Lobb and Vincent Alsop, as well as William Penn.

Then James proceded to make a more determined effort to promote Roman Catholicism, some of his measures being frontal attacks, others more indirect approaches from the flanks. Among the blatent elements of his *blitzkrieg* were the setting up of a Catholic Chapel Royal in Whitehall, and the starving of funds and encouragement for the Anglican Chapel Royal; the use of the newly created Catholic Chapel at Windsor Castle on his visits there, so that the St George's Chapel was likewise reduced to insignificance; the increase from one to four in the number of Vicars-Apostolic; the establishment of an Italian Papal Nuncio in London, who was consecrated bishop in the Chapel Royal; the proposal to the Pope that he should have three Cardinals to wait on him, and his fury when the Pope rejected the plan; and his appointment of thirteen Catholics to his Council. He also attempted by various devices to make other Catholic appointments elsewhere in the government, which included trying to appoint Catholics to posts which had hitherto been regarded as vital parts of the Anglican establishment, although he was hampered in this by the sheer unavailability of sufficient candidates of high enough standard. In addition, as we have noted, Anglican clergy were forbidden to preach anti-Catholic sermons, and even bishops were suspended for not complying with the enforcement of this ruling; the Anglican monopoly of publishing was breached, and a Catholic press was established, with royal licence, in Oxford; the King's printers in London and York were converted to Catholicism, and they started to publish Catholic books; an attempt was made to open the way for Catholics to matriculate and graduate at the universities without having to submit to Anglican formularies; and Catholics were appointed to important university posts. In central government James largely by-passed the completely Protestant foreign service, and conducted his secret and bumbling foreign policy with the aid of special Catholic agents; and Catholics were intruded into the armed forces in as large numbers as possible, and into local government posts. It was all very alarming to the by then fundamentally Protestant Church of England, and indeed to Protestants in general.

It was on 4 April 1687 that the King announced what was to be the cornerstone of his policy of appealing to Dissenters for support, a Declaration of Indulgence which suspended the execution of all the ecclesiastical penal laws and ordered that the oaths required of office-holders by the Test Act should no longer be imposed. But the King expected as a *quid pro quo* for such leniency, that the Dissenters would rally to his support in an intensified campaign to secure a Parliament that would repeal the Test and Corporation Acts. It seems that in such an expectation he was led astray by an over-estimate of the numbers of Dissenters upon whom he was placing such reliance, and by a more serious miscalculation about their response to his overture. They did not react with unanimous enthusiasm. Most of them were pleased to take advantage of the grant of toleration, despite their scruples concerning the constitutional propriety of an arbitrary suspension of parliamentary legislation. There were many, however, who were deeply suspicious of James' motives, and they harboured fears that they were merely being used as pawns in the King's ultimate objective of imposing long-term intolerant Catholicism. It was widely felt that Catholicism and toleration were incompatible. Both these doubts were voiced by the Marquis of Halifax in a *Letter to a Dissenter* which was published in the summer of 1687. The Dissenters, he argued, were 'to be hugged now, only that you may be the better squeezed at another time . . . This alliance between liberty and infallibility is bringing together the two most contrary things that are in the world. The Church of Rome doth not only dislike the allowing of liberty, but by its principles it cannot do it.'[10]

Nonetheless, it is by no means certain that James' campaign to pack Parliament was bound to fail. From the autumn of 1687, the King and his advisers, and notably, Sunderland and Jeffreys, began systematically to build up a powerful electoral organization in many constituencies. New Commissions of Peace were issued early in 1688, and only those Justices of the Peace were appointed who showed in response to three set questions that they had an acceptable attitude to the repeal of the Test and Corporation Acts. Those not considered suitably conformist in this matter were ejected and replaced largely by Dissenters. But all the efforts of James were of no consequence, because the packed Parliament never met. They nevertheless increased the suspicion of the Whigs and Tories, Anglicans and Protestant Dissenters that James' intentions were not agreeable to their interests. Then came two events in the first half of 1688 which cemented the alliance of all the leading Protestants against James.

On 27 April a second Declaration of Indulgence was issued, which was in effect the first one of 1687, with the addition of a promise of a Parliament in November. For reasons which it is difficult to fathom, for it was most audacious and fraught with potentially disastrous consequences, on 4 May James ordered that the Declaration should be read at the usual set services in the churches of London, and on 3 and 10 June in the rest of the country. It appears that he never expected serious resistance from the Anglican clergy. Most of their political allies whom the clergy consulted prevaricated, but seemed to think that the clergy should comply with the royal instruction, except Clarendon who advised a refusal. The clergy consulted among themselves at a meeting in Ely House, the London residence of the Bishop of Ely. They were concerned that the church should not appear pusillanimous, especially when so many laymen had recently lost office for refusing to countenance the abolition of religious laws. Sir John Lowther wrote that if the clergy complied in this something worse would certainly be imposed on them to ruin them and, having lost their reputation, they would fall unpitied; that they could never take an opportunity of refusing upon a more justifiable point; that their consenting to this, made their condition as precarious as that of any other Dissenters, who having no legal establishment, were forced to fly to the Declaration for protection.[11]

The foremost London clergy decided on 11 May to ask the bishops to petition the King. It was made clear in the final petition that the refusal to read the Declaration did not arise 'from any want of due tenderness to Dissenters; in relation to whom they are willing to come to such a temper, as shall be thought fit', but 'because that Declaration is founded upon such a dispensing power as hath often been declared illegal in Parliament'.[12] Hatred of Rome had once again proved to be a stronger force than the mutual antipathy of Anglicans and Dissenters.

Many of the clergy of the Church of England were canvassed, and by 17 May it was reckoned that there were almost seventy who would not comply with the King's edict. The next day the final petition was drawn up by William Sancroft, Archbishop of Canterbury, by Bishops Henry Compton of London, Thomas White of Peterborough, William Lloyd of Norwich, Francis Turner of Ely, Thomas Ken of Bath and Wells, Sir Jonathan Trelawney of Bristol and John Lake of Chichester, together with Edward Stillingfleet, Dean of St Paul's, Simon Patrick, Dean of Peterborough, John Tillotson, Dean of Canterbury, and later Archbishop of Canterbury, Thomas Tenison, vicar of St Martin in the Fields, and later Archbishop of Canterbury and Robert Grove, rector of St Andrew Undershaft. The petition was handed to the King. The Church of England had made a firm stand. The outcome was catastrophic, not for them but for the King and all he stood for. Events were moving fast. The confrontation between the church and the monarch, and with it the whole future political and religious destiny of the country, was moving to its climax.

The same night that the bishops presented their petition, a pirated earlier version was being hawked around the streets of London, and a few days later the final version was in print. At the beginning of June Sancroft and the seven bishops were charged with having published a false, malicious and seditious libel. Their trial was eagerly observed by the population of London. 'When, on Saturday 30 June, Sir Roger Langley, foreman of the jury, brought in a verdict of "not guilty", there was a most wonderful shout, that one would have thought the hall had cracked.' This glorious noise 'went out of the hall, which was crowded with people, and was taken up by the watermen, and in a moment, like a train of gunpowder set on fire, went up and down the river, and along the streets, to the astonishment even of those that contributed to it'. The city was jubilant. There were 'multitudes of bonfires' that night, and more celebrations as the news spread across the country; and 'very few villages throughout all England' did not rejoice at the bishops' acquittal.[13]

The second devastating event for James in these crucial months of 1688 was an occasion of joy for him; the birth of a son on 10 June. For Protestants it raised the spectre of a possible unlimited period of Catholic rule. For James himself, the birth of an heir simply strengthened his confidence immeasurably, and encouraged him to pursue his self-destructive course.

It is not appropriate for us to examine in detail the final train of events which culminated in the landing of William of Orange at Torbay on 5 November, the small resistance to him as he advanced towards London or as he entered the capital, the flight of James on 23 December, and the ease with which William assumed authority in matters political and ecclesiastical. The change of monarch went smoothly. The changes brought to the Church in England are matters for a further volume.

Roman Catholicism and the Dissenters

Although he was a self-confessed, dedicated and determined Roman Catholic, the Roman Catholics as a community did not fare well under the rule of James II. 'His short reign was so packed with rapid changes of royal policy and extraordinary, even mad, royal decisions and appointments that ordinary citizens found it impossible to keep abreast of developments or to understand what was happening. For most Catholics it seems to have been an experience in which bewilderment, fear and exhilaration were mixed in equal proportions.'[14] They had been sustained by the thought of James as King, and his accession had been greeted with joy and expectation. They were to find their hopes to a large extent in tatters when, after just under four years, the Catholic King, 'a sick and shattered man muffled for disguise in a thick boat-cloak, was assisted ashore from the trawler at Ambleteuse in France as a fugitive who had been deprived of his throne'.[15]

When James came to the throne he found a Church of England which had a rock-like solidity. The majority of educated English people would never have accepted Catholicism, although there was a very substantial minority of Protestants who were vulnerable to attack or allurement. At the time of the Popish Plot crisis there had been a small wave of conversions to Catholicism, drawn mainly from High Church Anglicans, former Whig zealots, former Dissenters and nominal Anglicans. After 1686 this wave somewhat increased in size. It included political converts like Lord Sunderland, the Earl of Yarmouth, Sir Thomas Strading, Sir Nicholas Butler and Sir Thomas Wright, all of whom smartly reverted to Anglicanism after 1688. Although there were converts during the period 1686 to 1688 who were sincere and who stood firm in the face of imprisonment, ostracism or even ruin, they were insufficient to convert a nation. Of the genuine converts, special mention should be made of John Dryden, for he was a supreme example of the kind of minority person to whom we have just referred, and he illustrates both the potential for conversion to Catholicism and the apprehension of intelligent and observant Catholics at the time about the course of events under the rule of James.

John Dryden (1631–1700) was clerk to Cromwell's chamberlain during the Republic, and in 1659 wrote *Heroic stanzas* in praise of the late Lord Protector.[16] At the Restoration he was a Royalist, who hailed the King with his *Astrea Redux*. As the reign of Charles II unfolded he moved further away from the Puritanism of his youth. He wrote a series of plays, but it was his narrative poetry which established him as the greatest figure in English literature in the second half of the seventeenth century. In 1668 he was appointed Poet Laureate. He rewarded the monarch amply with the writing in 1681–2 of *Absalom and Achitopel*, in which he made a devastating attack upon the Earl of Shaftesbury and the Whigs. It was the finest piece of political satire in the whole history of English verse.

In 1685 Dryden put himself under the instruction of James Corker, a convert Benedictine missioner in Clerkenwell, and became a Catholic. In 1687 he wrote *The Hind and the Panther*, which was a defence in heroic couplets of his new faith. 'He retained for good his total inability to base his faith on mystical experience. He was no Pascal, George Fox or Bunyan. He had no illusions about the actualities of Rome and English Catholicism. He did not share the belief in a Catholic revolution of James II or militant Catholics.' 'The Hind' (the Catholic Church) is the prey of 'the Panther' (the Church of England) and is: 'doomed to death, though fated not to die . . .'[17] With the Revolution he lost his Laureateship and his pension, his wife became insane, and his Catholic sons were exiles abroad. But he retained his acknowledged supremacy over the literary world, and he held fast to his Catholicism.

There were many Catholics who shared with Dryden a profound concern about the dangers in the speed and boldness with which James II demanded a drive for conversions. The Catholic clergy were embarrassed by the haste and zealousness of the King, for they knew from long experience that boldness could often be counter-productive, and that England was littered with lapsed converts. They concentrated their main effort on the lapsed and schismatics of a Catholic mind. As a consequence, by 1688, they could report a real, if rather modest, degree of success and the hope of a few thousand conversions by the 1690s, but they reckoned that a steady, undramatic and unhurried approach was essential. The reckless haste and aggressiveness of the King's actions in promoting Catholicism caused not only the priests but some of the Catholic leaders, including Lords Bellasis, Arundell and Dover and Bishop Leyburne, to protest more or less bluntly. Here and there a few Catholic gentry refused appointments as JPs; and some, either deliberately or by chance, stayed overseas.

Up to November 1687 it appeared that James would be succeeded on the throne by his elder daughter, the Princess Mary, and she and her husband, William, Prince of Orange, were Protestants. The wiser and more far-seeing Catholics were concerned that a precipitate Catholic drive would invite an equally strong Protestant backlash after the death of James. In such a situation John Leyburne counselled discretion, and the Pope urged caution. After the Queen gave birth to a son in June 1688 there was greater optimism among Catholics about the future, and many could not resist a feeling that providence was overruling the King's folly and opening a way to a great Catholic triumph. But this only tended to increase the atmosphere of acute tension among both

Catholics and Protestants; the prudent, whether Catholic or Protestant, were terrified that something awful, perhaps civil war, must be the outcome.

The decision by James II to woo the Dissenters by offering them freedom was in keeping with the policy of his father. Like his father, he 'preferred that they should owe their freedom to Declarations of Indulgence issued by the Crown, rather than by their making common cause with the Church of England'.[18] Many of the Church of England leaders, both clerical and lay, found such a policy difficult, if not impossible, to support. They were either so passionately conformist Church of England men and women, and so intolerant of Dissent, that any attempt to grant rights to the Dissenters was viewed as a betrayal of the established church, or they, together with many of the Dissenters themselves, believed that those who co-operated with the King were being deceived into supporting a move towards Catholic emancipation. The latter looked to a united Protestant front against the Roman Catholics.

At the local level even the most sympathetic Church of England incumbent found Dissenters exasperating, with their excessive zeal, which had been encouraged by the Declarations of Indulgence, with the surge in the building of meeting houses, and with the way the favouring of Dissenters undermined the status, authority and influence of the Church of England. There was nevertheless widespread realization that Dissent was becoming established as a force in the land, and that it had come to stay. 'The luckless James II thus not only gave the Dissenters freedom of worship for the last two years of his reign, he broke the back of Anglican intolerance and made possible the permanent toleration of Dissent once William of Orange had landed at Torbay and James had fled to France.'[19]

After the Revolution there was an immediate and pronounced move towards converting Dissent into recognized Nonconformity. In the election to the Convention Parliament in February 1689 there was an increase to thirty in the number of Members of Parliament who may have been Dissenters. The 1689 Toleration Act provided exemption from the penalties of the Elizabethan Act of 1593 and the Conventicle Act of 1670 for Protestant Trinitarian Dissenters who took the oaths of allegiance and supremacy and obtained a licence for their meetings; and those Nonconformist ministers who subscribed to thirty-six of the Thirty-Nine Articles were to be exempt from the penalties of the Act of Uniformity and of the Five Mile Act. In addition, Baptist ministers were excused subscription to the article on infant baptism and Quakers were permitted to make a declaration instead of taking the oaths. Only Roman Catholics and those who denied the doctrine of the Trinity were specifically excluded from the benefits of the Act. The 'Glorious Revolution' thus conferred freedom to worship in their own way on orthodox Dissenters, and the triumph of the Independent concept of toleration over the Presbyterian hopes of comprehension was assured. 'The Toleration Act of 1689 marked the end of the Church of England's claim to be the national church, the single all-inclusive church of the English people, after almost thirty years of struggle.'[20]

Religious beliefs and future prospects

The events I have just described heralded a new phase in the history of Nonconformity, and of the relationship of Nonconformity to the Church of England, and with it a new era in the history of the Church in England. Indeed, by 1688 there were many, interrelated, fundamental changes taking place in the religious sphere of the nation's life which can only be clearly discerned with hindsight.

First, it is evident that although social changes and the development of science and rationalism in the latter half of the seventeenth century resulted in increased scepticism, yet the population as a whole remained very religious.[21] 'More and more, explanations for phenomena were couched in natural rather than supernatural terms. Yet it would be the greatest exaggeration to suggest that these trends were the only ones apparent, let alone the dominant ones.'[22] For one thing, the rationalism which some have perceived as the accompaniment to the new science was typical of only a small minority of people. There was considerable opposition to the new surge of science exactly because it was associated with the radicalism of the 1650s and with the apparent growth of irreligion in Restoration England. The new science did not carry all before it, and neither was there any conflict between science and religion for most people. 'What can, however, be clearly seen is that by the mid seventeenth century the new intellectual developments had greatly deepened the gulf between the educated classes and the lower strata of the rural population.'[23]

The religiosity of the people continued to express itself in a variety of ways, and this included the persistence of folk religion of different kinds. Magical and superstitious beliefs loomed large in the lives of people, and especially among the lower socio-economic groups of

Elizabethan England, but so did they also among the same groups in the England of James II. It seems that atheism was almost as much a rarity at the end of our period as at the beginning of it.[24]

A good example of the persistence throughout the period of popular folk magic is the continued strong belief in witches and witchcraft. At a popular level a variety of magical activity, all representing an unacceptable brand of religion, might be lumped together under the blanket term of 'witchcraft'. 'Nevertheless, it is possible to isolate that kind of "witchcraft" which involved the employment (or presumed employment) of some occult means of doing harm to other people in a way which was generally disapproved of. In this sense the belief in witchcraft can be defined as the attribution of misfortune to occult agency. A witch was a person of either sex (but more often female) who could mysteriously injure other people.'[25] The damage done, which was technically called *maleficium*, took various forms. Normally, the witch was suspected of causing physical injury to other people, or of bringing about their death. The injury or death might also, more commonly, be inflicted on farm animals, or the witch might interfere with nature by preventing cows from giving milk, or by frustrating such domestic processes as making butter, cheese or beer. The witch's activities usually came under one of these heads, but there was a wide range of other possible hostile actions. To this popular belief in the power of maleficent magic, sixteenth and seventeenth-century England added the theological notion that the essence of witchcraft was adherence to the Devil. Throughout our period the belief in witchcraft in its various forms continued much the same as during the Middle Ages. The increasingly pervasive Protestant ethic and world-view, with its emphasis upon individual responsibility before God, and its condemnation of mediaeval superstitions; the increased rationalism which this new cosmology endorsed and promoted; and the rationalism which the new science and the 'rationalistic' philosophies encouraged, were not sufficient to prevent such survivals as the witchcraft and folk religion to which I have alluded.

Nonetheless, despite the fact that religious thinking, religious practices and religious institutions remained at the very centre of the life of English society, and the Christian religion was entrenched in the customs of the people and by the precept of the ruling classes, there were signs of a secularization process which was not to become acute until the twentieth century.[26] Some of the population, although an infinitesimally small part, showed evidence of acting less in response to religious motivation than had previously been almost universally the custom. They tended to assess the world in empirical and rational terms, and refused to allow the dogmas of the Christian church to dictate behaviour. They sought for non-religious explanations for the world around them, and they searched for non-religious laws which governed the physical universe. They were the fathers of the philosophers and scientists of the impending Age of Reason.

It is also arguable that the latter half of the seventeenth century witnessed the first, very slight, 'differentiation' of religious ideas and institutions from other parts of the social structure. Instead of religion providing the primary source of legitimation for the whole of society, it showed some indication of becoming increasingly a matter of private choice, restricted to the sphere of religiously interested participants. It began to lose something of its former public role, and its socially-acknowledged educational and welfare functions.

The Restoration period also heralded a change in world-views, initially on a very small scale, which was associated with the development of scientific methods and technology. Importance was increasingly attached to experimentation and the causal explanation of phenomena, and there was a decline in the importance given to any form of explanation and world-view which was not readily subject to such 'scientific' verification. Here was the beginning of that modern rejection by a minority of the population of the traditional religious cosmology which was comprehensive and all-embracing, and which provided a general framework of thinking.

In parallel with this, there was a discernable process of desacralization, even within the confines of the churches themselves. This had been growing in intensity and extensiveness since the first half of the seventeenth century, and had become more explicit and identifiable as the seventeenth century progressed.[27] It manifested itself in 'the Freethinking Republicans', with 'their indictmants of the priestcraft of the Church of England between 1660 and 1730' and, for example, in the seventeenth-century groundwork which was laid for the subsequent secular, comparative study of religions by the *philosophes* of the eighteenth-century French Enlightenment. The whole comparative approach to religion, which was to have such a devastating effect on the authority and acceptability of Christianity, was directly related to confessional disputes within Christianity, and to the historical criticism of the Bible which got under way in earnest in the seventeenth century.[28] 'While within Christendom, religious pluralism had provided the impetus for the comparison of "religions", from without, discoveries in the New World and the Pacific were calling into question biblical views of human history. This challenge to sacred history, reinforced by the writings of such thinkers as Spinoza, La Peyrere, and Hobbes, was to set the more radical of the rationalizing theologians on the path of biblical criticism. "Religions" thus came to be credited with a natural, rather than a sacred history.'[29]

The very concept of 'religion' had radical implications. It entailed the relocation of religious faith into a sphere in which its presumed substance could serve as an object of rational investigation. 'The new context for "religion" was the realm of nature.'[30] Herbert of Cherbury and the Cambridge Platonists were instrumental in developing the concept of 'natural religion' as a means of acknowledging and dealing with the 'problem' of global religious pluralism. And this way of approaching the study of 'religions' had a radical effect on the way nature was perceived. 'The development of a science of religion from this theological starting point was to begin with the desacralization of nature itself. God was banished from the world and from naturalistic explanations. Nature became independent of divine fiat, and was considered lawful on its own account.'[31] As new areas of the world were discovered, and as knowledge of the beliefs of other peoples became more widely and fully known there was seen to be a new challenge to Christianity. 'A "sceptical crisis" was developing in the first half of the seventeenth century about dealing with the polygenic and polytheistic evidences. The data indicating that the varieties of mankind could not be encompassed within biblical history, chronologically or geographically, and that the varieties of human belief could not square with the biblical account, raised very serious problems about the then accepted Jewish and Christian framework.'[32]

In all these ways, the end of the period I am covering may have seen the birth of modern secularization, and with it the emergence of the modern phase of humanism, agnosticism and atheism, but if this is so, it was all but dimly discernable; religion in its various manifestations still reigned supreme. The truly secular age lay well in the future.

Secondly, as we come to the end of our period, we are confonted by an established church which had come-of-age. During the confusing period we have covered, the Church of England had undergone a painful process of self-realization and the forging of a distinctive character and identity. By 1688 it was able to draw upon an ecclesiology which had developed and matured throughout one hundred and fifty years of varied fortunes. Consciously or unconsciously, and for most churchmen it was perhaps a vague ill-defined notion rather than a clear and articulated theory, there had emerged a theology of the nature and purpose of the church. Perhaps it was in the turmoil of the mid-seventeenth century that this Anglican ecclesiology and understanding of herself was especially clarified as the Church of England had to grapple with her own identity, her place in the life of the nation, and her relationship with Dissenters and Roman Catholics. Such issues had confronted the national church before, but the rapid succession of dramatic events, and the fearsome questioning of her role as a privileged church brought the issues into sharp focus. It was in such a context that the mid-seventeenth century Anglican divines struggled, some would say successfully, to find a way through the morass of equivocal ecclesiology which for so long had bedevilled their church. One of the most notable achievements of the Church of England in the Restoration period was the maintenance of a semblance of unity among the clergy. 'This was achieved by a realistic acceptance of the tensions and ambiguities within a body of shared Anglican belief, by allowing ecclesiological arguments to be pitched at a variety of levels to suit different audiences and different advocates, and by a pragmatic willingness to live with intellectual anomolies, confusions and evasions.'[33]

Thirdly, we discern at the end of our period a body of 'old' Nonconformity which had already achieved its essential structure, form and characteristics. The mid-seventeenth century had been a formative period for the Dissenters as for the established church. It was correlative to the Church of England situation we have just described. 'The growth of Presbyterianism and of the Congregationalists, Baptists, Quaker and other denominations during the central decades of that century could well be regarded as a second English Reformation.'[34] It, and similar developments in other Protestant countries, indicate that the Reformation of the sixteenth century set in motion forces which permitted, and possibly encouraged, a multiplicity of Christian religious forms, liberty of choice to the individual and freedom of worship even to minor and unpopular sects. Indeed, this raises the whole question, or series of questions, about the consequences of the 'Protestant ethic'. It is arguable that the advent of Protestantism may have been the early if involuntary stage in the emergence of modern 'democratic' government, and modern 'democratic' society. For our immediate purposes it is sufficient to note that by the end of our period, England 'was a society which enjoyed a plural, competitive, religious culture'.[35] By his granting of freedom of worship to the Dissenters during the last two years of his reign, James 'broke the back of Anglican intolerance and made possible the permanent toleration of Dissent'.[36]

The 'Glorious Revolution' was a key event for orthodox Dissenters. Although the 1689 Toleration Act conferred upon them only a measure of toleration, it was indicative of more that was to come. It gave them statutory freedom to worship in their own way, although it did not grant them civil liberty; it vindicated the Independent political theory, which was subsequently given classic expression by John Locke and others; and it marked the end of the pioneering, heroic age of Dissent.

Lastly, as we look back on the churches in England in 1688, we can see that just over the horizon there was another heroic age, not just for Nonconformity but also for at least part of the Church of England, which itself had its roots in the sixteenth and seventeenth centuries. Within less than half a century of the Glorious Revolution the Methodist and Evangelical Anglican revivals came like a breath of fresh air upon somewhat moribund churches. And such was their importance and impact that they can, with ample justification, be regarded as the third Protestant Reformation in England. The historical process is continuous and clear from the initial religious impulse of the Henrician Protestant Reformation to the eighteenth-century Evangelical revival and beyond. 'What do they know of the Reformation who have not met John Wesley and his friends or who have not sensed the devout and eventually beneficent forces at work in late Georgian England? On the one hand, the Methodist and Evangelical movements sprang almost directly from the spiritual impulses initiated by the Reformers; on the other, Protestant beliefs made interesting combinations with the secular thought of the Age of Reason.'[37] In both content and character there is a family likeness between some of the developments of the sixteenth, and perhaps more particularly of the seventeenth, century and those in the eighteenth and later centuries. 'The Wesleyan movement thus resumed, a century later, the move of Puritanism into the countryside, which the sects had started in the sixteen-fifties, but had not been strong enough to carry through.'[38] And in many other respects the Puritan Revolution was not defeated. The Puritan values it enshrined reappeared in various forms, some more obvious than others, throughout the following centuries, and they live on as part of the English heritage, and also as part of the individual and corporate psyche.

In 1689 there was little to indicate that so soon there would be such a remarkable and sustained revival of Christianity. But in retrospect it is possible to see some features in the life of the nation in the latter half of the seventeenth century which might have favoured such an out-pouring of spiritual life. There were negative elements, such as the perhaps almost inevitable swing of the pendulum to compensate for the prevailing and pervasive commonsensical, cerebral religion which dominated the Restoration and post-Restoration churches in England, and which was epitomized by the most successful book of the age, *The Whole Duty of Man*, and the Latitudinarian churchmanship which permeated the Church of England. Both of these emphasized the moral aspects of the Christian life at the expense of the more dynamic, life-transforming experiences which were to be offered in the gospel preached by the revivalists. The 'Latitude Men' stressed moderation. 'They loved the constitution of the Church and the liturgy [says Burnet]. They wished that things might have been carried on with more modera-tion, and they continued to keep a good correspondence with those who differed from them, and allowed a great freedom both in philosophy and divinity: from whence they were called men of Latitude, and, upon this men of narrower thoughts and fiercer tempers fastened upon them the name of Latitudinarians.'[39] They overlapped, but did not coincide with, the Cambridge Platonists, who themselves were mostly latitudi-narian in temper. And it was the Cambridge Platonists who were the most influential in setting the tone, and even the agenda, of academic philosophy, and to a lesser extent academic life as a whole, in the last half of the seventeenth century. Such a glut of rationalism left many yearning for something more vibrant and spiritually animated: the possibility of a personal faith which went beyond the cerebral and provided a deep, satisfying and lasting experience of God's mercy and goodness to individuals in their ordinary daily lives.

Then, of course, the Church of England lost many of its most enthusiastic, energetic, spiritually alert and able men either as a result of the ejections of the 1660s, or as a consequence of the departure of the Nonjurors. In an age when rationalism and reason were to the fore, the national church could ill afford to be deprived of those who might have helped it to redress the balance to some extent in favour of a more lively and stirring form of spirituality.

But there were also developments which positively paved the way for the impending revival. There were the largely unsung efforts and influence of the Nonjurors and sympathizers with them who remained, sometimes somewhat uneasily, within the established church;[40] there was the quiet but telling influence from the continent of Moravianism and various pietistic movements which became more significant as the seventeenth gave way to the eighteenth century; there was the lingering Puritan influence, mediated through an albeit limited number of scattered individuals who drew strength from a tradition which had suffered a serious decline since the mid-seventeenth century;[41] there was the growth of various forms of Dissent which, after 1688, was to manifest itself in a remarkable surge in the number of Nonconformist places of worship, some of them with large congregations, and some of them in areas which were to become centres of the impending revivals;[42] and there were the religious societies, especially in London, which kept alive within the established church a concern for vital personal faith and a relating of that faith to the social needs of the time. The London societies had been founded in 1678. In regular weekly meetings the members applied themselves to 'good discourses, and things wherein they might edify one another'.[43] They remained staunchly Church of England gatherings. The members assiduously guarded against any form of schism or faction by partaking of Church of England communion each month, by conscientiously attending public prayers and by obtaining the explicit approval of their superintendent Church of England clergyman for the introduction of any rule, prayer or change of practice. The societies represented a continuing possibility within the Church of England of a more profound and intense religious awareness and personal religious experience than was generally to be attained, with some notable exceptions, through the regular parish ministry. After a few decades, with the coming of Whitefield and the Wesleys, these religious societies became 'a channel through which the revival flowed until the stream became a torrent and burst the banks of the Establishment which had contained it'.[44]

Abbreviations

BJS	*British Journal of Sociology*
DNB	*Dictionary of National Biography*
EHR	*English History Review*
H	*History*
HJ	*Historical Journal*
HR	*Historical Research*
HT	*History Today*
JBS	*Journal of British Studies*
JEH	*Journal of Ecclesiastical History*
JHI	*Journal of Historical Ideas*
JMH	*Journal of Modern History*
MH	*Midland History*
NH	*Northern History*
NRS	*Northamptonshire Record Society*
P & P	*Past and Present*
SCH	*Studies in Church History*
SH	*Southern History*
TBGAS	*Transactions of the Bristol and Gloucestershire Archaeological Society*
TRHS	*Transactions of the Royal Historical Society*

Bibliography

Abbott, W.M., 'The Issue of Episcopacy in the Long Parliament, 1640–1648; The Reasons for Abolition' , Oxford D.Phil. thesis 1981

Abernathy, G.R., 'The English Presbyterians and the Stuart Restoration, 1648–1663', *Transactions of the American Philosophical Society*, 55, pt 2, 1965

Acheson, R.J., *Radical Puritans in England 1550–1660*, Harlow 1990

Addleshaw, G.W.O., *The High Church Tradition*, London 1941

Alexander, G., 'Bonner and the Marian Persecutions' in Christopher Haigh (ed), *The English Reformation Revised* , London 1987

Alexander, H.G., *Religion in England 1558–1662* , London 1968

Aston, Margaret, *Lollards and Reformation: Images and Literacy in Late Mediaeval Religion*, London 1984

Aveling, J.C.H., *The Handle and the Axe. the Catholic Recusants in England from the Reformation to Emancipation*, London 1976

Avis, P.D.L., *Anglicanism and the Christian Church – Theological Resources in Historical Perspective*, Edinburgh 1989

Aylmer, G.E., *Rebellion or Revolution? England from Civil War to Restoration*, Oxford 1986

Aylmer, Gerald, 'Did the Ranters exist?, *P & P*, 117, 1987, pp. 208–219

Barnard, Toby, *The English Republic 1649–1660*, Harlow 1982

Barratt, D.M., 'Conditions of the Parish Clergy from the Reformation to 1660 in the Dioceses of Oxford, Worcester and Gloucester', Oxford D.Phil. thesis 1950

Baxter, Richard, *Autobiography*, Everyman's Library edition 1931

Bebb, E.D., *Nonconformity and Social and Economic Life 1660–1800. Some problems of the Present as they appeared in the Past*, London 1935

Becker, Howard, *Systematic Sociology on the Basis of the Beziehungslehre und Gebildelehre of Leopold von Wiese*, New York 1932

Beckingsale, B.W., *Elizabeth I*, London 1963

Beddard, R.A., 'Sheldon and Anglican Recovery', *HJ*, 19, 1976

Beddard, R.A., 'The Restoration Church' in J.R. Jones (ed), *The Restored Monarchy, 1660–1688*, London 1979

Bennett, G.V., *The Tory Crisis in Church and State 1688–1730*, Oxford 1975

Bennett, G.V., 'The Seven Bishops: A Reconsideration', *SCR*, xv, 1978

Berger, Peter L., *The Sacred Canopy*, New York 1967

Berger, Peter L., *A Rumour of Angels*, London 1970

Berman, David, *A History of Atheism in Britain. From Hobbes to Russell*, London 1988

Bernard, George, 'The Church of England, *c.*1529–1642', *H*, 75, 1990, pp. 183–206

Bindoff, S.T., *Tudor England*, Harmondsworth 1950

Bolam, C.G., *The English Presbyterians: from Elizabethan Puritanism to Modern Unitarianism*, London 1968

Bosher, Robert S., *The Making of the Restoration Settlement. The Influence of the Laudians 1649–1662*, London 1951

Bossy, J., 'The Character of Elizabethan Catholicism', *P & P*, xxi, 1962

Bossy, John, *The English Catholic Community 1570–1850*, London 1975

Bossy, J., *Christianity in the West, 1400–1700*, Oxford 1985

Bourne, E.C.E., *The Anglicanism of William Laud*, London 1947

Bowker, M, *The Secular Clergy in the Diocese of Lincoln, 1495–1520*, Cambridge 1968

Bowker, M., *The Henrician Reformation: the Diocese of Lincoln under John Langland, 1521–1547*, Cambridge 1981

Bowle, John, *Charles I. A Biography*, London 1975

Brachlow, Stephen, 'The Elizabethan Roots of Henry Jacob's Churchmanship', *JEH*, 36, 1985

Brachlow, Stephen, *The Communion of Saints. Radical Puritan and Separatist Ecclesiology 1570–1625*, Oxford 1988

Braithwaite, William C., *The Beginnings of Quakerism*, London 1912

Braithwaite, William C., *The Second Period of Quakerism*, London 1919

Brigden, S., 'Youth and the English Reformation', *P & P*, 95, May 1982, pp. 37–67

Brigden, S., *London and the Reformation*, Oxford 1989

Brook,V.J.K., *A Life of Archbishop Parker*, Oxford 1962

Cameron, Euan, *The European Reformation*, Oxford 1991

Capp, Bernard, 'The Fifth Monarchists and Popular Millenarianism' in J.F. McGregor and B. Reay (eds), *Radical Religion in the English Revolution*, Oxford 1984

Capp, Bernard, 'Comment', *P & P*, 140, August 1993, pp. 164–171

Carlton, Charles, *Archbishop William Laud*, London 1987

Carlyle, Thomas, *Oliver Cromwell's Letters and Speeches with Elucidations*, London 1983 edition

Carpenter, E., *The Protestant Bishop*, London 1956

Champion, J.A.I., *The Pillars of Priestcraft Shaken. The Church of England and its Enemies 1660–1730*, Cambridge 1992

Chandos, John, *In God's Name. Examples of Preaching in England 1534–1662*, London 1971

Christianson, P., 'Reformers and the Church of England under Elizabeth I and the early Stuarts' with a comment by P. Collinson, *JEH*, 31, 1980, pp. 463–88

Clark, G. N., *The Later Stuarts 1660–1714*, Oxford 1934

Clark, Peter, *English Provincial Society from the Reformation to the Revolution: Religion, Politics and Society in Kent, 1500–1559*, London 1983

Clark, R., 'Anglicanism, Recusancy, and Dissent in Derbyshire, 1603–1670', Oxford D. Phil. thesis 1979

Clifton, R., 'Fear of popery' in Conrad Russell (ed), *The Origins of the English Civil War*, London 1973

Cohn, Norman, *The Pursuit of the Millennium: Revolutionary Millenarians and Mystical Anarchists of the Middle Ages*, London 1970

Collinson, Patrick, 'Episcopacy and Reform in the Later Sixteenth Century' in G. Cuming (ed), *Studies in Church History*, III, Cambridge 1966

Collinson, Patrick, *The Elizabethan Puritan Movement*, London 1967

Collinson, Patrick, *Archbishop Grindal, 1519–1583. The Struggle for a Reformed Church*, London 1979

Collinson, Patrick, *The Religion of Protestants. The Church in English Society 1559–1625*, Oxford 1982

Collinson, Patrick, *Godly People. Essays on English Protestantism and Puritanism*, London 1983

Collinson, Patrick, *The Birthpangs of Protestant England*, London 1988

Coward, Barry, *The Stuart Age*, London 1980

Cragg, G. R., *From Puritanism to the Age of Reason*, Cambridge 1950, 1966

Cressy, David, *Literacy and the Social Order: Reading and Writing in Tudor and Stuart England*, Cambridge 1980

Cressy, David, *Coming Over: Migration and Communication between England and New England in the Seventeenth Century*, Cambridge 1987

Cross, Claire, *Church and People 1450–1660. The Triumph of the Laity in the English Church*, London 1976

Cross, F. L., *The Oxford Movement and the Seventeenth Century*, London 1933

Cross, F. L. and Livingstone, E. A. (eds), *The Oxford Dictionary of the Christian Church*, 2nd edn, Oxford 1974

Cross, M. C., 'The Church in England, 1646–1660' in G. E. Aylmer (ed), *The Interregnum: The Quest for Settlement 1646–1660*, London 1972

Cruickshanks, Eveline (ed), *Ideology and Conspiracy: Aspects of Jacobitism, 1689–1759*, Edinburgh 1992

Cuming, G. J., *A History of Anglican Liturgy*, London 1969

Cuming, G. J., *The Godly Order*, Alcuin Club 1983

Curtis, M. H., 'The Hampton Court Conference and its Aftermath', *H*, 46, 1961

Cust, Richard, and Hughes, Ann, *Conflict in Early Stuart England. Studies in Religion and Politics 1603–1642* , London 1989

Davies, Evan, 'The Enforcement of Religious Uniformity in England, 1668–1700, with special reference to the Dioceses of Chichester and Worcester', Oxford D. Phil. thesis 1982
Davies, Godfrey, *The Early Stuarts 1603–1660*, Oxford 1937
Davies, Horton, *Worship and Theology in England* vol. I: *From Cranmer to Hooker, 1534–1603*, Princeton, NJ 1970
Davies, Horton, *Worship and Theology in England* vol. II: *From Andrewes to Baxter, 1603–1690*, Princeton, NJ 1975
Davies, Julian, *The Caroline Captivity of the Church. Charles I and the Remoulding of Anglicanism 1625–1641*, Oxford 1992
Davis, J. C., *Fear, Myth and History: the Ranters and the Historians*, Cambridge 1986
Davis, J. C., 'Cromwell's Religion' in J. S. Morrill (ed), *Oliver Cromwell and the English Revolution*, London 1990
Davis, J. C., 'Fear, Myth and Furore: Reappraising the "Ranters"', *P & P*, 129, November 1990, pp. 79–103
Davis, J. C., 'Reply', *P & P*, 140, August 1993, pp. 194–210
Davis, J. F., *Heresy and Reformation in the South-east of England, 1520–1559*, 1983
Dawley, Powel Mills, *John Whitgift and the Reformation*, London 1955
Dickens, A. G., *Lollards and Protestants in the Diocese of York 1509–1558*, Oxford 1959
Dickens, A. G., *The English Reformation*, London 1964
Dickens, A. G., review of J. J. Scarisbrick, *The Reformation and the English People*, Oxford 1984, in *JEH*, xxxvi, 1985, pp. 125–26
Doran, Susan and Durston, Christopher, *Pastors and People. The Church and Religion in England 1529–1689*, London 1991
Duffy, E., 'Primitive Christianity Revived: Religious Renewal in Augustan England', *SCH*, 14, 1977
Duffy, E., 'The godly and the multitude in Stuart England', *The Seventeenth Century 1*, London 1986
Duffy, Eamon, *The Stripping of the Altars. Traditional Religion in England 1400–1580*, Yale 1992
Dures, A., *English Catholicism, 1558–1642*, London 1983

Edwards, David L., *Christian England*, 3 vols, London 1981,1983,1984
Elton, G. R., *England under the Tudors*, London 1974
Elton, G. R., *Reform and Reformation*, London 1977
Elton, G. R., 'A High Road to Civil War?' in G. R. Elton, *Studies in Tudor and Stuart Politics and Government*, Cambridge 1974, 1983, vol. II, pp. 164–69

Emerson, Everett H., *English Puritanism from John Hooper to John Milton*, Durham, NC 1968

Every, G., *The High Church Party 1688–1718*, London 1956

Fielding, John, 'Arminianism in the Localities: Peterborough Diocese 1603–1642' in Kenneth Fincham (ed), *The Early Stuart Church 1603–1642*, London 1993

Fincham, K., 'Prelacy and Politics: Archbishop Abbot's defence of Protestant Orthodoxy', *HR*, 61, 1988

Fincham, Kenneth, *Prelate as Pastor. The Episcopate of James I*, Oxford 1990

Fincham, Kenneth (ed), *The Early Stuart Church 1603–1642*, London 1993

Fincham, K., 'Episcopal Government 1603–1640' in Kenneth Fincham (ed), *The Early Stuart Church 1603–1642*, London 1993

Fincham, K., and Lake, P., 'The Ecclesiastical Policy of King James I', *JBS*, 24, 1985; abbreviated and amended in 'The Ecclesiastical Policies of James I and Charles I' in Kenneth Fincham (ed), *The Early Stuart Church 1603–1642*, London 1993, pp. 23–49

Fines, J., 'Heresy Trials in the Diocese of Coventry and Litchfield, 1511–1512', *JEH*, xiv, 1963, pp. 160–67

Firth, C.H., *Oliver Cromwell and the Rule of the Puritans*, Oxford 1900

Firth, C.H., *The Last Years of the Protectorate*, 2 vols, London 1910

Fletcher, Anthony, *A County Community in Peace and War: Sussex 1600–1660*, London 1975

Fletcher, A., *Tudor Rebellions*, 3rd edn, London 1983

Fletcher, 'Oliver Cromwell and the godly nation' in John Morrill (ed), *Oliver Cromwell and the English Revolution*, London 1990

Foster, A., 'Church Policies of the 1630s' in Richard Cust and Ann Hughes (eds), *Conflict in Early Stuart England: Studies in Religion and Politics 1603–42*, Harlow 1989

Foster, A., 'The Clerical Estate Revitalized' in Kenneth Fincham (ed), *The Early Stuart Church 1603–1642*, London 1993, pp. 139–160

Fox, George, *The Journal of George Fox*, London 1975 edition

Foxe, John, *Book of Martyrs*, London 1868 edition

Fraser, Antonia, *Mary Queen of Scots*, London 1970

Fraser, Antonia, *Cromwell Our Chief of Men*, London 1973

Fraser, Antonia, *King Charles II*, London 1979

Frere, W.H., *The English Church in the Reigns of Elizabeth and James I (1558–1625)*, London 1904

Gairdner James, *A History of the English Church in the Sixteenth Century from the Accession of Henry VIII to the Death of Mary*, London 1903

Gardiner, S.R., *The History of England 1603–42*, 10 vols, London 1883–34

Gardiner, Samuel Rawson, *The Constitutional Documents of the Puritan Revolution 1625–1660*, Oxford 1889

Gardiner, S. R., *The History of the Great Civil War*, 4 vols, London 1893

George, Charles, H., 'Puritanism as History and Historiography', *P & P*, 41, 1968, pp. 77–104

Gibb, M. A., *John Lilburne. The Leveller. A Christian Democrat*, London 1947

Gibbons, B. J., 'Comment', *P & P*, 140, August 1993, pp. 178–194

Gilley, Sheridan and Sheils, W. J (eds), *A History of Religion in Britain. Practice and Belief from Pre-Roman Times to the Present*, Oxford 1994

Godfrey, Elizabeth, *Social Life under the Stuarts*, London 1904

Goldie, Mark, 'Danby, the Bishops and the Whigs' in Tim Harris, Paul Seaward and Mark Goldie (eds), *The Politics of Religion in Restoration England*, Oxford 1990

Goring, J. J., 'The Reformation of the Ministry in Elizabethan Sussex', *JEH*, 34, 1983

Greaves, Richard, *Religion and Society in Elizabethan England*, Minneapolis 1981

Green, I. M., *The Re-establishment of the Church of England 1660–1663*, Oxford 1978

Green, I. M., ' "England's Wars of Religion"? Religious Conflict and the English Civil Wars' in J. van den Berg and P. G. Hoftijzer (eds), *Church, Change and Revolution*, Brill 1991

Green, Ian, 'Anglicanism in Stuart and Hanoverian England' in Sheridan Gilley and W. J. Sheils (eds), *A History of Religion in Britain*, Oxford 1994

Green, V. H. H., *Religion at Oxford and Cambridge. A History c. 1160–1960*, London 1964

Grell, Ole Peter, Israel, Jonathan I. and Tyacke, Nicholas, *From Persecution to Toleration. The Glorious Revolution and Religion in England*, Oxford 1991

Guy, John, *Tudor England*, Oxford 1988

Haigh, C., *Reformation and Resistance in Tudor Lancashire*, Cambridge 1975

Haigh, Christopher, 'Puritan evangelism in the reign of Elizabeth I', *EHR*, xcii, 1977, pp. 30–58

Haigh, Christopher, 'Anticlericalism and the English Reformation', *H*, 68, 1983

Haigh, Christopher (ed), *The Reign of Elizabeth I*, London 1984

Haigh, Christopher, 'The Church of England, the Catholics and the People' in Christopher Haigh (ed), *The Reign of Elizabeth I*, London 1984

Haigh, C., 'Revisionism, the Reformation and the History of English Catholicism' with a comment by P. McGrath, *JEH*, 36, 1985, pp. 394–406

Haigh, Christopher (ed), *The English Reformation Revised*, London 1987

Haigh, Christopher, 'The Continuity of Catholicism in the English Reformation' in Christopher Haigh (ed), *The Reformation Revised*, London 1987, pp. 176–208

Haigh, Christopher, *English Reformations*, London 1993

Haines, Roy M., 'Aspects of the Episcopate of John Carpenter, Bishop of Worcester, 1444–1476', *JEH*, 19, 1968

Haley, K.H.D., *The First Earl of Shaftesbury*, Oxford 1968

Haller, William, *The Rise of Puritanism*, New York 1938

Haller, William, *Liberty and Reformation in the Puritan Revolution*, New York 1955

Harper-Bill, Christopher, *The Pre-Reformation Church in England 1400–1530*, London 1989

Harris, Tim, Seaward, Paul and Goldie, Mark (eds), *The Politics of Religion in Restoration England*, Oxford 1990

Harris, Tim, 'Introduction: Revising the Restoration' in T. Harris, P. Seaward and M. Goldie (eds), *The Politics of Religion in Restoration England*, Oxford 1990

Harrison, Peter, *'Religion' and the Religions in the English Enlightenment*, Cambridge 1990

Hart, A.T., *The Life and Times of John Sharp*, London 1949

Hauguard, W.P., *Elizabeth and the English Reformation*, Cambridge 1968

Heal, Felicity and O'Day, Rosemary (eds), *Church and Society in England: Henry VIII to James I*, London 1977

Heal, Felicity, *Of Prelates and Princes: A Study of the Economic and Social position of the Tudor Episcopate*, Cambridge 1980

Heath, P., *Medieval Clerical Accounts*, St Anthonys Hall, York, Borthwick Paper 16, 1964

Heath, P., *The English Parish Clergy on the Eve of the Reformation*, London 1969

Hibbard, Caroline M., 'Early Stuart Catholicism', *JMH*, 52, i, March 1980

Higham, Florence, *Catholic and Reformed. A Study of the Anglican Church 1559–1662*, London 1962

Hill, Christopher, *Economic Problems of the Church. From Archbishop Whitgift to the Long Parliament*, Oxford 1956

Hill, Christopher, *Puritanism and Revolution*, London 1958

Hill, Christopher, *The Century of Revolution*, London 1961

Hill, Christopher, *Society and Puritanism in Pre-Revolutionary England*, London 1964

Hill, Christopher, *Who's Who in History*, vol. III: *England 1603 to 1714*, Oxford 1965

Hill, Christopher, *God's Englishman. Oliver Cromwell and the English Revolution*, London 1970

Hill, Christopher, *The World Turned Upside Down. Radical Ideas during the English Revolution*, London 1972

Hill, Christopher, 'The Religion of Gerrard Winstanley', *P & P*, supp. 5, 1978

Hill, C., 'Archbishop Laud's Place in English History' in C.Hill, *A Nation of Change and Novelty*, London 1990, pp. 56–81

Hill, Michael, *A Sociology of Religion*, London 1973

Hilton, J.A., 'Catholicism in Elizabethan Northumberland', *NH*, 13, 1977, pp. 44–58

Hilton, J.A., 'The Cumbrian Catholics', *NH*, 16, 1980, pp. 40–58

Hirschberg, D.R., 'The Government and Church Patronage in England, 1660–1760', *JBS*, 20, 1980–1

Hirst, Derek, *Authority and Conflict. England 1603–1658*, London 1986

Hirst, D., 'The Failure of Godly Rule', *P & P*, 132, 1991

Hoak, D.E., *The King's Council in the Reign of Edward VI*, Cambridge 1976

Hobbes, Thomas, *Leviathan* , Cambridge 1991 edition

Holmes, Geoffrey (ed), *Britain After the Glorious Revolution, 1689–1714*, London 1969

Holmes, Geoffrey, *Augustan England: Professions, State and Society 1680–1730*, London 1982

Holmes, Geoffrey, *The Making of a Great Power. Late Stuart and Early Georgian Britain, 1660–1722*, London 1993

Holmes, P., *Resistance and Compromise: The Political Thought of Elizabethan Catholics*, Cambridge 1982

Hooker, Richard, *Of the Laws of Ecclesiastical Polity*, Everyman's Library edition 1907

Houlbrooke, R., *Church Courts and the People during the English Reformation, 1520–1570*, Oxford 1979

Hudson, W.S., *The Cambridge Connection and the Elizabethan Settlement of 1659*, Durham, NC 1980

Hughes, Ann, *The Causes of the English Civil War*, Basingstoke 1991

Hunt, William, *The Puritan Movement. The Coming of Revolution in an English County*, Cambridge, Mass. 1983

Huntley, Frank Livingstone, *Bishop Joseph Hall, 1574–1656. A biographical and critical study*, Cambridge 1979

Hurwick, J.J., 'Dissent and Catholicism in English Society: a study of Warwickshire, 1660–1720', *JBS*, 16, 1976

Hutchinson, Lucy, *Memoirs of the Life of Colonel Hutchinson*, Everyman's Library edition 1908

Hutton, R., *The Restoration: a Political and Religious History of England and Wales, 1658–1667*, Oxford 1985

Hutton, Ronald, *Charles II King of England, Scotland, and Ireland*, Oxford 1991

Hutton, William Holden, *William Laud*, London 1895

Hutton, William Holden, *The English Church. From the Accession of Charles I to the Death of Anne (1625–1714)*, London 1903

Hyde, Edward, Earl of Clarendon, *The History of the Rebellion and Civil Wars in England*, 3 vols, Oxford 1702–4
Hylson-Smith, Kenneth, *High Churchmanship in the Church of England from the Sixteenth Century to the Late Twentieth Century*, Edinburgh 1993

Ingram, Martin, *Church Courts, Sex and Marriage in England, 1570–1640*, Cambridge 1987

Johnson, Paul, *Elizabeth I*, London 1974
Jones, J.R., *The First Whigs: the Politics of the Exclusion Crisis 1678–83*, Oxford 1961; reprinted with revisions 1970
Jones, J.R., *Country and Court. England 1658–1714*, London 1978
Jones, J.R. (ed), *The Restored Monarchy 1660–1688*, London 1979
Jones, R.Tudur, *Congregationalism in England 1662–1962*, London 1962

Kalu, Ogbu Uke, 'The Jacobean Church and Essex Puritans', Toronto Ph.D thesis 1972
Keeble, N.H., *The Literary Culture of Nonconformity in Later Seventeenth-Century England*, Leicester 1987
Kendall, R.T., *Calvin and English Calvinism to 1649*, Oxford 1979
Kent, J., *The Unacceptable Face: The Modern Church in the Eyes of the Historian*, London 1987
Kenyon, J.P., *Robert Spencer, Earl of Sunderland, 1641–1702*, London 1958
Kenyon, John, *The Popish Plot*, London 1972
Kenyon, J.P., *Stuart England*, Harmondsworth 1978
Kenyon, J.P., *The Stuart Constitution. Documents and Commentary*, Cambridge 1986
Knappen, M.M., *Tudor Puritanism. A Chapter in the History of Idealism*, 1939; reissued Gloucester, Mass. 1963
Knowles, Dom David, *The Religious Orders in England*, 3 vols, Cambridge 1948, 1955, 1959; *Vol III: The Tudor Age*
Krieder, Alan, *English Chantries. The Road to Dissolution* , Cambridge, Mass. 1979

Lacey, Douglas R., *Dissent and Parliamentary Politics in England, 1660–1689 A Study in the Perpetuation and Tempering of Parliamentarianism*, New Jersey 1969
Lake, P., 'The significance of the Elizabethan identification of the Pope as Antichrist', *JEH*, 31, 1980
Lake, P., *Moderate Puritans and the Elizabethan Church*, Cambridge 1982
Lake, P., 'Puritan identities', *JEH*, 35, 1984, pp. 112–23
Lake, P., 'Presbyterianism, the Idea of a National Church and the Argument from Divine Right' in P.Lake and M.Dowling (eds), *Protestantism and the National Church in Sixteenth-Century England*, London 1987

Lake, Peter, 'Calvinism and the English Church 1570–1635', *P & P*, 114, 1987

Lake, P., *Anglicans and Puritans? Presbyterianism and English Conformist Thought from Whitgift to Hooker*, London 1988

Lake, Peter, 'Anti-popery: the structure of prejudice' in Richard Cust and Ann Hughes (eds), *Conflict in Early Stuart England*, London 1989

Lake, Peter, Introduction to Geoffrey F. Nuttall, *The Holy Spirit in Puritan Faith and Experience*, London 1992

Lamont, W. M., *Godly Rule: Politics and Religion 1603–1660*, London 1969

Lamont, William and Oldfield, Sybil, *Politics, Religion and Literature in the Seventeenth Century*, London 1975

Lamont, William, 'The Rise of Arminianism Reconsidered', *P & P*, 107, May 1985, pp. 227–231

Legg, J. Wickham, *English Church Life. From the Restoration to the Tractarian Movement*, London 1914

Leys, M. D. R., *Catholics in England 1559–1829*, London 1961

Loach, J., 'The Marian Establishment and the Printing Press', *EHR*, c, 1986, pp. 138–41

Loach, Jennifer, *Parliament and the Crown in the Reign of Mary Tudor*, Oxford 1986

Loades, D. M., *The Oxford Martyrs*, London 1970

Loades, D. M., *The Reign of Mary Tudor*, London 1979

Loades, D. M., *Mary Tudor: A Life*, Oxford 1989

Loades, David, *Revolution in Religion: The English Reformation 1530–1570*, Cardiff 1992

Loades, David, *The Mid-Tudor Crisis, 1545–1565*, Basingstoke 1992

Lossky, Nicholas, *Lancelot Andrewes the Preacher (1555–1626). The Origins of the Mystical Theology of the Church of England*, Oxford 1991

MacCulloch, D., *Suffolk and the Tudors*, Oxford 1986

MacCulloch, Diarmaid, *The Later Reformation in England 1547–1603*, London 1990

Macnicol, D. C., *Robert Bruce. Minister in the Kirk of Edinburgh*, London 1907

McAdoo, H. R., *The Spirit of Anglicanism*, London 1965

McGee, J. S., *The Godly Man in Stuart England. Anglicans, Puritans and the Two Tables, 1620–1670*, New Haven 1976

McGee, J. Sears, 'William Laud and the outward face of religion' in R. De Molen (ed), *Leaders of the Reformation*, London 1984

McGrath, Patrick, *Papists and Puritans under Elizabeth Ist*, London 1967

McGrath, P., 'Elizabethan Catholicism: a Reconsideration', *JEH*, 35, 1984, pp. 414–28

McGregor, J. F. and Reay, B. (eds), *Radical Religion in the English Revolution*, Oxford 1984

McGregor, J.F., 'Comment', *P & P*, 140, August 1993, pp. 155–163

McGregor, J.F., 'Debate, Fear, Myth and Furore: Reappraising the Ranters', *P & P*, 140, August 1993

Manning, Brian, *The English People and the English Revolution*, London 1976

Manning, Brian, 'The Levellers and Religion' in J.F. Mcgregor and B. Reay (eds), *Radical Religion in the English Revolution*, Oxford 1984

Manning, Roger, B., *Religion and Society in Elizabethan Sussex*, London 1969

Manning, R.B., 'The Crisis of Episcopal Authority during the Reign of Elizabeth 1', *JBS*, 11, 1971, pp. 1–25

Marchant, R.A., *The Puritans and the Church Courts in the Diocese of York 1560–1642*, London 1960

Marshall, J., 'The Ecclesiology of the Latitude-Men 1660–1689: Stillingfleet, Tillotson and "Hobbism"', *JEH*, 36, 1985

Marshall, P., 'Attitudes of the English People to Priests and Priesthood, 1500–1553' , Oxford D.Phil. thesis 1990

Marshall, W.M., 'Episcopal Activity in the Hereford and Oxford Dioceses, 1660–1760', *MH*, 8, 1983

Martin, David, 'The Denomination', *BJS*, XIII, 1962

Matthew, David, *Catholicism in England. The Portrait of a Minority: Its Culture and Tradition*, London 1955

Matthews, A.G., *Calamy Revised, being a revision of Edmund Calamy's 'Account' of the Ministers and Others Ejected and Silenced, 1660-2*, Oxford 1934

Matthews, A.G., *Walker Revised*, Oxford 1948

Maycock, A.L., *Nicholas Ferrar of Little Gidding*, London 1938

Mayhew, G.J., 'The Progress of the Reformation in East Sussex, 1530–1559: the evidence from wills', *SH*, 5 , 1983, pp. 38–67

Miller, John, *Popery and Politics in England 1660–1688*, Cambridge 1973

Miller, John, *James II. A Study in Kingship*, Hove 1977

Milton, Anthony, *Catholic and Reformed: the Roman and Protestant Churches in English Protestant Thought, 1600–1640*, Cambridge 1993

More, Paul Elmer and Cross, Frank Leslie, *Anglicanism. The Thought and Practice of the Church of England, Illustrated from the Religious Literature of the Seventeenth Century*, London 1951

Morrill, John, 'The Church in England 1642–1649' in J.M. Morrill (ed), *Reactions to the English Civil War*, London 1982

Morrill, John, 'The religious context of the English civil war', *TRHS*, 5th series, vol. 34, 1984

Morrill, J., 'The Attack on the Church of England in the Long Parliament, 1640–1642' in D.Beales and G.Best (eds), *History, Society and the Churches*, London 1985

Morrill, John, 'The Ecology of Allegiance in the English Civil War', *JBS*, 26, 1987

Morrill, John (ed), *Oliver Cromwell and the English Revolution,* London 1990
Morrill, John, *The Nature of the English Revolution,* London 1993
Morton, A.L., *The World of the Ranters: Radical Religion in the English Revolution,* London 1970

Neale, J.E., *Queen Elizabeth,* London 1934
Neale, J.E., *Elizabeth I and her Parliaments 1559–1581,* London 1953
Neill, Stephen, *Anglicanism,* Harmondsworth 1958
Neill, Stephen, *A History of Christian Missions,* Harmondsworth 1964
New, John F.H., *Anglican and Puritan. The Basis of Their Opposition, 1558–1640,* London 1964
Nichols, Aidan, *The Panther and the Hind. A Theological History of Anglicanism,* Edinburgh 1993
Niebuhr, Richard H., *The Social Sources of Denominationalism,* New York 1929
Nuttall, G.F., *Visible Saints: the Congregational Way 1640–60,* Oxford 1957
Nuttall, G.F. and Chadwick, O. (eds), *From Uniformity to Unity, 1662–1962,* London 1962
Nuttall, Geoffrey F., *Richard Baxter,* London 1965
Nuttall, Geoffrey F., *The Holy Spirit in Puritan Faith and Experience,* Chicago 1992 edition

O'Day, R., *The English Clergy. The Emergence and Consolidation of a Profession 1558–1642,* Leicester 1979
O'Day, R. and Heal, F. (eds), *Continuity and Change: The personnel and administration of the Church in England 1500–1642,* Leicester 1976
O'Day, R. and Heal, F. (eds), *Princes and Paupers in the English Church 1500–1800,* Leicester 1981
O'Day, R., 'Anatomy of a Profession: the Clergy of the Church of England' in W.R. Prest (ed), *The Professions in Early Modern England,* London 1987
Ogg, David, *England in the Reign of Charles II,* 2 vols, Oxford 1934
Overton, J.H., *Life in the English Church (1660–1714),* London 1885
Overton, J.H., *The Nonjurors,* London 1902
Owens, W.R., (ed), *Seventeenth Century England. A Changing Culture,* Open University 1980
Oxley, J.E., *The Reformation in Essex,* London 1965

Packer, J.I., *Among God's Giants. The Puritan Vision of the Christian Life,* Eastbourne 1991
Packer, John W., *The Transformation of Anglicanism 1643–1660 with special reference to Henry Hammond,* Manchester 1969
Paget, Francis, *An Introduction to the Fifth Book of Hooker's Treatise of the Laws of Ecclesiastical Polity,* Oxford 1907

Pailin, David, 'Rational Religion in England from Herbert of Cherbury to William Paley' in Sheridan Gilley and W. J. Sheils (eds), *A History of Religion in Britain*, London 1988

Painter, Borden W., 'Anglican Terminology in Recent Tudor and Stuart Historiography', *AEH*, 56, 1987

Pallister, D. M., *The Age of Elizabeth. England under the Later Tudors 1547–1603*, London 1983

Parker, Kenneth L., *The English Sabbath: A Theological Study of Doctrine and Discipline from the Reformation to the Civil War*, Cambridge 1988

Platt, Colin, *The Parish Churches of Mediaeval England*, London 1981

Plowden, Alison, *Danger to Elizabeth. The Catholics under Elizabeth I*, London 1973

Pogson, R. H., 'Reginald Pole and the Priorities of Government in Mary Tudor's Church', *HJ*, 18, 1975

Pogson, R. H., 'Revival and Reform in Mary Tudors Church: A Question of Money' in Christopher Haigh (ed), *The English Reformation Revised*, London 1987, pp. 139–156

Pope, Liston, *Millhands and Preachers*, New Haven, Conn. 1942

Popkin, Richard H., 'The Deist Challenge' in O. P. Grell, J. I. Israel and N. Tyacke (eds), *From Persecution to Toleration*, Oxford 1991

Powell, K. G., 'The Beginnings of Protestantism in Gloucestershire', *TBGAS*, xc, 1971

Powell, K. G., 'The Social Background to the Reformation in Gloucestershire', *TBGAS*, xcii, 1973

Powell, K. G., 'The Marian Martyrs and the Reformation in Bristol', Bristol Branch of the Historical Association, Local History Pamphlet No. 31, 1972

Powicke, Maurice, *The Reformation in England*, Oxford 1941

Prothero, G. W. (ed), *Select Statutes and other Constitutional Documents illustrative of the reigns of Elizabeth and James I*, Oxford 1918

Rack, H. D., 'Religious Societies and the Origins of Methodism', *JEH*, 38, 1987, pp. 582–95

Redwood, John, *Reason, Ridicule and Religion. The Age of Enlightenment in England 1660–1750*, London 1976

Redworth, G., 'Whatever happened to the English Reformation?', *HT*, 37, 1987

Reese, M. M., *The Puritan Impulse. The English Revolution, 1559–1660*, London 1975

Reid, James, *Memoirs of the Westminster Divines*, 1811; Edinburgh 1982 edition

Rex, Richard, *Henry VIII and the English Reformation*, Basingstoke 1993

Richardson, C. F., *English Preachers and Preaching 1640–1670*, London 1928

Richardson, R.C., *Puritanism in North-West England: a regional study of the diocese of Chester to 1642*, Manchester 1972
Ridley, Jasper, *Elizabeth I* , London 1987
Roots, Ivan, *The Great Rebellion 1642–1660*, London 1966
Rowse, A.L., *The England of Elizabeth. The Structure of Society*, London 1950
Rowse, A.L., *Reflections on the Puritan Revolution*, London 1986
Rupp, E.G., *Religion in England, 1688–1791*, Oxford 1986
Russell, Conrad, *The Crisis of Parliaments. English History 1509–1660*, Oxford 1971
Russell, Conrad (ed), *The Origins of the Civil War* , London 1973
Russell, Conrad, *Parliaments and English Politics, 1621–1629*, Oxford 1979
Russell, Conrad, *The Causes of the English Civil War. The Ford Lectures Delivered at the University of Oxford 1987–1988*, Oxford 1990

Sampson, George, *The Concise Cambridge History of English Literature*, Cambridge 1941
Scarisbrick, J.J., *The Reformation and the English People*, Oxford 1984
Schwarz, M., 'Some Thoughts on the Development of a Lay Religious Consciousness in Pre-Civil War England' in G. Cuming and D. Baker (eds), *Popular Belief and Practice*, Studies in Church History, 8, Cambridge 1972
Scott, Jonathan, 'England's Troubles: Exhuming the Popish Plot' in T. Harris, P. Seaward and M. Goldie (eds), *The Politics of Religion in Restoration England*, Oxford 1990, pp. 107–131
Seaver, Paul S., *The Puritan Lectureships*, Stanford 1970
Seaver, Paul S., *Wallington's World. A Puritan Artisan in Seventeenth Century London*, London 1985
Seaward, Paul, 'Gilbert Sheldon, the London Vestries, and the Defence of the Church' in T. Harris, P. Seaward and M. Goldie (eds), *The Politics of Religion in Restoration England*, Oxford 1990
Sharpe, J., 'Scandalous and Malignant Priests in Essex: the Impact of Grassroots Puritanism' in C. Jones, M. Newitt and S. Roberts (eds), *Politics and People in Revolutionary England*, Oxford 1986
Sharpe, Kevin, 'Archbishop Laud', *HT*, 33,1983
Sharpe, K., *Politics and Ideas in Early Stuart England* , London 1989
Sharpe, Kevin, *The Personal Rule of Charles I*, New Haven 1992
Sheils, W.J., 'The Puritans in Church and Politics in the Diocese of Peterborough 1570–1610', London Ph.D thesis 1974
Sheils, W.J., 'Religion in Provincial Towns: Innovation and Tradition' in F. Heal and R. ODay (eds), *Church and Society in England*, London 1977, pp. 156–176
Sheils, W.J., 'The Puritans in the Diocese of Peterborough, 1558–1610', *NRS*, 1979
Sheils, W.J., *The English Reformation 1530–1570*, London 1989

Shriver, F., 'Hampton Court Revised: James I and the Puritans', *JEH*, 33, 1982

Smith, Nigel, 'Comment', *P & P*, 140, August 1993, pp. 171–177

Solt, Leo F., *Church and State in Early Modern England 1509–1640* , Oxford 1990

Somerset, Anne, *Elizabeth I*, London 1992

Speck,W.A., *Reluctant Revolutionaries. Englishmen and the Revolution of 1688* , Oxford 1989

Spufford, Margaret, *Contrasting Communities: English Villagers in the Sixteenth and Seventeenth Centuries*, Cambridge 1974

Spurr, John, ' "Latitudinarianism" and the Restoration Church', *HJ*, 31, 1988

Spurr, John, 'Virtue, Religion and Government: the Anglican Uses of Providence, in T. Harris, P. Seaward and M. Goldie (eds), *The Politics of Religion in Restoration England*, Oxford 1990

Spurr, John, *The Restoration Church of England, 1646–1689*, Yale 1991

Starkey, D., *The Reign of Henry VIII: Personalities and Politics*, London 1985

Stone, Lawrence, *The Causes of the English Revolution, 1529–1642*, London 1972

Swanson, R.N., *Church and Society in Late Medieval England*, Oxford 1989

Sykes, Norman, *Church and State in England in the Eighteenth Century*, Cambridge 1934

Symonds, Richard, *Alternative Saints. The Post-Reformation British People Commemorated by the Church of England*, London 1988

Tawney, R.H., *The Acquisitive Society*, London 1921

Tawney, R.H., 'The Rise of the Gentry', *Economic History Review* 1941

Tawney, R.H., *Religion and the Rise of Capitalism*, London 1944

Thomas, Keith, *Religion and the Decline of Magic. Studies in Popular Beliefs in Sixteenth and Seventeenth-Century England*, London 1971

Thomson, J.A.F., *The Later Lollards, 1414–1520*, Oxford 1965

Thomson, John A.F., *The Early Tudor Church and Society 1485–1529*, London 1993

Thompson, S., 'The Pastoral Work of the English and Welsh Episcopate, 1500–1558', Oxford D.Phil. thesis 1984

Tolmie, Murray, *The Triumph of the Saints: The Separate Churches of London 1616–49*, Cambridge 1977

Trevor-Roper, H.R., 'The Gentry 1540–1640', *Economic History Review Supplement I*, 1953

Trevor-Roper, H.R., *Historical Essays*, London 1957

Trevor-Roper, H.R., *Archbishop Laud 1573–1645*, London 1962

Trevor-Roper, Hugh, *Catholics, Anglicans and Puritans. Seventeenth-century essays*, London 1987

Troeltsch, Ernst, *Social Teachings of the Christian Churches*, 2 vols., New York edition 1931

Tuck, Richard, Introduction to Hobbes, *Leviathan,* Cambridge 1991 edition

Tyacke, Nicholas, 'Puritanism, Arminianism and counter-revolution' in Conrad Russell (ed), *The Origins of the Civil War,* London 1973

Tyacke, Nicholas, 'The Rise of Arminianism Reconsidered', *P & P,* 115, 1987, pp. 201–16

Tyacke, Nicholas, *Anti-Calvinists. The Rise of English Arminianism c. 1590–1640,* Oxford 1987

Tyacke, Nicholas, 'Archbishop Laud' in Kenneth Fincham (ed), *The Early Stuart Church 1603–1642,* London 1993, pp. 51–70

Underdown, David, *Revel, Riot and Rebellion. Popular Politics and Culture in England 1603–1660,* Oxford 1985

Underdown, David and Morrill, John, 'Debate: The ecology of allegiance', *JBS,* 26, 1987, pp. 451–79

Underwood, A. C., *A History of the English Baptists,* London 1947

Usher, Roland Greene, *The Reconstruction of the English Church,* 2 vols, London 1910

Walsh, John D., 'Religious Societies: Methodist and Evangelical 1738–1800', *SCH,* 23, 1986, pp. 279–302

Walsham, Alexandra, *Church Papists. Catholicism, Conformity and Confessional Polemic in Early Modern England,* The Royal Historical Society 1993

Walton, Izaak, *The Lives,* London 1847 edition

Walzer, Michael, *The Revolution of the Saints. A Study in the Origins of Radical Politics,* New York 1973

Wand, J. W. C., *The High Church Schism: Four Lectures on the Non-jurors,* London 1951

Watkin, E. I., *Roman Catholics in England from the Reformation to 1950,* Oxford 1957

Watt, Tessa, *Cheap Print and Popular Piety, 1550–1640,* Cambridge 1991

Watts, Michael, *The Dissenters. From the Reformation to the French Revolution,* Oxford 1978

Waugh, Evelyn, *Edmund Campion. Scholar, Priest, Hero, and Martyr,* Oxford 1980

Weber, Max, *The Protestant Ethic and the Spirit of Capitalism* (1904–5) trans. London 1930

Weber, Max, *General Economic History,* New York 1963 edition

Weber, Max, *The Sociology of Religion,* London 1965 edition

Wedgwood, C. V., *Strafford,* London 1938

Welsby, Paul A., *George Abbot,* London 1962

Welsby, Paul A., *Lancelot Andrewes 1555–1626,* London 1964

White, B. R., *The English Separatist Tradition,* Oxford 1971

White, P., 'The Rise of Arminianism Reconsidered', *P&P*, 101, 1983, pp. 34–54

White, Peter, 'A Rejoinder', *P & P*, 115, 1987, pp. 201–16

White, Peter, *Predestination, Policy and Polemic: Conflict and Concerns in the English Church from the Reformation to the Civil War*, Cambridge 1992

Whiting, R., 'Abominable Idols: Images and Image-breaking under Henry VIII', *JEH*, xxxiii, 1982, pp. 30–47

Whiting, R., ' "For the Health of my Soul": Prayers for the Dead in the Tudor South-West', *SH*, v, 1983

Whiting, Robert, *The Blind Devotion of the People: Popular Religion and the English Reformation*, Cambridge 1989

Whitman, A.O., 'The Re-Establishment of the Church of England 1660–1663', *TRHS*, 5, 1955

Wilkinson, John T., *1662 and After. Three Centuries of English Nonconformity*, London 1962

Willey, Basil, *The Seventeenth-Century Background*, London 1934

Williamson, James A., *The Tudor Age*, London 1979

Willson, David Harris, *King James VI & I*, London 1956

Wilson, B.R., *Sects and Society*, London 1961

Wilson, B.R., *Religion in Secular Society*, Harmondsworth 1966

Wilson, B.R., *Patterns of Sectarianism*, London 1967

Wilson, B.R., *Contemporary Transformations of Religion*, Oxford 1976

Woodward, Josiah, *An Account of the Rise and Progress of the Religious Societies in the City of London*, London 1701

Worden, Blair, 'Toleration and the Cromwellian Protectorate', *SCH*, 21, 1984

Worden, Blair, 'Providence and Politics in Cromwellian England', *P & P*, cix, 1985, pp. 55–99

Worden, Blair, 'Oliver Cromwell and the Sin of Achan' in Derek Beales and Geoffrey Best (eds), *History, Society and the Churches*, Cambridge 1985, pp. 125–45

Wormald, Jenny, 'James VI and I: two kings or one?', *H*, 68, 1983

Wormald, Jenny, 'Gunpowder, Treason and Scots', *JBS*, 24, May 1985, pp. 141–68

Wrightson, Keith, *English Society 1580–1680*, London 1981

Wrightson, K. and Levine, D., *Poverty and Piety in an English Village: Terling, 1525–1700*, London 1979

Yinger, Milton J., *Religion, Society and the Individual*, New York 1957

Youings, J.A., 'The Terms of the Disposal of the Devon Monastic Lands 1536–58', *EHR*, lxix, 1954

Youings, J.A., *The Dissolution of the Monasteries*, London 1971

Youings, Joyce, *Sixteenth-Century England*, Harmondsworth 1984

Zell, M., 'The Personnel of the Clergy in Kent during the Reformation', *EHR*, lxxxix, 1974

Notes

In general, works will be referred to only by author and shortened title. Details of date and place of publication will be found in Bibliography which precedes these Notes.

Acknowledgments

1. There have been very few comprehensive general accounts and analyses of the Church in England in the period 1558 to 1688 published during the last century. There is Frere, *The English Church in the Reigns of Elizabeth and James I (1558–1625)*, London 1904 and Hutton, *The English Church from the Accession of Charles I to the Death of Anne (1625–1714)*, London 1903, but they do not have the unity of single authorship, and they are almost entirely concerned with the Church of England. There is Higham, *Catholic and Reformed*, London 1962, which almost qualifies chronologically, but not in its width of coverage, for it is also confined to the Church of England. Alexander, *Religion in England 1558–1662*, London 1968, despite the title, likewise gives little space to non-Anglican religious traditions. And, of course, all of these works suffer inevitably from the passage of time, especially as the intervening years have transformed our perception of many aspects of the history of the churches in England in the period being considered. Edwards' excellent and widely appreciated three volume *Christian England*, London 1981, 1983, 1984 is broader in its scope than the present work, tends to concentrate rather more on theologians and persons of witness and prayer than the present book, and is not able, because of when it was published, to take account of the quite astonishing volume and range of studies, published and unpublished, which have proliferated in the succeeding years.

   Of the excellent works which cover parts of the period special mention should be made of Cross, *Church and People 1450–1660*, London 1976, Doran and Durston, *Pastors and People*, London 1991, Haigh, *English Reformations*, London 1993, MacCulloch, *The Later Reformation in England 1547–1603*, London 1990, Solt, *Church and State in Early Modern England 1509–1640*, Oxford 1990 and Spurr, *The Restoration Church of England, 1646–1689*, Yale 1991. Magnificent though these are, there exists a need for a more general overview of the whole period.

Introduction

1. The most important recent works which illustrate this entirely, or largely, include, Dickens, *The English Reformation*, London 1964, Elton, *Reform and Reformation 1509–1558*, London 1977, Parker, *The English Reformation to 1558*, Oxford 1950, and Powicke, *The Reformation in England*, Oxford 1941.
2. In addition to the works already cited, attention is drawn, merely as examples, to Collinson, *The Elizabethan Puritan Movement*, London 1967, Cust and Hughes (eds), *Conflict in Early Stuart England*, London 1989, Fincham (ed), *The Early Stuart Church 1603–1642*, London 1993, Hirst, *Authority and Conflict. England 1603–1658*, London 1986, and McGrath, *Papists and Puritans under Elizabth 1*, London 1967.
3. As there are literally dozens of references covering the topics mentioned in this and the following four paragraphs, I will not list them until I come to the appropriate place in the text.
4. Coward, *The Stuart Age*, p. xi.
5. Collinson, *Godly People*, p. 292.
6. MacCulloch, *The Later Reformation in England*, p. 6.
7. Doran and Durston, *Pastors and People*, p. 5.
8. Ibid., p. 197.
9. Weber, *The Protestant Ethic*, *General Economic History* and *The Sociology of Religion*.
10. Troeltsch, *Social Teaching of the Christian Churches*.
11. See Niebuhr, *The Social Sources of Denominationalism*.
12. See Becker, *Systematic Sociology*.
13. See Berger, *The Sacred Canopy*; Martin, 'The Denomination'; Niebuhr, *The Social Sources of Denominationalism* ; Pope, *Millhands and Preachers;* and Yinger, *Religion, Society and the Individual*.
14. Wilson, *Sects and Society* and *Patterns of Sectarianism*.
15. Spurr, *The Restoration Church of England*, p. 105.
16. Quoted in ibid., p. 107.
17. Dickens, *The English Reformation*, p. 277.
18. Williamson, *The Tudor Age*, p. 225.

1. Prelude

1. Loades, *The Mid-Tudor Crisis*, p. 161.
2. Haigh, *English Reformations*, p. 11.
3. Duffy, *The Stripping of the Altars*, p. 11
4. Ibid., p. 91.
5. Ibid., p. 338.
6. Swanson, *Church and Society in Late Medieval England*, p. ix.
7. Thomas, *Religion and the Decline of Magic*, p. 53.

8. Haigh (ed), Introduction to *The English Reformation Revised*, p. 3.
9. Harper-Bill, *The Pre-Reformation Church in England 1400–1530*, p. vii.
10. Swanson, *Church and Society in Late Medieval England*, p. 252.
11. Some of the most important and interesting local studies are, Barratt, 'Conditions of the Parish Clergy from the Reformation to 1660 in the diocese of Oxford, Worcester and Gloucester'; Bowker, *The Secular Clergy in the Diocese of Lincoln, 1495–1520* and *The Henrician Reformation: the Diocese of Lincoln under John Langland, 1521–1547*; Brigden, 'Youth and the English Reformation' and *London and the Reformation*; Clark, *English Provincial Society from the Reformation to the Revolution*; Davis, *Heresy and Reformation in the South-east of England, 1520–1559*; Fines, 'Heresy Trials in the Diocese of Coventry and Lichfield, 1511–1512'; Haigh, *Reformation and Resistance in Tudor Lancashire*; MacCulloch, *Suffolk and the Tudors*; Mayhew, 'The Progress of the Reformation in East Sussex 1530–1559'; Oxley, *The Reformation in Essex*; Spufford, *Contrasting Communities*; Whiting, 'Abominable Idols', ' "For the Health of my Soul" ' and *The Blind Devotion of the People*.
12. See the works listed under footnote 11.
13. Bowker, *The Henrician Reformation*, p. 181.
14. For examples of episcopal ministry in addition to those already cited, see Haines, 'Aspects of the Episcopate of John Carpenter, Bishop of Worcester, 1444–1476'; Houlbrooke, *Church Courts and People during the English Reformation*; O'Day and Heal (eds), *Continuity and Change*.
15. See especially Heath, *The English Parish Clergy on the Eve of the Reformation*.
16. Ibid., p. 103. This is a book to which the present comments are greatly indebted.
17. Scarisbrick, *The Reformation and the English People*.
18. See Haigh, 'Anticlericalism and the English Reformation'.
19. See especially Duffy, *The Stripping of the Altars*; Haigh (ed), Introduction to *The English Reformation Revised* and *English Reformations*.
20. Davis, *Heresy and Reformation*.
21. Sheils, *The English Reformation 1530–1570*, p. 1.
22. Swanson, *Church and Society in Late Medieval England*, pp. 259, 260.
23. See, for example, Oxley, *The Reformation in Essex*.
24. See footnote 11 for examples of local studies illustrating different aspects of clerical behaviour.
25. See Sheils, *The English Reformation 1530–1570*, p. 2.
26. See Bowker, *The Secular Clergy in the Diocese of Lincoln, 1495–1520* and 'The Henrician Reformation and the parish clergy' in Haigh (ed), *The English Reformation Revised*, pp. 75–93; Haigh, 'Anticlericalism and the English Reformation'; Heath, *The English Parish Clergy on the Eve of the Reformation*; O'Day and Heal (eds), *Continuity and Change*.

27. In addition to the references in footnote 26, see Haigh, *Reformation and Resistance in Tudor Lancashire*; P. Heath, *Medieval Clerical Accounts*; Colin Platt, *The Parish Churches of Mediaeval England*, London 1981.
28. See Houlbrooke, *Church Courts and the People during the English Reformation* and O'Day and Heal (eds), *Continuity and Change*.
29. Some of the main, and somewhat varying, interpretations of the extent, influence, character and significance of Lollardy are to be found in Aston, *Lollards and Reformation*; Davis, *Heresy and Reformation in the South-east of England*; Dickens, *Lollards and Protestants in the Diocese of York 1509–1558*; Haigh, *Reformation and Resistance in Tudor Lancashire*; Powell, 'The Beginnings of Protestantism in Gloucestershire'; Thomson, *The Later Lollards 1414–1520*
30. Dickens, *The English Reformation*, p. 59, and also see the works listed under footnote 29.
31. See Fines, 'Heresy Trials in the Diocese of Coventry and Litchfield, 1511–1512' and Loades, *The Mid-Tudor Crisis*.
32. Davis, *Heresy and Reformation in the South-east of England*, p. 5.
33. Dickens, *The English Reformation*, p. 152.
34. Ibid., p. 85.
35. Ibid., p. 106.
36. Elton, *England under the Tudors*, p. 131.
37. Youings, *The Dissolution of the Monasteries*, p. 14. See also Knowles, *The Religious Orders in England*, vols 2,3, and Krieder, *English Chantries*.
38. See Fletcher, *Tudor Rebellions*.
39. Youings, *The Dissolution of the Monasteries*, p. 14.
40. See O'Day and Heal (eds), *Continuity and Change*.
41. See references under footnote 37, and also Harper-Bill, *The Pre-Reformation Church in England* .
42. In addition to the references in footnote 37, see B.A. Hanawalt, 'Keepers of the Lights; Late Medieval English Parish Gilds', *Journal of Medieval and Renaissance Studies*, 14, 1984 and Rubin, 'Corpus Christi Fraternities and Late Medieval Piety', *SCH*, 23, 1986.
43. Whiting, 'Abominable Idols', p. 39, and also see Duffy, *The Stripping of the Altars*.
44. Dickens, *The English Reformation*, p. 160.
45. For the Prayer Books see Cuming, *A History of Anglican Liturgy* and *The Godly Order*; and Davies, *Worship and Theology in England*, vol.1.
46. Dickens, *The English Reformation*, p. 277.
47. See Davies, *Worship and Theology in England*, vol.1.; Davis, *Heresy and Reformation in the South-east of England*; and Sheils, *The English Reformation*, p. 45.
48. Swanson, *Church and Society in Late Medieval England*, p. 361.
49. Williamson, *The Tudor Age*, p. 225.

50. Loades, *The Oxford Martyrs*, p. 274.
51. See Loades, *The Mid-Tudor Crisis*, p. 153.
52. Collinson, *Archbishop Grindal*, p. 67.
53. See Solt, *Church and State in Early Modern England* , pp. 63, 64.
54. See especially Loach, *Parliament and the Crown in the Reign of Mary Tudor*.
55. Scarisbrick, *The Reformation and the English People*.
56. Haigh, *English Reformations*, pp. 208f.
57. See Pogson, 'Revival and Reform in Mary Tudor's Church'.
58. Loades, *The Mid-Tudor Crisis*, pp. 180, 181.
59. For a discussion of this point see Pogson, 'Reginald Pole and the Priorities of Government in Mary Tudor's Church'.
60. See Swanson, *Church and Society in Late Medieval England*, pp. 362, 363.

2. The Elizabethan Settlement

1. See D.M. Palliser, 'Popular Reactions to the Reformation during the years of uncertainty 1530–70' in Haigh (ed), *The English Reformation Revised*, p. 95.
2. Of the many biographies of Elizabeth I, special mention should be made of those by Beckingsale, Johnson, Neale, Ridley and Somerset.
3. See Neale, *Elizabeth 1 and her Parliaments*.
4. See Hudson, *The Cambridge Connection*, pp. 25, 110.
5. Williamson, *The Tudor Age*, p. 147.
6. Guy, *Tudor England*, p. 251.
7. Dickens, *The English Reformation*, p. 348.
8. Russell, *The Crisis of Parliaments*, p. 149.
9. Ibid., p. 156.
10. Prothero, *Select Statutes*, p. xxxi.
11. Collinson, *Archbishop Grindal*, p. 85.
12. MacCulloch, *The Later Reformation in England* , p. 30.
13. Ibid., p. 30.
14. For details of the new Prayer Book see Cuming, *A History of Anglican Liturgy* and *The Godly Order*.
15. Dickens, *The English Reformation*, p. 282.
16. Collinson, *The Elizabethan Puritan Movement*, p. 34. The present summary of the Injunctions owes much to Alexander, *Religion in England 1558–1662*, pp. 51, 52.
17. Collinson, *The Elizabethan Puritan Movement*, p. 34.
18. Collinson, *Archbishop Grindal*, pp. 99, 101.
19. Quoted in Manning, *Religion and Society in Elizabethan Sussex*, p. 46.
20. A good summary of the life and teaching of John Jewel is to be found in the *DNB*.

21. Loades, *Revolution in Religion,* p. 56.
22. Haigh, *English Reformations,* p. 252.
23. See Pallister, *The Age of Elizabeth,* pp. 382–384.
24. See W.J. Sheils, 'Religion in Provincial Towns'.
25. See Bowker, *The Secular Clergy in the Diocese of Lincoln: 1495–1520;* Zell, 'The Personnel of the Clergy in Kent during the Reformation'; Haigh, *Reformation and Resistance in Tudor Lancashire;* Heath, *Medieval Clerical Accounts* and *The English Parish Clergy on the Eve of the Reformation.*
26. Hill, *Economic Problems of the Church,* p. 111.
27. See Heal, 'Economic Problems of the Clergy' in Heal and O'Day (eds), *Church and Society in England,* p. 110.
28. For this example and quotation, see Pallister, *The Age of Elizabeth,* p. 386.
29. Figures quoted in Pallister, *The Age of Elizabeth,* p. 386.
30. Duffy, *The Stripping of the Altars,* p. 593.
31. See Haigh, *English Reformations,* pp. 291–3.
32. For some exploration of these themes, and related matters see Walsham, *Church Papists.* especially ch. 5.
33. See Collinson, *The Religion of Protestants,* especially pp. 94–5; MacCulloch, *The Later Reformation in England 1547–1603,* ch. 7, and O'Day, *The English Clergy,* ch. 4 and pp. 69–72.
34. Davies, *Worship and Theology in England,* vol. 1, p. 357.
35. Duffy, *The Stripping of the Altars,* and Whiting, 'Abominable Idols'.
36. For a discussion of the use of the term 'Anglicanism', see Painter, 'Anglican Terminology in Recent Tudor and Stuart Historiography'.
37. I will examine the *Laws of Ecclesiastical Polity* fully in the next chapter.

3. Elizabethan Puritanism and Separatism

1. See Lake, Introduction to Nuttall, *The Holy Spirit* and ch.2 n..36.
2. Haller, *The Rise of Puritanism,* and *Liberty and Reformation in the Puritan Revolution.*
3. Gardiner, *The History of England 1603–42,* 10 vols and *The History of the Great Civil War,* 4 vols.
4. Neale, *Queen Elizabeth* and *Elizabeth I and her Parliaments.*
5. Lake, Introduction to Nuttall, *The Holy Spirit,* pp. x,xi, and note 2.
6. Among Hill's many works, the most relevant in this context are *Puritanism and Revolution, Society and Puritanism in Pre-Revolutionary England,* and *The World Turned Upside Down.*
7. See Stone, *The Causes of the English Revolution.*
8. Russell (ed), *The Origins of the English Civil War.*
9. Collinson, *The Religion of Protestants, Godly People* and *The Birthpangs of Protestant England.*

10. In addition to the work cited in footnote 8, attention should be drawn to Russell, *The Crisis of Parliaments, Parliaments and English Politics* and *The Causes of the English Civil War* . The main relevant works of Morrill are 'The Church in England 1642–1649', 'The religious context of the English civil war', 'The Attack on the Church of England in the Long Parliament, 1640–1642' ,'The Ecology of Allegiance in the English Civil War', *Oliver Cromwell and the English* (ed) and *The Nature of the English Revolution*
11. Works in addition to those already cited will be considered in chapter 7 when I examine the course of events, and any possible underlying causes which lead to the onset of war.
12. See, for example, Nuttall, *The Holy Spirit* and Packer, *Among God's Giants.*
13. Packer, *Among God's Giants*, p. 41.
14. Collinson, *The Elizabethan Puritan Movement*, p. 12. This book is widely recognized as seminal in the study of Elizabethan Puritanism, and the present account is greatly indebted to it.
15. Ibid., p. 14.
16. See Packer, *Among God's Giants*, p. 41.
17. Ibid., p. 42.
18. Collinson, *The Elizabethan Puritan Movement*, p. 14.
19. Dickens, *The English Reformation*, p. 374.
20. Hill, *Society and Puritanism*, p. 47.
21. Packer, *Among God's Giants*, p. 32.
22. Ibid. As well as the general studies of Puritanism, to which reference has or will be made, there are a number of valuable regional studies, such as Goring, 'The Reformation of the Ministry in Elizabethan Sussex'; Haigh, 'Puritan evangelism in the reign of Elizabeth I'; Marchant, *The Puritans and the Church Courts in the Diocese of York 1560–1642;* Richardson, *Puritanism in North-West England*, Manchester 1972; and Sheils, *The Puritans in the Diocese of Peterborough 1558–1610.*
23. McGrath, *Papists and Puritans under Elizabeth Ist*, pp. 77, 78. This is a book to which the present chapter owes much.
24. Collinson, *The Elizabethan Puritan Movement*, p. 45.
25. See Strype, *Life and Acts of Matthew Parker*, Oxford 1821, I, p. 302, and Brook, *A Life of Archbishop Parker*, pp. 165f., to which reference is made in McGrath, *Papists and Puritans*, p. 85.
26. See Gee and Hardy (compilers), *Documents Illustrative of English Church History*, London 1910, pp. 467–75, quoted in McGrath, *Papists and Puritans*, p. 89.
27. See Collinson, *The Elizabethan Puritan Movement*, p. 72.
28. McGrath, *Papists and Puritans*, p. 93.
29. Collinson, *Godly People*, p. 246.

30. Ibid., pp. 257, 258.
31. Goring, 'The Reformation of the Ministry in Elizabethan Sussex', p. 346.
32. Collinson, *Godly People*, pp. 399, 400.
33. Lake, 'Presbyterianism, the Idea of a National Church and the Argument from Divine Right', p. 196.
34. Collinson, *The Elizabethan Puritan Movement*, p. 86.
35. Ibid., p. 86.
36. Prothero, *Select Statutes*, pp. 198, 199.
37. Alexander, *Religion in England,* p. 68.
38. Ibid., p. 80.
39. Ibid., p. 78.
40. Ibid.
41. See Collinson, *The Elizabethan Puritan Movement*, pp. 306, 307.
42. See Collinson, *Archbishop Grindal*, p. 168.
43. Watts, *The Dissenters*, p. 19.
44. White, *The English Separatist Tradition*, p. 29,
45. Ibid., p. 30.
46. Watts, *The Dissenters*, p. 26.
47. Quoted in Manning, *Religion and Society in Elizabethan Sussex*, p. 191.
48. Quoted in Collinson, *Archbishop Grindal*, p. 242.
49. Watts, *The Dissenters*, p. 277.
50. McGrath, *Papists and Puritans*, p. 305.
51. Watts, *The Dissenters*, p. 29.
52. See White, *The English Separatist Tradition*, p. 71.
53. Ibid., p. 40.
54. Watts, *The Dissenters*, p. 36.
55. Pierce, *John Penry*, London 1920, pp. 366, 385, quoted in Watts, *The Dissenters*, p. 39.
56. Knappen, *Tudor Puritanism*, pp. 314, 315.
57. Quoted in Collinson, *The Elizabethan Puritan Movement*, pp. 244, 245.
58. Ibid., pp. 246, 247.
59. In the present work the Everyman Library edition (1907) is used.
60. McGrath, *Papists and Puritans*, p. 315.
61. Ibid., pp. 316f.
62. Ibid., p. 317.
63. Dickens, *The English Reformation*, p. 376.
64. Thomas, *Religion and the Decline of Magic*.
65. Ibid., p. 191.
66. Ibid., p. 204.
67. Ibid., p. 204.
68. Knappen, *Tudor Puritanism*, pp. 379, 380.
69. See Haigh (ed), *The English Reformation Revised*; Haigh, *English Reformations* and Thomas, *Religion and the Decline of Magic*.

70. Haigh (ed), *The English Reformation Revised*, p. 24; Cressey, *Literacy and the Social Order:*, Seaver, *The Puritan Lectureships*, and Sheils, 'Religion in Provincial Towns'.
71. See Thomas, *Religion and the Decline of Magic*, pp. 4,5.
72. See especially Ingram, *Church Courts, Sex and Marriage in England*, p. 94; Collinson, *The Religion of Protestants*, ch.5, and Spufford, *Contrasting Communities*, pp. 319–44.
73. Quoted in Ingram, *Church Courts*, pp. 93, 94.
74. See Ibid., p. 94.
75. Collinson, *The Religion of Protestants*, p. 191.
76. Ingram, *Church Courts*, p. 1.
77. Ibid., p. 323.

4. *Elizabethan Roman Catholicism*

1. See especially Dickens, *The English Reformation*; Dickens, review of J.J. Scarisbrick, *The Reformation and the English People*; Bossy, 'The character of Elizabethan Catholicism', and *The English Catholic Community*.
2. Haigh is a central figure in expounding the revisionist interpretation of English Catholicism in the Tudor period, and the author most in mind in this paragraph. His key works on this topic are, 'The Church of England, the Catholics and the People' ; 'Revisionism, the Reformation and the History of English Catholicism'; 'The continuity of Catholicism in the English Reformation' in Haigh (ed), *The English Reformation Revised*, pp. 176–208, and *English Reformations*.
3. Haigh, 'The continuity of Catholicism in the English Reformation' in Haigh (ed), *The English Reformation Revised*, p. 182. See also Matthew, *Catholicism in England*, as Haigh largely returned to a traditional view found in Matthew. See also Duffy, *The Stripping of the Altars*, which is an important examination of the persistence of Catholic belief and practice.
4. See Aveling, *The Handle and the Axe*; McGrath, *Papists and Puritans* and McGrath, 'Elizabethan Catholicism: a Reconsideration'.
5. McGrath, 'Elizabethan Catholicism: a Reconsideration', p. 417.
6. Ibid., pp. 414–28.
7. See the various views on this period as represented by the authors cited in footnotes 1–4 above.
8. Thomas, *Religion and the Decline of Magic*, p. 206.
9. Among the local studies which are particularly relevant to Elizabethan Catholicism, which have not already been cited, attention is drawn to Hilton, 'Catholicism in Elizabethan Northumberland' and 'The Cumbrian Catholics'.

10. Haigh (ed), *The English Reformation Revised*, pp. 179, 180.
11. Ibid., p. 180.
12. Hilton, 'Catholicism in Elizabethan Northumberland'.
13. Fletcher, *A County Community in Peace and War*, p. 94.
14. Walsham, *Church Papists*, p. 1.
15. See Fletcher, *Tudor Rebellions*.
16. See especially Bossy, *The English Catholic Community* and also the *DNB*.
17. Williamson, *The Tudor Age*, p. 238.
18. These quotations are taken from McGrath, *Papists and Puritans*, pp. 69, 70.
19. See Williamson, *The Tudor Age*.
20. McGrath, *Papists and Puritans*, p. 100.
21. Haigh, *English Reformations*, p. 261.
22. Quoted in McGrath, *Papists and Puritans*, pp. 162, 163.

5. The Reign of James I

1. Hill, *Who's Who in History*, vol. III, p. 1.
2. For James' kingcraft see especially Wormald, 'James VI and I: two kings or one?'; and for his personal religious beliefs and practices and his ecclesiastical policy see particularly Fincham, *Prelate and Pastor*, and Fincham and Lake, 'The Ecclesiastical Policy of King James I', abbreviated and amended in 'The Ecclesiastical Policies of James I and Charles I' in Fincham (ed), *The Early Stuart Church 1603-1642*, pp. 23-49.
3. Fincham and Lake, 'The Ecclesiastical Policies of James I and Charles I', p. 25.
4. See Fincham, *Prelate and Pastor*.
5. Quoted in Fincham and Lake, 'The Ecclesiastical Policies of James I and Charles I' , p. 25.
6. The Millenary Petition, quoted in Prothero, *Select Statutes* , p. 413.
7. For this summary and the quotations it contains, see Prothero, *Select Statues*, pp. 413-416.
8. Usher, *The Reconstruction of the English Church*, I, pp. 308, 309, quoted in McGrath, *Papists and Puritans*, p. 346.
9. Russell, *The Crisis of Parliaments*, p. 262.
10. Higham, *Catholic and Reformed*, p. 39.
11. See Prothero, *Select Statutes,* pp. 416, 417.
12. Gardiner, *History of England, 1603-1642*.
13. Quotations are from White, 'The *via media* in the early Stuart Church' in Fincham (ed), *The Early Stuart Church*, p. 218.
14. Ibid., p. 217.
15. Gardiner, *History of England, 1603-1642*, vol.1, p. 157, quoted in Curtis, 'The Hampton Court Conference and its Aftermath', p. 1.

16. See Fincham, *Prelate as Pastor*, pp. 213–215.

17. Ibid, p. 291.

18. The following comments are especially indebted to Fincham, 'Prelacy and Politics'.

19. See Hyde, Earl of Clarendon, *The History of the Rebellion and Civil Wars in England*, vol.1. pp. 68–9, and Trevor-Roper, *Historical Essays*.

20. Tyacke, 'Puritanism, Arminianism and counter-revolution', 'The Rise of Arminianism Reconsidered' and *Anti-Calvinists*.

21. I will be exploring the interchange of opinions and theories in the next chapter.

22. This comment is based on Fincham, *Prelate as Pastor*, p. 18.

23. Hill, *Economic Problems of the Church*, p. 207.

24. See Fincham, *Prelate as Pastor*, ch. 6, and O'Day, *The English Clergy*, pp. 20, 136.

25. See Foster, 'The Clerical Estate Revitalized'.

26. Heal, 'Economic Problems of the Clergy' in Heal and O'Day (eds), *Church and Society in England*, p. 118.

27. Underdown, *Revel, Riot and Rebellion*, p. 43.

28. Hinde, *A Faithful Remonstrance of the Holy Life and Happy Death of John Bruen of Bruen Stapleford*, London 1641, p. 89, quoted in Underdown, *Revel, Riot and Rebellion*, p. 59

29. Collinson, *The Religion of Protestants*, p. 241.

30. Underdown, *Revel, Riot and Rebellion*, p. 58.

31. Green, 'Anglicanism in Stuart and Hanoverian England' in Gilley and Sheils (eds), *A History of Religion in Britain*, pp. 181, 182.

32. Quoted in Watts, *The Dissenters*, p. 42.

33. Powicke, *Henry Barrow and the Exiled Church of Amsterdam*, London 1910, p. 269, quoted in Watts, *The Dissenters*, p. 43.

34. *Works* (ed Whitley), vol. I, pp. 256f., quoted in Underwood, *A History of the English Baptists*, p. 36.

35. Underwood, *A History of the English Baptists*, p. 36.

36. Burgess, *John Smith, the Se-Baptist, Thomas Helwys and the First Baptist Church in England*, London 1911, pp. 137–8, quoted in Watts, *The Dissenters*, p. 44.

37. Powicke, *Henry Barrow and the Exiled Church of Amsterdam*, London 1910, pp. 254–8, quoted in Watts, *The Dissenters*, p. 44.

38. For the early Anabaptists, the messianic movements, and the Munster events, see Cohn, *The Pursuit of the Millennium*.

39. See Works (ed Whitley), vol. I, pp. xciv ff., quoted in Underwood, *A History of the English Baptists*, p. 38.

40. Watts, *The Dissenters*, p. 51.

41. Johnson, *A Christian Plea Concerning three Treatises*, London 1617, pp. 120–1, quoted in Watts, *The Dissenters*, p. 51.

42. Clark, *English Provincial Society from the Reformation to the Revolution*, p. 177, quoted in Collinson, *The Religion of Protestants*, p. 273.
43. Collinson, *The Religion of Protestants*, p. 273.
44. See Tolmie, *The Triumph of the Saints*, Cambridge 1977, pp. 1–27.
45. See Watts, *The Dissenters*, Oxford 1978, p. 53.
46. Tolmie, *The Triumph of the Saints*, p. 4.
47. Collinson, *The Religion of Protestants*, p. 274.
48. The comments in this section owe much to Doran and Durston, *Princes, Pastors and People*, p. 110.
49. Walker, *An Exhortation*, quoted in Richardson, *Puritanism in North-West England*, p. 84.
50. Packer, *Among God's Giants*, p. 129.
51. Hinde, *Life of John Bruen*, London 1641, pp. 56–7, quoted in Richardson, *Puritanism in North-West England*, p. 102.
52. Packer, *Among God's Giants*, p. 76. The details of the books cited are taken from Packer's most useful book.
53. Ibid., pp. 326, 327.
54. Ibid., p. 167.
55. Quoted in Coward, *The Stuart Age*, p. 73.
56. Packer, *Among God's Giants*, p. 387.
57. Seaver, *Wallington's World*, pp. 56, 57. The actual quotation refers to a time in the 1630s, but it is introduced here as I want to draw attention to an aspect of the Puritan world-view which is evident throughout the time from the reign of James I to the Restoration, and which provides one clue to the understanding of Puritanism in those years.
58. Lake, Introduction to Nuttall, *The Holy Spirit*, p. xix.
59. Nuttall, *The Holy Spirit*, pp. 9, 10.
60. See Underdown, *Revel, Riot and Rebellion*, especially ch. 5.
61. See especially Morrill, 'The Ecology of Allegiance in the English Civil War'.
62. Underdown, *A History of the English Baptists*, p. 52.
63. See Richardson, *Puritanism in North-West England*.
64. See Kalu, 'The Jacobean Church and Essex Puritans', Toronto Ph.D. thesis 1972, and Hunt, *The Puritan Movement*.
65. Quoted in McGrath, *Papists and Puritans*, p. 364.
66. J.R. Tanner, *Constitutional Documents of the Reign of James I*, p. 83, quoted in McGrath, *Papists and Puritans*, p. 367.
67. Wormald, 'Gunpowder, Treason and Scots', pp. 157, 161, 162.
68. Quotations are taken from Solt, *Church and State in Early Modern England*, pp. 149, 150.
69. See Aveling, *The Handle and the Axe*, p. 141.
70. Ibid., pp. 162, 163.

6. Arminianism and the Emergence of High Churchmanship

1. Jacobus Arminius, *Examen Modestum*, Leiden 1612, pp. 196, 220, quoted in Tyacke, *Anti-Calvinists*, p. 39.
2. This section owes much to Solt, *Church and State in Early Modern England*.
3. H. C. Porter, *Reformation and Reaction in Tudor Cambridge*, Cambridge 1958, pp. 344, 388, quoted in Tyacke, *Anti-Calvinists*, p. 31.
4. Hugh Trevor-Roper, *Catholics, Anglicans and Puritans*, p. 58.
5. Ibid.
6. Ibid., p. 60.
7. Ibid., p. 87.
8. The present comments are greatly indebted to Fincham and Lake, 'The Ecclesiastical Policies of James I and Charles I'.
9. Quoted in Higham, *Catholic and Reformed*, p. 97.
10. The key works in this interchange of views among historians are Bernard, 'The Church of England *c.*1529–*c.*1642'; Hill, 'Archbishop Laud's Place in English History'; Lake, 'Calvinism and the English Church 1570–1635'; Lamont, 'The Rise of Arminianism Reconsidered'; Russell, *The Origins of the English Civil War* and *The Causes of the English Civil War*; Sharpe, *Politics and Ideas in Early Stuart England* and *The Personal Rule of Charles I*; Tyacke, 'Puritanism, Arminianism and Counter-Revolution', 'The Rise of Arminianism Reconsidered' and *Anti-Calvinists*; White, 'The Rise of Arminianism Reconsidered', 'A Rejoinder', and *Predestination, Policy and Polemic*.
11. See the works by Tyacke cited in footnote 10 to see how, from 1973 onwards he has elaborated and refined his thesis. As an example of a later exposition of his main contentions see Fielding, 'Arminianism in the Localities: Peterborough Diocese 1603–1642' in Fincham (ed), *The Early Stuart Church*.
12. See the works of White in footnote 10 in which he criticized Tyacke's views, and those of like mind, including Fincham and Lake; and in this he was supported by Bernard, Hill and Sharpe.
13. Lake, 'Calvinism and the English Church 1570–1635', p. 32.
14. Collinson, *The Religion of Protestants*, p. 82.
15. Lake, 'Calvinism and the English Church 1570–1635', p. 33.
16. Lamont, *'The Rise of Arminianism Reconsidered'*, p. 227.
17. Fincham, *Prelate as Pastor*, p. 304.
18. Ibid.
19. Ibid.
20. See Hylson-Smith, *High Churchmanship in the Church of England*.
21. See Doran and Durston, *Pastors and People*, p. 27.
22. Fincham, 'Episcopal Government 1603–1640' in Fincham (ed), *The Early Stuart Church*, p. 77.

23. See Tyacke, *Anti-Calvinists*, p. 114.
24. Quoted in ibid., p. 107.
25. For the life and teaching of Lancelot Andrewes see especially Lossky, *Lancelot Andrewes the Preacher (1555–1626)*, Welsby, *Lancelot Andrewes 1555–1626*, and the *DNB*.
26. Lossky, *Lancelot Andrewes the Preacher*, p. 18.
27. Welsby, *Lancelot Andrewes*, pp. 266, 267.
28. Gardiner, *History of England, 1603–1644*, vol. II, p. 120.
29. Welsby, *Lancelot Andrewes*, p. 264.
30. Lossky, *Lancelot Andrewes*, p. 30.
31. Ibid.
32. Welsby, *Lancelot Andrewes*, p. 264.
33. Lossky, *Lancelot Andrewes*, p. 327.
34. Ibid., p. 332.
35. Ibid., p. 333.
36. Kenneth Hylson-Smith, *High Churchmanship in the Church of England*.
37. Lossky, *Lancelot Andrewes*, p. 326.
38. Welsby, *Lancelot Andrewes*, pp. 274, 275.

7. The Reign of Charles I to 1642

1. Useful comments on the historiography of the events and issues of the period covered by this chapter are to be found in Cust and Hughes, 'Introduction: after Revisionism' in Cust and Hughes (eds), *Conflict in Early Stuart England*; Haigh, Introduction to Haigh (ed), *The English Reformation Revised*; Hughes, *The Causes of the English Civil War*, and Russell, Introduction to Russell (ed), *The Origins of the Civil War*.
2. Cust and Hughes (eds), *Conflict in Early Stuart England*, p. 2.
3. Tawney, 'The Rise of the Gentry'.
4. Trevor-Roper, 'The Gentry 1540–1640'.
5. Hill, *Economic Problems of the Church*.
6. See footnotes 9 and 10 in my Introduction, to which must be added Tawney, *The Acquisitive Society*, and *Religion and the Rise of Capitalism*.
7. Russell, Introduction to Russell (ed), *The Origins of the Civil War*, p. 5.
8. See Elton, 'A High Road to Civil War?'
9. Foster, 'Church Policies of the 1630s'.
10. Hill, *Who's Who in History*, vol. III, p. 46. Of the recent biographies special mention should be made of Sharpe, *The Personal Rule of Charles I*.
11. Hill, *Who's Who in History*, vol. III, p. 46.
12. Hughes, *The Causes of the English Civil War*, p. 156.
13. Sharpe, *The Personal Rule of Charles I*, p. xvi.
14. Hirst, *Authority and Conflict*, p. 141.

15. Quoted in Tyacke, *Anti-Calvinists*, p. 166.
16. Ibid., p. 180. Some of the comments in this section are based on Carlton, *Archbishop William Laud*, and especially pp. 27, 28.
17. The quotations are taken from Hill, *Who's Who in History*, vol. iii, pp. 45f.
18. Recent works on Laud and Laudianism include Carlton, *Archbishop William Laud*; Cust and Hughes (eds), *Conflict in Early Stuart England*; Davies, *The Caroline Captivity of the Church*; Hylson-Smith, *High Churchmanship in the Church of England*; McGee, 'William Laud and the outward face of religion'; Sharpe, 'Archbishop Laud'; Trevor-Roper, *Archbishop Laud* and 'Laudianism and Political Power'; Tyacke, 'Archbishop Laud' in Fincham (ed), *The Early Stuart Church*.
19. Quoted in Coward, *The Stuart Age*, p. 150. The present summary of the religious beliefs and practices of Laud takes into account the in many ways somewhat controversial perspective of Carlton, *Archbishop William Laud*.
20. For this definition see Hill, *Who's Who in History*, vol. iii, p. 64.
21. Richardson, *Puritanism in North-West England*, p. 39.
22. Underdown, *Revel, Riot and Rebellion*, p. 78.
23. Davies, *The Caroline Captivity of the Church*, p. 131.
24. Ibid., p. 69.
25. Ibid., p. 206.
26. Underdowen, *Revel, Riot and Rebellion*, p. 130.
27. Davies, *The Caroline Captivity of the Church*, p. 54.
28. For a discussion of the different views on the sabbath see Parker, *The English Sabbath*.
29. Coward, *The Stuart Age*, p. 151.
30. Tyacke, 'Archbishop Laud' in Fincham (ed), *The Early Stuart Church*, p. 51.
31. Morrill, 'The religious context of the English civil war', p. 162.
32. For the life and teaching of Nicholas Ferrar and the story of Little Gidding see especially Maycock, *Nicholas Ferrar of Little Gidding*.
33. Maycock, *Nicholas Ferrar*, p. 199.
34. Louis L. Martz (ed), *George Herbert and Henry Vaughan*, Oxford 1986, p. xix.
35. For these comments see Davies, *Worship and Theology in England* vol. ii, p. 107.
36. Ibid., p. 110.
37. Sampson, *The Concise Cambridge History*, p. 198.
38. Ibid., p. 201.
39. Trevor-Roper, 'The Great Tew Circle' in Trevor-Roper, *Catholics, Anglicans and Puritans*, p. 166.
40. Ibid., pp. 168, 169.
41. Ibid., pp. 219, 227.
42. Roots, *The Great Rebellion*, p. 66.

43. The following comments are based on Haller, *Liberty and Reformation in the Puritan Revolution*.
44. Haller, *Liberty and Reformation,* p. 11.
45. Lake, Introduction to Nuttall, *The Holy Spirit,* p. xiii.
46. Coward, *The Stuart Age,* p. 74.
47. Tolmie, *The Triumph of the Saints,* p. 37, referred to in Coward, *The Stuart Age,* p. 74.
48. Watts, *The Dissenters,* p. 62.
49. Jones, *Congregationalism in England,* p. 24, quoted in Watts, *The Dissenters,* p. 64.
50. Sharpe, *The Personal Rule of Charles I,* p. 751.
51. Cressy, *Coming Over,* p. 106.
52. Sharpe, *The Personal Rule of Charles I,* p. 751.
53. Watts, *The Dissenters,* p. 65.
54. Underwood, *A History of the English Baptists,* p. 58.
55. Ibid., p. 63.
56. The quotations are taken from Watts, *The Dissenters,* pp. 87, 90.
57. Gibb, *John Lilburne,* p. 42.
58. Hill, *Who's Who in History,* vol. 111, p. 87.
59. Gibb, *John Lilburne,* p. 40.
60. Hill, *Who's Who in History,* vol. 111, p. 88.
61. Watts, *The Dissenters,* p. 66.
62. Ibid., p. 67.
63. For this analysis see Aveling, *The Handle and the Axe,* p. 154. This is a book to which this present section is much indebted.
64. For a full description of Henrietta Maria see Sharpe, *The Personal Rule of Charles I.*
65. Russell, *The Crisis of Parliaments,* p. 325.
66. Roots, *The Great Rebellion,* p. 24.
67. Ibid., pp. 24, 25.
68. Coward, *The Stuart Age,* p. 153.
69. Roots, *The Great Rebellion,* p. 27.
70. Ibid., p. 30.
71. Ibid., pp. 34, 35.
72. Coward, *The Stuart Age,* p. 166.
73. Quoted in Coward, *The Stuart Age,* p. 166.
74. Hirst, *Authority and Conflict,* p. 194.
75. Underdown, *Revel, Riots and Rebellion,* p. 140.
76. Hirst, *Authority and Conflict,* p. 209.
77. Ibid., p. 216.
78. Coward, *The Stuart Age,* p. 172.
79. See the works listed in the Introduction on this matter.
80. Morrill's works listed in the bibliography.

81. Morrill, *The Nature of the English Revolution*, pp. 277, 278.
82. Ibid., p. 36.
83. Ibid.
84. Ibid., pp. 36, 37
85. Collinson, *The Religion of Protestants*, p. 277.
86. See ibid., pp. 272, for these examples and quotations.
87. Underdown, *Revel, Riot and Rebellion*, p. 72.
88. Pailin, 'Rational Religion in England from Herbert of Cherbury to William Paley' .
89. On religious indifference, scepticism, agnosticism and atheism in the seventeenth century see Berman, *A History of Atheism in Britain*; Redwood, *Reason, Ridicule and Religion* and Underdown, *Revel, Riot and Rebellion*.
90. Green, 'Anglicanism in Stuart and Hanoverian England' in Gilley and Sheils (eds), *A History of Religion in Britain*, p. 182.
91. For these comments, see Green, loc.cit.

8. The Civil War and the Interregnum

1. Morrill, *The Nature of the English Revolution*, p. 34.
2. McGregor and Reay (eds), *Radical Religion in the English Revolution*, p. 5.
3. Russell, *Crisis of Parliaments*, p. 342. This book gives a good account of the course of events in the period under review in this chapter.
4. Coward, *The Stuart Age*, p. 175. This book also covers the events of the period 1642 to 1660 most helpfully.
5. Underdown, *Revel, Riot and Rebellion*, p. 4. For a full and useful discussion of this matter, see Underdown, pp. 1–8.
6. Morrill, *The Nature of the English Revolution*, pp. 224, 225, which is a summary of Underdown's argument.
7. Most notably by Morrill, 'The Ecology of Allegiance in the English Civil War'.
8. See, for example, Hill, *Society and Puritanism*; Manning, *The English People and the English Revolution*; Wrightson, *English Society, 1580–1680*; Wrightson and Levine, *Poverty and Piety in an English Village*.
9. Hutchinson, *The Life of Colonel Hutchinson*, quoted in Coward, *The Stuart Age*, p. 174.
10. Coward, *The Stuart Age*, pp. 201, 202.
11. Ibid., p. 206.
12. Morrill, 'The making of Oliver Cromwell' in Morrill (ed), *Oliver Cromwell and the English Revolution*, p. 19.
13. Quoted in Haller, *Liberty and Reformation in the Puritan Revolution*, pp. 211, 212.

14. Davis, 'Cromwell's Religion' in Morrill (ed), *Oliver Cromwell and the English Revolution*, p. 187.
15. Worden, 'Oliver Cromwell and the Sin of Achan' in Beales and Best (eds), *History, Society and the Churches*, p. 125. Worden has made a major contribution to our understanding of the religious experience, orientation and policy of Cromwell.
16. *A Declaration of his Highness the Lord Protector and the Parliament . . . for a Day of Solomn Fasting and Humiliation in the Three Nations*, London, [September] 1654, quoted in Worden, 'Oliver Cromwell and the Sin of Achan'.
17. Davis, 'Cromwell's Religion' in Morrill (ed), *Oliver Cromwell and the English Revolution*, p. 191.
18. Fletcher, 'Oliver Cromwell and the godly nation' in Morrill (ed), *Oliver Cromwell*, p. 231.
19. Roots, *The Great Rebellion*, p. 176.
20. Rushworth, *Historical Collections*, London 1721, iv, 450, quoted in Watts, *The Dissenters*, p. 83.
21. Packer, *Among God's Giants*, p. 203.
22. Quoted in ibid., p. 202.
23. Quoted in ibid., p. 203.
24. Quoted in ibid., p. 387.
25. Quoted in ibid., p. 204.
26. Quoted in ibid., p. 323.
27. Watts, *The Dissenters*, p. 92.
28. Packer, *Among God's Giants*, pp. 366, 367.
29. Watts, *The Dissenters*, pp. 98, 99.
30. See Underwood, *A History of the English Baptists*, p. 65.
31. Quoted in ibid., p. 65.
32. Quoted in ibid., p. 74.
33. McGregor and Reay (eds), *Radical Religion in the English Revolution*, p. 28.
34. For the matters raised in this section see especially McGregor, 'The Baptists: Fount of All Heresy' in McGregor and Reay (eds), *Radical Religion in the English Revolution*, pp, 23–63.
35. Watts, *The Dissenters*, p. 167.
36. Nuttall, *Visible Saints*, p. 163.
37. Packer, *Among God's Giants*, p. 251.
38. Ibid., p. 282.
39. The literature involved in an examination of religion in England in the years 1642–1660 is so great, especially with the many books and articles which have either given rise to academic debate or have promoted it, that no attempt will be made to list even the more general works. Attention will be directed to the salient contributions when the main topics of interest and importance are considered in the rest of this chapter.

40. Thomas, *Religion and the Decline of Magic*, p. 15.
41. Hill, *The World Turned Upside Down*, p. 91.
42. Ibid., p. 96.
43. Thomas, *Religion and the Decline of Magic*, p. 162.
44. Hill, *The World Turned Upside Down*, p. 96.
45. Capp, 'The Fifth Monarchists and Popular Millenarianism' in Mcgregor and Reay (eds), *Radical Religion in the English Revolution*, pp. 165, 189.
46. Ibid., p. 166. The Norman Yoke was a theory, propounded by Levellers and others. It postulated a high level of freedom in Anglo-Saxon England which was suppressed by the Norman Conquest. It was the post-Norman Conquest development of the ruling class and all the accompanying oppressions and injustices about which Levellers and others complained.
47. Adamson, 'Oliver Cromwell and the Long Parliament' in Morrill (ed), *Oliver Cromwell and the English Revolution*, p. 85.
48. Thomas, *Religion and the Decline of Magic*, p. 169.
49. See Capp, 'The Fifth Monarchists and Popular Millenarianism' in Mcgregor and Reay (eds), *Radical Religion in the English Revolution*, pp. 170f.
50. Watts, *The Dissenters*, pp. 117, 118.
51. See Manning, 'The Levellers and Religion' in McGregor and Reay (eds), *Radical Religion in the English Revolution*, p. 69.
52. Ibid., pp. 77, 78.
53. Aylmer, 'The Religion of Gerrard Winstanley' in McGregor and Reay (eds), *Radical Religion in the English Revolution*, p. 93.
54. Ibid., p. 95.
55. Ibid., p. 98.
56. For the quotation, see Hill, 'The Religion of Gerrard Winstanley', pp. 53, 56. For various views on the person and beliefs of Winstanley, see this article by Hill and, for example, George Juretic, 'Digger no Millenarian: The Revolutionizing of Gerrard Winstanley', *JHI*, xxxvi, 1975, pp. 268–280, and L. Mulligan, J.K. Graham and J. Richards, 'Winstanley: A Case for the Man as He Said He Was', *JEH*, xxviii, 1977, pp. 57–75
57. Coward, *The Stuart Age*, p. 80, quoting Dell.
58. Braithwaite, *The Beginnings of Quakerism*, p. 19. This is the standard work on the origins and early years of Quakerism, and is a book to which the present work owes much, not only for the account of Quakerism but for the description and analysis of the religious sects of the period under review; although it needs to be considered in the light of more recent studies.
59. Braithwaite, *The Beginnings of Quakerism*, p. 20.
60. For good expositions of the identification and interpretation of the Ranters as outlined in this present section, see Morton, *The World of the Ranters*, and Hill, *The World Turned Upside Down*, together with the main works

in the subsequent debate on who and what they were, of which the most important are J.C. Davis, *Fear, Myth and History: the Ranters and the Historians* and 'Fear, Myth and Furore: Reappraising the "Ranters"', and the various ensuing articles to which reference is made below.

61. Coward, *The Stuart Age*, p. 209.
62. Watts, *The Dissenters*, p. 183.
63. Davis, *Fear, Myth and History*, p. x.
64. McGregor, 'Debate, Fear, Myth and Furore: Reappraising the "Ranters"', p. 164.
65. Capp, 'Comment' in *P & P*, 140, November 1990, p. 171.
66. Davis, 'Reply', p. 194.
67. Quoted in Braithwaite, *The Beginnings of Quakerism*, p. 23.
68. Hill, *The World turned Upside Down*, p. 81.
69. Quoted in ibid., p. 83.
70. Ibid., p. 190.
71. McGregor, 'Seekers and Ranters' in McGregor and Reay (eds), *Radical Religion in the English Revolution*, pp. 122, 123.
72. Hill, *The World turned Upside Down*, p. 192.
73. Braithwaite, *The Beginnings of Quakerism*, p. 25, quoted in Hill, *The World turned Upside Down*, p. 186.
74. See Acheson, *Radical Puritans in England*, p. 61.
75. Braithwaite, *The Beginnings of Quakerism*, p. 26.
76. The following account of the life and teaching of George Fox, and the beginning of Quakerism, inevitably relies heavily on *The Journal* of George Fox as well as Braithwaite, *The Beginnings of Quakerism*.
77. George Fox, *The Journal*, pp. 11, 12.
78. Ibid., p. 33.
79. Ibid., p. 72.
80. Braithwaite, *The Beginnings of Quakerism*, p. 36.
81. George Fox, *The Journal*, p. 33.
82. Ibid., p. 34.
83. Ibid., p. 35.
84. Braithwaite, *The Beginnings of Quakerism*, p. 43.
85. Ibid., pp. 86, 94.
86. The following account of James Nayler owes much to Braithwaite, *The Beginnings of Quakerism*, and to Cross and Livingstone (eds), *The Oxford Dictionary of the Christian Church*, pp. 956, 957.
87. Lamb, 'A Quaker's Meeting' in *Essays of Elia*, quoted in Braithwaite, *The Beginnings of Quakerism*, p. 241.
88. Reay, 'Quakerism and Society' in McGregor and Reay (eds), *Radical Religion in the English Revolution*, p. 141.
89. Ibid., p. 161.
90. Spurr, *The Restoration Church of England*, p. 3.

91. The following account owes much to Morrill, 'The Church in England 1642–1649'.
92. Spurr, *The Restoration Church of England 1646–1689*, p. 3.
93. Ibid., p. 4.
94. Ibid., p. 5.
95. Doran and Durston, *Pastors and People*, pp. 154, 145.
96. See Morrill, 'The Church in England 1642–1649' in Morrill, *The Nature of the English Revolution*, pp. 148–175.
97. Spurr, *The Restoration Church of England 1646–1689*, p. 15.
98. Ibid., p. 10.
99. Morrill, 'The Church in England 1642–1649' in Morrill, *The Nature of the English Revolution*, pp. 166, 167.
100. Morrill, 'The Church in England 1642–1689' in Morrill, *The Nature of the English Revolution*, p. 174.
101. Hill, *The Century of Revolution*, p. 153.
102. Hill, *God's Englishman*, p. 121.
103. Aveling, *The Handle and the Axe*, p. 178.
104. See Thomas, *Religion and the Decline of Magic*; Morton, *The World of the Ranters*; Spufford, *Contrasting Communities*.
105. See Berman, *A History of Atheism in Britain*; Hill, 'Irreligion in the Puritan Revolution' in McGregor and Reay (eds), *Radical Religion in the English Revolution*, pp. 191–211; Redwood, *Reason, Ridicule and Religion*.
106. Edwards, *Gangraena*, London 1646, 1, p. 89, quoted in Tolmie, *The Triumph of the Saints*, p. 133.
107. See Tuck, Introduction to Hobbes, *Leviathan*, p. ix. The present work is indebted to this excellent article.
108. Ibid., pp. xviii., xxiii.

9. The Restoration and the Reign of Charles II

1. This brief resume of recent historiography owes much to Harris, Seaward and Goldie (eds), *The Politics of Religion in Restoration England*, pp. 1–28.
2. Jones, *The First Whigs*.
3. Haley, *The First Earl of Shaftesbury*; Kenyon, *Robert Spencer, Earl of Sunderland*; Miller, *Popery and Politics in England*; Miller, *James II*.
4. See especially Bosher, *The Making of the Restoration Settlement*, London 1951, A.Whiteman, 'The Re-establishment of the Church of England', *TRHS*, 5th series, vol. V, 1955; Abernathy, 'The English Presbyterians and the Stuart Restoration, 1648–63'; Green, *The Re-establishment of the Church of England 1660–63*; Cragg, *From Puritanism to the Age of Reason*; Lacey, *Dissent and Parliamentary Politics in England*; Nuttall and Chadwick (eds), *From Uniformity to Unity*; Watts, *The Dissenters*;

Bennett, 'The Seven Bishops: A Reconsideration' and *The Tory Crisis in Church and State*; Every, *The High Church Party*; Sykes, *Church and State in England in the Eighteenth Century*.

5. See especially Harris, Seaward and Goldie (eds), *The Politics of Religion in Restoration England*, and the references in that work.

6. For the full text of the Declaration of Breda see Gardiner, *The Constitutional Documents of the Puritan Revolution*, pp. 465–467. See also Kenyon, *The Stuart Constitution*.

7. Green, *The Re-establishment of the Church of England*.

8. Ibid., p. 9.

9. Bosher, *The Making of the Restoration Settlement*, p. xiv.

10. Seaward, 'Gilbert Sheldon, the London Vestries, and the Defence of the Church' in Harris, Seaward and Goldie (eds), *The Politics of Religion in Restoration England*, p. 50.

11. Morrill, 'The Church in England, 1642–1649'.

12. Hill, *Who's Who in History*, vol. III, pp. 210–216.

13. Spurr, *The Restoration Church of England*, p. 29.

14. Goldie, 'Danby, the Bishops and the Whigs' in Harris, Seaward and Goldie (eds), *The Politics of Religion in Restoration England*, p. 76.

15. Hutton, *The Restoration*, p. 144.

16. See Spurr, *The Restoration Church of England*, p. 35.

17. Coward, *The Stuart Age*, p. 249.

18. Lacey, *Dissent and Parliamentary Politics in England*, p. 24.

19. Watts, *The Dissenters*, p. 223.

20. See Bosher, *The Making of the Restoration Settlement*, p. 205, Braithwaite, *The Second Period of Quakerism*, p. 9, and Watts, *The Dissenters*, p. 223.

21. Watts, *The Dissenters*, p. 223.

22. Cross, *Church and People 1450–1660*, p. 224.

23. Spurr, *The Restoration Church of England*, p. 43.

24. Ibid.

25. Ibid.

26. Wilkinson, *1662 and After*, p. 54.

27. Richard Baxter, quoted in Wilkinson, *1662 and After*, p. 59 For the quotations see ibid., pp. 54,55 and Edmund Calamy, *An Account of the Ministers...who were ejected after the Restoration*, London 1713.

28. Keeble, *The Literary Culture of Nonconformity* , p. 68.

29. Spurr, *The Restoration Church of England*, p. 61.

30. Ibid., p. 62.

31. Ibid., p. 65.

32. Ibid., p. 68.

33. Ibid.

34. See Coward, *The Stuart Age*, p. 181.

35. Kenyon, *The Popish Plot*.

36. Quoted in ibid., p. 4.
37. Ibid., p. 7.
38. Ibid., p. 13.
39. Miller, *Popery and Politics in England,* p. 1.
40. Scott, 'England's Troubles: Exhuming the Popish Plot'.
41. Bedloe, *A Narrative and impartial discovery of the Horrid Popish Plot,* London 1679, p. 2, quoted in Scott, art. cit., p. 118.
42. Goldie, 'Danby, the Bishops and the Whigs' in Harris, Seaward and Goldie (eds), *The Politics of Religion in Restoration England,* p. 80.
43. Aveling, *The Handle and the Axe,* p. 180, a book to which the present section owes much.
44. Ibid., p. 188.
45. See ibid.
46. Spurr, *The Restoration Church of England,* p. 65.
47. Aveling, *The Handle and the Axe,* p. 221.
48. Watts, *The Dissenters,* p. 217.
49. Abernathy, 'The English Presbyterians and the Stuart Restoration, 1648–1663', p. 93.
50. Watts, *The Dissenters,* p. 248.
51. Ibid.
52. Jones, *Congregationalism in England,* p. 50, a book to which the present study inevitably owes much as it is the standard work on the history of English Congregationalism.
53. Watts, *The Dissenters,* p. 217.
54. Jones, *Congregationalism in England,* p. 56.
55. Ibid., p. 61.
56. Hill, *Who's Who in History,* vol. 111, p. 173.
57. Jones, *Congregationalism in England,* p. 71.
58. Ibid., p. 101.
59. Underwood, *A History of the English Baptists,* p. 89.
60. Ibid., p. 94.
61. Ibid., p. 97.
62. Wilkinson, *1662 and After,* p. 60.
63. See Watts, *The Dissenters,* p. 248.
64. Quoted in Underwood, *A History of the English Baptists,* p. 105.
65. Ibid., p. 106.
66. Hutton, *Charles II,* p. 153.
67. For this summary see Braithwaite, *The Second Period of Quakerism,* pp. 21, 22.
68. Ibid., p. 37.
69. See ibid., p. 38.
70. The following comments owe much to Lacey, *Dissent and Parliamentary Politics in England.*

71. See ibid., p. 17.
72. Ibid., p. 28.
73. Hill, *Who's Who in History*, vol. III, p. 227.
74. Spurr, *The Restoration Church of England*, p. 47.
75. Ibid.
76. Ibid., p. 48, and also see Spurr's references: Sir Roger L'Estrange, *Toleration Discussed*, London 1663, p. 86, and Sir Robert Pointz, *A Vindication of Monarchy*, London 1661, p. 35.
77. Seaward, 'Gilbert Sheldon, the London Vestries, and the Defence of the Church' in Harris, Seaward and Goldie (eds), *The Politics of Religion in Restoration England*, p. 69.
78. Beddard, 'Bishop Cartwright's Death-Bed', Bodleian Library Record, 11, 1984, p. 220, quoted in Spurr, *The Restoration Church of England*, p. 85.
79. For the life and thought of Henry Compton, see Carpenter, *The Protestant Bishop*.
80. Ibid., p. 42.
81. Wrightson and Levine, *Poverty and Piety in an English Village*.
82. Quoted in Spurr, *The Restoration Church of England*, p. 203.
83. Quoted in ibid, p. 166.
84. Pruett, *The Parish Clergy under the Later Stuarts*, pp. 23, 39–48. Other relevant studies include J.L. Salter, 'Warwickshire Clergy, 1660–1714', Birmingham Ph.D thesis 1975; E.A.O. Whiteman, 'The Episcopate of Dr Seth Ward, Bishop of Exeter (1662 to 1667) and Salisbury (1667 to 1688/89', Oxford D.Phil thesis 1951; Holmes, *Augustan England*, and O'Day, 'Anatomy of a Profession: the Clergy of the Church of England' in Prest (ed), *The Professions in Early Modern England*.
85. See Spurr, *The Restoration Church of England*, p. 198.
86. Ibid., p. 229.
87. Of particular help in the consideration of Anglican liturgical life in the period 1660 to 1685 is Davis, *Worship and Theology in England*, vol. II.
88. Green, 'Anglicanism in Stuart and Hanoverian England' in Gilley and Sheils (eds), *A History of Religion in Britain*, p. 185.
89. Ibid., p. 186.
90. Spurr, 'Latitudinarianism and the Restoration Church', p. 82.
91. Nuttall, *Richard Baxter*, p. 20, a book to which this section is indebted.
92. Quoted in ibid., p. 48.
93. See Nuttall, *The Holy Spirit*, p. 33.
94. Baxter, *The Divine Appointment of the Lord's Day*, London 1671, p. 124, quoted in Nuttall, *Richard Baxter*, p. 53.
95. Ibid., p. xxi.
96. Ibid.
97. Baxter, *The Reformed Pastor*, London 1656, p. 187, quoted in Wilkinson, *1662 and After*, p. 204.

98. See Keeble, *The Literary Culture of Nonconformity*, pp. 136, 137.
99. The following comments are based on Keeble, *The Literary Culture of Nonconformity*.
100. Ibid., p. 283.
101. Ibid., p. 284.

10. The Reign of James II and the Revolution

1. For the life and thought of James II particular attention is drawn to Miller, *James II*. Other works which cast light upon him include Bennett, *The Tory Crisis in Church and State* and 'The Seven Bishops. A Reconsideration'; Carpenter, *The Protestant Bishop;* Jones, *Country and Court;* Lacey, *Dissent and Parliamentary Politics in England;* and Speck, *Reluctant Revolutionaries.*
2. Miller, *James II*, pp. 58, 59.
3. Hill, *Who's Who in History*, vol. III, p. 308.
4. Quoted in Miller, *James II*, p. 120.
5. For the life and place in contemporary history of James, Duke of Monmouth, there is a useful summary in Hill, *Who's Who in History*, vol. III, pp. 299–301, and reference should also be made to the *DNB*, but also see Jones, *Country and Court.*
6. Hill, *Who's Who in History*, vol. III, pp. 299, 300.
7. Spurr, *The Restoration Church of England*, p. 88.
8. Coward, *The Stuart Age*, p. 296.
9. Quotation from Miller, *James II*, p. 170.
10. Quoted in Coward, *The Stuart Age*, p. 297.
11. Quoted in Spurr, *The Restoration Church of England*, p. 94.
12. Quotation in Coward, *The Stuart Age*, p. 298.
13. Sir John Lowther, *Memoir of the Reign of James II*, ed T. Zouch, York 1808, pp. 31, 32, quoted in Spurr, *The Restoration Church of England*, pp. 96,97.
14. Aveling, *The Handle and the Axe*, p. 222. This is a book to which the present account is greatly indebted.
15. Ibid.
16. For the life and works of John Dryden placed in an historical context see Aveling, *The Handle and the Axe*; Hill, *Whos Who in History*, vol. III; the *DNB*; and Nichols, *The Panther and the Hind.*
17. Aveling, *The Handle and the Axe*, pp. 230, 231.
18. Carpenter, *The Protestant Bishop*, p. 74.
19. Watts, *The Dissenters*, p. 259.
20. Spurr, *The Restoration Church of England*, p. 105.
21. See Thomas, *Religion and the Decline of Magic.*
22. Coward, *The Stuart Age*, p. 457.

23. Thomas, *Religion and the Decline of Magic*, pp. 797, 798.
24. See Berman, *A History of Atheism in Britain;* Redwood, *Reason, Ridicule and Religion;* and Tuck, Introduction to Hobbes, *Leviathan.*
25. Thomas, *Religion and the Decline of Magic*, pp. 518, 519.
26. For the following brief sociological review of the concept of secularization see especially Berger, *The Sacred Canopy*, and *A Rumour of Angels;* Will Herberg, *Protestant, Catholic, Jew*, New York 1955, Hill, *A Sociology of Religion*, 1973, Thoms Luckmann, *The Invisible Religion*, New York 1967, Shiner, 'The Concept of Secularization in Empirical Research', *Journal for the Scientific Study of Religion*, Vol. vi, no.2, 1967, pp. 207–220, Wilson, *Religion in Secular Society*, Wilson, *Contemporary Transformations of Religion.*
27. The following comments owe much to Champion, *The Pillars of Priestcraft Shaken*, and especially to Harrison, *'Religion' and the Religions in the English Enlightenment.*
28. See K. Scholder, *The Birth of Modern Critical Theology*, London 1990.
29. Harrison, *'Religion' and the Religions*, p. 3.
30. Ibid., p. 5. And see pp. 5f. of that work for a development of the concept and its relation to the Enlightenment in general, as well as to the Reformation and its aftermath.
31. Ibid., p. 60.
32. Popkin, 'The Deist Challenge', in Grell, Israel and Tyacke (eds), *From Persecution to Toleration*, p. 196.
33. Spurr, *The Restoration Church of England*, p. 107.
34. Dickens, *The English Reformation*, p. 392.
35. Spurr, *The Restoration Church of England*, p. 229.
36. Watts, *The Dissenters*, p. 259.
37. Dickens, *The English Reformation*, p. 329.
38. Hill, *Society and Puritanism*, p. 484.
39. Quoted in Rupp, *Religion in England*, p. 33.
40. For the Nonjurors see Cross, *The Oxford Movement* ; Overton, *Life in the English Church* and *The Nonjurors*; Rupp, *Religion in England*; Wand, *The High Church Schism. Four Lectures on the Non-jurors.*
41. A useful introduction to the continued influence of the Puritans is Packer, *Among God's Giants.*
42. See Holmes, *The Making of a Great Power*, pp. 353f., and Bennett, 'Conflict in the Church', in Holmes (ed), *Britain After the Glorious Revolution*, pp. 163f.
43. For the religious societies see especially Duffy, Primitive Christianity Revived; Rack, 'Religious Societies and the Origins of Methodism'; and Walsh, 'Religious Societies: Methodist and Evangelical'.
44. Woodward, *An Account of the Rise and Progress of the Religious Societies*, p. 23.

Index